WEST ACADEMIC PUBLISHING'S LAW SCHOOL ADVISORY BOARD

PRINCIPLES OF INVESTIGATIVE CRIMINAL PROCEDURE

Second Edition

Leslie W. Abramson
Frost Brown Todd Professor of Law Emeritus
Louis D. Brandeis School of Law
University of Louisville

CONCISE HORNBOOK SERIES™

WEST ACADEMIC

860 Blue Gentian Road, Suite 350
Eagan, MN 55121
1-877-888-1330

Published in the United States of America

ISBN: 979-8-89209-988-2

For Ren, Rhys, Charlie, and Amelia

Preface

For law students of constitutional criminal procedure, *Principles of Investigative Criminal Procedure* will assist them in learning about Fourth Amendment, Fifth Amendment, Sixth Amendment, and grand jury issues associated with criminal investigations. This volume is an effort to provide a comprehensive, though "Concise", treatise for law students and attorneys.

The materials discuss and analyze the criminal procedure jurisprudence of the United States Supreme Court and lower courts, with extensive use of primary source material that affects judges, prosecutors, defense counsel, and criminal defendants. Discussions relate to breakthrough decisions like *Miranda v. Arizona* and *Strickland v. Washington*, as well as lower court cases adding a nuance to topics already well-developed in prior Court decisions.

"The Court" is a phrase used hundreds of times as a shorthand reference to the work of the United States Supreme Court. Footnotes provide specific page citations in United States Reports for a quick reference to Westlaw. The coverage of this book extends to United States Supreme Court decisions through the 2023–2024 Term.

For the preparation of the first edition in 2022, I am grateful to Sue Eng Ly, a 2019 graduate of the University of Louisville Louis D. Brandeis School of Law and a member of the California Bar, for her quality research assistance. Both editions of this book appear with the support of Carol B. Armstrong, as well as Ren, Rhys, Charlie and Amelia.

My editors at West Academic Publishing, Danny Buteyn, Megan Hoffman, and others, deserve special thanks for their patience during the process of writing and editing. To all, I am grateful. If anyone has suggestions for improving this edition, please notify me at les.abramson@louisville.edu.

Leslie W. Abramson

April 2025

Summary of Contents

Table of Contents

PRINCIPLES OF INVESTIGATIVE CRIMINAL PROCEDURE

Second Edition

Chapter 1

EXCLUSIONARY RULE

Table of Sections

§ 1.1 Introduction

The exclusionary rule is a device by which evidence obtained in violation of a defendant's constitutional rights is inadmissible at the defendant's trial. The effects of the rule can result in the dismissal of criminal charges, especially when the rule applies to the clinching piece of evidence through illegal search, interrogation, or identification procedures. The rule also prohibits the use of evidence in certain circumstances in which a defendant's rights have been violated but the violation does not rise to the level of a constitutional infringement.[1]

However, "mere violation of a government regulation or internal policy" does not trigger application of the exclusionary rule. While police regulations may be stricter than the constitution requires, those regulations do not expand the scope of the constitution.[2] For example, in *Whren v. United States*,[3] the Court held that because a vehicle stop by plainclothes officers in an unmarked vehicle violated police regulations, that stop was not unconstitutional.

The purposes served by the exclusionary rule vary according to the nature of the right which has been infringed and the kind of evidence which has been obtained. For example, the exclusionary rule in relation to pretrial identification is intended to protect against unduly suggestive procedures which might otherwise impugn the integrity of the factfinding process.[4] The rule is also intended to deter police misconduct and to preserve the integrity of the judicial process in the area of confessions.[5] For incriminating statements, the exclusionary rule operates to insure the voluntariness of incriminating statements and to prevent the use of coercive techniques, thus serving to promote the integrity both of the factfinding process and of the judicial process.[6]

By contrast, in the case of an illegal arrest, search, or seizure, the rule may result in the exclusion of evidence that is usually reliable. For example, in *Stone v. Powell*,[7] the Court held that Fourth Amendment violations are different from Fifth or Sixth Amendment violations, i.e., illegal searches and seizures do not "impugn the

[1] See Oregon v. Elstad, 470 U.S. 298 (1985) (*Miranda* exclusionary rule is broader than the Fifth Amendment itself). See Chapter 12.

[2] See Virginia v. Moore, 553 U.S. 164 (2008).

[3] 517 U.S. 806 (1996).

[4] Foster v. California, 394 U.S. 440 (1969); Stovall v. Denno, 388 U.S. 293 (1967).

[5] Brown v. Illinois, 422 U.S. 590, 599 (1975).

[6] *Id.*, at 603.

[7] 428 U.S. 465 (1976).

integrity of the fact-finding process or challenge evidence as inherently unreliable."[8]

§ 1.2 History, Rationales, Scope, and Alternatives

A. History of the Rule

The exclusionary rule did not become effective at the same time as the Bill of Rights in 1791. Because constitutional amendments were not explicit about remedies for violations, even if the police violated a person's Fourth Amendment rights, suppression of the illegally obtained evidence was not automatic. Until 1886, the only remedies available to victims of illegal searches were civil suits for actual damages based on trespass or a replevin action for return of the goods seized. The latter type of litigation was not successful if the items seized were contraband or the fruits of a crime. Those objects were forfeited to the State, without regard for the seizure's legality.

In 1914, the Court in *Weeks v. United States*[9] explicitly recognized an exclusionary rule in federal criminal cases, as part of its supervisory powers over the federal courts. Nearly fifty years later, in *Mapp v. Ohio*,[10] the Court applied the rule to the States via the Fourteenth Amendment. The Court has significantly expanded the availability of the exclusionary rule by holding that most aspects of the first eight amendments to the U.S. Constitution apply to the State prosecutions through the Fourteenth Amendment Due Process Clause.[11]

As the breadth of its availability has expanded beyond the Fourth Amendment, the legal foundation for the exclusionary rule has blurred since the Court stamped it as constitutionally-based when it was first applied to the States in *Mapp v. Ohio*. In *Mapp*, the Court explains that the exclusionary rule is "part and parcel of the Fourth Amendment's limitation upon [governmental] encroachment of individual privacy."[12] Less than two decades later, *United States v. Calandra* pulled back on its *Mapp* statement and described the

---

8 Stone v. Powell, 428 U.S. 465, 479 (1976).

9 232 U.S. 383 (1914).

10 367 U.S. 643 (1961).

11 See, e.g., Mapp v. Ohio, 367 U.S. 643 (1961) (Fourth Amendment seizure); Ker v. California, 374 U.S. 23 (1963) (Fourth Amendment search); Malloy v. Hogan, 378 U.S. 1 (1964) (Fifth Amendment self-incrimination); Benton v. Maryland, 395 U.S. 784 (1969) (Fifth Amendment double jeopardy); Gideon v. Wainwright, 372 U.S. 335 (1963) (Sixth Amendment counsel); Pointer v. Texas, 380 U.S. 400 (1965) (Sixth Amendment confrontation); Duncan v. Louisiana, 391 U.S. 145 (1968) (Sixth Amendment jury trial); Baze v. Rees, 553 U.S. 35 (2008) (Eighth Amendment excessive bail); Robinson v. California, 370 U.S. 660 (1962) (Eighth Amendment cruel punishment).

12 *Mapp v. Ohio*, 367 U.S. at 651.

exclusionary rule as "a judicially-created remedy designed to safeguard Fourth Amendment rights generally through its deterrent effect, rather than a personal constitutional right of the party aggrieved."[13]

Which view is correct? The Fourth Amendment states that the people shall be protected against "unreasonable" searches and seizures. But it does not allude to the possibility or requirement of excluding evidence for a violation. By comparison, the Fifth Amendment does require exclusion of evidence obtained in violation of a defendant's privilege against incrimination: "No person. . . shall be compelled in any criminal case to be a witness against himself. . . ." Without an explicit command, the Court could choose to apply an exclusionary rule in criminal cases if to do so is considered fundamental and necessary to Due Process.

B. Rationales for Excluding Evidence

Whether as originally adopted or in its application to the States, the rule has not been free from criticism. Many have advocated abolition of the exclusionary rule because, for example, the rule's operation of barring evidence is too high a price for society to pay, i.e., the notion that the "criminal is to go free because the constable has blundered."[14] Critics also wonder why society should be responsible for the misbehavior of individuals such as police officers by releasing factually guilty persons when the exclusionary rule is applied. The same critics are dismissive of the argument that Government must "play the game" by the rules and cannot profit from its illegal acts.

The fundamental argument supporting the exclusionary rule is deterrence, i.e., police are deterred from illegal conduct if they know that evidence obtained by illegal means will be suppressed. Critics of the rule believe that the deterrence goal is plausible only if the police responsible for constitutional violations are prosecuted; currently, individual police misbehavior is rarely prosecuted.

The rule's detractors rebut the deterrence rationale by observing that (1) it applies only when criminal charges follow; it does not prevent police harassment or abuse; (2) no direct sanctions are used to punish the State actors whose illegal conduct results in exclusion of evidence; the immediate sanction of excluding evidence affects prosecutors directly; (3) the time lag between police misconduct and judicial disposition fails to deter, i.e., by the time a judge rules evidence inadmissible due to police misconduct, the wrongdoers are likely to have committed additional mistakes; and (4) the rule is too

---

[13] United States v. Calandra, 414 U.S. 338, 348 (1974).

[14] People v. Defore, 150 N.E. 585 (N.Y. 1926).

broad, relating to both inadvertent errors of judgment and deliberate and flagrant violations.

Other concerns relate to judicial integrity and police education. Proponents of the exclusionary rule believe that it prevents a court from becoming a party to police illegality. Foes of the rule believe that the rule makes the court a party to permitting a guilty person to go free. Proponents of the rule believe that, before abandoning the rule, further attempts may increase its public acceptance, e.g., (1) by improving police training and explaining mistakes quickly to the offending officers; (2) forming a compensation system for victims of police illegality, and/or disciplinary actions against offending police. The rule's opponents think that no matter how many ways that the rule is modified, judicial decisions about issues like search and seizure and police interrogation are so unclear that police officers cannot understand or follow them in the developing, numerous contexts of police-citizen encounters.

Critics further argue that the exclusionary rule operates to exclude the most credible evidence in a case. It is a rule that aids only the guilty, e.g., physical evidence obtained during an illegal search is no less reliable than when police obtain it legally. Proponents agree, but counter that police who are willing to use any method to convict a defendant would never be looking for worthless evidence. In sum, critics view the exclusionary rule not as a constitutional requirement, but as an experimental step in the tradition of the common law that is unworkable and irrational.

Although *Mapp* stressed that the issue was not the effectiveness of the exclusionary rule or the ineffectiveness of alterative remedies, the Court's strained constitutional arguments implicitly decided that the exclusion of evidence is the only effective sanction. Without exclusion as a sanction, the Court perhaps decided that the right to be free from unreasonable searches is a "dead letter."

C. Scope of the Rule

The exclusionary rule does not establish a *per se* rule of exclusion forbidding the use of all illegally obtained evidence in all situations. Instead, courts balance the interest of deterrence against the societal costs of suppressing probative evidence, concluding that in certain circumstances suppression is inappropriate.[15]

While the exclusionary rule applies at criminal trials, at other stages of the criminal justice process courts have held that the exclusionary rule is inapplicable. For example, a preliminary hearing

---

[15] See, e.g., Massachusetts v. Sheppard, 468 U.S. 981 (1984); United States v. Leon, 468 U.S. 897 (1984); Michigan v. DeFillippo, 443 U.S. 31 (1979).

stage of a criminal case follows the defendant's arrest and his initial appearance in court. Judges do not apply the exclusionary rule to suppress evidence in federal preliminary hearings and in most States as well. At a preliminary hearing, a presiding judge decides whether probable cause exists that a crime was committed, and whether the accused committed the offense. If the relatively lesser judicial officers find probable cause at preliminary hearings, the case proceeds to the next stage of proceedings conducted in that jurisdiction, e.g., a grand jury to return an indictment, or a prosecutor files an information with the trial court where the trial of the charges occurs.

At an *ex parte* grand jury proceeding, prosecutors question witnesses without the presence of either the target of the investigation or that person's counsel. In *United States v. Calandra*,[16] a grand jury witness objected to questioning that was based on information acquired by an earlier illegal search of his premises. The Court disagreed, holding that the Fourth Amendment exclusionary rule does not apply to grand jury proceedings. Bearing in mind the secrecy and the *ex parte* nature of the grand jury, applying the exclusionary rule "would seriously impede the grand jury" by requiring suppression hearings on "issues only tangentially related to the grand jury's primary objective," i.e., to decide whether probable cause exists to issue an indictment. Because illegally seized evidence is already excludable at trial, additional exclusion at the grand jury stage, "would deter only police investigation consciously directed toward the discovery of evidence solely for use in a grand jury investigation."[17] "Any incremental deterrent effect which might be achieved by extending the [exclusionary] rule to grand jury proceedings is uncertain at best."[18] It is ironic that the grand jury can consider illegally obtained evidence, but the trial jury would not hear that same evidence.

The exclusionary rule also is unavailable to challenge the evidence supporting an indictment. *Costello v. United States* held that "neither the Fifth Amendment nor any other constitutional provision prescribes the kind of evidence upon which grand juries must act."[19] After his indictment, the defendant moved to dismiss the charges in the indictment because of the amount and quality of the evidence presented to the grand jury. The Court rejected the defendant's self-incrimination challenges to grand jury indictments. As with *Calandra*, grand jury traditions preclude any practical method for deciding Fourth and Fifth Amendment issues in an

---

16 414 U.S. 338 (1974).

17 United States v. Calandra, 414 U.S. 338, 351 (1974).

18 *Id.*

19 Costello v. United States, 350 U.S. 359, 362 (1956).

adversary setting either *before* evidence is heard by the grand jury, or *after* a grand jury indicts. In either context, challenges to the evidence heard by the grand jury would require a complex evaluation of every piece of evidence heard by the grand jurors.

During trials, courts on occasion have refused to apply the exclusionary rule because its "substantial social costs" outweighed its "deterrence benefits." In *Hudson v. Michigan*,[20] the Court held that the exclusionary rule did not apply to evidence obtained in executing a search warrant when the only police violation related to a failure to observe the "knock-and-announce" requirements for entering the premises to be searched. The social costs of applying the exclusionary rule included the "constant flood" of suppression motions claiming a violation of the doctrine for conduct that related to whether the police waited long enough before entering or were justified in not waiting long enough. By contrast, the benefits were minimal, because of the (1) lack of incentive to violate the rule, and (2) availability of civil rights remedies for violations.

Applying the exclusionary rule at trial was also deemed inappropriate in *Herring v. United States*[21] when an arresting officer reasonably believed that there was an outstanding arrest warrant for the defendant, but that belief was wrong due to a negligent bookkeeping entry by another police employee because the warrant was withdrawn five months earlier. "To trigger the exclusionary rule, police conduct must be sufficiently deliberate that exclusion can meaningfully deter it, and sufficiently culpable that such deterrence is worth the price paid by the justice system."[22] The Court stated that "the error was the result of isolated negligence attenuated from the arrest."

Operation of the exclusionary rule also affects other major parts of the criminal justice system, e.g., the plea bargaining process. Proponents argue that the rule encourages plea bargaining when prosecutors fear either the suppression of vital evidence, or making bad law on appeal (through reversals of convictions), even if the evidence is not suppressed at trial. Opponents point to the delay in plea bargaining resulting from pretrial suppression hearings to determine whether evidence should be excluded at a forthcoming trial. If the evidence is excluded, the prosecutor's case is weakened and a dismissal is more likely. If the defendant loses the motion to suppress, bargaining may resume.

---

[20] 547 U.S. 586 (2006). See § 1.5, discussing a "Knock-and-Announce" Violation.

[21] 555 U.S. 135 (2009).

[22] Herring v. United States, 555 U.S. 135, 144 (2009).

Even *after* a defendant's conviction, the exclusionary rule may be inapplicable to issues presented to a court. For example, in *Pennsylvania Bd. of Probation and Parole v. Scott*,[23] the Court held that the exclusionary rule is inapplicable in parole revocation proceedings. Although a parole officer illegally searched the residence of a known parolee, the Court opted for total inapplicability of the exclusionary rule in parole board hearings. The majority declared that the cost of the exclusionary rule that would alter "the traditionally flexible, administrative nature of parole revocation proceedings," and was not worth the "minimal" deterrence that would result. The Court reasoned that a parole officer would be deterred by the risk of evidence exclusion at a parole hearing, because he is "not engaged in the competitive enterprise of ferreting out crime," and could be sufficiently deterred by "departmental training and discipline and the threat of damage actions."[24]

D. Alternatives to the Rule

During the past half century, the frequency of dismissals has produced increased support for the modification or abolition of the exclusionary rule. Like plea bargaining, not everyone is eager to support proposals to modify the exclusionary rule. One proposal would continue the rule only for charges with shorter sentences, but the rule could not be used in serious cases like homicide and robbery. Those favoring this alternative argue that dangerous people would never be released into the community. Opponents ask whether this alternative approach might encourage overcharging suspects with more serious offenses, or possibly encourage police to violate the Fourth Amendment because they are freed from the rule's constraints in the most serious cases, i.e., those cases in which the exclusionary rule has the greatest deterrent effect.

Calls for modification or rejection of the exclusionary rule for the most part have been unsuccessful. Despite widespread criticism, the exclusionary rule has survived, though not with the same constitutional grounding as when *Mapp* was decided in 1961. The Court continues to believe that "nothing else works" to deter police misconduct.

Public opinion as a method of correcting police misconduct is problematic for two reasons. First, the "public" is unaware of most cases when police misconduct occurs. Second, because case law discussing the rule involves defendants who are guilty of the charged offense, little public sympathy exists for their constitutional claims.

---

[23] 524 U.S. 357 (1998).

[24] Pennsylvania Bd. of Probation and Parole v. Scott, 524 U.S. 357, 368, 369 (1998).

Criminal prosecution as an effective remedy for police who engage in wrongdoing is generally dismissed as impractical. In exercising their discretion, prosecutors rarely seek charges against police. While an occasional criminal prosecution may deter misconduct by others, the infrequency of prosecutions dilutes whatever deterrence could follow an unlikely conviction.

Police review boards, whether composed exclusively of police or local citizens, are rarely effective. Peers have difficulty sanctioning their colleagues, and civilian review boards usually do not identify with the police conduct that is under scrutiny. Moreover, such panels often lack the legal authority, e.g., subpoena power, to enforce their own recommendations for discipline.

Civil lawsuits against police officers and the governmental entity for which they work typically are insufficient or ineffective. Damages are sought under 42 U.S.C. § 1983 against state and municipal employees, or under *Bivens v. Six Unknown Named Agents*[25] against federal law enforcement agents. However, recovery is unlikely, because the officers' good faith is typically a complete defense for individual defendants (but not for the governments unit),[26] damage recoveries against individual officers are rarely enforceable, and case precedent for monetary relief against a governmental unit is available only to the extent that its "policy or custom, whether made by its lawmakers or by those whose edicts or acts may fairly be said to represent official policy, inflicts the injury. . . ."[27]

§ 1.3 Limitations on the Rule's Application

A. Private Actors

As noted in the foregoing discussion, one purpose of the exclusionary rule is to discourage official misconduct. The Bill of Rights affects persons acting in a governmental capacity. While the typical search involves a police officer searching a person or a place, the State action requirement necessary for a constitutional violation is also satisfied. For example, the Fourth Amendment applies to school officials, or a licensing authority is searching to ensure compliance with State law.[28] Civil as well as criminal justice system

---

25 403 U.S. 388 (1971).

26 Owen v. City of Independence, 445 U.S. 622 (1980).

27 Monell v. Department of Social Services of the City of New York, 436 U.S. 658, 694 (1978).

28 See, e.g., New York v. Burger, 482 U.S. 691 (1987); O'Connor v. Ortega, 480 U.S. 709 (1987).

officials must comply with constitutional search and seizure limitations.[29]

Because agency principles may apply to constitutional violations, evidence illegally obtained by private persons acting with or as the agents of law enforcement may be inadmissible. For example, in *Abel v. United States*,[30] a hotel manager consented to the FBI search of the defendant's hotel room after check-out. The evidence obtained from the cooperative or coercive action between the police officers and private citizens was subject to the exclusionary rule.[31] The warrantless search was proper, because the manager had the authority to consent and had exclusive right to possession of the room.

By contrast, a search by a private person acting in a private capacity only does not implicate Fourth Amendment concerns. It is not that such a search is necessarily reasonable; instead, a purely private search, whether reasonable or unreasonable, is none of the Fourth Amendment's concern. Merely because the evidence from such a search is offered at a criminal trial does not convert the prior search from a private act into State action. What matters is not the purpose of the search; it is the involvement of the Government in the search process. *United States v. Jacobsen*[32] held that no Fourth Amendment violation occurred when employees of a private freight carrier opened a damaged package, examined its contents, discovered plastic bags filled with white powder, and *then* called a federal agent who took a trace sample of the powder and tested it.

A middle ground may arise between a purely private search and a cooperative private-public search situation, discussed above. If a private person with access to a container opens it and, after finding incriminating information or objects, sends the container or information to the police, is the search made by a private person or public official? *Jacobsen* noted that no Fourth Amendment search occurs there as long as the police "learn nothing that had not previously been known during the private search." If the private search produced incriminating information but the police "learn nothing" else seems to be an impractical and unlikely situation and standard.[33]

---

29 See New Jersey v. T.L.O., 469 U.S. 325 (1985).

30 362 U.S. 217 (1960).

31 See Abel v. United States, 362 U.S. 217 (1960). See, e.g., Skinner v. Railway Labor Executives' Association, 489 U.S. 602 (1989); Smith v. Maryland, 442 U.S. 735 (1978).

32 466 U.S. 109 (1984).

33 *United States v. Jacobsen*, 466 U.S. at 120.

B. "Silver Platter" Doctrine

Because the constitutional limitation on obtaining evidence is intended to deter all public officers, an unlawful seizure of evidence by an agent of one sovereignty or governmental unit is not cleansed of its taint merely because the fruits of the action are handed to another sovereignty or governmental unit "on a silver platter." For example, In *Elkins v. United States*,[34] State police conducted an illegal search; the Court held that the evidence illegally obtained therefrom was also inadmissible in the defendant's federal trial.

C. "Good Faith" Exception

The good faith exception to the exclusionary rule allows illegally obtained evidence to be admitted during the prosecutor's case-in-chief because the police reasonably relied on the issuance of a search warrant. The Court endorsed the exception in *United States v. Leon*,[35] holding that

> the Fourth Amendment exclusionary rule should be modified so as not to bar the use in the prosecution's case in chief of evidence obtained by officers acting in reasonable reliance on a search warrant issued by a detached and neutral magistrate but ultimately found to be unsupported by probable cause.[36]

In *Leon*, the police sought a search warrant for the suspect's home based on police surveillance. After the judge issued a warrant, the search produced large amounts of illicit drugs. After Leon's indictment, a judge granted his motion to suppress the drugs because the affidavit for the warrant failed to establish probable cause. The Government appealed, and the Court recognized a good faith exception to the exclusionary rule. The Court reasoned that any constitutional harm comes solely from the illegal search and seizure, not from the use of the illegally obtained evidence in a criminal proceeding. Because the exclusionary rule is a judicially created remedy rather than an individual right, courts must decide whether to apply that rule by balancing the costs of excluding the evidence against the probable deterrent effect of exclusion on police misconduct.

When the police execute a search warrant issued by a judge, exclusion to deter the police is ordinarily inappropriate. Because the officer justifiably relied on the prior judgment of the judge in issuing the warrant, "there is no police illegality." From there, it was

---

34 364 U.S. 206 (1960).

35 468 U.S. 897 (1984).

36 United States v. Leon, 468 U.S. 897, 900 (1984).

relatively simple to conclude that "the marginal or nonexistent benefits produced by suppressing evidence obtained in objectively reasonable reliance on a subsequently invalidated search warrant cannot justify the substantial costs of exclusion."[37]

Leon concluded that the costs of the exclusionary rule outweighed the benefits, and recognized the good faith exception. The costs of exclusion allow the guilty defendant to go unpunished or to receive a reduced sentence, as well as public disrespect for the law. Using the balancing test, when an officer in good faith has relied upon a neutral judge's facially valid warrant, the deterrent effect of the exclusionary rule is not served by excluding the evidence.[38]

The Court has used *Leon*'s rationale and discussion to identify additional contexts when the good faith exception applies. For example, the Court has continued to use the *Leon* criteria for whether a police officer has acted in good faith: (1) the officer's expert opinion; (2) the staleness of the warrant; (3) whether the officer sought a prosecutor's advice in preparing affidavits; (4) whether a judge issued a warrant; and (5) whether competent judges could disagree as to the existence of probable cause.[39]

The Court has extended *Leon* in both warrant and non-warrant situations. Although *Leon* indicated that the good faith exception usually does not apply if a police officer did not have a warrant, or was not trying to obtain a warrant though he had had ample time to obtain one, the Court did note a potential for applying Leon to a broader area than warrants, i.e., the exclusionary rule "cannot be expected, and should not be applied, to deter objectively reasonable law enforcement activity."[40]

The Court applied the good faith exception to a *non-warrant* case in *Illinois v. Krull*.[41] There, the police relied on a statute authorizing a specific search, but the statute violated the Fourth Amendment. The Court reasoned that "[t]he approach used in *Leon* is equally applicable to the present case." Applying the exclusionary rule when police reasonably rely on a statute would "have as little deterrent effect on the officers' actions" as in *Leon*. "[L]legislators, like judicial officers, are not the focus of the rule," because there "is nothing to indicate that applying the exclusionary rule to evidence seized pursuant to the state prior to the declaration of its invalidity will act

---

[37] *Id.*, at 922.

[38] *Id.*, at 919.

[39] *Id.*, at 926; United States v. Fama, 758 F.2d 834, 838 (2d Cir. 1985).

[40] *United States v. Leon*, 468 U.S. at 919.

[41] 480 U.S. 340 (1987).

as a significant, additional deterrent"[42] to the occasional enactment of a statute later determined to be unconstitutional.

The Court also extended *Leon* to other warrant situations. In *Arizona v. Evans*,[43] a police officer pulled over a vehicle after seeing the vehicle going the wrong way on a one-way street. After the driver could not produce a driver's license because it was suspended, the officer ran the license number through a database and found an outstanding arrest warrant for the driver. Because the driver dropped a hand-rolled cigarette that smelled like marijuana, the officer searched the vehicle and found a bag of marijuana. After the driver was charged with possession of illegal drugs, the police learned that the arrest warrant had been quashed but has remained in the database only because of a clerical error. The trial court granted the defendant's motion to exclude the marijuana from evidence because it was discovered during the course of an illegal arrest. The Court applied *Leon*'s good faith exception, because the "threat of exclusion of evidence could not be expected to deter such individuals."[44]

In *Herring v. United States*,[45] a police officer contacted a county sheriff about active arrest warrants for the defendant. When the sheriff's clerk reported an existing warrant, the officer arrested the defendant who possessed drugs and a firearm at the time of his arrest. Defendant's motion to suppress alleged that the warrant had been withdrawn five months earlier, but was never removed from the database. The Court concluded that the exclusionary rule was inapplicable because the police "error was the result of isolated negligence attenuated from the arrest."[46] If this were a case where "systemic errors were demonstrated, it might be reckless for officers to rely on an unreliable warrant system." The Court refused to exclude the evidence, because the benefits of negligent police recordkeeping did not outweigh the costs of excluding the evidence. In addition, the officer had reasonably relied on the warrant, and no evidence showed that the error was deliberate or part of a pervasive database problem.

In *Davis v. United States*,[47] Court used the same cost-benefit analysis in concluding that the exclusionary rule not applicable when

---

[42] Illinois v. Krull, 480 U.S. 340, 352 (1987).

[43] 514 U.S. 1 (1995).

[44] Arizona v. Evans, 514 U.S. 1, 15 (1995). See State v. Malecha, 3 N.W.3d 566 (Minn. 2024) (endorses Justice Ginsburg's *Evans* dissent for applying exclusionary rule developed under state constitution; good-faith exception does not extend to a search and arrest based on quashed warrant that appears active to law enforcement due to clerical error o court administration).

[45] 555 U.S. 135 (2009).

[46] Herring v. United States, 555 U.S. 135, 137 (2009).

[47] 564 U.S. 229 (2011).

"the police conduct a search in compliance with binding precedent that is later overruled."[48] Because the exclusionary rule was inapplicable when the police reasonably relied upon a search warrant (*Leon*) and a statute later determined to violate the Fourth Amendment (*Krull*), the Court held that the same conclusion should apply to "searches conducted in objectively reasonable reliance on binding appellate precedent" that is later overruled. "[S]uppression would do nothing to deter police misconduct in these circumstances, and . . . it would come at a high cost to both the truth and the public safety."[49]

A Fourth Amendment violation "does not necessarily mean that the exclusionary rule applies."[50] "The extent to which the exclusionary rule is justified by . . . deterrence principles varies with the culpability of the law enforcement conduct."[51] The rule applies when the police misconduct is deliberate, reckless, grossly negligent, or resulted from systematic negligence. The post-*Leon* cases have consistently held that, based on the type of alleged error, any deterrent effect that exclusion would have on the conduct of the police did not justify the social cost of excluding the evidence.

D. Exceptions to the Good Faith Exception

In addition to announcing the good faith exception to the exclusionary rule, the *Leon* Court described four exceptions (to the exception!) when the good faith exception does not apply. None of these exceptions includes a concern for the police officer's state of mind or bad faith, either of which is insufficient for suppressing evidence.[52]

The first listed exception relates to a situation when the issuing judge has been misled by information in an affidavit that the officer knew was false or would have known was false but for his reckless disregard of the truth.[53] These situations usually relate to knowing (rather than reckless) falsehoods about an informant's identity and credibility, or how recently the informant had seen contraband like drugs in a location. Recklessness tends to be inferred when omitted information is essential to assessing the legality of a search.

---

[48] Davis v. United States, 564 U.S. 229, 232 (2011).

[49] *Id.*, at 232.

[50] *Herring v. United States*, 555 U.S. at 150.

[51] *Id.*, at 143.

[52] Scott v. United States, 436 U.S. 128 (1978).

[53] *United States v. Leon*, 468 U.S. at 923. See § 4.5(C), discussing *Franks v. Delaware*.

Leon's second exception occurs when the issuing judge wholly abandoned his judicial role.[54] *Lo-Ji Sales, Inc. v. New York*[55] is the only case cited by the Court; in that case a judge issued a warrant to seize an obscene film and then accompanied the officers on the raid of the adult bookstore where they believed the film was stored. The case law deals with a judge's failure to act in a detached and neutral manner, such as (1) a part-time magistrate who shares a law practice with the prosecutor, (2) a judge being paid for every search warrant that he issued, or (3) a judge fails to display judicial independence by not reading the supporting affidavit or warrant that is issued.

Third, an exception also applies if the officer relied on the warrant based on an affidavit "so lacking in indicia of probable cause to render official belief in its existence entirely unreasonable."[56] In effect, this standard is about what a reasonably well-trained officer would know, and it applies both to those providing information to the affiant, persons who obtained the warrant and those who executed it.

A well-trained officer knows the types of information that an affidavit must contain to satisfy the probable cause standard in *Illinois v. Gates*, e.g., establishing a confidential informant's reliability, the sources of his information and the basis of his knowledge. He also knows (1) the technical requirements for a valid warrant in the jurisdiction, (2) the distinctions between probable cause to search and probable cause to arrest, (3) that the mere presence of unnamed and undescribed persons does not allow a search of those persons, and (4) the minimum requirements for seizing various types of contraband that are the subject of the specific warrant.

The last *Leon* exception requires suppression of an otherwise good faith warrant that is so facially deficient that no reasonable officer who is responsible for executing the warrant could have believed that the search warrant was valid.[57] For example, in *Groh v. Ramirez*,[58] the face of the warrant failed to state or list what items were to be seized. A similar defect would be the absence of specificity for items or persons to be searched. The requirement arguably is not

---

54 *United States v. Leon*, 468 U.S. at 923. See, e.g., United States v. Parker, 373 F.3d 770 (6th Cir. 2004) (trial commissioner also worked as administrative assistant in county jail was not neutral and detached).

55 442 U.S. 319 (1979).

56 *United States v. Leon*, 468 U.S. at 923, quoting Brown v. Illinois, 422 U.S. 590, 611 (1975) (Powell, J., concurring in part). See, e.g., United States v. Bershchansky, 788 F.3d 102 (2d Cir. 2015) (failure to name defendant or particularize place to be searched).

57 *United States v. Leon*, 468 U.S. at 923. See, e.g., United States v. Doyle, 650 F.3d 460 (4th Cir. 2011) (facially deficient for failure to state when alleged crimes were committed).

58 540 U.S. 551 (2004).

satisfied if there is any facial deficiency, no matter how minor it may be. The warrant should not be dependent on judicially created ideas such as curing overbroad documents.

Some State courts have rejected the good faith exception under State constitutional law, because the Court decided *Leon* as a matter of *federal* constitutional law. These States disagree with the Court's deterrence analysis, concluding that the approach does not exist under their constitutions. In those States, the unconstitutional conduct of a federal agent with a warrant is subject to the good faith exception, but the same evidence by a municipal officer would not be admissible.

E. Federal Habeas Corpus

When a federal habeas corpus petitioner had a full and fair opportunity in State court to litigate his Fourth Amendment claim, the exclusionary rule does not apply, per *Stone v. Powell*.[59] "Even if one rationally could assume that some additional incremental deterrence effect would be presented in isolated cases, the resulting advance of the legitimate goal of furthering Fourth Amendment rights would be outweighed by the acknowledged costs to other values vital to a rational system of criminal justice."[60] Subsequent decisions by the Court have refused to extend the *Stone*'s Fourth Amendment limitation to other Bill of Rights' issues.[61]

F. Other Exceptions

The exclusionary rule is usually inapplicable in civil cases. When Los Angeles police illegally seized evidence, *United States v. Janis*[62] permitted the evidence to be used in a federal civil tax proceeding for back taxes. The rule also does not apply in civil deportation proceedings.[63]

Besides prison time, criminal defendants increasingly face statutory forfeiture of instrumentalities used in their commission of specified criminal activity (e.g., cars, boats and airplanes used for drug smuggling transportation or homes used to store contraband). While the exclusionary rule continues to apply to civil forfeiture proceedings because these proceedings are deemed "quasi-criminal" in nature, the leading cases were decided before the Court began in

---

59 428 U.S. 465 (1976).

60 Stone v. Powell, 428 U.S. 465, 493–94 (1976).

61 See, e.g., Withrow v. Williams, 507 U.S. 680 (1983) (*Miranda* challenge); Rose v. Mitchell, 443 U.S. 545 (1979) (grand jury discrimination); Jackson v. Virginia, 443 U.S. 307 (1979) (insufficient evidence challenge).

62 428 U.S. 433 (1976).

63 Immigration & Naturalization Service v. Lopez-Mendoza, 468 U.S. 1032 (1984).

the 1970s to limit the rule's application to situations where incremental deterrence of police conduct is achieved.[64] Whenever the Court revisits this line of cases, it may take a different judicial stance on the issue.

Ker v. Illinois[65] and *Frisbie v. Collins*[66] stand for the proposition that the "body" or identity of a defendant or respondent in a criminal or a civil proceeding is never itself suppressible as a fruit of an unlawful arrest.

§ 1.4 Impeachment

A. Impeachment with Illegally Obtained Evidence

The exclusionary rule applies to the prosecution's presentation of evidence during its case-in-chief at trial. However, even though evidence is inadmissible during the prosecutor's presentation, that same evidence may be introduced by the prosecution to "impeach" a defendant's credibility during cross-examination. Several examples suffice.

In *Harris v. New York*[67] the defendant during direct examination denied the charge of selling drugs. The trial court then allowed the prosecutor to impeach the defendant's credibility by offering a statement obtained in violation of *Miranda*. The Court held that statements that were derived from improper *Miranda* warnings nevertheless could be used to impeach the defendant. Strategically, while a defendant has a constitutional right to testify at trial, the prosecutor's ability to impeach him, even with illegally obtained evidence, may affect his decision to testify.

> The impeachment process here undoubtedly provided valuable aid to the jury in assessing petitioner's credibility, and the benefits of this process should not be lost, in our view, because of the speculative possibility that impermissible police conduct will be encouraged thereby. Assuming that the exclusionary rule has a deterrent effect on proscribed police conduct, sufficient deterrence flows when the evidence in question is made unavailable to the prosecution in its case in chief.
>
> Every criminal defendant is privileged to testify in his own defense, or to refuse to do so. But that privilege cannot be construed to include the right to commit perjury. . .

---

64 One 1958 Plymouth Sedan v. Commonwealth of Pennsylvania, 380 U.S. 693 (1965).

65 119 U.S. 436 (1886).

66 342 U.S. 519 (1952).

67 401 U.S. 222 (1971).

> Having voluntarily taken the stand, petitioner was under an obligation to speak truthfully and accurately, and the prosecution here did no more than utilize the traditional truth-testing devices of the adversary process.[68]

After *Harris*, prosecutors could use most types of illegally obtained evidence to impeach a defendant's direct testimony. When prosecutors impeach a defendant's direct or cross-examination testimony with illegally obtained statement admitting to the charged offense, prior to impeachment with an illegally obtained confession, the prosecution must establish that the confession was given voluntarily, i.e., not in violation of Due Process.[69] In *Harris*, the police did not give the defendant complete *Miranda* warnings but he did not "claim that the statements made to the police were coerced or involuntary." In *Oregon v. Hass*,[70] the police advised the defendant of his rights, and continued to question him even after he requested counsel. The Court saw no difference between *Hass* and *Harris*, because "inadmissibility would pervert the constitutional right into a right to falsify free from the embarrassment of impeachment evidence from the defendant's own mouth."[71]

In *United States v. Havens*,[72] the Court enlarged the impeachment opportunity, permitting impeachment of statements elicited on cross-examination when cross-examination was "reasonably suggested" by the defendant's direct testimony. The defendant testified during cross-examination that he did not own an incriminating t-shirt that had been illegally seized by the Government. The Court held that the prosecution properly cross-examined the defendant about the t-shirt because he had denied owning it.

> In terms of impeaching a defendant's seemingly false statements with his prior inconsistent utterances or with other reliable evidence available to the government, we see no difference of constitutional magnitude between the defendant's statements on direct examination and his answers to questions put to him on cross-examination that are plainly within the scope of the defendant's direct examination.[73]

---

[68] Harris v. New York, 401 U.S. 222, 225 (1971).

[69] Mincey v. Arizona, 437 U.S. 385 (1978). See Chapters 12 & 13, discussing constitutional grounds for challenging a defendant's incriminating statements.

[70] 420 U.S. 714 (1975).

[71] Oregon v. Hass, 420 U.S. 714, 723 (1975).

[72] 446 U.S. 620 (1980).

[73] United States v. Havens, 446 U.S. 620, 627 (1980).

Despite the forgoing discussion, impeachment with illegally obtained evidence from either a defendant's direct testimony or statements elicited on cross-examination is prohibited when either type of testimony is given in response to a grant of immunity. For example, in *New Jersey v. Portash*,[74] grand jury statements made under a grant of immunity were inadmissible in a later criminal trial, even for impeachment purposes. The Court distinguished *Hass* and *Harris*, because those defendants did not claim that their illegally obtained statements were coerced or involuntary. Because the Court regarded immunized testimony as "the essence of coerced testimony,"[75] it refused to permit impeachment with immunized statements.

Most recently in *Kansas v. Ventris*,[76] police violated the defendant's Sixth Amendment right to counsel by placing an informant in the defendant's cell to hear his incriminating statements. The Court concluded that the defendant's right to counsel was violated "at the prior critical stage which produced the inculpatory evidence," and permitted the use of the overheard statements for impeachment. Like *Harris*, the Court stated that *Ventris* did "not involve. . . the prevention of a constitutional violation, but rather the scope of the remedy for a violation that has already occurred."[77]

The use of illegally obtained evidence to impeach applies only to the defendant's testimony; it cannot be used to impeach other defense witnesses.[78] The rationale for the limitation is that permitting impeachment of all defense witnesses would compromise the deterrent effect of the exclusionary rule.

B. Impeachment About Pretrial Silence

Prosecutors sometimes may attempt to impeach a defendant a trial by asking about his pretrial silence. Prosecutors cannot ask about a defendant's post-arrest silence *after* he received his *Miranda* warnings, either to impeach or as substantive evidence of guilt.[79] In *Doyle v. Ohio*,[80] the Court held that impeachment by defendant's post-arrest silence after he had received the *Miranda* warnings was impermissible. Not only is "every post-arrest silence. . . insolubly

[74] 440 U.S. 450 (1979).

[75] New Jersey v. Portash, 440 U.S. 450, 459 (1979).

[76] 556 U.S. 586 (2009).

[77] Kansas v. Ventris, 556 U.S. 586, 593 (2009).

[78] James v. Illinois, 493 U.S. 307 (1990).

[79] Wainwright v. Greenfield, 474 U.S. 284 (1986) (substantive evidence); Doyle v. Ohio, 426 U.S. 610 (1976) (impeachment).

[80] 426 U.S. 610 (1976).

ambiguous" because it "may be nothing more than the arrestee's exercise of [his] *Miranda* rights," but use of the silence to impeach "would be fundamentally unfair" given the fact that the warnings carry the implicit "assurance that silence will carry no penalty."[81]

Several later cases distinguished *Doyle*. *Greer v. Miller*[82] held that *Doyle* is violated only when post-warning silence is actually used for impeachment purposes. The prosecution asked the defendant on cross-examination why he hadn't "told this story to anybody when you got arrested." The trial court sustained defense counsel's immediate objection, and told the jury to "disregard questions . . . to which objections were sustained." The Court held that there was no *Doyle* violation, because the court had not permitted the prosecutor " 'to undertake impeachment on' " or " 'to call attention to' [defendant's] silence" and the fact of that silence therefore "was not submitted to the jury as evidence from which it was allowed to draw any permissible inference."[83]

Other cases distinguished Doyle based on the timing of the arrest or the giving of *Miranda* warnings. In *Jenkins v. Anderson*,[84] the Court approved of using the defendant's pre-arrest silence to impeach his self-defense claim for two weeks after the crime. The Court permitted impeachment by the defendant's prior inconsistent statements in *Anderson v. Charles*[85] after *Miranda* warnings, because "a defendant who voluntarily speaks after receiving *Miranda* warnings has not been induced to remain silent."[86] *Fletcher v. Weir*[87] permitted the use of the defendant's post-arrest silence not preceded by *Miranda* warnings to impeach the defendant, because this was not "a case where the government had induced silence by implicitly assuring the defendant that his silence would not be used against him."[88]

Salinas v. Texas[89] addressed whether a defendant's silence, in response to police questioning at a time when he had not been placed in custody and had not been given the *Miranda* warnings, is admissible in the prosecutor's case-in-chief as evidence of defendant's guilt. In *Salinas*, the plurality concluded that the defendant's Fifth Amendment claim failed because he did not expressly invoke the

---

81 Doyle v. Ohio, 426 U.S. 610 (1976).

82 483 U.S. 756 (1987).

83 Greer v. Miller, 483 U.S. 756, 774–75 (1987).

84 447 U.S. 231 (1980).

85 447 U.S. 404 (1980).

86 Anderson v. Charles, 447 U.S. 404, 408 (1980).

87 455 U.S. 603 (1982).

88 Fletcher v. Weir, 455 U.S. 603, 606 (1982).

89 570 U.S. 178 (2013) (plurality opinion).

privilege in response to the police questioning.[90] This, they explained, is because the general rule that a witness who "desires the protection of the privilege . . . must claim it"

§ 1.5 "Knock-and-Announce" Violation

Police officers with a search warrant ordinarily must knock on the door and announce their purpose before entering the premises. In *Hudson v. Michigan*,[91] after knocking the police waited only three to five seconds to enter and search the defendant's residence. Despite deciding that the wait time was too brief before entering after the knock and announcement of their presence, the Court refused to suppress the objects and other information learned by the police during the search.

Applying a cost-benefit analysis, the Court decided that the exclusionary rule should not be indiscriminately applied. Its use should be limited to situations "where its remedial objectives are thought most efficaciously served," i.e., "where its deterrence benefits outweigh its substantial social costs."[92] The Court observed that its knock-and-announce rule was intended to prevent violence, property damage, and impositions on privacy, not to prevent police from conducting a search for which they have a valid warrant.

The 2020 police murder of Breonna Taylor in Louisville, Kentucky, produced nationwide State and municipal legislative attempts to abolish the knock-and-announce practice. Continued use of the knock-and-announce practice has dramatically shown that the effect of the Court's language in reality has cost lives, as it has discounted the exclusionary rule.

§ 1.6 Standing to Exclude Evidence

When the police obtain evidence by conduct that violates the Fourth, Fifth, or Sixth Amendment, and they seek to use it against a defendant in a criminal case, the defendant must establish that he has standing to object. Any defendant has standing of the type contemplated by the Article III "case or controversy" requirement, because he has a real interest in the case and can be relied on, as much as anyone could, to litigate all the factual and legal questions.

---

[90] In State v. Lovejoy, 89 A.3d 1066, 1075 (Me. 2014), noting the *Salinas* split, the court held that there was a sufficient showing of defendant's "invocation of his right against self-incrimination" where he "terminated a telephone conversation with the investigating detective upon stating that he wanted to speak with a lawyer, and then did not return the detective's subsequent telephone calls," thus "provid[ing] sufficient information to demonstrate his invocation of his right against self-incrimination."

[91] 547 U.S. 586 (2006).

[92] Hudson v. Michigan, 547 U.S. 586, 591 (2006).

But it is thought too costly to require the exclusion of unconstitutionally obtained evidence at the request of a defendant who was not himself directly injured by the police misconduct at the time of the police activity.

If there is a calculation of social costs and benefits, is there another categorical method for determining the cases for which standing is required for a defendant to suppress evidence. For example, why not disregard standing and order exclusion when the police conduct was deliberate or severe, or where the crime charged was not serious? Or, why not abolish standing completely?[93] Eliminating a standing requirement would redirect the focus on the allegation of police misconduct, instead of mandating proof of injury to the defendant from the misconduct. Unless and until such changes occur, the case law defines standing requirements, some of which are easy to administer and some are complex.

A defendant has standing to challenge the admission of illegally obtained evidence only if the defendant's personal constitutional rights were violated. A person who lacks standing cannot challenge offered evidence, even if it was illegally obtained. Two examples illustrate the principle. In *United States v. Payner*,[94] the prosecution introduced documents illegally seized from the briefcase of a bank officer against the defendant, who lacked standing to request exclusion of the documents because the illegal search did not violate his own constitutional rights. In *Alderman v. United States*,[95] although illegally wiretapped conversations occurring on a homeowner's premises could not be introduced against the defendant homeowner, they were admissible against coconspirators and codefendants whose rights were not violated by the illegal search.

To enable a defendant to establish standing and to challenge evidence that he is seeking to quash, suppression hearing statements made by him to make that constitutional challenge are not admissible at a later trial on his substantive guilt of the offense charged.[96]

A. Standing in Fifth and Sixth Amendment Cases

The easier standing cases relate to the admissibility of confessions and identification procedures, because generally only a person from whom an incriminating statement has been illegally obtained has standing to challenge its admissibility. Another person

---

93 See Alderman v. United States, 394 U.S. 165, 208 (1969) (Fortas, J., concurring).

94 447 U.S. 727 (1980).

95 394 U.S. 165 (1969).

96 Simmons v. United States, 390 U.S. 377 (1968).

implicated by the confessor lacks standing to challenge it.[97] Likewise, only a person who is subjected to improper identification procedures may challenge the admission into evidence of the resulting evidence.

B. Standing in Fourth Amendment Cases

The Court has adopted the position that the phrase, "reasonable expectation of privacy," embodies two separate but related principles. First, as discussed in the next Chapter, the concept of "Fourth Amendment activity"[98] asks whether the challenged police activity constituted a search or seizure, and whether an invasion of constitutionally protected privacy has occurred. Second, the standing cases look to *whose* privacy has been violated, focusing on the capacity of the individual to assert the claim. Together, standing is about establishing a nexus between the area searched and the defendant seeking to raise the Fourth Amendment issue.

The interrelationship between the issues is as follows. Proving standing shows Fourth Amendment activity, i.e., the specific defendant's standing verifies a reasonable expectation of privacy. However, establishing that there is Fourth Amendment activity by the police does not guarantee that the particular defendant will have standing. If there is no Fourth Amendment activity, there is no need to worry about the standing issue, because the exclusionary rule applies only to Fourth Amendment activity, i.e., to find that there is no Fourth Amendment activity is to conclude that no one has standing to challenge the police conduct.

If the police enter a person's house, they may have violated a reasonable expectation of privacy, but a defendant may not have standing to object to that illegal entry if *this defendant* had no reasonable expectation of privacy in the premises. (In other cases, such as aerial overflight cases, there will be no search at all and thus a court will never reach the question of standing.) The question of whether personal rights have been violated is a separate question from whether a search has occurred, even though both questions are governed by the same test of reasonable expectation of privacy.

C. Rakas v. Illinois

Most of the controversy on standing issues relates to Fourth Amendment problems. A defendant has standing to challenge the fruits of the search or seizure only when he has a reasonable expectation of privacy in the area searched or in the evidence seized. By contrast, a person cannot complain about the reasonableness or

---

[97] See People v. Varnum, 66 Cal. 2d 808, 427 P.2d 772 (1967) (suspects' statements could be used against another defendant).

[98] See Chapter 2, discussing Fourth Amendment Activity.

legality of a search or seizure of premises, property or person of *another* person.[99] For example, a driver is seized from the moment his vehicle comes to a halt on the side of the road. A passenger in that vehicle has standing to object to such constitutional violations and to have any property suppressed that is found in the vehicle, if any of the following is unreasonable: (1) the stopping of the vehicle; (2) the length of a passenger's detention; or (3) the passenger's removal from the vehicle. A defendant's motion to suppress must establish that his own Fourth Amendment rights were violated by the challenged search or seizure.

In *Rakas v. Illinois*,[100] after a robbery, the police stopped the suspected getaway vehicle, which the owner was driving and in which the defendant was a passenger. During a search of the vehicle, the police found a box of rifle shells in the glove compartment and a sawed-off rifle under the front passenger seat and arrested the defendant. The passengers stated that the gun and shells did not belong to them. Before trial, the defendant moved to suppress the rifle and shells on Fourth Amendment grounds. The trial court denied the motion because the defendant had no standing to object to the vehicle search, because he did not own either the car or the rifle and shells.

On appeal, the Court held that Fourth Amendment rights are personal to the defendant and cannot be vicariously asserted. A defendant's rights have not been invaded by an illegal search of someone else's premises or property. The defendant in *Rakas* lacked standing to challenge the search of a glove compartment and the area under the passenger seat. A passenger normally would lack a legitimate expectation of privacy in those areas.

Before *Rakas*, part of the prevailing standing principles was to grant automatic standing to a person who was "legitimately on the premises" when the search occurred.[101] The Court later decided that the phrase was too broad for measuring Fourth Amendment rights, and changed the argument by saying that a defendant would have Fourth Amendment standing to challenge a search only if he had a legitimate expectation of privacy in the premises he was using. The reverse approach would be to deny standing to a person who cannot assert a property or a possessory interest in the area searched or an interest in the property seized. In *Rakas*, that person would lack

---

99 Rakas v. Illinois, 439 U.S. 128 (1978).

100 439 U.S. 128 (1978).

101 Jones v. United States, 362 U.S. 257 (1960), overruled by United States v. Salvucci, 448 U.S. 83 (1980).

standing, i.e., no legitimate expectation of privacy in the glove compartment or the area under the vehicle's passenger seat.

It is important that the passengers in *Rakas* denied ownership of the gun and the shells. Even if there were nothing illegal about the vehicle stop or the removal of the passengers from the vehicle, a passenger still has standing to complain about any search of his personal effects in the vehicle. Because *Rakas* dealt only with the passengers in the vehicle, the Court did not address whether the vehicle owner had a stronger interest in the vehicle even if he was absent at the time of the stop or search.

As long as the owner has not abandoned the vehicle or made a bailment of the vehicle, he has standing to challenge any evidence seized from the stop or search of the vehicle. The owner's family members and others who share in the use of the vehicle with the owner also may have standing if they regularly travel in the vehicle or keep their effects there, even if they were absent from the stop and search of the vehicle.

Two years after *Rakas* in *United States v. Salvucci,*[102] the Court put the *Jones* "automatic standing" concept to rest. Defendants were charged with possession of stolen mail. Federal authorities had seized the stolen checks that were at the center of the indictment during a search of the defendant's mother's apartment. The defendants moved to suppress the checks because the affidavit in support of the search warrant did not show probable cause. The trial court granted the motion and the appellate court affirmed, relying on the "automatic standing" theory in *Jones v. United States,*[103] without regard to whether the defendant had any reasonable expectation of privacy in the apartment.

The Court overruled *Jones* and held that a defendant charged with possessory crimes has standing to use the exclusionary rule only if his own Fourth Amendment rights were violated. With *Jones* overruled, the prosecution more easily can rely on *Rakas* and prove the charged crime, but also assert that its conduct did not deprive this defendant of his Fourth Amendment rights. Specifically in *Salvucci,* the Government simultaneously showed that the defendant had a possessory interest in the checks that were seized, while denying that he had any expectation of privacy in his mother's apartment.

In standing cases, it is important to isolate which police act is objectionable. If the defendant in *Rakas* had challenged the stop of the vehicle in which he was riding or had challenged the seizure of

---

[102] 448 U.S. 83 (1980).

[103] 362 U.S. 257 (1960).

his person,[104] he would probably have had standing to challenge the evidence seized as a fruit of the violation of his personal rights. As it was, however, he challenged the legitimacy of the search of the vehicle, in which he had no reasonable expectation of privacy.

D. Other Fourth Amendment Standing Cases

The standing test relates to whether the defendant claims a proprietary interest in the items seized and whether he had a legitimate expectation of privacy in the area searched. For example, a person has no reasonable expectation of privacy in a stolen vehicle, and thus lacks standing to challenge the search of the vehicle.

In *Rawlings v. Kentucky*,[105] police officers had an arrest warrant for someone else, but when they arrived at that person's residence, they found another resident along with others. As they searched the residence looking for the person named in the warrant, the officer smelled marijuana smoke and saw marijuana seeds in plain view. Two officers left but returned in less than an hour with a search warrant for the entire residence.

After an officer read the search warrant and gave *Miranda* warnings to the occupants, he ordered one occupant to empty her purse. As illegal drugs fell from the purse, the purse's owner told the defendant "to take what was his" and he immediately claimed ownership. After the officer searched the defendant, finding $4500 in cash along with a knife, he was arrested. The trial court denied his motion to suppress the drugs and money, as well as his statements claiming the drugs when the police saw the drugs.

On appeal from his conviction, the Court held that the defendant had no expectation of privacy in his friend's purse; even though he claimed ownership of the drugs seized from her purse, he had no prior access to it or the right to exclude others from it. The Court observed that, while the defendant's ownership of the drugs was one fact to be considered, "arcane" concepts of property law do not control the ability to claim the protections of the Fourth Amendment. Still, a privacy interest in the place searched is the crucial factor, rather than an ownership interest in the items seized, i.e., a defendant cannot use the exclusionary rule where his property is located when he lacks a privacy interest.

By contrast, in *Byrd v. United States*,[106] the defendant's girlfriend rented a car and immediately turned it over to the

---

[104] See Berkemer v. McCarty, 468 U.S. 420 (1984) (a passenger in a car stopped by the police had standing to challenge the stop; stopping a vehicle and detaining its occupants constitutes a seizure).

[105] 448 U.S. 98 (1980).

[106] 584 U.S. 395 (2018).

defendant who was later stopped with forty-nine bricks of heroin in the trunk. The Government claimed that only authorized drivers of rental vehicles have standing, i.e., legitimate expectations of privacy in those vehicles. This view misread *Rakas*, which did not hold that passengers could never have an expectation of privacy in vehicles. Instead, the Court relied on Justice Powell's concurrence in *Rakas* that a "distinction . . . may be made in some circumstances between the Fourth Amendment's rights of passengers and the rights of an individual who has exclusive control" of a vehicle or "of its locked compartments."[107]

Byrd noted "that, as a general rule, someone in otherwise lawful possession and control [with the attendant right to exclude] of a rental car has a reasonable expectation of privacy in it even if the rental agreement does not list him or her as an authorized driver."[108] The Court favorably compared Byrd's expectation of privacy in the rented vehicle to "whether the defendant's friend owned or leased the apartment he permitted the defendant to use in his absence."[109] The reasonable expectation of privacy does not depend on whether the defendant owns or rents a vehicle.[110]

The Court has also addressed standing issues for invitees and overnight guests. In *Minnesota v. Carter*,[111] a police officer peered through a gap in the renter's closed blinds to observe the defendant and the apartment renter bagging cocaine. After his arrest, the defendant moved unsuccessfully to suppress the drugs seized from the apartment. The Court held that the defendant did not have the requisite standing, because he failed to show that he personally had an expectation of privacy in the apartment and that his expectation was reasonable.

The Court looked to several factors to evaluate the standing issue, e.g., the purely commercial nature (bagging cocaine) of the transaction, the relatively short time that the defendant had been in the apartment, and a lack of prior connection with the renter. This defendant's status as an invitee fell somewhere on a continuum between an overnight guest (the *Olson* case discussed in the next paragraph) and someone merely legitimately on the premises (who has no standing). The Court concluded that a person using another person's apartment to cut cocaine lacked privacy rights there and therefore lacked standing.

---

107 *Rakas v. Illinois*, 439 U.S. at 154 (Powell, J., concurring).

108 Byrd v. United States, 584 U.S. 395, 398–99 (2018).

109 See United States v. Jones, 565 U.S. 400 (2012).

110 *Byrd v. United States*, 584 U.S. at 408.

111 525 U.S. 83 (1998).

In *Minnesota v. Olson*,[112] the police suspected the defendant of driving the getaway vehicle in a robbery-murder. After the police found the murder weapon and the murderer, they went to the home of two women where the police thought the defendant was staying. During a telephone call with one of the women, the police could hear a male voice say, "Tell them I left." The police entered the home without consent, found the defendant in a closet, and arrested him. He soon made an inculpatory statement that the trial judge refused to suppress. After his conviction, he appealed.

The Court held that the defendant had standing to challenge the legality of the warrantless entry into the home. His status as an overnight guest staying in a home with the permission of the owner gave him a reasonable expectation of privacy there and entitled him to suppression of any evidence obtained by an unlawful entry into the premises. Combining *Carter* (a commercial guest) and *Olson* (an overnight guest), if Carter was on the premises (for the first time) to prepare baggies of cocaine but had brought his overnight bag to stay until the next day, would the Court have held that he had standing to challenge a search that occurred the following morning?

Summarizing, how does a defendant sustain his burden to prove that he has standing for challenging a violation of his Fourth Amendment rights? A multifactor approach regarding an objective expectation of privacy as used in *Carter* includes whether the defendant has: (1) claimed property ownership currently or in the past; (2) a possessory interest or exclusive interest in the thing seized; (3) a possessory interest in the place searched, temporarily or permanently; (4) the right to exclude others from that place;[113] (5) a subjective expectation that the place would remain free from governmental invasion;[114] (6) taking normal precautions to maintain privacy;[115] and (7) common authority over property or premises in order to give valid consent to an intrusion.[116]

E. Standing Under Trial Court's Supervisory Power

Standing to challenge the admissibility of evidence is sometimes granted under the trial court's supervisory power, but that standing concept "is applied with some caution even when the defendant

---

112 495 U.S. 91 (1990).

113 See Rawlings v. Kentucky, 448 U.S. 98 (1980).

114 *Id.*

115 See Katz v. U.S., 389 U.S. 347 (1967). See Chapter 2, discussing Fourth Amendment Activity.

116 United States v. Matlock, 415 U.S. 164 (1974). See Chapter 8, discussing Consent Searches.

asserts a violation of his own rights."[117] In *United States v. Payner*,[118] at the defendant's bench trial for tax fraud, he moved to suppress a loan guarantee agreement in which he pledged funds in a foreign bank account that he denied maintaining. The trial court found the defendant guilty, but it then ruled that the Government had discovered the loan agreement through an illegal search, thereby suppressing all the Government's evidence other than the defendant's tax return. Because of the suppression, the trial court set aside the conviction.

Although the defendant lacked Fourth Amendment standing to challenge the illegal search, the trial court used its inherent supervisory power to exclude the evidence tainted by the search. The Court agreed that the defendant lacked Fourth Amendment standing, because the search of the bank officer's briefcase did not violate the defendant's legitimate expectation of privacy. However, the search did violate the rights of a third party—the bank officer.

The Court also held that the supervisory power of the trial court was improperly invoked, because that power does not apply when admissible evidence is seized unlawfully from a third party who is not before the court.

> We conclude that the supervisory power does not authorize a federal court to suppress otherwise admissible evidence on the ground that it was seized unlawfully from a third party not before the court. . . . The values assigned to the competing interests do not change because a court has elected to analyze the question under the supervisory power instead of the Fourth Amendment. In either case, the need to deter the underlying conduct and the detrimental impact of excluding the evidence remain precisely the same.[119]

§ 1.7 Fruit of the Poisonous Tree Doctrine

A. Nature of the Doctrine

The exclusionary rule requires the suppression of any evidence that is either the direct or indirect result of illegal police conduct. Suppose a person is arrested and a search incident to the arrest reveals illegal drugs. The "fruit of the poisonous tree" doctrine precludes *both* the admissibility of evidence which is the direct result of a violation of the defendant's rights (here, the arrest), *and* any

---

117 United States v. Payner, 447 U.S. 727, 734–35 (1980).

118 447 U.S. 727 (1980).

119 *Id.*, at 735–36.

evidence obtained by an exploitation of that violation (here, the drugs found during the search incident to the arrest).

The doctrine is especially useful for defendants who lack standing to challenge the alleged fruit of the original violation. For example, if a confession was obtained from codefendant A as a result of an illegal seizure of codefendant B, codefendant B cannot directly attack the admissibility of A's confession because B lacks standing. However, under the fruit of the poisonous tree doctrine, B can prevent the admission of A's confession if B has standing to challenge B's own illegal seizure, which violated B's rights, and if B can show a direct link between B's illegal seizure and A's confession.[120]

Suppose the police arrest a suspect and then find drugs during a search incident to arrest of the arrestee's clothing. A defendant must prove three things in order to use the fruit of the poisonous tree doctrine. First, he has standing to challenge the original violation,[121] i.e., here, the arrest. Second, the defendant must prove that the original police activity violated his rights, i.e., the arrest. For example, in *Hayes v. Florida,*[122] when the police lacked probable cause to arrest the defendant, fingerprints obtained from his illegal investigative detention at the police station were inadmissible as the fruit of an illegal detention. And in *Florida v. Royer,*[123] after the police illegally confined the defendant, his consent to search his luggage was invalid as fruit of an unlawful confinement. Finally, the defendant must prove that the evidence sought to be admitted against him, i.e., the drugs, was obtained as a result of the illegal arrest. The burden of proving that evidence is not the fruit of the poisonous tree is on the prosecution. If all three steps are not met, the defendant seeking to suppress some piece of evidence must directly challenge its admissibility rather than using the indirect method of the fruit of the poisonous tree doctrine, i.e., challenge directly what was found during the search incident, separate from the legality of the arrest.

In *Silverthorne v. United States,*[124] federal officers unlawfully seized documents from the defendants. After a federal judge ordered the documents returned to them, the federal prosecutor directed the grand jury to subpoena the same documents. The Court held that the subpoenas were invalid.

---

[120] See Wong Sun v. United States, 371 U.S. 471 (1963).

[121] See § 1.6, discussing Standing to Exclude Evidence.

[122] 470 U.S. 811 (1985).

[123] 460 U.S. 491 (1983).

[124] 251 U.S. 385 (1920).

> The essence of a provision forbidding the acquisition of evidence in a certain way is that not merely evidence so acquired shall not be used before the Court but that it shall not be used at all. Of course this does not mean that the facts thus obtained become sacred and inaccessible. If knowledge of them is gained from an independent source they may be proved like any others, but the knowledge gained by the Government's own wrong cannot be used by it in the way proposed.[125]

In *Wong Sun v. United States*,[126] after federal agents broke down the door of defendant's laundry and chased him down the hall, they arrested James Wah Toy without probable cause; Toy made incriminating statements to the federal drug agents about selling narcotics; his statements also led the agents to Johnnie Yee, from whom they seized an ounce of drugs. Yee then claimed that he had purchased the drugs from Toy and another man known to Yee as "Sea Dog." Toy identified Sea Dog as Wong Sun and directed the agents to where he lived. Wong Sun was quickly arrested; several days after his release he returned to the police station and he gave the agents a written confession. At their trial, the agents relied on Toy's oral statements and Wong Sun's written confession. All three men were convicted of violating federal drug laws.

An important threshold issue for the Court was to reject the fruit of the poisonous tree concept as simply a "but-for" standard. The Court declined to "hold that all evidence is 'fruit of the poisonous tree' simply because it would not have come to light but for the illegal actions of the police."[127] As if to emphasize that it was not applying a but-for test, the Court held that Wong Sun's confession was untainted by the illegal police entry and his illegal arrest. Wong Sun confessed after his release from custody and then voluntarily returned to the station two days later.

The Court described its task as determining "whether, granting establishment of the primary illegality, the evidence to which instant objection is made has been come at by exploitation of that illegality or instead by means sufficiently distinguishable to be purged of the primary taint."[128] The Court held that the arrests of both Wong Sun and Toy violated the Fourth Amendment because probable cause was lacking. Using the fruit of the poisonous tree doctrine, a statement made by Toy immediately following the illegal entry and arrest was clearly not voluntary under Due Process. The drugs discovered

---

125 Silverthorne Lumber Co. v. United States, 251 U.S. 385, 392 (1920).

126 371 U.S. 471 (1963).

127 *Wong Sun v. United States*, 371 U.S. at 487–88.

128 *Id.*, at 488.

during the search of Yee and based on information in Toy's statement also were inadmissible against Toy.

What about the admissibility of Wong Sun's confession as the fruit of his arrest? He had standing to challenge his own arrest. There was no probable cause for his arrest. But the confession was not the fruit of the illegal arrest, because the connection between the arrest and the confession was so attenuated that it could not be considered tainted by the illegal arrest. After his release, he waited several days to return and confess. Thus, to suppress the confession, Wong Sun's only path was to challenge his confession on its merits.

In *Arizona v. Evans*,[129] the Court found that suppression of the fruits of a vehicular search was unnecessary, although the arrest preceding the search was based on a warrant that in fact had been quashed.

> The core rationale consistently advanced by this Court for extending the exclusionary rule to evidence that is the fruit of unlawful police conduct has been that this admittedly drastic and socially costly course is needed to deter police from violations of constitutional and statutory protections. This Court has accepted the argument that the way to ensure such protections is to exclude evidence seized as a result of such violations notwithstanding the high social cost of letting persons obviously guilty go unpunished for their crimes. On this rationale, the prosecution is not to be put in a better position than it would have been in if no illegality had transpired.
>
> By contrast, the derivative evidence analysis ensures that the prosecution is not put in a worse position simply because of some earlier police error or misconduct.[130]

Courts have recognized three exceptions to operation of the fruit of the poisonous tree doctrine; if the prosecutor establishes that: (1) the evidence was obtained from a source independent of the primary illegality, i.e., the "fruit" was actually located by means unrelated to the illegal source; (2) the evidence inevitably would have been discovered in the course of the investigation, i.e., the "fruit" would have been located by means unrelated to the illegality; or (3) the connection between the challenged evidence and the illegal conduct is so attenuated that it dissipates the taint of the illegal action, i.e., the "fruit" is sufficiently removed in time, place, or logic from the illegal source. These exceptions are discussed below.

---

[129] 514 U.S. 1 (1995).

[130] Nix v. Williams, 467 U.S. 431, 442–43 (1980).

B. Exceptions: Independent Source

The essence of the exclusionary rule is that illegally seized evidence is inadmissible in court. However, when the police obtain knowledge of the same facts through an independent source, the prosecution is not barred from attempting to prove such facts.[131] In *Wong Sun,* the Court cited *Silverthorne's* suggestion that "the exclusionary rule has no application" when "the Government learned of the evidence 'from an independent source.' "[132] With the independent source exception, not even the "but for" standard can be met, clearly showing that the evidence is not derived from a prior violation.

In *Segura v. United States,*[133] drug agents began tracking the defendants after receiving information about their involvement in drug trafficking. After observing one of them deliver a bulky package to another person in a parking lot, the agents followed the package recipient to her apartment and stopped her. After finding cocaine on her person, she admitted purchasing cocaine from one of the defendants.

When the agents applied for a search warrant for that apartment, they were told that a warrant would not issue until the following day. But they also were told to secure the premises to prevent evidence destruction. The agents later arrested one defendant in the lobby of the apartment building and took him to the apartment, where they knocked and entered without permission when another defendant opened the door. While they conducted a limited security check of the premises, they noticed drug paraphernalia in plain view. Two agents remained in the apartment after two suspects were taken into custody. Almost a full day later, due to "administrative delay," the search warrant issued. The agents found cocaine and drug sale records.

On appeal from their convictions, the Court upheld the pre-warrant and warrant seizures, applying the independent source exception. The police discovered the evidence post-entry, pursuant to a valid warrant. The information for that warrant was known *before* the earlier initial entry and came from sources *unconnected* with the entry. Thus, the evidence was not the fruit of the earlier illegal entry, because the legality of the original entry was irrelevant. The independent source doctrine applied both "to evidence obtained for the first time during an independent lawful search" and "to evidence

---

131 Silverthorne Lumber Co. v. United States, 251 U.S. 385 (1920).

132 *Wong Sun v. United States,* 371 U.S. at 487, quoting *Silverthorne Lumber Co. v. United States,* 251 U.S. at 392.

133 468 U.S. 796 (1984).

initially discovered during, or as a consequence of an unlawful search, but later obtained independently from activities untainted by the initial illegality."[134]

In *United States v. Crews*,[135] a robbery and assault victim quickly gave the police a complete description of her assailant. Days later, the police saw a person matching the description in an area near the crime scene. The police detained the defendant at a police station where he was questioned, photographed, and then released. The victim identified the suspect from the photo as the perpetrator. After the suspect was taken into custody again, the victim identified him in a court-ordered lineup. Following a motion to suppress by the now-indicted defendant, the trial court ruled that probable cause did not support the initial detention, and suppressed the photo and lineup identifications.

However, the trial court stated that the victim's ability to identify the suspect was based on her independent recollection and untainted by the intervening identifications; therefore she could still identify the suspect in court. After his conviction, the defendant appealed. The Court held that police knowledge of the defendant's identity and the victim's independent recollection predated the illegal detention and thus were not tainted by the later constitutional violation.

The Court discussed factors a court must consider when deciding whether to suppress an in-court identification as the fruit of an illegal arrest.[136] If the victim's identity was known long before any official misconduct, his presence in court was not traceable to the constitutional violation, and the victim's ability to reconstruct a mental image of the assailant was in no way affected by his arrest. The witness's courtroom identification of the defendant rested on an independent recollection of the encounter with the defendant.

C. Exceptions: Inevitable Discovery

The Supreme Court formally endorsed the inevitable discovery exception to the fruit of the poisonous tree doctrine in *Nix v. Williams*.[137] Although the defendant's illegally obtained confession led to a quick discovery of the murder victim's body, the prosecution had proved that a search party already was approaching the actual location of the body and would have found it. Thus, even if the

---

[134] Murray v. United States, 487 U.S. 533, 537 (1988).

[135] United States v. Crews, 445 U.S. 463 (1980).

[136] See Chapter 14, discussing Identification Procedures.

[137] 467 U.S. 431 (1984).

defendant had not confessed, the evidence pertaining to the discovery and condition of the victim was properly admitted.

Inevitable discovery is said to be a variation of the independent source exception, discussed in the previous section. While the independent source exception relates to whether the police in fact acquired evidence through an untainted source, inevitable discovery addresses whether the prosecution can prove that evidence found due to an earlier violation would inevitably have been discovered lawfully. Compared to the independent source exception, the inevitable discovery doctrine is based on speculation that the evidence would have been discovered legally rather than on a belief that a legally independent source existed in fact.

The facts in *Nix* were the same as in the seminal Sixth Amendment interrogation case of *Brewer v. Williams*.[138] Law enforcement had begun looking for the murder victim's body even before the police had illegally obtained a statement from the defendant about the body's location.

> The trial court concluded that the State had proved by a preponderance of the evidence that, if the search had not been suspended and [the defendant] had not led the police to the victim, her body would have been discovered "within a short time" in essentially the same condition as it was actually found.[139]

The State appellate court had discussed inevitable discovery as a two-part analysis: whether the police had acted in bad faith to hasten discovery of the evidence, and whether the evidence would have been discovered by lawful means. Because that court found that the police had not acted in bad faith, it did not reach the inevitable discovery prong.

However, the Court rejected a bad faith proof requirement, stating that it

> would place courts in the position of withholding from juries relevant and undoubted truth that would have been available to police absent any unlawful police activity. . . . [T]hat view would put the police in a worse position than they would have been in if no unlawful conduct had transpired. And . . . it wholly fails to take into account the

---

138 430 U.S. 387 (1977). See § 13.2, discussing Sixth Amendment Confession cases.

139 *Nix v. Williams*, 467 U.S. at 437–38. See United States v. Lauria, 70 F.4th 106 (2d Cir. 2023) (government must prove that it inevitably would have discovered the challenged evidence through independent means and not simply that it *could* have discovered the evidence if it had fixed flaws in the warrant affidavits it submitted).

> enormous societal cost of excluding truth in the search for truth in the administration of justice.[140]

The Court turned to the benefits of an inevitable discovery exception to the fruit of the poisonous tree analysis.

> Fairness can be assured by placing the State and the accused in the same positions they would have been in had the impermissible conduct not taken place. However, if the government can prove that the evidence would have been obtained inevitably and, therefore, would have been admitted regardless of any overreaching by the police, there is no rational basis to keep that evidence from the jury in order to ensure the fairness of the trial proceedings. In that situation, the State has gained no advantage at trial and the defendant has suffered no prejudice. Indeed, suppression of the evidence would operate to undermine the adversary system by putting the State in a worse position than it would have occupied without any police misconduct.[141]

If "the prosecution can establish by a preponderance of the evidence that the information ultimately or inevitably would have been discovered by lawful means, . . . the deterrence rationale has so little basis that the evidence should be received."[142]

D. Exceptions: Attenuation

Evidence that would not have been discovered but for police misconduct may be admissible if it is sufficiently attenuated from the illegal action, i.e.,

> when the connection between unconstitutional police conduct and the evidence is remote or has been interrupted by some intervening circumstance, so that "the interest protected by the constitutional guarantee that has been violated would not be served by suppression of the evidence obtained."[143]

The attenuation exception asks whether the connection between the illegal activity and the evidence obtained is so attenuated that the evidence can no longer be considered tainted. If so, the deterrent value of the exclusionary rule is also attenuated, and the cost of exclusion outweighs the benefit of deterrence. With attenuation, the facts of each case must be examined, asking whether illegal conduct

---

140 *Id.*, at 445.

141 *Id.*, at 446–47, quoting United States v. Ash, 413 U.S. 300, 315 (1973).

142 *Nix v. Williams*, 467 U.S. at 432.

143 Hudson v. Michigan, 547 U.S. 586, 593 (2006).

has in some manner resulted in procurement of evidence, and if so, whether that improper activity played a *de minimis* role?

In *Wong Sun v. United States*, although the defendant Wong Sun was initially arrested without probable cause, he had been released for several days after his arrest before returning to the police station voluntarily to make a statement. Despite the initial illegal arrest, his statement was admissible, because "the connection between the arrest and the statement had 'become so attenuated as to dissipate the taint.' "[144]

In *Brown v. Illinois*,[145] two detectives arrested the suspect without probable cause and then gave him the *Miranda* warnings that yielded two confessions. Those confessions were allegedly the fruit of the illegal arrest. The defendant made his first confession to police only two hours after the illegal arrest and without any significant intervening event such as a court appearance, consultation with counsel, or release from custody.[146] Later that same evening, a prosecutor repeated the *Miranda* warnings and questioned Brown; he again confessed.

The Court held that *Miranda* warnings alone would not always break the causal chain between a Fourth Amendment violation and a defendant's subsequent statement. The deterrent effect of the exclusionary rule would be diluted substantially if *Miranda* warnings were held sufficient to purge the taint of a violation, i.e., police would be encouraged to violate Fourth Amendment rights and then use *Miranda* warnings to cure the taint of the violation. Whether a confession after an illegal arrest is admissible must be decided on a case-by-case basis. Thus, the Court's holding was confined to the facts, pointing to the State court's "error in assuming that the *Miranda* warnings, by themselves, under *Wong Sun* always purge the taint of an illegal arrest."[147]

In determining whether the connection between an illegal tree and a subsequently obtained fruit (here, a confession) is attenuated, courts generally apply several factors articulated in *Brown v. Illinois*: temporal proximity between the "tree" and the "fruit," the presence of intervening circumstances for attenuating the connection between the tree and the fruit, and the purpose and flagrancy of the police misconduct. In cases where the fruit is an incriminating statement,

---

144 *Wong Sun v. United States*, 371 U.S. at 491.

145 422 U.S. 590 (1975).

146 *Id.*, at 604.

147 *Id.*, at 605.

the analysis requires as a prerequisite that the statement was voluntary under Due Process standards.[148]

Applying those factors, the Court stated that Brown's statement was separated by less than two hours, there was no intervening event of significance, and the police had purposely violated Brown's rights by arresting him without probable cause. As a result of applying the factors, the Court ruled that the trial court had erred by admitting Brown's statements into evidence.

Live testimony as fruit. While the cases applying the attenuation rule often concern the admissibility of physical evidence, e.g., a weapon found during a search incident to an illegal arrest, it is also used in other situations. In *United States v. Ceccolini*,[149] while a police officer was talking with an employee of a flower shop, he noticed an envelope that contained betting slips. In response to a question about who owned the envelope, the employee named the defendant. She repeated that testimony to a grand jury, after the defendant had denied any gambling involvement.

In his trial for perjury, the employee testified against the defendant who was found guilty. However, the trial court granted his motion to suppress her testimony as the fruit of an illegal search at the flower shop. Unlike most fruit of the poisonous tree cases, the alleged fruit in *Ceccolini* was live witness testimony. That fact compelled the Court to comment that the evidence showed that her testimony "was an act of her own free will," and was "in no way coerced or induced by official authority as a result of the officer's search of the betting slips."[150]

The Court then turned to the *Brown* factors and held that, although her trial testimony was the fruit of that search, it was sufficiently attenuated from the search to allow its admission. "Substantial periods of time elapsed between the time of the illegal search and the initial contact with the witness, on the one hand, and between the latter and the testimony at trial on the other."[151] The witness's testimony traced back to the search that produced the betting slips. No evidence existed "to suggest that [the officer] entered the shop or picked up the envelope with the intent of finding tangible evidence bearing on an illicit gambling operation."[152] The Court concluded by observing that excluding live witness testimony

---

[148] Brown v. Illinois, 422 U.S. 590, 601 (1975).

[149] 435 U.S. 268 (1978).

[150] United States v. Ceccolini, 435 U.S. 268, 279 (1978).

[151] *Id.*, at 280.

[152] *Id.*

is so costly to the prosecution that only a close connection between the testimony and the illegal conduct justifies exclusion.

Incriminating statement as fruit. In *Dunaway v. New York*,[153] the facts were parallel to those in *Brown*: the police seized the suspect without probable cause, and detained and interrogated him without legal justification. During the interrogation after *Miranda* warnings, the defendant made incriminating statements and drew sketches that implicated himself in the crime. The Court ruled that the connection between the unconstitutional police activity and the statements and sketches was not sufficiently attenuated under the *Brown* factors to allow their use against the defendant at trial. The defendant "was seized without probable cause in the hope that something might turn up." Specifically, the Court found that "[n]o intervening events broke the connection between the [defendant's] illegal detention and his confession,"[154] reaching the same conclusion as *Brown* for the same reasons.

In *Rawlings v. Kentucky*,[155] the Court noted that the defendant received *Miranda* warnings immediately prior to making the challenged incriminating statement. His spontaneous reaction to the discovery of drugs was freely made and unaffected by his illegal detention. Considering the brief 45-minutes between the arrest and confession, the Court concluded that the time lapse was sufficient to purge the taint of an illegal arrest. As to other parts of the *Brown* test, the Court did not acknowledge any significant intervening event, or any purposeful or flagrant misconduct requiring the exclusion of Rawlings' statement.

Like the other cases, *New York v. Harris*[156] assessed whether a confession is the fruit of an illegal arrest. But the Court distinguished the prior cases because the arrests in those cases were made without probable cause. Like *Brown*, though, the defendant confessed twice. The police entered his home without his consent to question him about a murder, but without an arrest warrant in violation of *Payton v. New York*.[157] After he confessed to the murder, he was arrested and taken to the police station where the police repeated the process of warning him and taking his written confession. The Court held that the first confession was the fruit of the *Payton* violation. As to the second violation, it held that a confession away from the home's

---

153 442 U.S. 200 (1979).

154 Dunaway v. New York, 442 U.S. 200, 218, 219 (1979).

155 448 U.S. 98 (1980).

156 495 U.S. 14 (1990).

157 445 U.S. 573 (1980).

interior cannot be the fruit of a *Payton* violation, which involves an illegal search of the home but not an illegal arrest.

> [S]uppressing the statement taken outside the house would not serve the purpose of the rule that made [Harris's] in-house arrest illegal. The warrant requirement for an arrest in the home is imposed to protect the home, and anything incriminating the police gathered from arresting [Harris] in his home, rather than elsewhere, has been excluded, as it should have been; the purpose of the rule has thereby been vindicated.[158]

There was no necessary connection between the search of the home and the later confession made outside the home at the station house.

In *Utah v. Strieff*,[159] the police corroborated an anonymous tip about drug activity at a specific residence, stopping the defendant as he exited the residence. After checking for warrants, they arrested him based on an outstanding traffic warrant. A search incident to the arrest revealed drugs on his person. Because no valid grounds existed for stopping the defendant, the prosecution argued that any connection between the groundless stop and discovery of the drugs was attenuated. Before applying the *Brown* factors, the Court assumed (due to the State's concession of the point) that the officer lacked reasonable suspicion to stop the defendant.

The Court applied the *Brown* factors to conclude that the connection between the unconstitutional conduct and the discovery of evidence was sufficiently attenuated to uphold admissibility of the drugs. The temporal proximity between the unlawful stop and the search incident to arrest for drugs was "only minutes" and favored the defendant, instead of the "substantial time" between an unlawful act and when the police obtain evidence, recognized by an earlier decision.[160]

The second factor of intervening circumstance favored the prosecution: the discovery of a pending warrant unrelated to the stop that compelled police to arrest the defendant. Citing precedent, the Court decided that the existence of a valid warrant issued before the officer began his investigation favored finding that the connection between unlawful conduct and the discovery of evidence is "sufficiently attenuated to dissipate the taint."[161]

---

[158] New York v. Harris, 495 U.S. 14, 20 (1990).

[159] 579 U.S. 232 (2016).

[160] Kaupp v. Texas, 538 U.S. 626, 633 (2003).

[161] Segura v. United States, 468 U.S. 796, 815 (1984).

The third factor of purpose and flagrancy supported attenuation, because the police officer at most was negligent in executing a groundless stop. The officer had made two good-faith mistakes by not knowing when the defendant had entered the drug house or how long the defendant remained there. The Court held that the evidence discovered on the defendant's "person was admissible because the unlawful stop was sufficiently attenuated by the pre-existing arrest warrant."[162]

Consecutive confessions. When the Court has examined cases involving *consecutive* confessions, the first unwarned and the second warned, it has reached conflicting results. The Court did not discuss attenuation explicitly in either case, but in effect it still decided whether the second confession was attenuated from the unwarned confession. In effect, the issue in both cases was whether a *Miranda* violation of failing to warn a suspect before a first confession poisoned the second, derivative confession. In one case, *Oregon v. Elstad,*[163] the failure to warn was described as a technical violation, while in the other case, *Missouri v. Seibert,*[164] the failure to warn was an intentional strategy to persuade the suspect to confess after having admitted to a crime before warnings were finally given.

In *Elstad*, the police spoke to a young suspect at his home about a burglary before arresting him and taking him to the police station. All the suspect had said at home was that he was present at the crime scene. The Court described the failure to warn at the home as an "oversight" that

> may have been the result of confusion as to whether the brief exchange qualified as "custodial interrogation" or . . . may simply have reflected . . . reluctance to initiate an alarming police procedure before [an officer] had spoken with [Elstad]'s mother.[165]

At the stationhouse, the suspect received his *Miranda* warnings and gave a full confession. The Court held that the second confession was admissible and voluntary. The Court ruled that any connection between the two statements was "speculative and attenuated."[166] *Seibert* later described the *Elstad* failure to warn "as a good-faith *Miranda* mistake, not only open to correction by careful warnings

162 Utah v. Strieff, 579 U.S. 232, 242 (2016).

163 470 U.S. 298 (1985).

164 542 U.S. 600 (2004).

165 Oregon v. Elstad, 470 U.S. 298, 315–16 (1985).

166 *Id.*, at 313.

before systematic questioning in that particular case, but posing no threat to warn-first practice generally."[167]

In *Seibert,* the Court criticized a "question-first" strategy, which "is to render *Miranda* warnings ineffective by waiting for a particularly opportune time to give them, after the suspect has already confessed."[168] A mother was convicted of being an accessory in killing a mentally retarded child who was living with her and her children. After the police arrested her, they used the question-first approach as directed by a superior officer. She was questioned without *Miranda* warnings until she confessed, and then she received the warnings. Police asked her to sign a waiver form and resumed the questioning with the intent to have her repeat the pre-break statements. The Court criticized the police strategy and held that the post-warning confession was inadmissible.

Physical evidence as fruit. In *United States v. Patane,*[169] police deliberately violated *Miranda* in the hope of obtaining statements that would lead them to *physical* evidence. It was the first case to discuss the admissibility of physical evidence as the fruit of a statement obtained in violation of *Miranda.* As a convicted felon, the defendant was prohibited from possessing a firearm. In addition, he was under a no-contact restraining order issued to protect his ex-girlfriend. Police arrested the defendant for violating the restraining order after speaking to him. The defendant interrupted the *Miranda* warnings, after the right to remain silent warning was given, saying that he knew his rights.

The police asked him about the gun he possessed, to which he responded, "I am not sure I should tell you anything about the Glock because I don't want you to take it away from me." Finally, the defendant told the officers the location of the gun and consented to the officer's request to retrieve it. On appeal from his conviction for being a felon in possession of a firearm, the Court held that the gun was admissible. Although there was substantial evidence that the *Miranda* violation was designed to facilitate discovery of the evidence, the Court applied *Elstad* and held that the physical evidence acquired as a result of the *Miranda* violation was admissible.

Justice Kennedy's concurrence noted the superior value of physical evidence as the fruit of illegal conduct over incriminating

---

167 Missouri v. Seibert, 542 U.S. 600, 615 (2004). See Chapter 12, discussing the *Miranda* confession cases.

168 *Id.*, at 611.

169 542 U.S. 630 (2004). When a defendant's confession is involuntary, applying *Elstad*, even physical evidence would likely be suppressed as the fruit of the poisonous tree.

evidence of questioned reliability. "Admission of nontestimonial physical fruits even more so than the post-warning statements to the police in *Elstad* does not run the risk of admitting into trial an accused's coerced incriminating statements against himself."[170]

§ 1.8 Harmless Constitutional Error

When a constitutional error possibly contributed to a conviction, it is presumed to be prejudicial unless the reviewing court can declare that the error was harmless beyond a reasonable doubt. In *Chapman v. California*,[171] repeated references to the defendant's failure to testify violated the Fifth and Fourteenth Amendments as reversible error. The prosecutor's error and the judge's jury instructions could not be shown beyond a reasonable doubt to have had no part in the jury's decision. If other evidence of guilt is so overwhelming that the defendant would have been convicted even without the constitutional violation, the violation is harmless.[172]

All constitutional violations are subject to harmless error analysis,[173] except for denial of assistance of counsel at trial,[174] denial of trial by an impartial factfinder, and failure to disclose exculpatory evidence.[175] Trial errors occurring during the presentation of the case to the trier of fact can be assessed in the context of other evidence to determine whether it is harmless beyond a reasonable doubt. On the other hand, structural defects in the constitution of the trial mechanism cannot be held harmless.[176]

---

170 United States v. Patane, 542 U.S. 630, 645 (2004) (Kennedy, J., concurring).

171 386 U.S. 18 (1967).

172 Chapman v. California, 386 U.S. 18 (1967).

173 Satterwhite v. Texas, 486 U.S. 249 (1988).

174 See United States v. Gonzalez-Lopez, 548 U.S. 140 (2006) (deprivation of choice of counsel not subject to harmless error analysis).

175 Kyles v. Whitley, 514 U.S. 419 (1995). See Neder v. United States, 527 U.S. 1 (1999) (erroneous omission from jury instruction of element of offense is subject to harmless error review).

176 See, e.g., Hedgpeth v. Pulido, 555 U.S. 57 (2008) (a defective jury instruction is subject to harmless error review). See Washington v. Recuenco, 548 U.S. 212 (2006) (*Apprendi* error is subject to harmless error analysis); Neder v. United States, 527 U.S. 1 (1999) (erroneous omission from jury instruction is subject to harmless error); Sullivan v. Louisiana, 508 U.S. 275 (1993) (constitutionally deficient reasonable doubt instruction cannot be harmless error).

Chapter 2

FOURTH AMENDMENT ACTIVITY

Table of Sections

§ 2.1 Introduction

The Fourth Amendment applies only to conduct that can be classified as a search or a seizure; it protects what an individual legitimately seeks to preserve as private.[1] If a person does not have a reasonable expectation of privacy or there is no physical trespass involved, the Fourth Amendment is inapplicable and law

---

[1] See California v. Hodari D., 499 U.S. 621 (1991) (contraband abandoned by defendant was lawfully recovered by police).

enforcement has no obligation to comply with constitutional requirements. However, if a reasonable expectation of privacy does exist or State actors are physically trespassing, law enforcement must satisfy Fourth Amendment requirements such as probable cause. This Chapter discusses the threshold issue of Fourth Amendment activity.

A court determines the reasonableness of a search by considering the following factors to balance the need for the particular search against the personal rights that the search entails: (1) the scope of the intrusion; (2) the manner in which the search is conducted, i.e., the type of search performed, by whom the search was conducted, the existence of risk, pain or trauma to the suspect, and the skills required to conduct the search; (3) the justification for initiating the search; and (4) the place in which the search is conducted.[2] For example, in *United States v. Knights*,[3] a probationer's acceptance of a search condition for his probation significantly reduced his expectation of privacy. Because the State has an interest in apprehending criminal law violators, law enforcement may focus on probationers. Thus, a warrantless search of a convicted person who was on probation was supported by reasonable suspicion and was reasonable under the Fourth Amendment.

§ 2.2 What Is a Search?

A. Katz v. United States

The Supreme Court's decisions have described two approaches for defining a Fourth Amendment search: (1) the defendant has a reasonable or legitimate expectation of privacy in the place or object of the search, or (2) Government officials have physically trespassed on a constitutionally protected area to gather information. Although a person has no privacy interest in criminal activity, the Fourth Amendment protects such activity anyway because it not known before a search that illegal activity will be discovered.

Katz v. United States[4] described a search as a visual observation or physical intrusion which infringes upon a person's expectation of privacy. In *Katz*, federal agents without a warrant placed an electronic listening device on the outside of a public telephone booth to record Katz's conversations about illegal gambling. The Court rejected the argument that no search occurred, because there was no infringement of Katz's property rights.

---

2 Bell v. Wolfish, 441 U.S. 520 (1979).

3 534 U.S. 112 (2001).

4 389 U.S. 347 (1967).

> For the Fourth Amendment protects people, not places. What a person knowingly exposes to the public, even in his own home or office, is not a subject of Fourth Amendment protection. . . But what he seeks to preserve as private, even in an area accessible to the public, may be constitutionally protected.[5]

The reach of the Fourth Amendment "cannot turn upon the presence or absence of physical intrusion onto any given enclosure." Instead, "a person in a telephone booth. . . who occupies it, shuts the door behind him, and pays the toll that permits him to place a call is surely entitled to assume that the words he utters into the mouthpiece will not be broadcast to the world."[6]

B. Justice Harlan's Concurrence

The applicable *Katz* test for more than the past half-century derives from Justice Harlan's concurrence.

> The question, however, is what protection [the Fourth Amendment] affords to those people. Generally, as here, the answer to that question requires reference to a "place." My understanding of the rule that has emerged from prior decisions is that there is a twofold requirement, first that a person have exhibited an actual (subjective) expectation of privacy and, second, that the expectation be one that society is prepared to recognize as "reasonable." Thus, a man's home is, for most purposes, a place where he expects privacy, but objects, activities, or statements that he exposes to the "plain view" of outsiders are not "protected" because no intention to keep them to himself has been exhibited. On the other hand, conversations in the open would not be protected against being overheard, for the expectation of privacy under the circumstances would be unreasonable.[7]

The expectation of privacy must not only be reasonable but also protect something that the defendant has a right to possess.

Justice Harlan emphasizes the need for examining the defendant's "subjective" perspective on his claim of privacy. If the defendant makes that initial showing, the Court then looks at whether the type and degree of privacy claimed by the defendant is recognized as objectively "reasonable." That objective issue is the factor litigated in most privacy cases.

---

5 Katz v. United States, 389 U.S. 347, 351 (1967).

6 *Id.*, at 352.

7 *Id.*, at 361 (Harlan, J., concurring).

C. Fourth Amendment Privacy

Litigants will ask the Court to recognize and protect privacy as a constitutional right through Fourth Amendment warrant or warrantless requirements. A person's behavior may determine whether the person has a privacy interest. For example, loud talking in a phone booth where passersby can easily overhear the telephone conversation likely would justify a judicial finding that the person abandoned any privacy interest in the conversation.

However, the Court emphasized that when Katz closed the door to the telephone booth, he showed a privacy interest. If he never closed the door, did he adequately have a privacy interest in the conversations that followed? Would *Katz* have presented a different case if there was no phone booth, but instead the public telephone was attached to a wall, with side barriers extending outward? Suppose that Katz testified that he had waited for the area near the phone to be deserted before having a telephone conversation? Suppose that Katz made the call from a booth with the door closed, but the booth was connected with a dozen other booths located near the most crowded intersection in the United States?

The Court also recognized a privacy interest in the social context in which it occurs. Because the contents of a 1960s telephone conversation in a closed telephone booth were unlikely to be circulated or overheard, a court likely would decide that the speaker could expect that Government agents would not have access to the conversation even through secret means like a wiretap. The Court also looked at the privacy interest by an individual as an interest shared by many others. *Katz* refers to the desirability of constitutional perception of the need to promote "private communications" through the "vital role"[8] of a public telephone.

The Government's argument against a privacy interest would have led to unregulated wiretaps with no judicial oversight provided by the exclusionary rule; the backup argument was that the warrant requirements do not apply to wiretaps if the wiretap is limited in scope and duration, and Government agents believed that illegal evidence would possibly be disclosed in the wiretapped conversations.

D. Post-*Katz* Case Law

Since *Katz*, the Court's decisions have assessed the reasonable expectation of privacy in several settings. For example, although passengers on airplanes, trains or buses reasonably may expect fellow passengers to handle or move carry-on baggage, a police

---

8 *Katz v. United States*, 389 U.S. at 352.

officer's squeeze or "probing tactile examination" of soft-sided luggage constitutes a search.[9] Other examples of a search:

- The use of a sense-enhancing, thermal imaging device to which the public does not have access (a) to explore details about the interior of private home, (b) without the inhabitant's knowledge or consent, is a search. *Kyllo v. United States.*[10]
- A warrantless urine test as a diagnostic test to obtain evidence of a person's criminal conduct is a search, requiring the patient's consent or a warrant. *Ferguson v. City of Charleston.*[11]
- Moving a piece of equipment from one place to another, or even to turn it, is a search when it is unrelated to the objective of an authorized intrusion. *Arizona v. Hicks.*[12]
- Taking a sample of a person's blood by piercing the skin is a search. *Birchfield v. North Dakota.*[13]

A physical trespass is also a search. In *United States v. Jones,*[14] the Supreme Court (re)introduced the physical trespass test as an alternative method of defining protected Fourth Amendment interests. In *Jones*, Government agents who suspected the defendant of illegal drug trafficking attached a tracking device to the underside of his wife's vehicle while it was located in a public parking area. For a month, the device monitored and recorded all travels of that vehicle, and the Government tried to introduce the travel data at Jones' trial.

Even without any showing that the agents had violated Jones' reasonable expectation of privacy, the Court held that the agents' actions nevertheless amounted to a search by applying common law trespass doctrines that predated *Katz*. The expectation of privacy standard in *Katz* had not changed the earlier[15] principle that the Government cannot engage in a physical intrusion of a constitutionally protected area in order to obtain information.[16] The

---

9 Bond v. U.S., 529 U.S. 334 (2000).

10 533 U.S. 27 (2001).

11 532 U.S. 67 (2001).

12 480 U.S. 321 (1987).

13 579 U.S. 438 (2016).

14 565 U.S. 400 (2012).

15 See Silverman v. United States, 365 U.S. 505 (1961); Goldman v. United States, 316 U.S. 129 (1942).

16 See *United States v. Jones*, 565 U.S. at 404. Compare United States v. Esqueda, 88 F.4th 818, 827 (9th Cir. 2023) ("because the officers' physical entry was expressly licensed and therefore itself permissible, the officers' use of recording

Court observed that *Katz's* reasonable expectation of privacy standard was *an addition, not a substitute for*, the common-law trespass test. Four Justices concurred in *Jones*, comparing this longer surveillance with shorter periods.

> [R]elatively short-term monitoring of a person's movements on public streets accords with expectations of privacy that our society has recognized as reasonable,". . . "the use of longer term GPS monitoring in investigations of most offenses impinges on expectations of privacy" [where, as here,] "for four weeks". . . .[17]

Examples of the *Jones* physical trespass test to define a search have included:

- The use of a drug dog at the front door to discover drugs in the defendant's residence is a search. The police officers were on private property within the defendant's curtilage and their purpose was to conduct a search, neither explicitly nor implicitly permitted by the homeowner. *Florida v. Jardines*.[18]
- No search occurs through use of a State's system of attaching a device to track a sex offender's movements. *Grady v. North Carolina*.[19]
- Using a robbery suspect's cell-site location information to track his movements for more than four months was an unlawful search without a search warrant. *Carpenter v. United States*.[20]
- *Jones* observed that the earlier case of *California v. Ciraolo*[21] upheld flyover surveillance by airplanes and helicopters in a "physically nonintrusive manner," i.e., no search had occurred.

An essential component of a Fourth Amendment claim now requires that: (1) one's own personal "effects" have been trespassed (e.g., the trespassory nature of the secret installation of a GPS device on a person's automobile), or (2) the defendant's expectation of privacy was impinged. The reasonable expectation of privacy test and

---

equipment once inside did not transform their physical presence into a Fourth Amendment search").

[17] United States v. Jones, 565 U.S. 400, 430 (2012) (Alito, J., concurring).

[18] 561 U.S. 1 (2013).

[19] 575 U.S. 306 (2015).

[20] 585 U.S. 296 (2018).

[21] 476 U.S. 207 (1986).

the physical trespass test are alternative methods for measuring Fourth Amendment activity.

§ 2.3 What Is a Seizure?

The language and scope of the Fourth Amendment includes not only searches but also seizures. A *Katz* search may occur with or without an accompanying seizure. The privacy interest discussed in *Katz* related to a search, and later decisions recognized that Fourth Amendment protections may include a seizure without a search.[22] Seizures relate to interests in property possession (e.g., seizing tangible items) and a person's liberty (e.g., an arrest). *United States v. Place*[23] represents both type of seizure interests; police interfered with the defendant's "possessory interest in his luggage" for ninety minutes and they interfered with his "liberty interest in proceeding with his itinerary."

A seizure in the Fourth Amendment context requires some meaningful interference with an individual's liberty or possessory interest.[24] In *Katz*, the Government was seizing Katz's recorded telephone conversations. His defense counsel had to persuade the Court of two points: (1) to apply the Fourth Amendment to a wiretap type of intrusion that involved the seizure described above, and (2) to suppress the evidence of those conversations at his trial, because federal agents had failed to follow the process of seeking a search warrant supported by probable cause.

A. Seizure of Persons

An arrest requires *either* physical force . . . *or*, where that is absent, *submission* to the assertion of authority."[25] That seizure of an individual requires that an officer's use of physical force or show of authority is with the intent to restrain.[26] In *Torres v. Madrid*,[27] the police shot a person who was fleeing in her car, but she continued to escape despite her wounds. In her civil case for damages, she asserted that the police used excessive force. Although lower courts held that no seizure had occurred, the Court held that "application of physical

---

[22] See, e.g., Soldal v. Cook County, 506 U.S. 56 (1992).

[23] 462 U.S. 696 (1983).

[24] See, e.g., United States v. Jacobsen, 466 U.S. 109 (1984); Illinois v. Lidster, 540 U.S. 419 (2004).

[25] California v. Hodari D., 499 U.S. 621, 626 (1991) (emphasis in original).

[26] Accidental force does not qualify as a seizure. Torres v. Madrid, 592 U.S. 306 (2021).

[27] 592 U.S. 306 (2021).

force to the body of a person with intent to restrain is a seizure, even if the force does not succeed in subduing the person."[28]

A seizure is a single act, and not a continuous fact. A seizure by force without consent "lasts only as long as the application of force," and therefore the suspect may be seized "for the instant that bullets struck her." If a fleeing suspect was seized illegally but subsequently discarded contraband after he escaped, he may be able to suppress the contraband as the fruit of a Fourth Amendment violation.

If an officer engages in a nonphysical show of authority, a seizure occurs only if a reasonable person would not feel free to leave and actually submits to the assertion of authority.[29] By manifesting authority in some way, an officer adds to the inherent pressure in a police-citizen encounter. Police conduct such as drawing a weapon, touching a citizen, the threatening presence of multiple officers, or language or tone suggesting a demand rather than a request all constitute seizures.

- That the defendant did not feel free to leave a location does not mean that the person was seized. Under the totality of circumstances, a show of authority without submission to that authority is not a "seizure" of the person. *Florida v. Bostick*.[30]
- A vehicle stop to obtain information about an earlier hit-and-run is a Fourth Amendment "seizure." *Illinois v. Lidster*.[31]
- A police car driving parallel to a running pedestrian does not constitute a seizure of the pedestrian. *Michigan v. Chesternut*.[32]

In *United States v. Drayton*,[33] officers conducted a routine, suspicionless drug investigation of bus passengers. The Court held that the officers did not have to disclose to the passengers that they had the right not to cooperate and to refuse to consent to searches. Applying the principle from *Bostick*, the Court found that, provided a reasonable person would understand that he is free to leave, police officers can approach bus passengers at random to ask questions and to request their consent to search.

---

28 Torres v. Madrid, 592 U.S. 306 (2021).

29 See Brendlin v. California, 551 U.S. 249 (2007) ("any reasonable passenger would have understood the police officers to be exercising control to the point that no one in the car was free to depart without police permission").

30 501 U.S. 429 (1991).

31 540 U.S. 419 (2004).

32 486 U.S. 567 (1988).

33 536 U.S. 194 (2002).

B. Seizure of Property

Seizures of property may relate to the commission of an offense, contraband, fruits of a crime, or property intended for use as a means of committing a crime,[34] as well as business or personal papers.[35] In *Katz*, the Government and the defense initially focused on the question of whether a telephone booth is a protected "area" in a property sense. If it is, the Fourth Amendment would govern any official intrusion into the area, and if it is not, the Fourth Amendment does not apply. The *Katz* opinion does not reveal that defense counsel modified their argument in the reply brief and at oral argument, urging the Court not to rely on the "constitutionally protected area" concept and instead to protect the right to conversational privacy in any context in which it is reasonable to conclude that the parties intend a conversation to be confidential.[36]

The following post-*Katz* cases required the Court to decide whether a seizure of property had occurred.

- The seizure of personal business records does not offend the Fifth Amendment privilege against self-incrimination. *Andresen v. Maryland*.[37]
- The admitted seizure and destruction of trace amounts of the defendants' property was deemed not to be a "seizure" because it was not a "meaningful" interference, but instead it had "at most" "a *de minimis* impact on any protected property interest." *United States v. Jacobsen*.[38]
- Recording the serial numbers observed by police on stereo equipment is not a seizure. *Arizona v. Hicks*.[39]

A seizure of property during an arrest requires probable cause for the arrest, and police may take the property for later use as evidence or for safekeeping. To seize property during a stop, police

[34] See Warden v. Hayden, 387 U.S. 294 (1967).

[35] The contents of "[l]etters and sealed packages . . . in the mail are as fully guarded from examination and inspection . . . as if they were retained by the parties forwarding them in their own domiciles." Ex parte Jackson, 96 U.S. (6 Otto) 727 (1878). As long as a package is "closed against inspection," the Fourth Amendment protects its contents, "wherever they may be," and the police must obtain a warrant to search it just "as is required when papers are subjected to search in one's own household." California v. Greenwood, 486 U.S. 35, 46 (1988) (Brennan, J., dissenting).

[36] See David A. Sklansky, Katz v. United States, the Limits of Aphorism, in Criminal Procedure Stories (Carol S. Steiker, ed. 2006).

[37] Andresen v. Maryland, 427 U.S. 463 (1976). Certain exceptions apply to a seizure of foreign objects or blood in a person's body. See, e.g., Schmerber v. California, 384 U.S. 757 (1966). See Chapter 10, discussing Exigent Circumstances.

[38] United States v. Jacobsen, 466 U.S. 109 (1984).

[39] 480 U.S. 321 (1987).

must have reasonable suspicion and the seizure must be brief in order for police to determine whether to release the stopped person or to arrest him.

Permissible seizures of objects are justified by police (1) pursuant to a warrant when a judge, after finding probable cause, has issued a search warrant for particularly described items, (2) during execution of a search warrant or an arrest warrant when an object is seized, even though it was not described in the warrant, or (3) without a warrant when the incriminating nature of the object was immediately apparent and the search was otherwise legal. The first and second situations are discussed in the next Chapter discussing search warrants;[40] the third circumstance is discussed in the next section of this Chapter.

Summarizing: A search or seize of persons or property by police or other law enforcement personnel constitutes Fourth Amendment activity, and that conduct is subject to constitutional restrictions under the Fourth Amendment. On the other hand, if law enforcement has not engaged in a search or a seizure, there is no Fourth Amendment activity. When there is no such activity, the Fourth Amendment is inapplicable and law enforcement personnel do not have to comply with concepts like probable cause.

§ 2.4 Plain View and Other Sensory Perceptions

A. Plain View

Plain view requires that the: (1) objects seized were plainly visible; (2) viewer had a right to be in his location for viewing the object; and (3) incriminating nature of the object was immediately apparent to the viewer. Fourth Amendment activity conducted pursuant to "plain view" is "better understood, therefore, not as an independent 'exception' to the warrant clause, but simply as an extension of an already ongoing search or other lawful activity."[41]

The first requirement of plain view is that the objects were plainly visible by direct observation. *Katz* cited with approval *United States v. Lee*[42] where the Court held that use of a Coast Guard cutter's searchlight to see aboard a schooner at night was not a search, i.e., "what a person knowingly exposes to the public. . . is not a subject of Fourth Amendment protection."[43] Thus, artificial illumination by police in a position where he has a right to be does not constitute a search. Because *Lee* compared the use of the searchlight "to the use

40 See Chapter 4, discussing Search Warrants.

41 Texas v. Brown, 460 U.S. 730, 738–39 (1983).

42 274 U.S. 559 (1927).

43 *Katz v. United States,* 389 U.S. at 351.

of a marine glass or a field glass,"[44] modern cases have concluded that the use of binoculars does not, *per se*, constitute a search. Eyesight may be enhanced artificially through the use of common devices such as flashlights to illuminate at night things that could be seen with the naked eye during daylight; the same idea applies to enhancing equipment like an aerial camera or a telescope. "Nothing in the Fourth Amendment prohibited the police from augmenting the sensory faculties bestowed upon them at birth with such enhancement as science and technology afforded them."[45]

In *Texas v. Brown*,[46] the Court held that shining a flashlight to illuminate the interior of the defendant's car did not violate the Fourth Amendment. However, Fourth Amendment activity occurs when the police enhance the senses into new senses by using sophisticated machines. In *Katz*, Government agents, acting without a warrant, used an electronic device to listen to and record a conversation in a public telephone booth; the Court held that use of the device violated the individual's legitimate expectation of privacy and therefore constituted an illegal search and seizure.[47]

The second requirement for a plain view seizure is that the viewer must have had a right to be in position for the view. As *Brown* noted, " 'plain view' provides grounds for seizure of an item when an officer's access to an object has some prior justification under the Fourth Amendment."[48]

> Thus, police may perceive an object while executing a search warrant, or they may come across an item while acting pursuant to some exception to the warrant clause. Alternatively, police may need no justification under the Fourth Amendment for their access to an item, such as when property is left in a public place.
>
> It is important to distinguish "plain view" . . . from an officer's mere observation of an item left in plain view. Whereas the latter generally involves no Fourth Amendment search, the former generally does implicate the Amendment's limitations upon seizures of personal property. The information obtained as a result of observation of an object in plain sight may be the basis for probable cause or reasonable suspicion of illegal activity. In

---

44 United States v. Lee, 274 U.S. 559, 563 (1927).

45 United States v. Knotts, 460 U.S. 276, 282 (1983).

46 460 U.S. 730 (1983).

47 See, e.g., Katz v. United States, 389 U.S. 347 (1967).

48 Texas v. Brown, 460 U.S. 730, 738 (1983).

turn, these levels of suspicion may, in some cases, justify police conduct affording them access to a particular item.[49]

Prior, independent justification for police presence includes performing legal searches for other purposes. For example, in *Washington v. Chrisman*, when university police arrested the defendant and accompanied him to his dorm room to obtain identification, they seized a pipe and marijuana seeds in plain view without violating the Fourth Amendment.[50]

While standing on a public sidewalk, suppose the police look through a large window of a residence and see drugs on a table. The observation itself, from a place where they had a right to be, may provide probable cause to obtain a warrant to search the house for drugs, even though they lacked either a search warrant or exigent circumstances to justify an immediate entry. In *Texas v. Brown*, an officer's observation of narcotics in the defendant's car during a routine driver's license checkpoint was not a search and did not violate Fourth Amendment.[51]

Third, plain view requires that the incriminating nature of the item seized be immediately apparent.[52] The police do not have to be unusually certain about the evidentiary value of the item seized, but probable cause is necessary.[53] However, the incriminating character of the contents of a container must be apparent without a physical inspection of the interior[54] or visual prying into a hidden area.

Evidence need not be discovered "inadvertently" for plain view to apply. In *Horton v. California*,[55] an officer applied for a warrant to search for weapons and stolen property, but the warrant authorized only a search for stolen property. The officers executing the warrant did not find the stolen property but found weapons in plain view. The Court held that the fact that the officers knew about the weapons and hoped to find them did not invalidate the search. The Court stated further that the police must "not only . . . be lawfully located in a

---

49 *Id.*, at 738 n.4.

50 455 U.S. 1 (1982). Obviously, if the original activity is unlawful, the plain view search also falls as being the fruit of the poisonous tree. See, e.g., Coolidge v. New Hampshire, 403 U.S. 443 (1971) (the plain view exception did not justify a seizure of the defendant's car when a search warrant was invalid). See Chapter 1, generally discussing the Exclusionary Rule, and § 1.7 specifically discussing the Fruit of the Poisonous Tree Doctrine.

51 *Texas v. Brown*, 460 U.S. at 740.

52 See Coolidge v. New Hampshire, 403 U.S. 443 (1971).

53 Arizona v. Hicks, 480 U.S. 321 (1987).

54 See Coolidge v. New Hampshire, 403 U.S. 443 (1971).

55 496 U.S. 128 (1990).

place from which the object can be plainly seen, but . . . must also have a lawful right of access to the object itself."[56]

B. Plain Smell

Plain smell is another potential example of using a device to enhance sensory perception and to facilitate surveillance. Plain smell need not be by a human; trained dogs are permissible. Exposing luggage or the exterior of a vehicle located in a public place to a dog trained to detect drugs or other contraband is not a Fourth Amendment search.[57] *United States v. Place*[58] emphasized that a "canine sniff is *sui generis;*" unlike any other investigative procedure, it "discloses only the presence or absence of. . . a contraband item" and "does not expose noncontraband items that otherwise would remain hidden from public view."[59]

A dog sniff of a container "discloses only the presence or absence of. . . a contraband item" and "does not expose noncontraband items that otherwise would remain hidden from public view."[60] By contrast, a dog sniff of a person is likely regarded as a search due to its intrusive nature. The Court concluded in *Illinois v. Caballes*[61] that no search occurred from a dog sniff "on the exterior of [defendant's] car while he was lawfully seized for a traffic violation."[62] The Court distinguished a dog sniff from *Kyllo v. United States*' technological monitoring for the presence of drugs: "The legitimate expectation that information about perfectly lawful activity will remain private is categorically distinguishable from [the defendant's] hopes or expectations concerning the nondetection of contraband in the trunk of his car."[63]

The use of dogs to sniff evidence has led to mixed outcomes. For example, in *Florida v. Harris,*[64] an alert by a drug-detection dog that had been certified by a bona fide organization was presumptively sufficient to establish probable cause. By contrast, in *Florida v. Royer,*[65] investigating officers impermissibly detained a defendant when the use of dogs trained to detect presence of controlled

---

56 Horton v. California, 496 U.S. 128, 137 (1990).

57 Illinois v. Caballes, 543 U.S. 405 (2005); United States v. Place, 462 U.S. 696 (1983).

58 462 U.S. 696 (1983).

59 *United States v. Place*, 462 U.S. at 707.

60 *Id.*

61 543 U.S. 405 (2005).

62 *Illinois v. Caballes*, 543 U.S. at 409.

63 *Id.*, at 410. See § 2.5(A) and § 2.6(A) for a discussion of *Kyllo v. United States.*

64 568 U.S. 237 (2013).

65 460 U.S. 491 (1983).

substances in luggage would have been a more expeditious alternative.

Florida v. Jardines[66] held that use of a drug dog at the front door to discover drugs in defendant's residence was a search, using the *Jones* property-rights approach. The Court's analysis asked whether the police investigated in a "constitutionally protected area." After the Court stated that the police were on the curtilage rather than in open fields, the next inquiry asked whether the investigation was "accomplished through an unlicensed physical intrusion."[67] When the Court said the officers had "a purpose to conduct a search, which is not what anyone would think he had license to do," their conduct appears to have been a search that had to satisfy Fourth Amendment standards.

C. Plain Feel

Plain feel may apply during a warrantless seizure of contraband, or during an otherwise valid frisk of a suspect. The seizure is reasonable if the officer's sense of touch makes it *immediately* apparent that the felt object is contraband. In *Minnesota v. Dickerson,*[68] an officer's frisk of a suspect's clothing went beyond its permissible scope to locate weapons that could be used to injure the officers or others.[69] After determining that an item within the pocket of the clothing was not a weapon, the officer continued to manipulate the object; its seizure was therefore unconstitutional, even though its identity was unclear. The officer's continued exploration of [the defendant's] pocket after having concluded that it contained no weapon was unrelated to 'the sole justification of the' frisk which was "the protection of the officers and others nearby."[70] In the *Dickerson* context, "officers will less often be able to justify seizures of unseen contraband," thereby negating the probable cause necessary to seize the object.

Bond v. United States[71] also involved an effort to justify a "plain feel" of soft luggage on the overhead shelves of a bus that had been lawfully stopped. The Court rejected an analogy to the plain view cases because a physical invasion "is simply more intrusive than purely visual inspection."[72] The Court also recognized that "travelers are particularly concerned about their carry-on luggage" that they

66 569 U.S. 1 (2013).

67 Florida v. Jardines, 569 U.S. 1, 7 (2013).

68 508 U.S. 366 (1993).

69 See Chapter 9, discussing Stop and Frisk.

70 Minnesota v. Dickerson, 508 U.S. 366, 378 (1993).

71 529 U.S. 334 (2000).

72 Bond v. United States, 529 U.S. 334 (2000).

use "to transport personal items that, for whatever reason, they prefer to keep close at hand."[73] Because the police conduct intruded on the defendant's reasonable expectation of privacy, it was an illegal search. While a bus passenger "expects that other passengers and bus employees may move [the luggage] for one reason or another," "he does not expect that other passengers or bus employees will, as a matter of course, feel the bag in an exploratory manner,"[74] as the federal agent did.

§ 2.5 What Places Are Protected?

A. The Home and Its Curtilage

Almost a century ago, *Hester v. United States*[75] held that the Fourth Amendment protects both the home and the land commonly used in connection with it, known as the "curtilage."[76] Later case law held that there is no reasonable expectation of privacy in open or public areas of private property beyond the curtilage, i.e., the discovery of items in these areas does not constitute a search and therefore Fourth Amendment standards are inapplicable.

In *Kyllo v. United States*,[77] the Court held that the use of a sense-enhancing, thermal imaging device to which the public does not have access, in order to explore details about the interior of a private home without the inhabitant's knowledge, is a search within the meaning of the Fourth Amendment and therefore is presumptively unreasonable without a warrant. *Florida v. Jardines*[78] held that use of a drug dog at the front door of a residence to discover drugs there was a search, because that private property search was within the "curtilage" rather than in "open fields." In deciding the case, the Court answered two questions: whether the police investigation happened "in a constitutionally protected area," and whether it was "accomplished through an unlicensed physical intrusion."[79]

If property is within the curtilage (rather than open fields), a police intrusion is a search if the defendant has shown a reasonable expectation of privacy there. *United States v. Dunn*[80] offered its understanding of where the boundary exists between the home and curtilage, on the one hand, and the so-called "open fields." The extent

---

73 *Id.*, at 337–38.

74 *Id.*, at 338–39.

75 265 U.S. 27 (1924).

76 Oliver v. U.S., 466 U.S. 170 (1984).

77 533 U.S. 27 (2001). See § 2.6(A), discussing how monitoring technology can reveal illegal activities within the home.

78 569 U.S. 1 (2013).

79 Florida v. Jardines, 569 U.S. 1, 7 (2013).

80 United States v. Dunn, 480 U.S. 294 (1987).

of a home's curtilage is determined by reference to four factors: the proximity to the home, whether the area is included within an enclosure surrounding the home, the nature of the area's uses to which the area is put, and the steps taken by the resident to protect the area from observation by people passing by.

The *Dunn* Court concluded that a barn and immediately adjoining lands were outside the curtilage: they were sixty yards from the residence, outside a fence surrounding the house, "not being used for intimate activities of the home," and not protected from observation from nearby open fields. While porches, decks and grounds adjacent to the home that are bounded by fences have Fourth Amendment protection, police may observe what occurs in those areas from places where they have a right to be, e.g., on the street.

Fourth Amendment protections do not apply to public areas such as streets or parks. For example, in *California v. Greenwood*,[81] the Court held that no Fourth Amendment activity occurs when the police inspect and seize garbage bags left on the street at the curb outside the defendant's house. Two arguments supported its conclusion. First, by voluntarily turning over the bags on the curb rather than on their property, the defendants had "no legitimate expectation of privacy in information" that was voluntarily turned over to the third parties. Second, the defendants lost their expectation of privacy by exposing "their garbage to the public" on the street to be picked up by a garbage collector, "who might himself have sorted through [it] or permitted others, such as the police, to do so."[82]

No reasonable expectation of privacy exists in information that is readily visible to the public. Placing the garbage bags at the curb made them "readily accessible to animals, children, scavengers, snoops, and other members of the public." "[T]he police cannot be reasonably be expected to avert their eyes from evidence of criminal activity that could have been observed by any member of the public."[83] Because garbage hidden in opaque bags is not literally exposed to the public, the Court was referring to a *risk* of exposure; the contents were constructively exposed for Fourth Amendment purposes. Once the expectation of privacy is lost, it does not matter whether the search occurs at the curb or later at a landfill. The majority and dissenting Justices differed on what society is prepared to accept as reasonable.

---

81 486 U.S. 35 (1988).

82 California v. Greenwood, 486 U.S. 35, 40–41 (1988).

83 *Id.*, at 41.

Using the *Greenwood* facts, suppose the defendant leaves the garbage bags in the garage instead of at the curb. The garbage in the garage is still on the curtilage in a private area. Although trash collectors have implicit permission to take trash from the garage area on the curtilage, where the public is excluded, the police lack that permission and cannot seize the bags without probable cause. However, if the collector takes the bags from the garage and gives it to the police, no search has occurred unless the collector already was cooperating with or working for the police. If the trash is located on the street beyond the curtilage or at a landfill, the police could search the contents for evidence because there was no Fourth Amendment activity.

The police may be on the curtilage of private property without a warrant only to the extent that the public may do so. Courts regard the main entrance of a residence, including driveways and walkways as properly "invadable" curtilage, because it is an area that is open to the public. Law enforcement personnel thus have an implied license to knock on the front door of a residence in order to speak with the occupants about a crime, an investigation, or a matter of public welfare. The police can walk on a person's driveway as the access route to the house. However, without a warrant or grounds for a warrantless search, they cannot depart from that access area in order to engage in unreasonable and intrusive viewing.

Police sometimes use a "knock and talk" procedure to have a consensual encounter with the resident on the approach to the main entrance of the residence. Once at the front door, police observations from a "knock and talk" may be used to spot evidence in plain view or to support probable cause for a warrant. The procedure is used to investigate the resident of the property, provided the officer goes only where he has a legal right to be. "Knock and talk" procedures are commonly violated when conducted at a back door that is not the main entryway, or when officers are unlawfully located on a defendant's backyard patio without the resident's consent. Observations by the police of incriminating evidence or activities while they are unlawfully on the curtilage are inadmissible.

B. Above the Curtilage

Unlike Fourth Amendment activity *on* the curtilage, other cases have addressed a person's expectation of privacy *above* the curtilage. For example, in *California v. Ciraolo*,[84] even though the defendant's marijuana crop was within the fenced curtilage of his residence, naked-eye aerial observation of curtilage from aircraft in public navigable airspace is reasonable. Because the observations "took

---

[84] 476 U.S. 207 (1986).

place within public navigable airspace" and were of "plants readily discernible to the naked eye as marijuana," no search occurred. "Any member of the public flying in this airspace who glanced down could have seen what these officers observed."[85]

Florida v. Riley[86] relied upon *Ciraolo*, likewise finding that no search occurred. *Riley* upheld the helicopter surveillance at 400 feet, and *Ciraolo* involved a fixed-wing aircraft at 1,000 feet. The Court, however, refused to declare "that an inspection of the curtilage of a house from an aircraft will always pass muster under the Fourth Amendment simply because the plane is within the navigable airspace specified by law."[87]

Similarly, while the Court in *Dow Chemical Co. v. United States*[88] held that the use of sophisticated cameras to record open field activity from an airplane was not a search, it cautioned that a different result might be possible if the surveillance were of "an area immediately adjacent to a private home, where privacy expectations are most heightened." Some places like an industrial plant may fall "somewhere between 'open fields' and curtilage, but lacking some of the critical characteristics of both."[89]

While the Court hinted that physical entry of such land would constitute the curtilage, it held that as to aerial surveillance the place was "more comparable to an open field," meaning such surveillance was not a search.[90] The result might have been different if the surveillance involved "highly sophisticated surveillance not generally available to the public, such as satellite technology."[91] The Court also limited the approved surveillance by commenting that "no objects as small as 1/2-inch diameter such as a class ring, for example, are recognizable, nor are there any identifiable human faces or secret documents captured in such a fashion as to implicate more serious privacy concerns."[92]

---

[85] California v. Ciraolo, 476 U.S. 207, 213–14 (1986).

[86] 488 U.S. 445 (1989).

[87] Florida v. Riley, 488 U.S. 445, 451 (1989). See State v. McKelvey, 544 P.3d 632, 645 (Ak. 2024) (Alaskans have a reasonable expectation that authorities will not examine curtilage of their homes from aircraft with high-powered optics [to detect unlicensed marijuana growing operation]; court examines "the utility of the conduct as a technique of law enforcement"; fact that other images of curtilage are available online does not make defendant's expectation of privacy in the curtilage unreasonable; warrant required to observe curtilage of home that is protected from ground-level observation).

[88] 476 U.S. 227 (1986).

[89] *Dow Chemical Co. v. United States*, 476 U.S. at 236.

[90] *Id.*, at 239.

[91] *Id.*, at 238.

[92] *Id.*, at 238 n.5.

C. Open Fields or Areas

The area beyond the curtilage, called "open fields," is unprotected from Governmental personnel arbitrarily entering that property, even in violation of trespass laws and free from Fourth Amendment inquiry. If property is *within* the curtilage (rather than open fields), Governmental intrusion constitutes a Fourth Amendment search if a defendant has shown an expectation of privacy. *Oliver v. United States*[93] held that Fourth Amendment protections do not extend to open fields or areas beyond the curtilage. "[A]n individual may not legitimately demand privacy for activities conducted out of doors in fields, except in the area immediately surrounding the home."[94] Police can arbitrarily enter open fields to observe, free of Fourth Amendment scrutiny.

In open fields, it does not matter how a person tries to display a reasonable expectation of privacy, i.e., fencing land and posting "No Trespassing" signs are not decisive in assessing the legitimacy of subjective expectations of privacy, because they do not create a reasonable expectation of privacy in open fields. Likewise, a warrantless search of the woodland area beyond the curtilage is valid.[95] The police may also lawfully observe land from the air without raising issues of whether their observations constitute a search.[96] In other words, if a defendant has no expectation of privacy for aerial surveillance of open areas, no search occurs. Similarly, marijuana plants observable by the naked eye from public airspace are not constitutionally protected.[97]

As noted, *Dunn* held that a barn sixty yards from the main residence was not adjacent to the house and therefore was not part of the curtilage. The barn was used for purposes unrelated to the home, and the barn area was not protected from observation. Police officers in *Dunn* ignored both exterior and interior fences constructed of barbed wire before approaching the barn. At the barn, police shined a light through a window and saw drug equipment, without a search warrant or exigent circumstances. The interior of the barn was protected by Fourth Amendment standards; the police could shine a light into the interior but not enter the barn.

On two occasions, they reentered the land without a warrant to search the farm. Similarly, if Dunn had parked his vehicle in an open field beyond the curtilage, the police could look in the vehicle's

---

93 466 U.S. 170 (1984).

94 Oliver v. United States, 466 U.S. 170, 178 (1984).

95 See Oliver v. United States, 466 U.S. 170 (1984).

96 See Florida v. Riley, 488 U.S. 445 (1989).

97 California v. Ciraolo, 476 U.S. 207 (1986).

windows to acquire information to support a warrant. The Court held that there was no privacy right in the barn under the circumstances. The federal agents used the information they had learned to obtain a warrant for searching the barn's interior.

If the barn had had a telephone, could the Government have tapped that phone without a warrant *and* without probable cause? If there is no privacy interest in the barn, Katz was entitled to more Fourth Amendment protection in a public phone booth than Dunn on private property that is closed off to the public. If everything outside the curtilage is unprotected by the Fourth Amendment, there would seem to be no reason why Government agents could not hide transmitters and cameras outside the curtilage and engage in permanent surveillance.

D. Business Premises

The portions of business premises that are open to the public are considered to be public areas, which may be searched by police without invading any right of privacy of the owners or occupants. For example, in *Maryland v. Macon*,[98] police officers "action in entering the bookstore and examining the wares that were intentionally exposed to all who frequent the place of business did not infringe a legitimate expectation of privacy and hence did not constitute a search within the meaning of the Fourth Amendment."[99] Purchasing some magazines for sale in the store is not a Fourth Amendment "seizure," because the defendant "voluntarily transferred any possessory interest he may have had in the magazines to the purchaser upon the receipt of the funds."[100]

However, a search may not be conducted in areas or compartments within a business premises which are not open or accessible to the public at the time of the search.[101] In *G.M. Leasing Corp. v. United States*,[102] while law enforcement may seize automobiles from public streets, parking lots, and other open places that did not violate a reasonable expectation of privacy, federal agents' entry of corporate offices to seize tax books and records from a private office was illegal. The Court denied the Government's argument "that the warrant protections of the Fourth Amendment do not apply to invasion of privacy in furtherance of tax collection."[103]

---

[98] 472 U.S. 463 (1985).

[99] Maryland v. Macon, 472 U.S. 463, 469 (1985).

[100] *Id.*, at 463.

[101] See, e.g., Mancusi v. DeForte, 392 U.S. 364 (1968) (warrantless search of a union office); Recznik v. City of Lorain, 393 U.S. 166 (1968) (search of store, its basement, and a separate upstairs suite after hours).

[102] 429 U.S. 338 (1977).

[103] G.M. Leasing Corp. v. United States, 429 U.S. 338, 356 (1977).

Open areas of an industrial plant complex between buildings are comparable to an open field; taking aerial photos of the plant from an aircraft in navigable airspace is not a search prohibited by the Fourth Amendment.[104]

§ 2.6 Technology for Monitoring

A. Monitoring Conditions

Kyllo explicitly recognized that the thermal imaging device used to detect heat on the exterior surface of the home is only one kind of "technology." The likely development of other technologies required the Court to create guidelines for the future use of such devices in a residence and other structures. The Court also stated an updated version of a search for the age of technology:

> obtaining by sense-enhancing technology any information regarding the interior of the home that could not otherwise have been obtained without physical "intrusion into a constitutionally protected area" constitutes a search where (as here) the technology in question is not in general public use.[105]

The Government argued that the thermal imager was limited to detecting "only heat radiating from the external surface of the house" and "did not detect private activities occurring in private areas."[106] However, the Court rejected that distinction. "The Fourth Amendment draws 'a firm line at the entrance to the house' to require clear specification of those methods of surveillance that require a warrant. . . . In the home . . . all details are intimate details, because the entire area is held safe from prying government eyes."[107] A residence is a place where "privacy expectations are most heightened."[108] When

> the Government uses a device that is not in general public use, [such as a thermal imager,] to explore details of the home that would previously been unknowable without physical intrusion, the surveillance is a "search" [under the Fourth Amendment] and is presumptively unreasonable without a warrant.[109]

---

104 Dow Chemical Co. v. United States, 476 U.S. 227 (1986).

105 Kyllo v. United States, 533 U.S. 27, 34 (2001).

106 *Id.*, at 35, 37.

107 *Id.*, at 40.

108 *Id.*, at 33.

109 *Id.*, at 35.

The *Kyllo* dissenters argued that there was no search in this case through use of a high-tech thermal imager. While the majority conceded that it was arguable that "no 'significant' compromise of the homeowner's privacy" occurred, it decided that it was better to interpret the reasonable expectation of privacy consistent with the Framer's interests, "and in a manner which will conserve public interests."[110]

The majority noted that a "workable" line does not differentiate "off-the-wall" from "through-the-wall" intrusions, and does not distinguish intimate from non-intimate home activities.[111] The Court held that the "reasonable expectation of privacy" applies to a home, even though *Katz* had stated that the Fourth Amendment "protects people not places." *Kyllo* reiterated a property reference just as *Oliver* had applied the expectation of privacy protection for the curtilage but not open fields.

Prior to *Kyllo*, the Court had addressed limits for technological surveillance of a defendant's residence and curtilage. Like microphones and cameras, police use beepers as an effective method to monitor movement. In *United States v. Knotts*,[112] the police arranged with a chloroform seller to put a beeper inside one of the chloroform containers that was thereafter sold to the suspect. The Court held that no search had occurred, reasoning that the surveillance "amounted principally to the following of an automobile on public streets and highways."[113] If the police had accomplished its investigation by visual surveillance, there would have been no search because one "traveling in an automobile on public thoroughfares has no reasonable expectation of privacy in his movements from one place to another,"[114] and "scientific enhancement of this sort raises no constitutional issues which visual surveillance would not also raise."[115] The *Knotts* Court upheld information from the beeper as long as it was not used "to reveal information as to the movement of the . . . [container] within the [defendant's premises]."[116]

A year later, the Court applied the *Knotts* limitation in *United States v. Karo*[117] to limit beeper use to track movements up to a house and after a vehicle or other container leaves a house. However, the Government cannot use the beeper to track movement inside the

110 *Id.*, at 40.

111 *Id.*, at 39.

112 460 U.S. 276 (1983).

113 United States v. Knotts, 460 U.S. 276, 281 (1983).

114 *Id.*

115 *Id.*, at 285.

116 *Id.*

117 468 U.S. 705 (1984).

house. The Court indicated that its decision conclusion would be otherwise where the beeper monitoring "reveals information that could not have been obtained through visual surveillance,"[118] e.g., when the item to which the beeper is attached remains within private premises.

The Court applied the same rationale to police aerial observations of open fields with a "conventional" mapping camera. While the police could engage in the same conduct as the "flying public" by observing marijuana growing in a greenhouse, they could not obtain information of "intimate details connected with the use of the home or the curtilage."[119]

While *Kyllo* constructed procedures for the future usage of "advancing technology" in law enforcement, it left two important questions for lower courts. First, is the warrantless use of thermal imaging or similar technology acceptable in *non-residential* contexts, e.g., commercial structures, residences where occupants also perform their job duties, unoccupied buildings? Second, how do lower courts determine when the "technology in question is not in general public use"? What factors are relevant to deciding whether a device has become generally available to the public?

In *United States v. Poller*,[120] officers approached a car outside a building that was under surveillance. Using his Apple iPhone in camera mode to see through the dark tinted windows of the car, an officer saw two guns inside the car. The court held that no search occurred under *Kyllo*, because cell phone cameras are in general public use.

> [C]ellphones are "now such a pervasive and insistent part of daily life that the proverbial visitor from Mars might conclude they were an important feature of human anatomy." Similarly, cameras are in general public use, as now more than ever, cameras are ubiquitous, found in the hands and pockets of virtually all Americans, on the doorbells and entrances of homes, and on the walls and ceilings of businesses. . . . [A] Google search for the terms "iPhone camera tinted windows" yields a litany of local television news and automotive magazine or blog articles . . . explaining that thieves can use cell phone cameras to see through tinted windows.
>
> . . .

118 United States v. Karo, 468 U.S. 705, 707 (1984).

119 *Florida v. Riley*, 488 U.S. at 452.

120 682 F.Supp.3d 226, 231 (D. Conn. 2023).

> [T]he use by law enforcement of technology that is in general public use does not—without more—violate a person's reasonable expectation of privacy. . . . Accordingly, the detectives did not violate Poller's reasonable expectation of privacy by using an iPhone to see through the tint of the windows on his car.[121]

B. Monitoring a Suspect's Movements

Increasingly, the Government investigates criminal behavior by relying on technology to monitor the suspect's current or past movements. Because modern cultural customs include carrying a cell phone for various purposes, police often track the movements of a cell phone (and thus the owner of the phone) through acquisition of cell-site location information [CSLI].[122] Although acquisition of the data is simple, obtaining it constitutes a Fourth Amendment search that normally requires issuance of a warrant. *United States v. Jones* had "already recognized that individuals have a reasonable expectation of privacy in the whole of their physical movements." *Carpenter v. United States* invalidated the Government's acquisition of cell-site data that proved a robbery suspect's movements.

> [I]ndividuals . . . compulsively carry cell phones with them all the time. [W]hen the Government tracks the location of a cell phone it achieves near perfect surveillance, as if it had attached an ankle monitor to the phone's user.
>
> Moreover, the retrospective quality of the data here gives police access to a category of information otherwise unknowable. . . . With access to CSLI, the Government can now travel back in time to retrace a person's whereabouts, subject only to the retention policies of the wireless carriers, which currently maintain records for up to five years. . . . Unlike with the GPS device in *Jones,* police need not even know in advance whether they want to follow a particular individual, or when.
>
> Whoever the suspect turns out to be, he has effectively been tailed every moment of every day for five years, . . .
>
> . . . From the 127 days of location data it received, the Government could, in combination with other information, deduce a detailed log of Carpenter's movements, including when he was at the site of the robberies. And the

---

121 *Id.*, at 231–232.

122 CSLI refers to the information collected as a cellphone identifies its location to nearby cell towers. CSLI from nearby cell towers can indicate a cell phone's approximate location. With information from multiple cell towers, a technique called "triangulation" is used to locate a cell phone with greater accuracy.

> Government thought the CSLI accurate enough to highlight it during the closing argument of his trial.
>
> At any rate, the rule the Court adopts "must take account of more sophisticated systems that are already in use or in development." While the records in this case reflect the state of technology at the start of the decade, the accuracy of CSLI is rapidly approaching GPS-level precision.[123]

Most lower courts have confined *Carpenter* to its facts.[124]

Courts also have held that a person has a reasonable expectation of privacy in his personal cell phone, including all record and text messages.[125] However, lower courts have permitted police to conduct warrantless searches of cell phones in cases involving drug trafficking, where evidence of the crime is likely stored on the phones, recent call records can easily be destroyed, and cell phones enable drug smugglers to develop methods that could endanger officers and the public.

C. Third-Party Doctrine

A person has no legitimate expectation of privacy in information that he voluntarily turns over to third parties, "even if the information is revealed on the assumption that it will be used only for a limited purpose."[126] The Fourth Amendment does not prohibit the government from accessing that information without a warrant. The rationale is that, in revealing information to another, the defendant takes the risk that the information will be conveyed by that person to law enforcement officials.[127] In *Carpenter v. United States*, the Court declined to extend the rule to cell-site records that convey "a detailed and comprehensive record of [a] person's movements," but the third-party doctrine continues to apply to

---

123 Carpenter v. United States, 585 U.S. 296 (2018).

124 Compare United States v. Tuggle, 4 F.4th 505 (7th Cir. 2021) (use of pole camera installed on public property to surveil suspect's home was not search, regardless of duration) with Commonwealth v. Mora, 150 N.E.3d 297 (2020) (long-term use of camera installed on utility pole for targeted surveillance of person's home constituted a search). See also United States v. Moore-Bush, 36 F.4th 320 (1st Cir. 2022) (en banc) (First Circuit divides evenly on whether use of pole cameras in public space for eight months to surveil a home constitutes a search).

125 See Riley v. California, 573 U.S. 373 (2014); Chapter 6, discussing Search Incident to Arrest.

126 *Carpenter v. United States*, 585 U.S. 296 (2018). See Smith v. Maryland, 442 U.S. 735, 743–44 (1979); United States v. Miller, 425 U.S. 435, 443 (1976).

127 See United States v. Contreras, 905 F.3d 853 (5th Cir. 2018) ("the third-party doctrine applies to business records that might incidentally reveal location information" such as basic subscriber information. On the other hand, if the Government hacks into a person's computer to learn his IP address, that conduct constitutes a search and must comply with the Fourth Amendment.

"business records that might incidentally reveal location information," including telephone numbers and bank records.[128]

D. Fourth Amendment and Email

The Sixth Circuit has found an expectation of privacy in the contents of emails. Taking a different approach to the seizure of the contents of personal emails stored by an ISP, *United States v. Warshak*[129] affirmed the issuance of an injunction that prohibiting the seizure of the contents of personal emails without notice and an opportunity to be heard. *Warshak* distinguished *Smith v. Maryland,* recognizing increased protection for email contents. Like telephone communications, the expectation of privacy in the contents is not reduced just because the phone company or an ISP could access the contents of e-mails and phone calls.

Warshak held that email is ordinarily protected by the Fourth Amendment. "Given the fundamental similarities between email and traditional forms of communication" such as letters, "it would defy common sense to afford emails lesser Fourth Amendment protection."

> Email is the technological scion of tangible mail, and it plays an indispensable part in the Information Age. Over the last decade, email has become so pervasive that some persons may consider it to be an essential means or necessary instrument for self-expression, even self-identification. It follows that email requires strong protection under the Fourth Amendment; otherwise, the Fourth Amendment would prove an ineffective guardian of private communication, an essential purpose it has long been recognized to serve. As some forms of communication begin to diminish, the Fourth Amendment must recognize and protect nascent ones that arise.[130]

If email is the functionally equivalent of a letter or a phone call, government agents cannot force a commercial Internet Service Provider (ISP) to turn over the contents of an email without

---

[128] Carpenter v. United States, 585 U.S. 296 (2018). Relying on the third party doctrine, circuit courts have found no expectation of privacy in business records of a blockchain transaction records. See, e.g., United States v. Gratkowski, 964 F.3d 307 (5th Cir. 2020) (defendant had no privacy interest in his information located on virtual currency's block-chain).

[129] 631 F.3d 266 (6th Cir. 2010).

[130] United States v. Warshak, 631 F.3d 266, (6th Cir. 2010). Other decisions agree with Warshak that electronic messaging is subject to the Fourth Amendment. See, e.g., United States v. Ali, 870 F.Supp.2d 10, 39 (D.D.C. 2012) (emails); State v. Hinton, 280 P.3d 476, 483 (2012), rev'd on other grounds, 319 P.3d 9 (Wash. 2014) (text messages). See also Riley v. California, 573 U.S. 373 (2014) (suggesting that internet provider has Fourth Amendment protection).

triggering the Fourth Amendment. The police cannot burst into a post office and intercept a letter, unless they get a warrant absent a warrantless exception.[131]

[131] Compare United States v. Trader, 981 F.3d 961 (11th Cir. 2020) (the Government did not need a search warrant to request e-mail address and internet protocol addresses connected with user's profile from third party providing messaging service; the user lacked a reasonable expectation of privacy in e-mail and Internet protocol addresses, by voluntarily sharing with his app provider and logging onto the app; no Fourth Amendment activity occurred).

Chapter 3

PROBABLE CAUSE

Table of Sections

§ 3.1 Introduction

Probable cause is an important component of the Fourth Amendment: ". . . and no Warrants shall issue, but upon probable cause." It applies to both clauses of the Fourth Amendment. For most searches and seizures, probable cause is sufficient to permit intrusions into circumstances where individuals have a legitimate expectation of privacy. It is measured by the information available to law enforcement prior to an arrest or search; what is learned afterwards is irrelevant to *that* arrest or search. As police gather more information, they may have probable cause to arrest a different person or search a different location.

While the police would be more effective if they could search anyone or anywhere, for any reason, what did the Framers of the Bill of Rights intend by selecting "probable cause" as the standard for arrest or search?

> "The substance of all the definitions" of probable cause "is a reasonable ground for belief of guilt." And this "means less than evidence which would justify condemnation" or conviction, as Marshall, C.J., said for the Court more than a century ago. Since Marshall's time, [probable cause] has come to mean more than bare suspicion: Probable cause exists where "the facts and circumstances within [the officers'] knowledge and of which they had reasonably trustworthy information [are] sufficient in themselves to warrant a man of reasonable caution in the belief that" an offense has been or is being committed.
>
> These long-prevailing standards seek to safeguard citizens from rash and unreasonable interferences with privacy and from unfounded charges of crime. They also seek to give fair leeway for enforcing the law in the community's protection. Because many situations which confront officers in the course of executing their duties are more or less ambiguous, room must be allowed for some mistakes on their part. But the mistakes must be those of reasonable men, acting on facts leading sensibly to their conclusions of probability.[1]

If searches were allowed without probable cause, it would be difficult to preserve the privacy of individuals. The probable cause standard has become a privacy line between the police and the citizens. The probable cause requirement is described as "the best compromise that has been found for accommodating"[2] the often opposing interests of privacy and effective law enforcement.

The necessity of probable cause is apparent in "straight search" issues but it is also necessary in derivative search questions. For example, in a search incident to arrest, the validity of the search is dependent upon the validity of the arrest[3]—the latter requiring probable cause.

In *Camara v. Municipal Court*,[4] the Court devised a less demanding form of probable cause that requires a "balancing" of "the need to search against the invasion which the search entails."

---

1 Brinegar v. United States, 338 U.S. 160, 175–76 (1949).

2 *Id.*, at 176.

3 See Chapter 6, discussing Search Incident to Arrest.

4 387 U.S. 523 (1967).

Initially, the Court approved its use for housing inspection warrants, i.e., "'probable cause' to issue a warrant to inspect must exist if reasonable legislative or administrative standards for conducting an area inspection are satisfied with respect to a particular dwelling."[5] Since *Camara*, the balancing approach is used to uphold other types of administrative or regulatory searches.[6]

§ 3.2 Defining Probable Cause

Courts often do not draw a distinction between searches and arrests when citing authority for their probable cause findings. The distinction, however, is particularly significant in search cases when information must establish a nexus between the things sought, the criminal activity, and the time and place of the search. In *Sgro v. United States*,[7] the Court held that probable cause must be based on facts closely related to the time that a warrant issues. Probable cause requires more than bare suspicion but less than "beyond a reasonable doubt" needed to support a conviction at trial. In *Massachusetts v. Upton*,[8] the Court held that the affidavit for the search warrant provided the requisite probable cause for its issuance, even though it did not possess the certainty associated with formal trials.

A. Probable Cause to Search

Probable cause to search exists when, at the time the judge issues a warrant or the police officer performs the search, there are reasonably trustworthy facts and circumstances that are sufficient, using the totality of the circumstances, to lead a reasonable person to believe that there is a fair probability that the items sought constitute fruits, instrumentalities, or evidence of crime, and will be present at the time and place of the search. For example, in *Illinois v. Gates*,[9] the Court held that the totality of circumstances established probable cause, based on an anonymous letter coupled with the corroboration of an informer's tip.

B. Probable Cause to Arrest

Probable cause to *arrest* exists when, at the time the judge issues the warrant or the police officer makes the arrest, there are reasonably trustworthy facts and circumstances sufficient, using the totality of the circumstances, to lead a reasonable person to believe

---

[5] Camara v. Municipal Court, 387 U.S. 523, 538 (1967).

[6] See Chapter 11, discussing Administrative and Special Needs Searches.

[7] 287 U.S. 206 (1932).

[8] 466 U.S. 727 (1984). See Brinegar v. United States, 338 U.S. 160 (1949) (despite variations in detail, ultimate facts constituted probable cause when taken together).

[9] Illinois v. Gates, 462 U.S. 213 (1983).

there is a fair probability that the suspect is committing or has committed an offense.[10] Probable cause to arrest also is defined as a "reasonable ground for belief of guilt" and requires that belief of guilt to be "particularized with respect to the person to be searched or seized."[11] For example, in *Maryland v. Pringle*,[12] following a suspect's consent to search a vehicle, the police recovered cash and cocaine of which none of the vehicle's occupants admitted ownership. The Court held that the police may reasonably infer that people found in a vehicle containing evidence of crime are engaged in a jointly undertaken criminal enterprise and arrest all of them. The facts supported an inference of probable cause that any or all of the occupants possessed the cocaine solely or jointly.

Probable cause has both objective and subjective components. However, it is mostly an objective, flexible, common-sense standard[13] dealing with reasonableness and probabilities as understood by persons knowledgeable in the field of law enforcement, i.e., the evidence must be seen and weighed as understood by those versed in the field of law enforcement.[14] As for the subjective components of probable cause, a police officer can rely on his training and experience as he learns information firsthand, from informants, from citizens, or from other officers, e.g., police know from their training that deodorizers are frequently used to mask the odor of narcotics.

C. Important Connections with a Crime

Probable cause to search for the fruits, instrumentalities, or evidence of a crime requires some connection with a criminal offense. While contraband is self-evident, a search for otherwise noncriminal items should have a probable cause basis as to why the items are to be seized. In *Arizona v. Hicks*,[15] the Court stated that what was lacking was "probable cause to believe the [stereo] equipment was stolen was required." Similarly, where the police want to search a place for certain items, there must be probable cause to believe the items are present at the place to be searched, i.e., there must be a nexus between criminality and the place to be searched. The *Hicks* majority rejected the option of recognizing a third category of police conduct that would fall between plain view requiring no probable cause and a "full-blown search" that required probable cause.[16]

---

10 *Id.*

11 Maryland v. Pringle, 540 U.S. 366, 371 (2003).

12 540 U.S. 366 (2003).

13 Texas v. Brown, 460 U.S. 730, 735 (1983).

14 United States v. Cortez, 449 U.S. 411 (1981).

15 480 U.S. 321, 328 (1987).

16 *Id.*, at 328–29.

The issue of connection to crime is also relevant to an arrest, i.e., why the police believed the defendant was violating the law.

D. An Example of Probable Cause

The following excerpt is from *Carroll v. United States*.[17] As you read this Chapter, consider whether these facts support probable cause under the current constitutional standards.

> Grand Rapids is about 152 miles from Detroit, and that Detroit and its neighborhood along the Detroit river, which is the international boundary, is one of the most active centers for introducing illegally into this country spirituous liquors for distribution into the interior. It is obvious from the evidence that the prohibition agents were engaged in a regular patrol along the important highways from Detroit to Grand Rapids to stop and seize liquor carried in automobiles. They knew or had convincing evidence to make them believe that the Carroll boys, as they called them, were so-called "bootleggers" in Grand Rapids; i.e., that they were engaged in plying the unlawful trade of selling such liquor in that city. The officers had soon after noted their going from Grand Rapids halfway to Detroit, and attempted to follow them to that city to see where they went, but they escaped observation. Two months later these officers suddenly met the same men on their way westward presumably from Detroit. The partners in the original combination to sell liquor in Grand Rapids were together in the same automobile they had been in the night when they tried to furnish the whisky to the officers, which was thus identified as part of the firm equipment. They were coming from the direction of the great source of supply for their stock to Grand Rapids, where they plied their trade. That the officers, when they saw the defendants, believed that they were carrying liquor, we can have no doubt. . . .[18]

The Court held that probable cause existed to search the vehicle, and affirmed the conviction.

§ 3.3 Sources of Probable Cause

When considering the presence or absence of probable cause, the police officer's expertise[19] and experience[20] are to be taken into account. In *United States v. Ortiz*, the Court stated that "officers are

---

17 267 U.S. 132 (1925).

18 Carroll v. United States, 267 U.S. 132, 160 (1925).

19 United States v. Ortiz, 422 U.S. 891 (1975).

20 Johnson v. United States, 333 U.S. 10 (1948).

entitled to draw reasonable inferences from these facts in light of their knowledge of the area and their prior experience with aliens and smugglers."[21] *Johnson v. United States* stated that probable cause may be based upon a distinctive odor where the officer is "qualified to know the odor."[22] Usually, a trained and experienced officer will have probable cause in circumstances when a layman would not, e.g., an officer identifies an illegal substance by smell,[23] feel, or sight. In *Brinegar v. United States*,[24] the Court noted that:

> For a variety of reasons relating not only to probative value and trustworthiness, but also to possible prejudicial effect upon a trial jury and the absence of opportunity for cross-examination, the generally accepted rules of evidence throw many exclusionary protections about one who is charged with standing trial for crime. Much evidence of real and substantial probative value goes out on considerations irrelevant to its probative weight but relevant to possible misunderstanding or misuse by the jury. . . .
>
> In dealing with probable cause, however, as the very name implies, we deal with probabilities. These are not technical; they are the factual and practical considerations of everyday life on which reasonable and prudent men, not legal technicians, act. The standard of proof is accordingly correlative to what must be proved.[25]

In *Brinegar*, the Court did not identify the degree of probability needed other than to say that "more than bare suspicion" and "less than evidence which would justify . . . conviction"[26] was required. Probable cause must be shown on the basis of facts rather than mere conclusions.[27] For example, facts which would contribute to a bad reputation may be taken into account.[28]

A. Arresting/Searching Police

Whether probable cause exists in a given case rests ultimately on the source of the information and whether the facts are sufficient to show probable cause either to arrest or to search. The issue is perhaps best defined by example. While the determination of

---

[21] *United States v. Ortiz*, 422 U.S. at 897.

[22] *Johnson v. United States*, 333 U.S. at 13.

[23] *Id.*, at 16.

[24] 338 U.S. 160 (1949).

[25] *Brinegar v. United States*, 338 U.S. at 173, 175.

[26] *Id.*, at 175.

[27] Aguilar v. Texas, 378 U.S. 108, 113 (1964).

[28] Jones v. United States, 362 U.S. 257, 271 (1960), overruled on other grounds by United States v. Salvucci, 448 U.S. 83 (1980).

probable cause is primarily objective, the experience of the officer is a relevant consideration that may afford probable cause, for example, in detecting drugs. In *Texas v. Brown*,[29] because the officer's experience made him aware that balloons tied in the same manner as the defendant's balloon were used to carry narcotics, he had probable cause to believe defendant's balloon contained an illicit substance. The officer's experience need only form a probability, however, and not a certainty. There are common instances where firsthand information by a police officer is part of the probable cause mix. A typical situation occurs when police observe a person in possession of property and conclude from the surrounding circumstances that the property is stolen.

Another situation may occur when officers come upon suspected illegal property. The question is whether a sufficient amount of information is present to justify the conclusion that the property is contraband. The training or expertise of an officer is relevant to this issue, as well as the officer's ability to perceive that the item is contraband. In *United States v. Ortiz*,[30] the Court stated that "officers are entitled to draw reasonable inferences from [the] facts in light of their knowledge of the area and their prior experience."[31] While the perception need not be a certainty, there must be some factor indicative of a contraband's nature.

A person's association with a place or another person also may be a factor in determining probable cause to arrest. For example, in *Ker v. California*,[32] the police observed the defendant contact a drug trafficker, who was known to traffic in drugs because of his continuing presence at a place where drug dealing was openly and repeatedly conducted. In *United States v. Di Re*,[33] after one person told a Government investigator that he was to buy counterfeit ration coupons from another person at a specific place, the investigator followed a vehicle to the particular place where he found the first person holding the counterfeit coupons. The Court determined that there was no probable cause to arrest a third person who was a passenger in the buyer's vehicle.

> The argument that one who "accompanies a criminal to a crime rendezvous" cannot be assumed to be a bystander, forceful enough in some circumstances, is farfetched when the meeting is not secretive or in a suspicious hide-out but in broad daylight, in plain sight of passersby, in a public

---

29 Texas v. Brown, 460 U.S. 730 (1983).

30 422 U.S. 891 (1975).

31 United States v. Ortiz, 422 U.S. 891, 897 (1975).

32 See Ker v. California, 374 U.S. 23, 41 (1963).

33 332 U.S. 581 (1948).

> street of a large city, and where the alleged substantive crime is one which does not necessarily involve any act visibly criminal. If [the passenger] had witnessed the passing of papers from hand to hand, it would not follow that he knew they were ration coupons, and if he saw that they were ration coupons, it would not follow that he would know them to be counterfeit. Indeed it appeared at the trial to require an expert to establish that fact. Presumptions of guilt are not lightly to be indulged from mere meetings.[34]

Perhaps a person is more likely to have been more than a bystander when the offense includes an "act visibly criminal."[35] When criminal activity is not apparent to the bystander, the police should emphasize the association to indicate that that person is an accomplice.

Maryland v. Pringle[36] distinguished *Di Re* when police stopped a vehicle for speeding in the early morning hours, and obtained the driver's consent to search the vehicle. There, he found more than $750 cash in the glove compartment and five baggies of cocaine in the backseat. After he told the three occupants that he would arrest them all unless someone admitted ownership of the drugs, the "men offered no information regarding the ownership of the drugs or money." The defendant later was convicted based on his admission that the drugs belonged to him, and the Court held that the confession was not the fruit of an unlawful arrest because there was probable cause for the arrest.

> We think it an entirely reasonable inference from these facts that any or all three of the occupants had knowledge of, and exercised dominion and control over, the cocaine. Thus a reasonable officer could conclude that there was probable cause to believe Pringle committed the crime of possession of cocaine, either solely or jointly.[37]

Because probable cause requires far less proof than the conviction standard of proof, there was arguably enough evidence that Pringle was likely individually guilty. The Court explained that all three defendant were in joint possession of the money and drugs by stating that

> it was reasonable for the officer to infer a common enterprise among the three men. The quantity of drugs and cash in the car indicated the likelihood of drug dealing, an enterprise to which a dealer would be unlikely to admit an

---

[34] United States v. Di Re, 332 U.S. 581, 593 (1948).

[35] *Id.*, at 593.

[36] 540 U.S. 366 (2003).

[37] Maryland v. Pringle, 540 U.S. 366, 372 (2003).

innocent person with the potential to furnish evidence against him.[38]

Observation of what reasonably appears to be a person's furtive gestures when strangers or the police approach strongly indicates guilt. *Peters v. New York*[39] suggested that deliberately furtive actions are strong indicia of mens rea; when connected with a police officer's specific knowledge about a suspect's relation to the evidence of crime, those gesture are proper factors in the probable cause proof to make an arrest. Frequently, the furtive gesture appears to be hiding an item such as drugs.

A related issue is flight of the person. While flight alone is insufficient for probable cause, it is some indication of criminal activity. In *Illinois v. Wardlow*,[40] the defendant began running from police when he noticed them. The Court commented that flight would support at least a reasonable suspicion sufficient to stop the person.

> Headlong flight, wherever it occurs—is the consummate act of evasion; it is not necessarily indicative of wrongdoing, but it is certainly suggestive of such. In reviewing the propriety of an officer's conduct, courts do not have available empirical studies dealing with inferences drawn from suspicious behavior, and we cannot reasonably demand scientific certainty from judges or law enforcement officers where none exists.[41]

An officer who comes upon a person engaged in possible criminal activity may question the person. Evasive responses to such questions may be considered in determining probable cause.[42] The nature of the area where the suspected criminal activity is occurring is also a relevant consideration. Likewise, the time when suspected activity takes place, e.g., 3:00 a.m. as opposed to 3:00 p.m., is often a factor for probable cause. Another way for an officer to support his credibility is to point to weapons seized during either a stop based on reasonable suspicion or an interview with the perpetrator.

The prior experience of the officer with a particular defendant is sometimes considered. A defendant's prior "reputation" alone is an insufficient basis upon which to base a finding of probable cause.[43] In addition, as with stops, the reasonableness of an arrest does not depend on the subjective motives of the officers making the arrest.

---

38 *Id.*, at 373.

39 392 U.S. 40 (1968).

40 528 U.S. 119 (2000).

41 Illinois v. Wardlow, 528 U.S. 119, 124–25 (2000).

42 See, e.g., Michigan v. DeFillippo, 443 U.S. 31, 37 (1979).

43 *Brinegar v. United States*, 338 U.S. at 162–63.

For example, in *Arkansas v. Sullivan*,[44] the Court noted that a traffic arrest cannot be invalidated by the fact that it was a pretext for search, because probable cause is the sole standard for measuring a seizure's legality. Regarding reputation, an alert by a drug-detection dog certified by a bona fide organization is presumptively sufficient to establish probable cause.[45]

B. Hearsay

Probable cause to arrest or search may be based upon secondhand information. Hearsay is permissible as long as there is a substantial basis for believing that: (1) the source of the hearsay is credible, and (2) there is a factual basis for the information furnished. The ease of establishing probable cause from hearsay varies somewhat depending on the source of the information, i.e., where the source is a citizen-witness, another officer, or an informant. However, the use of hearsay does not always satisfy probable cause. For example, in *Taylor v. Alabama*,[46] a warrantless arrest illegal when based on a tip from informant who had never given similar information to an officer, did not provide that officer with a sufficient basis for information, because it did not provide any details of a crime.

The reliability of information from citizen-witnesses is judged by a different standard than from the typical criminal informant. When the source of information is a known citizen-witness, it is presumed to be reliable. In *Jaben v. United States*,[47] the Court held that a judge was justified in accepting an IRS agent's factual allegations about another agent's observations without requiring supporting documents. The Court distinguished a tax evasion case from a narcotics case, where informants are less credible.

> [U]nlike narcotics informants, for example, whose credibility may often be suspect, the sources in this tax evasion case are much less likely to produce false or untrustworthy information. Thus, whereas some supporting information concerning the credibility of informants in narcotics cases or other common garden varieties of crime may be required, such information is not so necessary in the context of the case before us.[48]

A police officer may obtain information from other police to establish probable cause, because the veracity of the informing officer

---

44 532 U.S. 769 (2001).

45 Florida v. Harris, 568 U.S. 237 (2013).

46 See Taylor v. Alabama, 457 U.S. 687 (1982).

47 See Jaben v. United States, 381 U.S. 214 (1965).

48 *Id.*, at 224.

is presumed. In *United States v. Ventresca*, the events described in the search warrant affidavit were from the affiant's fellow officers. The Court upheld the warrant. "Observations of fellow officers of the Government engaged in a common investigation are plainly a reliable basis for a warrant applied for by one of their number."[49]

In *Whiteley v. Warden*,[50] the Court observed that police normally are entitled to assume that officers requesting aid in executing an arrest warrant had provided the judge with sufficient information to support a judicial assessment of probable cause. However, when the officers requesting aid did not offer such information to judge, an arrest is illegal. In *Whiteley*, a police officer arrested two men in response to a police radio bulletin that an arrest warrant for them had issued in another part of the state.

> We do not, of course, question that the Laramie police were entitled to act on the strength of the radio bulletin. Certainly police officers called upon to aid other officers in executing arrest warrants are entitled to assume that the officers requesting aid offered the magistrate the information requisite to support an independent judicial assessment of probable cause. Where, however, the contrary turns out to be true, an otherwise illegal arrest cannot be insulated from challenge by the decision of the instigating officer to rely on fellow officers to make the arrest.[51]

Under *Whiteley*'s so-called "fellow officer" rule, police may rely on a communication through official channels requesting that an arrest or a search be made. As long as there is an original basis for probable cause, officers may rely upon the collective knowledge of law enforcement personnel. For example, in *United States v. Hensley*,[52] the Court stated that "if a flyer or bulletin has been issued on the basis of articulable facts supporting a reasonable suspicion that the wanted person has committed an offense, then reliance on that flyer or bulletin justifies a stop to check identification."

C. Informants

An informant is distinguishable from an ordinary citizen who may be a witness to a crime. The totality of the circumstances rule includes the requirements of "basis of knowledge" and "veracity." The informant's veracity can be established by showing either the credibility of the informant or his reliability on a given occasion. The

---

49 United States v. Ventresca, 380 U.S. 102, 111 (1965).

50 401 U.S. 560 (1971).

51 Whiteley v. Warden, 401 U.S. 560, 568 (1971).

52 United States v. Hensley, 469 U.S. 221, 232 (1985).

basis of the informant's knowledge can be satisfied by either direct information or self-verifying detail. Particularly where either veracity or knowledge is lacking, an informant can be "enhanced" by police investigation to corroborate the information.

Suppose that someone calls the police and relates 8–10 details about a criminal procedure professor and his class meetings. The information predicts that the professor teaches class at a particular time and place, that he'll be carrying a gray-covered book (the casebook for the course), and drugs in his pocket. If the police corroborate all but the existence of the drugs and tell the judge that they corroborated all other facts, would there be probable cause for a search warrant or arrest warrant? If a reasonable judge would not issue a warrant, something more than corroboration is needed. What is it?

§ 3.4 Using Informants' Information

A. Proving Veracity

In a series of cases, the Court has addressed the use of informants and their hearsay information to establish probable cause for the issuance of search warrants. In *Aguilar v. Texas*,[53] the search warrant affidavit stated: "Affiants have received reliable information from a credible person and do believe that heroin, marijuana, barbiturates, and other narcotics and narcotic paraphernalia are being kept at the above described premises for the purpose of sale and use contrary to the provisions of the law." The Court concluded that the affidavit failed to meet Fourth Amendment requirements:

> Although an affidavit may be based on hearsay information and need not reflect the direct personal observations of the affiant, the magistrate must be informed of some of the underlying circumstances from which the informant concluded that the narcotics were where he claimed they were, and some of the underlying circumstances from which the officer concluded that the informant, whose identity need not be disclosed, was "credible" or his information "reliable." Otherwise, "the inferences from the facts which lead to the complaint" will be drawn not "by a neutral and detached magistrate," as the Constitution requires, but instead, by a police officer "engaged in the often competitive enterprise of ferreting out crime," or, as in this case, by an unidentified informant.[54]

---

53 378 U.S. 108 (1964).

54 Aguilar v. Texas, 378 U.S. 108, 114–15 (1964).

Courts applied *Aguilar*'s two-pronged test to determine probable cause issues for search or arrest warrants or for warrantless arrests or searches. For the "basis of knowledge" prong, the judge had to determine whether the informant had a basis for his allegations that a certain person had been involved in criminal conduct or that evidence of crime would be found at a certain place. The "veracity" prong required the judge to decide the inherent credibility of the informant or the reliability of his information.

For identifiable informants, a prosecutor can prove honesty by demonstrating accurate past performance. For example, in *McCray v. Illinois*,[55] the Court held that officers had probable cause to arrest, because the informant's reliability was sufficiently demonstrated. The officers testified that the informant had supplied information leading to arrests and convictions fifteen times. Although merely concluding the informant's reliability is inadequate, a statement that the person has furnished reliable information in the past is sufficient. A common technique is to allege that the informant has "given accurate information in the past." Should that be adequate? That statement would be *technically* true even if the information had nothing to do with criminal behavior and the police asked its best informant, "What colors are in the American flag?" Should that method of proving informant reliability be concerning? What would you think about basing informants' reliability on *that* specific question?

What would be the best method for proving the reliability of an informant? "This informant's reliable knowledge has led to convictions in the past." Do other methods set a useful standard for assessing reliability? A judge might conclude that an informant has veracity by asking whether his reports had led to one arrest or conviction in the past. Concentrating only on the information that has led to past arrests or convictions may miss an important point. How often has the informant's past knowledge been *in*accurate, or has not led to arrests or convictions? This type of questioning might lead to another useful method of evaluating credibility. Are there circumstances to assure that the information he gives is honest? Perhaps, if the informant will gain something (e.g., a reward or immunity from prosecution) only if the information is accurate.

Even if no statements about past performance are available, e.g., as with an anonymous informant, a statement by the informer against his own interest may show probable cause, because admissions of crime carry their own indicia of credibility, e.g., by identifying himself as an accomplice or revealing the location of the

---

55 386 U.S. 300 (1967).

fruits of the crime, or because, if his statement were untrue, he could be punished for perjury or false swearing. In *United States v. Harris*,[56]

> the warrant's affidavit recited extrajudicial statements of a declarant, who feared for his life and safety if his identity was revealed, that over the past two years he had many times and recently purchased "illicit whiskey." These statements were against the informant's penal interest, for he thereby admitted major elements of an offense under the Internal Revenue Code.
>
> Common sense in the important daily affairs of life would induce a prudent and disinterested observer to credit these statements. People do not lightly admit a crime and place critical evidence in the hands of the police in the form of their own admissions. Admissions of crime, like admissions against proprietary interests, carry their own indicia of credibility—sufficient at least to support a finding of probable cause to search. . . . [H]ere the informant's admission that over a long period and currently he had been buying illicit liquor on certain premises, itself and without more, implicated that property and furnished probable cause to search.[57]

B. Proving Knowledge

To satisfy the second prong for probable cause based on hearsay, the prosecutor can prove the informant's knowledge, either directly or indirectly. A direct showing demonstrates that the informant knows about the underlying circumstances supporting his probable cause conclusion, whether by his direct observation of suspicious conduct, or information from another informant, e.g., hearsay based on hearsay.

Indirect proof of the informant's knowledge may flow from the self-verifying detail in the informant's tip itself, e.g., the informant's information describes not only the vehicle's make used to transport drugs, but also the vehicle's color, model, hood ornament, unique tires, and special hubcaps. Such specific information connecting a defendant to a crime strongly suggests that the informant had personal knowledge (rather than casual rumor) of the facts meeting that description. For example in *Draper v. United States*,[58] the informant's information was both detailed and corroborated by a

[56] 403 U.S. 573 (1971).

[57] United States v. Harris, 403 U.S. 573, 583–84 (1971).

[58] 358 U.S. 307 (1959).

narcotics agent. "The information given to narcotic agent Marsh by "special employee" Hereford [aka the informant] may have been hearsay to Marsh, but . . . Marsh would have been derelict in his duties had he not pursued it."[59] *Spinelli* observed that the Hereford provided a sufficient basis of knowledge from the information provided.

> The detail provided by the informant in *Draper v. United States* provides a suitable benchmark. While Hereford, the Government's informer in that case did not state the way in which he had obtained his information, he reported that Draper had gone to Chicago the day before by train and that he would return to Denver by train with three ounces of heroin on one of two specified mornings. Moreover, Hereford went on to describe, with minute particularity, the clothes that Draper would be wearing upon his arrival at the Denver station. A magistrate, when confronted with such detail, could reasonably infer that the informant had gained his information in a reliable way. Such an inference cannot be made in the present case. Here, the only facts supplied were that Spinelli was using two specified telephones and that these phones were being used in gambling operations. This meager report could easily have been obtained from an offhand remark heard at a neighborhood bar.[60]

C. *Gates*: The Current Probable Cause Standard

Illinois v. Gates[61] displaced *Aguilar*'s relatively rigid two-pronged approach with the "totality of circumstances" method. The Court believed that the *Aguilar/Spinelli* test was too rigid, because it improperly permitted "these two elements such independent status."[62] Since *Gates*, the "credibility" and "basis of knowledge" prongs now are simply two of the factors considered in the totality of circumstances.

In *Gates*, the police received an anonymous tip about drug trafficking between Florida and Chicago. Gates' wife would drive a car to Florida, leave it to be loaded with drugs, and return to Chicago by airliner. Gates would then fly to Florida and drive the drug-filled car back to Chicago. Under these facts, neither prong under *Spinelli* was satisfied. The anonymous tip revealed nothing about the

---

59 Draper v. United States, 358 U.S. 307, 312–13 (1959).

60 Spinelli v. United States, 393 U.S. 410, 416–17 (1969), overruled on other grounds by Illinois v. Gates, 462 U.S. 213 (1983).

61 462 U.S. 213 (1983).

62 Illinois v. Gates, 462 U.S. 213, 233 (1983).

informant's credibility, and this tip provided no hints about the informant's basis of knowledge. Without the information from the informant, the remaining information could not satisfy probable cause.

> [W]e conclude that it is wiser to abandon the "two-pronged test" established by our decisions in *Aguilar* and *Spinelli*. In its place we reaffirm the totality of the circumstances analysis that traditionally has informed probable cause determinations. The task of the issuing magistrate is simply to make a practical, common-sense decision whether, given all the circumstances set forth in the affidavit before him, including the "veracity" and "basis of knowledge" of persons supplying hearsay information, there is a fair probability that contraband or evidence of a crime will be found in a particular place. And the duty of a reviewing court is simply to ensure that the magistrate had a "substantial basis for . . . conclud[ing]" that probable cause existed. We are convinced that this flexible, easily applied standard will better achieve the accommodation of public and private interests that the Fourth Amendment requires than does the approach that has developed from *Aguilar* and *Spinelli*.[63]

Instead of applying the "hypertechnical" *Aguilar* test, then, *Gates* applied a "totality of circumstances" test that includes but is not limited to credibility and basis of information. Equally significant is the Court's statement that "a deficiency in one" category in one factor, e.g., credibility, may be offset by a strong showing in another factor, e.g., basis of knowledge.[64] As an example, *Gates* stated that if

> a particular informant is known for the unusual reliability of his predictions of certain types of criminal activities in a locality, his failure, in a particular case, to thoroughly set forth the basis of his knowledge surely should not serve as an absolute bar to a finding of probable cause based on his tip.[65]

Florida v. Harris,[66] thirty years after *Gates*, unanimously reversed a State court's decision holding in favor of *Gates'* "flexible, common-sense standard" and "all-things-considered approach":[67]

---

63 *Id.*, at 238–39.

64 *Id.*, at 233.

65 *Id.*

66 568 U.S. 237 (2013).

67 Florida v. Harris, 568 U.S. 237, 240, 244 (2013).

> The [lower] court should allow the parties to make their best case, consistent with the usual rules of criminal procedure. And the court should then evaluate the proffered evidence to decide what all the circumstances demonstrate. If the State has produced proof from controlled settings that a dog performs reliably in detecting drugs, and the defendant has not contested that showing, then the court should find probable cause. If, in contrast, the defendant has challenged the State's case (by disputing the reliability of the dog overall or of a particular alert), then the court should weigh the competing evidence.[68]

Probable cause existed in *Harris* because the State showed that the dog "had successfully completed two drug-detection courses and maintained his proficiency through weekly training exercises,"[69] while defendant's evidence of two false alerts to his vehicle might be attributable to defendant who regularly used meth and transferred the odor to a door handle.

D. Corroboration of Information

Police often corroborate informants by independent investigation to support their informant's knowledge. For example, an informant's description of an imminent drug deal permits a finding of probable cause if the officers soon find persons or vehicles described by the informant. *Spinelli*'s facts created a twofold problem for the prosecution: there was no showing about *why* the informant was reliable, and there also was no showing of *how* the tipster obtained his information. Not only did the prosecution lose the case, but the facts revealed a fundamental weakness in the Court's analysis—how to establish the veracity of an *anonymous* informant? A court cannot presume that an anonymous informant is reliable. The increasing reliance on anonymous informants led to *Spinelli*'s failure as a binding precedent. Without the tip, ruled that the police lacked probable cause. Compare the *Gates* facts: the police knew that Gates' wife drove a car to a place in Florida that was the site of many drug purchases. Gates then flew to Florida and drove the car back to Chicago.

Draper v. United States[70] had held that, where an informant provided the description and location of defendant with great detail, and an officer verified all the information given except whether defendant had drugs on his person, the officer had probable cause to arrest the suspect. As mentioned, Hereford the reliable informant

---

68 *Id.*, at 247–48.

69 *Id.*, at 249.

70 Draper v. United States, 358 U.S. 307 (1959).

told drug agent March that Draper (1) would return from Chicago by train on one of two specified days, (2) had a particular physical description, (3) would wear certain clothing, (4) would be carrying a tan zipper bag, and (5) habitually walked fast. The agent surveilled the train station, arrested the described person when he appeared, and thereby discovered drugs. The *Draper* Court stressed that

> Marsh had personally verified every facet of the information given him by Hereford except whether petitioner had accomplished his mission and had the three ounces of heroin on his person or in his bag. And surely, with every other bit of Hereford's information being thus personally verified, Marsh had "reasonable grounds" to believe that the remaining unverified bit of Hereford's information—that Draper would have the heroin with him—was likewise true.[71]

Justice White's concurrence in *Gates* attested to *Draper*'s importance in a totality of circumstances approach to probable cause.

> The fact that the informer was able to predict, two days in advance, the exact clothing Draper would be wearing dispelled the possibility that his tip was just based on rumor or "an off-hand remark heard at a neighborhood bar." Probably Draper had planned in advance to wear these specific clothes so that an accomplice could identify him. A clear inference could therefore be drawn that the informant was either involved in the criminal scheme himself or that he otherwise had access to reliable, inside information.[72]

Gates used *Draper* to conclude that, even though the tip was inadequate on its own, independent police work had corroborated the details of the Gates' activities to support a conclusion of probable cause. *Gates* even accepted corroboration of *innocent* activity to support probable cause. "In making a determination of probable cause the relevant inquiry is not whether particular conduct is 'innocent' or 'guilty,' but the degree of suspicion that attaches to particular types of non-criminal acts."[73]

Gates decided that (1) the facts obtained by independent investigation were suspicious, because "Florida is well-known as a source of narcotics and other illegal drugs," (2) Gates' activity "is as suggestive of a pre-arranged drug run, as it is of an ordinary vacation trip" (3) "corroboration of the letter's predictions that the Gates' car would be in Florida, that Lance Gates would fly to Florida in the next

---

71 *Id.*, at 313.

72 *Illinois v. Gates*, 462 U.S. at 270 (White, J., concurring).

73 *Id.*, at 243 n.13.

day or so, and that he would drive the car north toward Bloomingdale all indicated, albeit not with certainty, that the informant's other assertions also were true," and (4) the details in the letter concerned "future actions of third parties ordinarily not easily predicted," suggesting the letter writer "also had access to reliable information of the Gates' alleged illegal activities."[74]

In effect, *Gates* decided that if the police corroborate all of the innocent information in the tip, the lower court finding of probable cause should also be presumed correct about the Gates' trafficking in drugs. What if the police corroboration shows that the informant is right about half the facts and wrong about the rest? Would *Gates* then support the same conclusion that the tipster was correct about the drug trafficking?

Let's briefly return to the criminal procedure professor's problem that a tipster has provided a few facts that the police easily corroborate about her location and appearance. Does that mean the tip also must have been correct about the probable cause for his drug possession?

There "are so many variables in the probable cause equation that one determination will seldom be a useful 'precedent' for another."[75] In summary, here are the component parts of *Gates* and the probable cause standard of totality of the circumstances. It includes but is not limited to veracity, basis of knowledge, and police corroboration. For veracity, probable cause relates to why a person with information is reliable, and is shown by either (1) general credibility, either as presumptively honest (police), or demonstrably honest (through accurate information in the past), or (2) the reliability of a particular piece of information (such as a statement against interest). The basis of a person's knowledge relates to how the informant obtained the information. The basis of his knowledge is shown either (1) directly, by describing the underlying circumstances of observation from which he concluded probable cause existed, or (2) indirectly, through police corroboration or by the self-verifying, sufficient detail of the information itself that a judge would know that the person was relying on more than casual rumor or the suspect's general reputation.

From *Gates*, it appears that corroboration is sufficient if it provides a reasonable basis to conclude that the informant knows what he is talking about. The corroboration function is satisfied even if the facts corroborated do not deal with criminal activity; in that situation, though, the tip will have to show why the facts indicate

---

74 *Id.*, at 243–45.

75 *Id.*, at 239.

criminality. A factual basis may be found from fair "inferences" from the given facts although, before with *Aguilar/Spinelli*, specificity as to how the information was obtained was required. *Gates* also appears to make warrants easier to obtain than *Aguilar*: (1) when there is a strong prong and a weak prong, but no corroboration, or (2) when a tip is not sufficient on its own to establish probable cause, but the tip is corroborated of criminal or noncriminal activity.

In addition to redefining the standard that a judge should apply in deciding whether probable cause exists (prospectively, to issue a search or arrest warrant) or existed (after the fact of the arrest or search, with or without a warrant), the Court discussed the level of scrutiny that a reviewing court should apply to the trial judge's decision. The Court rejected the notion that a court should engage in a trial *de novo* of the probable cause issue, instead holding that the reviewing court pay "great deference" to the magistrate's judgment. "[T]he duty of a reviewing court is simply to ensure that the magistrate had, assessing only whether the judge had 'a substantial basis' . . . for concluding that probable cause existed."[76]

Gates both eliminated the bright-line rules of *Aguilar/Spinelli*, *and* demanded deference to the magistrate's decision, thereby reducing the role of a reviewing court to enforce the probable cause standard. In addition, the Court did not specify a level of probability that represents a "fair probability." The likely result will of those two changes result in the unlikelihood that a reviewing court can overcome the required deference to the magistrate's decision to conclude that the magistrate's finding was both incorrect and lacked a substantial basis.

E. Revealing Informant's Identity

The prosecution may try to keep an informant's identity confidential, out of fear for his safety or a desire for his continued effectiveness as an informant, or both. The name of the person need not be disclosed in an affidavit for a search warrant when making an arrest, or when the informant's information is not used at trial. The case law establishes that Due Process does not require disclosure of an informant's identity at a pretrial hearing where guilt is not determined.

In *McCray v. Illinois*,[77] the officer testified that his informant had given information about drug activities often, resulting in numerous arrests and convictions. On cross-examination, the officer even named some of the persons who were convicted. Because the

[76] *Id.*, at 238–39.

[77] 386 U.S. 300 (1967).

officer's testimony satisfactorily described for the court the circumstances from which he concluded that the informant was credible, the Court held that probable cause had existed for the arrest. However, *McCray* refused to rule that defendants are always entitled to learn the informant's identity, leaving to the judge's discretion "to decide whether he needs such disclosure as to the informant in order to decide whether the officer is a believable witness."[78]

§ 3.5 When Probable Cause Is Determined

Probable cause is an independent judgment that is determined either at the time of the issuance of the warrant by the judge or at the time of the arrest or search by a law enforcement officer in warrantless situations. Hindsight cannot be used to justify a search. The validity of the search must be viewed in light of the circumstances existing at the time the search or arrest was made. Even if probable cause exists, the police are not constitutionally required to act immediately and may wait to gather further information prior to an arrest or to seeking an indictment. Even with probable cause, law enforcement may still lack the quantum and quality of proof necessary to support a later conviction.[79]

The warrant procedure locks in the government to the probable cause information recited in the warrant and the supporting affidavit. Later events cannot revise the earlier judicial conclusion that probable cause did or did not exist. However, when probable cause initially is deficient, later events may support the probable cause necessary to make a warrantless arrest or otherwise to proceed with a prosecution.

A. Time of Information

Ordinarily, time is not a factor in determining probable cause to arrest, because probable cause will continue to exist for an indefinite period assuming that no contrary facts appear. However, probable cause to search requires current information about the location of the items sought. The issue for search probable cause is whether the information is too stale to furnish probable cause. When the information is too old, the items may not be in the place originally stated for probable cause. For example, *Andresen v. Maryland*[80] held that a three-month gap between the facts used to seek a warrant and the issuance of the warrant did not make the information stale.[81]

---

78 McCray v. Illinois, 386 U.S. 300, 308 (1967).

79 Hoffa v. United States, 385 U.S. 293 (1966).

80 427 U.S. 463 (1976).

81 Andresen v. Maryland, 427 U.S. 463, 478 n.9 (1976).

No bright-line time period controls the case law on stale information for probable cause to search. A time period between the observation of criminal behavior and the application for a warrant which could have been as little as two days or as much as thirty days, is insufficient for probable cause. On the other hand, definite time periods of up to two weeks have on occasion been upheld.[82] There is little reason to search on the basis of stale information when it is simple enough to update it by making an additional observation either to confirm the prior information or to obtain fresher and perhaps stronger information.

Instead of measuring staleness solely by counting the days on a calendar, some courts consider the following variables:

> the character of the crime (chance encounter in the night or regenerating conspiracy?), the criminal (nomadic or entrenched?), the thing to be seized (perishable and easily transferable or of enduring utility to its holder?), the place to be searched (mere criminal forum of convenience or secure operational base?).[83]

B. Anticipatory Warrants

Probable cause may exist not only at the time the warrant issues, but it may exist in the future based on prospective probable cause in the form of a specified triggering condition. *United States v. Grubbs*[84] initially stated that "when an anticipatory warrant is issued, 'the fact that the contraband is not presently located at the place described in the warrant is immaterial, so long as there is probable cause to believe that it will be there when the search warrant is executed.' "[85] The Court then held that a warrant may issue even though the contraband is not currently at the particular location, as long as probable cause will exist once the contraband will be on the premises at the time that police execute the warrant.

For anticipatory warrants, the supporting affidavit must provide sufficient information to evaluate both aspects of the probable cause determination. While the triggering condition does not have to be set forth in the warrant itself, two prerequisites of probability must be satisfied: "probable cause exists to believe the triggering condition will occur," and, if the triggering condition

---

[82] See United States v. Harris, 403 U.S. 573 (1971).

[83] United States v. Christian, 893 F.3d 846, 858 (6th Cir. 2018), quoting United States v. Spikes, 158 F.3d 913, 923 (6th Cir. 1998).

[84] 547 U.S. 90 (2006).

[85] United States v. Grubbs, 547 U.S. 90, 96 (2006).

occurs, a fair probability exists "that contraband or evidence of a crime will be found in a particular place."[86]

The *Grubbs* warrant authorized the search of a residence based upon an affidavit stating that the warrant would be executed when a child pornography video (that the defendant ordered from an undercover postal inspector) was received and physically taken into the defendant's home. Two other affidavits described the defendant's residence and the items to be seized. If the triggering event, such as delivery of contraband that establishes prospective probable cause had not occurred, i.e., if no delivery was made, the search warrant would have been invalid and it could not or should not have been executed.

86 *Id.*, at 97.

Chapter 4

SEARCH WARRANTS

Table of Sections

§ 4.1 Introduction

The Fourth Amendment's Warrant Clause requires that "no Warrants shall issue, but upon probable cause supported by Oath or affirmation, and particularly describing the place to be searched, and the persons of things to be seized." American courts profess a strong preference for warrants, especially search warrants. However, the decisions from the past fifty years reveal that warrant preference is unrealized. The Court has discovered many exceptions to its warrant preference where the need for a quick police response to exigent circumstances requires warrantless searches or seizures.

Suppose the police chase a vehicle carrying a wanted felon and stop it very close to the local courthouse. Should we expect the officer to detain the suspect while an affidavit is written to support an arrest warrant to formally arrest the suspect? Or, suppose the police have already arrested the suspect in his truck. Without Court-created warrantless searches, imagine the time necessary to detain the suspect while the police prepare an affidavit for a warrant to search the vehicle. Some States have experimented with dial-a-warrant or other practices to expedite the issuance of arrest or search warrants. Despite the judicial preference for extensive warrant use, the realities of modern policing often cannot accommodate the desire for warrants. This Chapter describes the process by which judges approve search warrants, as well as search warrants' execution.

§ 4.2 Warrants Defined and Distinguished

A search warrant protects important Fourth Amendment search and seizure interests relating to a suspect's reasonable expectation of privacy.[1] An arrest warrant protects against police seizures of the suspect, while search warrants guard against searches of areas where a person has a reasonable expectation of privacy.[2] The issuance of a search warrant requires probable cause to believe that an item linked with criminal behavior[3] is located at a particular location.[4]

§ 4.3 Search Warrants

A. Applicable Federal Rule

Federal Rule of Criminal Procedure 41(c) permits issuance of search warrants to search and seize "(1) evidence of a crime; (2)

---

1 Katz v. U.S., 389 U.S. 347, 360 (1967) (Harlan, J., concurring). See Chapter 2, discussing expectations of privacy and the Fourth Amendment.

2 See Chapter 5, discussing Arrests, with and Without Warrants.

3 See Warden v. Hayden, 387 U.S. 294 (1967).

4 Steagald v. U.S., 451 U.S. 204, 213 (1981).

contraband, fruits of a crime, or other items illegally possessed; (3) property designed for use, intended for use, or used in committing a crime; or (4) a person to be arrested or a person who is unlawfully restrained."[5]

A search warrant is a written order signed by a judge or other authorized officer, directing any peace officer acting within the territorial limits of authority to search for property and to bring it before the appropriate court. The items that may be sought and seized under a warrant are virtually limitless. However, searches into a person's body may be so intrusive that they first require an adversary court procedure rather than an *ex parte* search warrant.

B. Requirements for a Warrant

Following the Fourth Amendment language, the Court has recognized three requirements in the Fourth Amendment for a valid warrant: the warrant must (1) be based on probable cause; (2) be supported by a sworn affidavit; and (3) contain a particular description of the place to be searched or the items to be seized.[6] Search warrants usually focus on the premises of persons who are suspected of criminal activity, although premises may be searched without implicating any particular person. Warrants may also focus on the premises of third persons not directly associated with criminal activity.

While preferring warrants over warrantless searches, courts recognize that even search warrants are subject to abuse. Certain constitutional provisions must be followed. Even when part of a warrant requires the suppression of evidence seized pursuant to that portion of the warrant, items described in the valid parts of the warrant or lawfully seized during its execution are admissible evidence.

§ 4.4 Obtaining a Search Warrant

The typical application procedure for a warrant is *ex parte*, without the presence or participation of a defense attorney or the target of a criminal investigation. A prosecutor or a police officer presents a judge with an application for a warrant in the form of a sworn affidavit. The judge reads the affidavit and decides whether to issue a warrant; the applicant often brings a partially completed warrant form that the judge can sign after reading the information that the police have filled in the blanks. The judge may modify or delete language with which he disagrees.

---

[5] Fed.R.Crim.P. 41(c).

[6] See Groh v. Ramirez, 540 U.S. 551 (2004).

A. Authority to Issue a Search Warrant

The Fourth Amendment requires that search warrants must be issued by a "neutral and detached magistrate." Statutes and court rules further define the persons with authority to issue a search warrant. While that person must be neutral and detached to make an unbiased decision about probable cause, that person does not have to be an attorney. In *Shadwick v. City of Tampa,*[7] a court clerk was authorized by statute to issue warrants for city violations. The Court held that lay clerks who work within the judicial branch under the supervision of municipal court judges are qualified to determine probable cause issues. While a "magistrate" does not have to be an attorney, the person issuing a warrant

> must meet two tests. He must be neutral and detached, and he must be capable of determining whether probable cause exists for the requested arrest or search. . . Whatever else neutral and detached might entail, it is clear that they require severance and disengagement from activities of law enforcement.[8]

Reviewing courts may be more adept at recognizing when a judge does *not* act in a neutral and detached manner. The

> placement of this checkpoint between the Government and the citizen implicitly acknowledges that an "officer engaged in the often competitive enterprise of ferreting out crime" . . . may lack sufficient objectivity to weigh correctly the strength of the evidence . . . against the individual's interests in protecting his own liberty.[9]

In *Connally v. Georgia,*[10] the Court held that the State fee system compensating a justice of the peace for each warrant issued was unconstitutional. The judge's

> financial welfare. . . is enhanced by positive action and is not enhanced by negative action. The situation, again, is one which offers "a possible temptation to the average man as a judge . . . or which might lead him not to hold the balance nice, clear and true between the State and the accused." It is, in other words, another situation where the defendant is subjected to what surely is judicial action by an officer of a court who "has a direct, personal, substantial,

---

7 Shadwick v. City of Tampa, 407 U.S. 345, 350 (1972).

8 *Id.*

9 Steagald v. U.S., 451 U.S. 204, 212 (1981) (quoting Johnson v. U.S., 333 U.S. 10, 14 (1948)).

10 429 U.S. 245 (1977).

pecuniary interest" in his conclusion to issue or to deny the warrant.[11]

Courts also are adept at spotting cases where an official such as an attorney general who actively oversees criminal investigations and is the chief trial prosecutor cannot be regarded as a neutral and detached magistrate.[12]

B. Jurisdiction to Issue a Search Warrant

The authority of a statutorily empowered official to issue a search warrant is not limited to the district or circuit in which he is elected or appointed. A State judge may issue search warrant to search outside the limits of the official's jurisdiction but still within State boundaries. In some States, appointed judicial officials may have the authority to issue search warrants only for the county in which they reside or to which they are temporarily assigned.

C. Detaining Persons Pending Issuance of a Warrant

During the time it takes to seek a search warrant, police may reasonably prevent a person from entering an area for which the police are requesting the warrant. A reasonable seizure often depends on the police having both probable cause to believe that the person's home contains evidence of a crime, and good reason to fear that, unless restrained, the person would destroy the evidence before the warrant is obtained or executed. Any detention must be for no longer than necessary for police, acting with diligence, to obtain the warrant.[13]

In *Illinois v. McArthur*,[14] the Court held that restricting access to the area for which the police are seeking a search warrant is reasonable, and hence lawful, in light of four enumerated circumstances:

> "the police had probable cause to believe that [his] trailer home contained evidence of a crime and contraband, namely, unlawful drugs"; "the police had good reason to fear that, unless restrained, [he] would destroy the drugs before they could return with a warrant," concluding that even before the requested consent to search he realized his angry wife had informed the police about the drugs; "the police made reasonable efforts to reconcile their law enforcement

---

11 Connally v. Georgia, 429 U.S. 245, 250 (1977), quoting Bennett v. Cottingham, 290 F.Supp. 759, 762–63 (N.D.Ala. 1968), aff'd, 393 U.S. 317 (1969).

12 Coolidge v. New Hampshire, 403 U.S. 443 (1971).

13 Illinois v. McArthur, 531 U.S. 326 (2001).

14 531 U.S. 326 (2001).

needs with the demands of personal privacy" by imposing "a significantly less restrict restraint" than a warrantless search of the premises; and "the police imposed the restraint for a limited period of time, namely, two hours."[15]

§ 4.5 Application for Search Warrant

A. Affidavit

The Fourth Amendment requires that a warrant must be based on probable cause, "supported by Oath or affirmation." The affiant for a warrant is committing to a public record the information known before the search, so that after the search occurs there is no confusion between what the affiant knew before and after the search. An affidavit is a written statement of fact under oath sworn to or affirmed by the person making it through reliable electronic means or before some person who has authority under the law of that jurisdiction to administer the oath.

Before approving and signing the warrant, the person authorized to issue it must review the affidavit and make a determination of probable cause based upon its contents. To aid in this determination, the person making the affidavit usually appears before the judicial officer and executes it under oath in a notary's presence.

> [A]n otherwise insufficient affidavit cannot be rehabilitated by testimony concerning information possessed by the affiant when he sought the warrant but not disclosed to the issuing magistrate. A contrary rule would, of course, render the warrant requirements of the Fourth Amendment meaningless.[16]

Fed.R.Crim.P. 41 authorizes a judge to question the affiant about information when the judge is concerned about whether the affidavit alone satisfies probable cause. Such questioning is recorded and becomes a part of the affidavit, thereby assuring a more careful decision about probable cause and the scope of a search under the warrant. Supplemental testimony potentially raises further issues, e.g., whether the (1) supplemental testimony is recorded, (2) Oath was properly administered, and (3) court can make an independent judgment about probable cause with others nearby. In States that do not permit a judge to supplement the affidavit with oral testimony, the grounds for issuing a warrant are effectively restricted to the "four corners of the affidavit."

---

15 *Illinois v. McArthur*, 531 U.S. at 331–32.

16 Whiteley v. Warden, 401 U.S. 560, 565 n.8 (1971).

B. Construing the Affidavit

The affidavit must establish probable cause for issuing the search warrant, as well as meeting certain minimal requirements.[17] The affiant's experience in law enforcement, although not essential, is helpful. The affidavit must indicate that the material sought is subject to seizure, and that there is a connection between the criminal activity and the person or place to be searched. Information may derive directly from the affiant's own observations, or it may come from others.

The information in the affidavit does not have to be admissible at a trial, because the Federal Rules of Evidence do not apply to the issuance of federal search warrants.[18] Where information from others is lacking or is minimal, the affidavit should include corroboration of the others' factual claims. Because the timing of information is relevant, the affidavit must include the time period within which the information came to light. As mentioned, while extrinsic evidence is usually not admissible to supply deficiencies in the affidavit, a trial judge may properly consider matters outside the affidavit such as whether the good faith exception to the exclusionary rule applies. Affidavits must be read in a common-sense manner and should not be hypertechnically construed.[19]

A judge is not merely a "rubber stamp" for signing off on warrant applications by the police or a prosecutor. A judge must use his experience to apply common sense and to make reasonable inferences from the affidavit. However, the common-sense approach does not dispense with constitutional guarantees. To encourage the police to seek warrants, reviewing courts generally defer to a prior determination of probable cause. In *United States v. Leon*,[20] for example, the Court held that a trial court will not exclude evidence obtained pursuant to a subsequently invalidated search warrant when the officer executing the warrant reasonably relied on the judge's determination of probable cause and the technical sufficiency of the warrant.

C. Contesting a Facially Valid Affidavit

Although an affidavit is a material prerequisite to the issuance of a search warrant, it can be challenged (but not until after the warrant is executed, given that the issuing process is *ex parte*) on two

---

17 See Chapter 3, discussing Probable Cause.

18 Fed.R.Evid. 1101(d)(3).

19 Illinois v. Gates, 462 U.S. 213, 236 (1983), quoting United States v. Ventresca, 380 U.S. 102, 109 (1965).

20 United States v. Leon, 468 U.S. 897 (1984).

grounds. First, the affidavit may be challenged on its face by accepting all of its statements as true, and arguing that those facts nevertheless fail to satisfy probable cause. The law of probable cause controls whether the affidavit's language was properly issued.

Franks v. Delaware[21] controls the legal analysis for the second challenge, comprising the affidavit argument; the defendant must make a preliminary showing that there are deliberately *or* recklessly false statements by the affiant in the affidavit that cannot be used to establish probable cause for a search warrant. A statement that is shown by the defendant to be simply wrong or to have been negligently made will not be stricken from the affidavit. Material that was deliberately or recklessly omitted by the affiant may be added to the affidavit and considered by a reviewing court.

A "defendant must point out specifically the portion of the warrant affidavit that is claimed to be false,"[22] and give "a statement of supporting reasons. Affidavits or sworn or otherwise reliable statements of witnesses should be furnished, or their absence explained."[23] Once the defendant makes the required preliminary showings, a hearing is held. However, no hearing is needed unless "the alleged false statement is necessary to the finding of probable cause."[24]

At a *Franks* hearing, if the defendant proves that the remaining affidavit information is insufficient to support a finding of probable cause without the tainted affidavit portions, the court must declare the warrant invalid.[25] On the other hand, if the remaining affidavit information still satisfies probable cause, despite other lies that may have been included in the affidavit, the search warrant is valid. By contrast, if the affidavit contained statements which are the results of mere "negligence or innocent mistake," the affidavit fails to support a conclusion of deliberate falsity or reckless disregard for the truth under *Franks*.[26]

The problems of proving an erroneous statement fall into two general areas. The first area is where the affiant says his own observations afforded probable cause and those remarks are shown to be false. That issue is limited to the affiant's own activity. The second problem area arises when if the affiant says he received

---

21 438 U.S. 154 (1978). Comparing *Franks* and *Leon* issues, *Franks* applies when the affidavit is allegedly defective due an error by the police. *Leon* applies when the search warrant allegedly is defective due to an error by the issuing magistrate.

22 Franks v. Delaware, 438 U.S. 154, 171 (1978).

23 *Id.*

24 *Id.*

25 *Id.*

26 *Id.*

information from an informant. The implications of the *Franks* declaration are that the deliberate falsity or recklessness must be "that of the affiant, not of any nongovernmental informant."[27] That comment suggests that a defendant who was the target of the investigation cannot raise the issue of whether the informant lied to the officer. If an officer is the affiant, the defendant's argument still may relate to whether the officer lied by not accurately repeating what the informant said or why the officer believed the informant was reliable.

§ 4.6 Form of the Warrant

If the issuing official is satisfied that there is probable cause to believe that grounds for the warrant application exist, a search warrant issues. The warrant is a command to search for the designated items which are to be preserved pending the directions from the appropriate court. In general, a search warrant must meet certain constitutional requirements as to specific descriptions of the place to be searched and the property to be seized.

The Fourth Amendment's particularity requirement makes general searches illegal, (1) assuring the propriety of government interference *only* with persons, places, or things in which it has presented a valid interest, usually by way of the affidavit, and (2) reducing the likelihood that, after execution of a warrant, officials will assert that what was found is precisely what the warrant authorized. Perfection in describing the place to be searched or the things to be seized is not required; it is sufficient "if the description is such that the officer with a search warrant can, with reasonable effort, ascertain and identify the place intended."[28] If the warrant is deficient in the identification or description, the affidavit may supplement an inadequate description in the warrant if the affidavit is incorporated by reference into the warrant and accompanies the warrant.[29]

A. Place to Be Searched

"The requirement that warrants shall particularly describe the things to be seized makes general searches under them impossible and prevents the seizure of one thing under a warrant describing another."[30] Avoiding general warrants (derisively known as "fishing expeditions") excludes the search of places not contemplated by the

---

27 *Id.*

28 Steele v. United States, 267 U.S. 498, 503 (1925).

29 See Groh v. Ramirez, 540 U.S. 551, 558 (2004); Massachusetts v. Sheppard, 468 U.S. 981, 990 n.7 (1984).

30 Marron v. United States, 275 U.S. 192, 196 (1927).

warrant.[31] For example, in *Maryland v. Garrison*,[32] the search warrant mistakenly approved a search of two apartments, instead of what was thought to have been only one apartment. (Prior to execution of the warrant, the *Leon* good faith exception applied, unless the executing officers knew or should have known that the premises were described too broadly.) The error was not obvious to the executing officers until they were already executing the warrant. Evidence found in plain view in the unintended apartment, though, was held to have been reasonably seized, because although there was a mistake, the executing officers did not know and could not have reasonably been expected to know that the premises were described too broadly. The Court conditioned the permissibility of the mistaken search if the police left the premises as soon as they learned they were in the wrong place (even though they would prefer to keep looking for evidence of criminal behavior).

Another example of a concern about general warrants relates to the recent uses of "geofence warrants." Geofence warrants are a powerful and controversial tool that enables law enforcement to compel technology companies to search through vast databases of users' historical location data to determine who have been at a specific location at a given time. When police request a geofence warrant, they specify a location and period of time, after which a judge approves the warrant for a tech company like Google to conduct a sweeping electronic search of location databases that provide a list of cell phones and affiliated users at or near a specific area during a time period.

United States v. Smith[33] held that geofence location data violates the Fourth Amendment as invasive, especially because a geofence retroactively tracks *anyone* within Google's "Location History," regardless of whether a particular person is suspicious or moving within the area. *Smith* held that geofence warrants 1) constitute general warrants that are categorically prohibited, 2) are intrusive given the omnipresence of location history data, and 3) violate defendant's reasonable expectation of privacy in their respective data.[34]

---

[31] Maryland v. Garrison, 480 U.S. 79, 84 (1987).

[32] 480 U.S. 79, 84 (1987).

[33] 110 F.4th 817 (5th Cir. 2024).

[34] 107 F.4th 319 (4th Cir. 2024). Instead of striking geofence warrants as a Fourth Amendment violation, the Fourth Circuit in United States v. Chatrie, 107 F.4.th 319 (4th Cir. 2024) upheld the trial court's denial of defendant's motion to suppress, because 1) no Fourth Amendment search ever occurred, 2) the defendant had no reasonable expectation of privacy because the Government accessed two hours' worth of Chatrie's location information that he voluntarily exposed to Google.

United States v. Davis[35] is an example of the random ways in which geofence warrants can function. The Eleventh Circuit held that a carjacking defendant lacked standing to contest a geofence warrant. The search did not reveal any information about data on *his own* device, displayed only his limited movements in public areas, and did not include his home. The geofence warrant disclosed a third party's Gmail account listed in someone else's name on a phone that the defendant did not own or exclusively used. Even if a person has a privacy interest in data on his own phone, he lacks that interest in data on someone else's phone. For those reasons, the defendant could not argue a privacy interest in the data that would have given him Fourth Amendment standing.

The simple test of the legal sufficiency of a search warrant description is whether it is sufficiently definite and certain to guide officers who can reasonably determine and recognize the place intended. Put another way, a search warrant is defective if: (1) it is vague in describing the place to be searched or what may be seized, or (2) it authorizes a search of a larger area than what the probable cause described in the affidavit has indicated.

The names of the city, county, and State where the premises are located are usually adequate without further description. The absence of any reference to city, county, or state is permissible if the premises are otherwise sufficiently described. However, the absence of either type of description renders the warrant invalid.

Descriptions of premises in urban areas often include the name of the person and a street number, but street numbers alone may be sufficient as long as it cannot be shown that more than one house in that city had the same number and street. Even when two houses share the same house number, the description is sufficient if the warrant states which of the two houses is to be searched. Without the house number, in less urban areas the premises may be described by reference, e.g., name of owner, county, shore of the Mississippi River.

Premises are sometimes described by the exterior appearance. Minor discrepancies between the warrant description and the executing officer's description of the premises are not crucial, as long as the warrant description was sufficient enough that the officer went to the proper place to execute the warrant. Warrants often describe the premises to be searched by the name of the owner, but the identity of the occupant or owner is unnecessary to search an otherwise properly described premises. A warrant is defective where there is no description of the premises or recitation of the owner's name.

---

[35] 109 F.4th 1320 (11th Cir. 2024).

B. Multiple-Occupancy Structures

A search warrant directed against a multi-unit dwelling is invalid unless it describes the subunit intended to be searched with sufficient specificity to exclude the search of an unintended subunit, e.g., a hotel. The mere fact that a defendant's premises are in the same building as other premises under the control of a person named in a search warrant does not bring the former premises within the terms of the warrant when neither the defendant nor the premises is described in the warrant or its affidavit. As mentioned, *Maryland v. Garrison*[36] held that a good faith factual mistake by the police in executing the warrant does not invalidate a search of the area thought to be included within the facially valid scope of the warrant. The officers' failure to realize the warrant's overbreadth was objectively reasonable.

C. Vehicles to Be Searched

A search warrant may specify vehicles to be searched along with the premises. Where warrants describe a particular vehicle, a full description is usually given, i.e., make, model, year, color, license plate number, and vehicle identification number (VIN). A description of the vehicle is sufficient for a search of its contents and any containers within the vehicle.

D. Things to Be Seized

A search warrant must not only specify where to search but must also specify what items to seize. "The requirement that warrants shall particularly describe the things to be seized makes general searches under them impossible and prevents the seizure of one thing under a warrant describing another," i.e., "nothing is left to the discretion of the officer executing the warrant."[37] Courts acknowledge that some subject matter limitation must exist. *Groh v. Ramirez* noted that "a court may construe a warrant with reference to a supporting application or affidavit if the warrant uses appropriate words of incorporation, and if the supporting document accompanies the warrant."[38]

On occasion, the Court has approved a detailed description of items to be seized, coupled with the phrase " 'together with other fruits, instrumentalities . . . of crime at this (time) unknown' " as not being *too* general.[39] *Andresen v. Maryland*[40] upheld the phrase

---

[36] 480 U.S. 79 (1987).

[37] Marron v. United States, 275 U.S. 192, 196 (1927).

[38] Groh v. Ramirez, 540 U.S. 551, 557–58 (2004).

[39] Andresen v. Maryland, 427 U.S. 463, 479 (1976).

[40] *Id.*, at 479–82.

"evidence of other crimes," because when read in context the warrant authorized seizure of only evidence that was relevant to the specific crimes described elsewhere in the warrant.

E. Description of Persons to Be Seized

A search warrant, not an arrest warrant, is required to enter the home of a third person to search for another individual accused of a crime. Executing an arrest warrant for the suspect who is believed to be a guest in another person's home does not justify a warrantless search of the third party's home.[41] Thus, the search warrant should include a sufficiently specific description of the accused person.

F. Signature of Issuing Officer

A search warrant must bear the signature of the issuing officer. Otherwise, the warrant is void. A mistake in describing the judge's title does not invalidate an otherwise lawful signature.

§ 4.7 Execution of the Search Warrant

While most attacks on search warrants concentrate on the validity of the warrant and its supporting affidavit, aspects of executing the warrant may affect the lawfulness of any seizure.

A. Who May Execute the Warrant?

Any officer acting within the territorial limits of his authority may execute a search warrant, the same standard as for arrest warrants. Although a search warrant may address specific peace officers, any peace officer in the jurisdiction may serve it. To avoid confusion, a search warrant often directs its execution to "all peace officers."

B. When May the Search Warrant Be Executed?

Federal law requires certain additional requirements for executing a search warrant at night,[42] and State standards at times specify the timing of a warrant's execution. For example, if a search is begun during the daylight, it may continue until it is completed even though night falls during the interim.

C. Expiration of the Warrant

A search warrant should be executed promptly after it issues in order to avoid the extinction of probable cause that might accompany an unreasonable delay. A federal search warrant must be executed

41 Steagald v. U.S., 451 U.S. 204 (1981).

42 Fed.R.Crim.P. 41(a)(1).

no more than fourteen days after it issues. The same warrant cannot be executed more than once.

D. "Knock-and-Announce" Entry Standards

"[T]he common law principle of announcement . . . is an element of the reasonableness inquiry under the Fourth Amendment."[43] At common law, when an officer appears to execute a search warrant at a private building, he should "knock and announce" his intentions to conduct a search.[44] That common law standard became a part of the Fourth Amendment reasonableness inquiry. The purpose of the requirement is threefold: (1) to limit police intrusion upon the inhabitants' privacy, i.e., providing an opportunity for the inhabitant to consent to the search and thereby speed the warrant's execution, (2) to protect officers who might be mistaken for unlawful intruders if they were to enter a residence unannounced, and (3) to prevent the physical property damage by providing the person living there with the chance to admit the police.

Besides knocking and announcing, police should also exhibit the search warrant to the person who is in control of either the premises or the object of the search. The display of the warrant or notice of its existence gives the officer the color of law authority that is necessary to compel compliance by the person in control of the premises or the object of the search. In *Bumper v. North Carolina*,[45] the Court found that consent to search was invalid when the officer had already falsely asserted that he had a warrant to search *and* that the occupant therefore could not resist the search.

The knock-and-announce standard has three components: (1) the police loudly announce their presence to be heard by the occupants, (2) the police loudly announce their purpose to be heard by the occupants, and (3) the delay prior to entry that is sufficient for the occupants to respond and answer the door. In *Wilson v. Arkansas*,[46] the Court held that, in evaluating the reasonableness of a search pursuant to a warrant, the announcement by officers of their presence and authority was one factor to be considered. Countervailing law enforcement interests include a threat of physical harm to the police, pursuit of a recently escaped arrestee, as well as reason to believe that evidence would be destroyed if advance notice was given. The Court left to lower courts the development of criteria to decide the reasonableness of such searches.

---

[43] Wilson v. Arkansas, 514 U.S. 927, 934 (1995).

[44] The common-law principle of announcement is "embedded in Anglo-American law." Miller v. United States, 357 U.S. 301, 313 (1958).

[45] 391 U.S. 543 (1968).

[46] 514 U.S. 927 (1995).

In *United States v. Ramirez*,[47] the Court upheld a police entry without notice because the person inside the residence

> was a prison escapee with a violent past who reportedly had access to a large supply of weapons. He had vowed that he would "not do federal time." The police certainly had a reasonable suspicion that knocking and announcing their presence might be dangerous to themselves or to others.[48]

The reasonableness of the officers' decision to dispense with a knock-and-announce procedure is to be evaluated just before a no-knock entry.

In *Richards v. Wisconsin*,[49] the police knocked on the defendant's hotel room door, claiming falsely to be a maintenance man. The defendant opened the door slightly, saw a uniformed officer, and slammed the door which the police immediately kicked in. "These actual circumstances—[defendant's] apparent recognition of the officers combined with the easily disposable nature of the drugs justified the officers' ultimate decision to enter without first announcing their presence and authority."[50] Although drug investigations frequently involve both the threat of physical violence to officers and the likely destruction of evidence if advance notice of the police presence is given, *Richards* held that such circumstances do not justify dispensing with a case-by-case evaluation of the manner in which a no-knock search is executed.

> [W]hile drug investigation frequently does pose special risks to officer safety and the preservation of evidence, not every drug investigation will pose these risks to a substantial degree. For example, a search could be conducted at a time when the only individuals present in a residence have no connection with the drug activity and thus will be unlikely to threaten officers or destroy evidence. . . .
>
> A second difficulty with permitting a criminal-category exception to the knock-and-announce requirement is that the reasons for creating an exception in one category can, relatively easily, be applied to others. Armed bank robbers, for example, are, by definition, likely to have weapons, and the fruits of their crime may be destroyed without too much difficulty. If a *per se* exception were allowed for each category of criminal investigation that included a

47 523 U.S. 65 (1998).

48 United States v. Ramirez, 523 U.S. 65, 71 (1998).

49 520 U.S. 385 (1997).

50 Richards v. Wisconsin, 520 U.S. 385, 396 (1997).

> considerable-albeit hypothetical-risk of danger to officers or destruction of evidence, the knock-and-announce element of the Fourth Amendment's reasonableness requirement would be meaningless.[51]

In *Richards*, the circumstances showed that officers believed that the defendant might destroy the evidence if given further opportunity.

However, even when there are violations of knock-and-announce rules, courts should not suppress evidence found by the police during the execution of the warrant. In *Hudson v. Michigan*,[52] evidence found during the execution of a search warrant was held to be admissible despite a violation of the Court's knock-and-announce rules. The "interests protected by the knock-and-announce requirement are quite different [than the warrant requirement]—and do not include the shielding of potential evidence from the government's eyes."[53] Evidence seized in violation of knock-and-announce rules "was not the fruit of the fact that the entry was not preceded by knock-and-announce."[54]

E. Entry to Serve a No-Knock Warrant

Because the knock-and-announce common law principle is an element of the Fourth Amendment reasonableness inquiry,[55] the requirements may be relaxed in two circumstances: (1) when an officer justifiably believes that the suspect already knows about the officer's presence and purpose so that announcing would be a "useless gesture;"[56] and/or (2) when an officer reasonably suspects that following the knock-and-announce standard "would be dangerous or futile, or . . . would inhibit the effective investigation of the crime."[57] If either of these circumstances exists, police may dispense with the knock-and-announce requirement and substitute what has become known as a "no-knock" entry to serve the warrant. Because judicial approval of a no-knock warrant is a case-by-case process, the suspected crime does not automatically determine whether a no-knock entry is appropriate.

Although judges usually do not consider whether to dispense with the knock-and-announce rules in issuing a warrant, as part of the process seeking a search warrant an officer could still inform the judge of sufficient information favoring a no-knock entry due to the

[51] *Id.*, at 393–94.

[52] 547 U.S. 586, 593 (2006).

[53] Hudson v. Michigan, 547 U.S. 586, 593 (2006).

[54] *Id.*, at 601.

[55] *Wilson v. Arkansas*, 514 U.S. at 934.

[56] Miller v. United States, 357 U.S. 301, 310 (1958).

[57] Richards v. Wisconsin, 520 U.S. 385, 394 (1997).

danger, futility, or threat to an effective investigation of following those rules. For example, the judge might prescribe a no-knock entry in the warrant itself after the officer tells the judge about either prior threats of violence to the police by the residents, or the presence of weapons in the building.

Even if a judge does not approve of a no-knock entry, the officer, as an alternative, could ask the judge to approve a specific time frame after knocking and before forcibly entering. Because warrants usually omit a specific time period for waiting, most cases depend on after-the-fact police testimony about assessing the reasonableness of the situation on-site as they waited for a person to answer the door before knocking it down to gain entry.

Assuming that notice is given, how long must the officer wait prior to a forcible entry? *United States v. Banks*[58] addressed that issue. When there is "no reason to suspect an immediate risk of frustration or futility in waiting at all," it is important "to give a person inside the chance to save his door," meaning "the reasonable wait time may well be longer when police make a forced entry, since they ought to be more certain the occupant has had time to answer the door."[59] From the Court's language, the defendant here was not someone likely to need time to answer the door.

> what matter[ed to this defendant] is the opportunity to get rid of cocaine, which a prudent dealer will keep near a commode or kitchen sink. . . That is, when circumstances are exigent because a pusher may be near the point of putting his drugs beyond reach, it is imminent disposal, not travel time to the entrance, that governs when the police may reasonably enter; since the bathroom and kitchen are usually in the interior of a dwelling, not the front hall, there is no reason generally to peg the travel time to the location of the door.[60]

Though noting that the "call is a close one" in *Banks*, the Court held that forcible entry by police executing a search warrant after knocking, announcing their purpose, and waiting 15–20 seconds for admittance was not unreasonable under the Fourth Amendment.

F. Detention and Search of Persons

The case law describes which persons at the scene of a search warrant being executed can be arrested, searched, detained, or frisked. The typical search warrant does not mention anyone by

---

[58] 540 U.S. 31 (2003).

[59] United States v. Banks, 540 U.S. 31, 41 (2003).

[60] *Id.*, at 40.

name to be searched. The police cannot automatically search a person who is on the premises while the police execute the warrant, but whose name is not stated on the face of the warrant.

However, persons named in the warrant can be searched, given that warrant naming the person was issued based on probable cause. In *Ybarra v. Illinois*,[61] the State claimed that the police should have to show only reasonable suspicion (rather than probable cause) to prove that the person had suspected objects on his person. The Court rejected the argument and held that the proper standard of probable cause was lacking for the police search. As for a frisk for weapons, unnamed persons may be frisked only when the officer reasonably believes or suspects that weapons are in their possession.[62]

May the police detain and frisk a person unnamed in the warrant or affidavit who is in the immediate vicinity of the warrant's execution? In *Michigan v. Summers*,[63] the Court approved the police detention (without an arrest) of a person who is on the premises when a search warrant for contraband is being executed.

> In assessing the justification for the detention of an occupant of premises being searched for contraband pursuant to a valid warrant, both the law enforcement interest and the nature of the "articulable facts" supporting the detention are relevant. Most obvious is the legitimate law enforcement interest in preventing flight in the event that incriminating evidence is found. Less obvious, but sometimes of greater importance, is the interest in minimizing the risk of harm to the officers. Although no special danger to the police is suggested by the evidence in this record, the execution of a warrant to search for narcotics is the kind of transaction that may give rise to sudden violence or frantic efforts to conceal or destroy evidence. The risk of harm to both the police and the occupants is minimized if the officers routinely exercise unquestioned command of the situation. Finally, the orderly completion of the search may be facilitated if the occupants of the premises are present. Their self-interest may induce them to open locked doors or locked containers to avoid the use of force that is not only damaging to property but may also delay the completion of the task at hand.[64]

---

[61] Ybarra v. Illinois, 444 U.S. 85 (1979).

[62] *Id.*, at 92–93. See Chapter 9, discussing Stop and Frisk.

[63] 452 U.S. 692 (1981).

[64] Michigan v. Summers, 452 U.S. 692, 702–03 (1981).

The police may even handcuff the detainee when the warrant authorizes a search for weapons and there is a need to detain multiple occupants.

Bailey v. United States[65] held that *Summers* is limited to instances in which "an occupant was detained within the immediate vicinity of the premises to be searched;" the police may not detain a person who has left the immediate vicinity of the premises in question before the search warrant is executed. The Court applied *Summers'* "three important law enforcement interests that, taken together, justify the detention of an occupant who is on the premises during the execution of a search warrant: officer safety, facilitating the completion of the search, and preventing flight."[66]

On the *Bailey* facts, a defendant who was away from the vicinity of the premises to be searched "posed little risk to the officers at the scene. If Bailey had rushed back to his apartment, the police could have apprehended and detained him under *Summers*. [A]fter Bailey drove away from [the search area], he was not a threat to the proper execution of the search."[67] To illustrate the relatively minor intrusion of a defendant at the search site, the Court described the defendant's detention away from the search scene.

> The detention here was more intrusive than a usual detention at the search scene. Bailey's car was stopped; he was ordered to step out and was detained in full public view; he was handcuffed, transported in a marked patrol car, and detained further outside the apartment. These facts illustrate that detention away from a premises where police are already present often will be more intrusive than detentions at the scene.[68]

G. Scope and Intensity of Search

Where police can execute a search warrant depends on the things and places named in the warrant's description. A description of premises authorizes a search of all buildings attached to the described building, but the officers may not search portions of the premises which are maintained separately from the described premises. Recall though that in *Maryland v. Garrison*,[69] the Court found that a good faith mistake in executing a search warrant did not

---

65 568 U.S. 186 (2013).

66 Bailey v. United States, 568 U.S. 186, 194 (2013).

67 *Id.*, at 196, 197.

68 *Id.*, at 200.

69 480 U.S. 79 (1987).

prohibit the admission of evidence seized prior to discovery of the mistake.

The requirement of particularity in a warrant determines the scope of the search. A search for described premises also contemplates the search of personal effects of the person occupying the premises, if those effects might reasonably contain the items described in the warrant. If a search warrant indicates that the items sought were stolen televisions, the officer is not authorized to rummage through desk drawers and other places too small to hold these items.

For example, in *Harris v. United States*,[70] the Court noted the inevitability of looking at documents not referred to in a warrant. "In searches for papers, it is certain that some innocuous documents will be examined, at least cursorily, in order to determine whether they are, in fact, among those papers authorized to be seized."[71] Searching closets, desks, and other containers does not exceed the scope of a warrant's search authority if at least one of the items named in the warrant could be concealed there. "The same meticulous investigation which would be appropriate in a search for two small cancelled checks could not be considered reasonable where agents are seeking a stolen automobile or an illegal still."[72] Once the items named in the search warrant have been found, the search should cease.

H. What May Be Seized

In addition to items specifically named in the warrant, officers frequently seize other unnamed items. Whether these other seizures are proper initially depends on whether the property is in plain view, i.e., "only where it is immediately apparent to the police that they have evidence before them; the 'plain view' doctrine may not be used to extend a general exploratory search from one object to another until something incriminating at last emerges."[73]

> Where, once an otherwise lawful search is in progress, the police inadvertently come upon a piece of evidence, it would often be a needless inconvenience, and sometimes dangerous—to the evidence or to the police themselves—to

---

70 331 U.S. 145 (1947), overruled by Chimel v. California, 395 U.S. 752 (1969).

71 Andresen v. Maryland, 427 U.S. 463, 482 n.11 (1976).

72 Harris v. United States, 331 U.S. 145, 152 (1947).

73 Coolidge v. New Hampshire, 403 U.S. 443, 466 (1971). See § 2.4(A), discussing Plain View.

> require them to ignore it until they have obtained a warrant particularly describing it.[74]

An officer may likewise seize items being used in the commission of a crime other than what is set forth in the warrant. The seizure of an object like a container does not require an immediate search of its contents. As long as the warrant is not a subterfuge for the seizure of unnamed items, the seizure of those unnamed items is valid.

I. Return of the Search Warrant

Upon the completion of executing a search warrant, the executing officer should record on the warrant the date and hour of its execution and make an inventory of all items seized under its authority. The purpose of the return is to provide evidence of the actions of the officer to assist in any court proceedings challenging the search. As a matter of Due Process, an officer taking property under a warrant must leave a copy of the warrant and a receipt for the property taken either on the premises or with the person from whose premises the property is taken.

> [W]hen law enforcement agents seize property pursuant to warrant, due process requires them to take reasonable steps to give notice that the property has been taken so the owner can pursue available remedies for its return. Individualized notice that the officers have taken the property is necessary . . . because the property owner would have no other reasonable means of ascertaining who was responsible for his loss.[75]

Failure to make a return or the making of an improper return, though, does not destroy the validity of the search if it was in fact conducted in a lawful manner.

The search warrant and the affidavit should be carefully preserved for filing with the appropriate court, although no specific law requires their filing. However, both must be proven by the prosecution in a suppression hearing to justify the search and seizure.

§ 4.8 Comprehensive Motion to Suppress

[Court and Parties]

---

[74] *Coolidge v. New Hampshire*, 403 U.S. at 467–68.

[75] City of West Covina v. Perkins, 525 U.S. 234, 240 (1999).

MOTION TO SUPPRESS

Defense counsel requests the Court to suppress certain property which the United States may introduce in the case before the Court. This motion is made pursuant to Fed.R.Crim.P. 41.

The defendant will show that on or about [date], certain property, to wit: [Defendant] was unlawfully seized and taken from [him/her] by certain officers of the United States whose true names are unknown to defendant.

The defendant will further show that the search and seizure of the above-described property was unreasonable and illegal and in violation of the Fourth Amendment to the Constitution of the United States and for the following reasons:

1. The search was allegedly conducted with an illegal search warrant.

2. The judge had no authority to issue the search warrant.

3. The application for the warrant was illegal because [it was applied for by an unauthorized person, and/or the affiant was not examined under oath, and/or the application is not in the form of a written and signed affidavit, and/or the affidavit is not signed by the affiant's true name].

4. The affidavit supporting the search warrant is illegal because [no time is stated as to when the alleged activity took place, and/or the time stated is too remote, and/or the affidavit bears a later date than the warrant].

5. The affidavit does not state probable cause because [no experience of the police officer is shown, and/or the named items are not shown to be subject to seizure, and/or there is no connection between the criminal activity and the place to be searched, and/or the information is based on hearsay and there is no showing as to the basis of knowledge of the information or the informant's basis of knowledge, and/or no corroboration is stated].

6. The search warrant [does not incorporate the affidavit and/or does not have an affidavit].

7. The search warrant does not name or describe the person or place to be searched with sufficient certainty and the warrant is thus a general warrant.

8. The search warrant authorizes the search of multiple premises.

9. The search warrant authorizes the search of multiple buildings.

10. The search warrant authorizes the search of vehicles for which there was no probable cause.

11. The search was conducted on the defendant's person, but the warrant only authorized a search of premises.

12. The search warrant did not sufficiently describe the defendant to authorize a search of his person.

13. The search warrant does not state with particularity the items to be seized and authorizes a general warrant.

14. The search warrant authorized the seizure of additional items for which no probable cause existed.

15. The original search warrant cannot be produced by the United States.

16. The issuing judge did not retain a copy of the search warrant.

17. The search warrant and/or the copies were not endorsed by the judge as to the date of issuance.

18. The search warrant and/or the copies do not bear the name of the officer to whom the warrant was delivered for execution.

19. The judge did not sign the warrant.

20. The search warrant was amended after it was issued.

21. The officer executing the warrant had no authority to do so.

22. The officer to whom the warrant was directed did not participate in the execution of the warrant.

23. The search warrant was executed more than once.

24. The warrant was not executed promptly.

25. In executing the search warrant, the officers used unreasonable force.

26. In executing the search warrant, the officers did not give notice of their authority and purpose.

27. In executing the search warrant, the officers detained and searched persons who were strangers to the process.

28. The scope and intensity of the search was beyond that authorized by the warrant and was unreasonable.

29. Items not named in the warrant were seized which were not in plain view.

30. No execution of the warrant is noted on its face.

31. No inventory of the property taken was noted on the warrant.

32. The return of the warrant was improper because [it was too long after the search, and/or the return is inaccurate, and/or there is no specificity as to the items taken].

33. The officer making the return is [not the same one who was authorized to make the search, and/or unknown, he/she having failed to note his/her name on the return].

Based upon the above grounds, the defendant requests that the above-described property be suppressed in any criminal proceeding [and that the property be returned to the defendant]

____

Counsel for Defendant

[Certificate of Service]

Chapter 5

ARRESTS, WITH AND WITHOUT WARRANTS

Table of Sections

---

§ 5.1 Introduction

The traditional arrest is defined as the seizure of a person in order to subject the person to the jurisdiction of the court in a criminal prosecution.[1] In *Florida v. Royer*,[2] the Court stated that the police have seized an individual if, in view of all the circumstances surrounding the incident, a reasonable person would have believed that he was not free to leave.

> Examples of circumstances that might indicate a seizure, even where the person did not attempt to leave, would be the threatening presence of several officers, the display of a weapon by an officer, some physical touching of the person to the citizen, or the use of language or tone of voice indicating that compliance with the officer's request might be compelled.[3]

California v. Hodari D. stated the current principle: "[a]n arrest requires *either* physical force . . . *or*, where that is absent, submission to the assertion of authority."[4] Applying its test, the Court found that no arrest occurred until the defendant was tackled; until then no physical force was applied and the defendant did not comply with a show of authority.

It is often necessary to determine when and whether an arrest occurs, which may require the prosecution to justify a search by stating that a lawful arrest has occurred. Conversely, the defendant may argue that he was arrested in order to prove that a resulting seizure or confession occurred while he was in custody; that seizure or confession would be illegal as the fruit of the poisonous tree if the arrest were unlawful.[5]

The fact a defendant was arrested in violation of the Fourth Amendment does not affect the jurisdiction of the court to subject that person to trial,[6] i.e., an "illegal arrest or detention does not void a subsequent conviction."[7] *Frisbie v. Collins*[8] stated that "[t]here is nothing in the Constitution that requires a court to permit a guilty person rightfully convicted to escape justice because he was brought to trial against his will."[9]

---

1 Terry v. Ohio, 392 U.S. 1, 17 (1968). See Brower v. County of Inyo, 489 U.S. 593, 596 (1989) (a seizure is a willful acquisition of physical control).

2 460 U.S. 491 (1983).

3 United States v. Mendenhall, 446 U.S. 544, 554 (1980).

4 California v. Hodari D., 499 U.S. 621, 626 (1991) (emphasis in the original).

5 See § 1.7, discussing Fruit of the Poisonous Tree Doctrine.

6 Gerstein v. Pugh, 420 U.S. 103 (1975); Frisbie v. Collins, 342 U.S. 519 (1952). See Ker v. Illinois, 119 U.S. 436 (1886).

7 Gerstein v. Pugh, 420 U.S. 103, 119 (1975).

8 342 U.S. 519 (1952).

9 Frisbie v. Collins, 342 U.S. 519, 522 (1952).

§ 5.2 Authority to Arrest

An arrest may be made: (1) by a peace officer acting under an arrest warrant;[10] (2) by a peace officer without an arrest warrant; or (3) by a private person. The statutory authority to arrest depends to a large extent on whether the offense for arrest is a felony or misdemeanor and whether the offense is committed in the presence of an officer.

A. Felonies

As a general rule, an officer may make a warrantless arrest for a felony whether or not the offense is committed in the officer's presence. A peace officer at common law could make a warrantless arrest for a felony when he had "reasonable grounds to believe" that a felony had been committed and that the prospective arrestee had committed the felony. Because the constitutional probable cause standard is the equivalent of the common law, all States permit police officers to arrest a person for the commission of a felony, even if there is time for obtaining an arrest warrant.

B. Misdemeanors

The common law standard for arresting a person for a misdemeanor was that a peace officer may conduct a warrantless arrest for the misdemeanor of breaching the peace committed in his presence. Otherwise, an arrest warrant was required to arrest for other misdemeanors committed in the officer's presence or for any misdemeanor committed outside the officer's presence. *Atwater v. City of Lago Vista*[11] was a civil rights case where the plaintiff claimed damages for being arrested for seat belt violations punishable by a fine only. She claimed that her misdemeanor arrest violated the Fourth Amendment, because a seat belt violation falls short of satisfying the common law breach of the peace limitation for warrantless misdemeanor arrests.

The Court held that, unlike the common law, the Fourth Amendment does not limit warrantless misdemeanor arrests made on an in-presence basis to those offenses constituting a breach of the peace. The Court rejected the plaintiff's argument that the Framers' view of the Fourth Amendment tracked the common law, ruling that the understanding of the common law rule at the time was not consistently understood to include the breach of the peace restriction. The existing "history, if not unequivocal, has expressed a decided majority view that the police need not obtain an arrest warrant

10 See the discussion in § 5.6, Arrest Warrants.

11 532 U.S. 318 (2001).

merely because a misdemeanor stopped short of violence or a threat of it."[12]

Most States have expanded the standard for a warrantless arrest to include *any* misdemeanor committed in the officer's presence; other States permit warrantless misdemeanor arrests under emergency circumstances. A few States have removed the "in the presence" standard altogether, so that the warrantless standard is the same for felonies and misdemeanors. Elsewhere, the term "in the presence" is important in distinguishing the legality of arrests for a felony and a misdemeanor.

The standard for arrest is whether there is probable cause to believe that an offense is being committed in the officer's presence, along with the facts and circumstances. A crime is committed in an officer's presence when he is apprised thereof by the exercise of one or more of the five senses; when the officer acquires direct personal knowledge of a criminal act, he may lawfully arrest the person committing it. Thus, when a peace officer sees, smells or hears evidence that leads to a belief that a crime is in progress, the officer may effect an arrest.

C. Arrest Under Exigent Circumstances

A warrantless arrest is not invalid merely because there was time to obtain a warrant. With the limited exception of a warrantless arrest in a person's home, the warrantless arrest of a person does not require the presence of exigent circumstances.[13] Put another way, without exigent circumstances, an arrest warrant is necessary to enter the home of the arrestee who resides there.

Payton v. New York,[14] held that the Fourth Amendment "prohibits the police from making a warrantless and nonconsensual entry into a suspect's home in order to make a routine felony arrest."[15] "It is a 'basic principle of Fourth Amendment law' that searches and seizures inside a home without a warrant are presumptively unreasonable."[16] By contrast, "objects such as weapons or contraband found in a public place may be seized by the police without a warrant."[17] "[A]n entry to arrest and an entry to search for and to seize property implicate the same interest in

---

12 *Id.*, at 345.

13 Payton v. New York, 445 U.S. 573 (1980). See United States v. Watson, 423 U.S. 411 (1976).

14 445 U.S. 573 (1980).

15 *Payton v. New York*, 445 U.S. at 576.

16 *Id.*, at 586.

17 *Id.*, at 586–87.

preserving the privacy and the sanctity of the home, and justify the same level of constitutional protection."[18]

> [A]ny differences in the intrusiveness of entries to search and entries to arrest are merely ones of degree rather than kind. The two intrusions share this fundamental characteristic: the breach of the entrance to an individual's home. The Fourth Amendment protects the individual's privacy in a variety of settings. In none is the zone of privacy more clearly defined than when bounded by the unambiguous physical dimensions of an individual's home—a zone that finds its roots in clear and specific constitutional terms: "The right of the people to be secure in their . . . houses . . . shall not be violated. . . ." In terms that apply equally to seizures of property and to seizures of persons, the Fourth Amendment has drawn a firm line at the entrance to the house. Absent exigent circumstances, that threshold may not reasonably be crossed without a warrant.[19]

There is also no need for a warrant if the arrested defendant was standing directly in the doorway of his residence,[20] but it probably is not enough that the door is open and the person to be arrested is clearly visible within the premises.

Payton also responded New York's argument that "only a search warrant based on probable cause to believe the suspect is at home at a given time can adequately protect the privacy interests at stake."[21]

> It is true that an arrest warrant requirement may afford less protection than a search warrant requirement, but it will suffice to interpose the magistrate's determination of probable cause between the zealous officer and the citizen. If there is sufficient evidence of a citizen's participation in a felony to persuade a judicial officer that his arrest is justified, it is constitutionally reason able to require him to open his doors to the officers of the law. Thus, for Fourth Amendment purposes, an arrest warrant founded on probable cause implicitly carries with it the limited authority to enter a dwelling in which the suspect lives when there is reason to believe the suspect is within.[22]

---

18 *Id.*, at 588.

19 *Id.*, at 589–90.

20 United States v. Santana, 427 U.S. 38 (1976).

21 *Payton v. New York*, 445 U.S. at 602.

22 *Id.*, at 602–03.

In *Welsh v. Wisconsin*,[23] the police entered the defendant's home without a warrant to arrest him for the offense of driving while intoxicated in the immediate vicinity only minutes before. The State claimed exigent circumstances for the police entry, i.e., a need to obtain evidence of the defendant's blood alcohol level, which the Court had previously found compelling in other circumstances.[24] Instead, the Court concluded "the best indication of the State's interest in precipitating an arrest" was the fact that the State had "chosen to classify the first offense for driving while intoxicated as a noncriminal, civil forfeiture offense for which no imprisonment is possible," holding that "a warrantless home arrest cannot be upheld simply because evidence of the petitioner's blood-alcohol level might have dissipated while the police obtained a warrant."[25]

When police enter a suspect's premises to execute an arrest warrant, they may not bring along others whose presence is unrelated to the purpose of the "authorized intrusion." *Wilson v. Layne*[26] held that the police violated the Fourth Amendment when they allowed members of the news media to accompany them as they entered a private residence to execute an arrest warrant.

D. Arrest in a Public Place

United States v. Watson[27] was "the first square holding that the Fourth Amendment permits a duly authorized law enforcement officer to make a warrantless arrest in a public place, even though he had adequate opportunity to procure a warrant after developing probable cause for arrest."[28] "[T]here is nothing in the Court's prior cases indicating that under the Fourth Amendment a warrant is required to make a valid arrest for a felony."[29]

> [W]e decline to transform this judicial preference [for arrest warrants] into a constitutional rule when the judgment of the Nation and Congress has for so long been to authorize warrantless public arrests on probable cause rather than to encumber criminal prosecutions with endless litigation with respect to the existence of exigent circumstances, whether it was practicable to get a warrant, whether the suspect was about to flee, and the like.[30]

---

23 466 U.S. 740 (1984).

24 Schmerber v. California, 384 U.S. 757 (1966).

25 Welsh v. Wisconsin, 466 U.S. 740, 754 (1984).

26 526 U.S. 603 (1999).

27 423 U.S. 411 (1976).

28 United States v. Watson, 423 U.S. 411, 427 (1976) (Powell, J., concurring).

29 *Id.*, at 416–17.

30 *Id.*, at 423–24.

A year earlier, *Gerstein v. Pugh*[31] made similar statements about dispensing with a warrant requirement for arrests. "[W]hile the Court has expressed a preference for the use of arrest warrants when feasible, it has never invalidated an arrest supported by probable cause solely because the officers failed to secure a warrant."[32] *Gerstein* held that an officer's arrest for probable cause warranted "a brief period of detention to take the administrative steps incident to arrest," when "the reasons that justify dispensing with the magistrate's neutral judgment evaporate," because there is "no longer any danger that the suspect will escape or commit further crimes while the police submit their evidence to a magistrate."[33] The Court held "that the Fourth Amendment requires a determination of probable cause as a prerequisite to extended restraint on liberty following arrest."[34] That decision must be made "promptly after arrest."[35] A later case declared that a probable cause decision within 48 hours of arrest was presumably reasonable, although a defendant could prove that any type of delay was unreasonably prejudicial; a longer delay then 48 hours is presumptively unreasonable with the burden on the Government to demonstrate the existence of a bona fide emergency or other extraordinary circumstance.[36]

E. Authority of Private Persons to Arrest

From State to State, the standards for a private person to make an arrest vary. The relevancy of the authority of private persons to arrest occurs when officers conduct an arrest beyond their territorial jurisdiction. A private person may make an arrest only if a felony has in fact been committed and he has probable cause to believe that the person being arrested has committed it. In making an arrest, a private person is acting as an agent of the State, and is thus subject to the Fourth Amendment prohibitions against unreasonable searches and seizures. By contrast, unlawful private searches and seizures which are conducted independent of an arrest are not sovereign acts within the meaning of State and the United States Constitutions.

---

31 420 U.S. 103 (1975).

32 Gerstein v. Pugh, 420 U.S. 103, 113 (1975).

33 *Id.*, at 114.

34 *Id.*

35 *Id.*, at 125.

36 County of Riverside v. McLaughlin, 500 U.S. 44, 57 (1991).

F. Judicial Review of Warrantless Arrest

Following a warrantless arrest, the defendant must be brought before a judge without unnecessary delay.[37] The failure to do so may have an impact on a confession,[38] but will not affect the validity of the arrest itself.[39]

G. Arrest for the "Wrong" Offense

An arrest is not rendered unlawful by the fact that an officer, who has authority to make an arrest for a particular offense, erroneously booked the accused for one offense when he had sufficient evidence of a different offense.

H. Use of Force

Unnecessary force or violence cannot be used to arrest.[40] The Court in *Tennessee v. Garner*[41] held that "[t]he use of deadly force to prevent the escape of all felony suspects, whatever the circumstances, is constitutionally unreasonable."[42] Fourth Amendment reasonableness standards apply to all claims that the police "have used excessive force—deadly or non-deadly—in the course of an arrest, investigatory stop, or other 'seizure' of a free citizen."[43] The Court declared that the excessive force issue is a case-by-case decision, with the following factors being relevant: "the severity of the crime at issue, whether the suspect poses an immediate threat to the safety of the officers or others, and whether [the defendant] is actively resisting arrest or attempting to evade arrest by flight."[44]

> The calculus of reasonableness must embody allowance for the fact that police officers are often forced to make split-second judgments—in circumstances that are tense, uncertain, and rapidly evolving—about the amount of force that is necessary in a particular situation.[45]

---

37 See County of Riverside v. McLaughlin, 500 U.S. 44 (1991) (48 hours after arrest is an appropriate outer boundary for presentation of an arrestee before a judge). *McLaughlin* applies retroactively. Powell v. Nevada, 511 U.S. 79 (1994).

38 See § 12.2, discussing Prompt Arraignment and Confessions.

39 Hitchcock v. United States, 580 F.2d 964 (9th Cir. 1978) (claim of unnecessary delay meritless where it was not a fundamental defect to justify relief).

40 See City and County of San Francisco v. Sheehan, 575 U.S. 600 (2015) (no clearly established Fourth Amendment rule exists regarding when police may shoot a person with mental illness).

41 471 U.S. 1 (1985).

42 Tennessee v. Garner, 471 U.S. 1, 11 (1985).

43 Graham v. Connor, 490 U.S. 386, 395 (1989).

44 *Id.*, at 396.

45 *Id.*, at 396–97.

The Court applied *Garner* to a high-speed chase by a deputy sheriff in pursuit of a person initially driving almost 20 mph above the speed limit. The chase ended in a crash that resulted in the driver's vehicle crashing and the driver becoming a quadriplegic. The Court held that the use of force was reasonable. The driver

> posed an actual and imminent threat to the lives of any pedestrians who might have been present, to other civilian motorists, and to the officers involved in the chase. It is equally clear that [the deputy's] actions posed a high likelihood of serious injury or death to respondent—though not the near *certainty* of death posed by, say, shooting a fleeing felon in the back of the head, or pulling alongside a fleeing motorist's car and shooting the motorist . . . We think it appropriate in this process to take into account not only the number of lives at risk, but also their relative culpability. It was [the driver], after all, who intentionally placed himself and the public in danger by unlawfully engaging in the reckless, high-speed flight that ultimately produced the choice between two evils that [the deputy sheriff] confronted.[46]

§ 5.3 Notice of Authority and Grounds for Arrest

An arrest is made when a person is placed under actual physical restraint or submits to the authority of the person making the arrest. The person making the arrest is required to inform the person to be arrested of the intention to effect an arrest and of the reason for the arrest. However, this information need not be given if the circumstances indicate that the person is aware of the basis for the arrest, if he resists arrest or otherwise renders it impractical or futile for the person making the arrest to convey the information.

The failure of the person making the arrest to announce an intention before attempting the arrest may deprive that person of the color of official authority to use force and may justify the person to be arrested in defending from an apparently lawless attack. However, the lack of notice of an intention to arrest does not render the arrest illegal in fact, and any evidence derived from the arrest is not required to be suppressed.

§ 5.4 Territorial Jurisdiction for Police to Arrest

The authority of a peace officer to make an arrest is ordinarily limited to the geographical boundaries of the governmental unit which he serves. However, a peace officer generally may conduct an

---

46 Scott v. Harris, 550 U.S. 372, 384 (2007).

arrest beyond those boundaries if the officer: (1) is in the boundaries of another governmental unit with which he has an agreement for cooperative action; or (2) was requested by a law enforcement agency to assist in any matter within the agency's jurisdiction.

What about pursuit of a suspect across State lines? At common law, law enforcement did not have the authority to arrest in another State, although an exception to this rule existed where the officer was in fresh pursuit of a person who had committed a felony. Under the Uniform Act on Fresh Pursuit, adopted in most States, a law enforcement officer from outside the State may enter the State "in fresh pursuit of a person in order to arrest him on the ground that he is believed to have committed a felony in such State."[47]

In addition, State residents who are federal law enforcement or investigative officers for the following federal agencies have the same powers and duties as any other peace officer in that State: Federal Bureau of Investigation, United States Secret Service, United States Marshal, Drug Enforcement Administration, Bureau of Alcohol, Tobacco and Firearms, United States Forest Service, Inspector General's Office of the Department of Agriculture, and the United States Customs Service.

§ 5.5 Comparing an Arrest with a Stop

A. Proof for an Arrest

Labeling the seizure of a person as a stop or as an arrest depends on what the police know at the time of the seizure. As discussed in Chapter 3, police must have probable cause to arrest a suspect, with or without a warrant, i.e., based on the totality of the circumstances so that a reasonable law enforcement officer would believe there is a fair probability that the suspect is committing or has committed an offense.

B. Proof for a Stop

In order to legally stop a person, the police may rely on less proof than for an arrest, i.e., a reasonable suspicion that, based on their experience, "criminal activity may be afoot."[48] After a stop, the police may learn information leading them to end the stop, because of their mistake in thinking that criminal activity had occurred, was occurring, or was about to occur. If so, the seized person can walk away because the stop and the focus on him ends. On the other hand, the police may learn information that replaces the reasonable

---

[47] Uniform Law on Fresh Pursuit (1937).

[48] Terry v. Ohio, 392 U.S. 1, 30 (1968). See Chapter 9, discussing Stop and Frisk.

suspicion needed for a stop with probable cause, i.e., a seizure that began as a stop has become an arrest.

C. Police Conduct After a Stop

The distinction between a stop and an arrest does not end with the quantum of proof necessary for each type of seizure. Whether there is a stop or an arrest determines what the police legally can do next.[49] From the case law, a stop must be brief, even if the suspect is confined. The short duration of a stop usually focuses on the officer's decision about reasonable suspicion that the suspect is armed and dangerous in order to conduct a frisk of his outer clothing for a weapon. The suspect may be moved from one place to another on the same premises. If a stop takes more time, the suspect is moved to another location, or a frisk produces a weapon or contraband, and the case law likely will then characterize the seizure as having become an arrest.

D. Police Conduct After an Arrest

When the police have probable cause to arrest a suspect, they have more options than after a stop. With probable cause, they may use weapons or physical force to subdue the suspect. Incident to the arrest, the police may conduct a full search of the suspect and the area within his immediate control[50] without first frisking the suspect's outer clothing. Police may seize anything they find, even if it relates to a different crime than the offense for which the arrest was made. An arrest carries no time restriction, the police may physically confine the arrestee, e.g., using handcuffs, and they may move him to another location like a police station for the purpose of fingerprinting.

§ 5.6 Arrest Warrants

The Supreme Court has long expressed a strong preference for the use of arrest warrants, although as previously discussed[51] it has declined to convert that preference into a constitutional standard. The Court prefers the warrant process because it "interposes an orderly procedure" involving "judicial impartiality" whereby "a neutral and detached magistrate" can make "informed and deliberate determinations"[52] on the issue of probable cause. The preference produces a slight distinction between the probable cause required when there is no warrant and that required when there is. *United*

---

49 See Chapter 9, discussing Stop and Frisk.

50 See Chapter 6, discussing Search Incident to Arrest.

51 See § 5.2(D).

52 Aguilar v. Texas, 378 U.S. 108, 110 (1964), abrogated by Illinois v. Gates, 462 U.S. 213 (1983).

States v. Ventresca stated that "in a doubtful or marginal case a search under a warrant may be sustainable where without one it would fail."[53] A court reviewing a warrant does not have to make "a *de novo* probable cause determination" but merely decides "whether the evidence viewed as a whole provided a 'substantial basis' for the magistrate's prior finding of probable cause."[54]

A. Application for an Arrest Warrant

Anyone may apply for an arrest warrant. The method of applying for an arrest warrant requires the signing of a written document called a complaint, which is a sworn affidavit alleging that a person has committed an offense and the essential facts constituting that offense. A conclusory information sworn to by a prosecutor will not suffice,[55] but an indictment "fair upon its face" returned by a "properly constituted grand jury . . . conclusively determines the existence of probable cause"[56] and requires issuance of an arrest warrant without further inquiry.

The standards for the affidavit of an arrest warrant are the same as those for a search warrant,[57] including the particularity requirement to describe the person to be arrested under the warrant. The typical arrest warrant specifies the name of the person to be arrested. Without an actual name for the arrestee, a "John Doe" or "Jane Doe" warrant must include sufficient information permitting the arresting office to identify the person to be arrested with certainty, e.g., personal appearance, race, gender, height and weight, and any peculiar physical features.

The complaint must contain information showing the jurisdiction of the court over the offense, and state specifically the facts upon which it is based. The judge (or a clerk authorized to issue a warrant) must examine the complaint and make an independent finding of probable cause. Prior to the issuance of a warrant, no notice or hearing is required, and the defendant has no right to be heard.

An arrest made pursuant to a previously issued warrant is not inevitably valid. In *Whiteley*, the Court explained that, while an officer is "entitled to assume" that the warrant was issued upon "the information requisite to support an independent judicial assessment of probable cause,"[58] if it turns out that this was not the case or that

---

[53] United States v. Ventresca, 380 U.S. 102, 106 (1965).

[54] Massachusetts v. Upton, 466 U.S. 727, 732–33 (1984).

[55] Albrecht v. United States, 273 U.S. 1, 5 n.1 (1927).

[56] Gerstein v. Pugh, 420 U.S. 103, 117 n.19 (1975).

[57] See Chapter 4, discussing Search Warrants; Aguilar v. Texas, 378 U.S. 108 (1964), abrogated by Illinois v. Gates, 462 U.S. 213 (1983).

[58] *Whiteley v. Warden*, 401 U.S. at 568.

the arrest was invalid in some other respect, the arrest cannot be upheld on the basis of the warrant.

When the reviewing official finds probable cause, he may issue either an arrest warrant or a summons stating the offense charged, as well as who should be apprehended for the offense. More than one warrant or summons may issue on a single complaint if the complaint alleged the commission of multiple offenses.[59]

B. Execution

An arrest warrant may be executed by any peace officer who does not have to have the warrant in his possession at the time of arrest. The arrest warrant is served/executed either actually or constructively by taking the person into custody (in the case of an arrest warrant), or commanding the person to appear before the appropriate court (in the case of a summons).

The arresting officer must advise the defendant of the offense charged and of the fact that a warrant has issued. The warrant and the complaint should be served at the time of arrest or soon thereafter. To effectuate an arrest, the officer may break into a building if after notifying the occupant of his purpose he is refused admittance or there is no response. A warrant must be presented in addition to the "knock-and-announce" rule.[60]

C. Using an Arrest Warrant in Another's Dwelling

Steagald v. United States held that an arrest warrant is insufficient to enter the dwelling of another person to look for the named defendant absent exigent circumstances.[61] The police entered the defendant's residence with an arrest warrant for another person. True, the arrest warrant legitimately authorized the police to arrest the other person either in public or in *his* own home, per *Payton v. New York*. The problem for the police was that they were using the authority of the *arrest* warrant to *search* for the other person in another person's home. When the judge authorized the arrest warrant, he was not authorizing the police to enter the defendant's home to arrest someone who did not reside there. For that purpose, the police would need a search warrant. In that circumstance, a search warrant is also needed to look for and to arrest the other person.

> [W]hile an arrest warrant and a search warrant both serve to subject the probable cause determination of the police to

---

59 Giordenello v. U.S., 357 U.S. 480 (1958).

60 See Chapter 4, discussing Search Warrants.

61 Steagald v. U.S., 451 U.S. 204 (1981).

> judicial review, the interests protected by the two warrants differ. An arrest warrant is issued by a magistrate upon a showing that probable cause exists to believe that the subject of the warrant has committed an offense and thus the warrant primarily serves to protect an individual from an unreasonable seizure. A search warrant, in contrast is issued upon a showing of probable cause to believe that the legitimate object of a search is located in a particular place, and therefore safeguards an individual's interest in the privacy of his home and possessions against the unjustified intrusion of the police.[62]

The rights of the person other than the arrestee are at issue. A defendant arrested with an arrest warrant in the home of a third person, may lack standing to contest the lawfulness of the arrest (as opposed to the search warrant).[63] The validity of a warrant affects both the lawfulness of the arrest and evidence thereby seized. After the execution of the warrant, the original warrant is taken to the judge along with the defendant. A notation of execution, called a "return," is made on the face of the warrant showing who served the warrant, as well as the date and time of service.

D. Challenging an Arrest Warrant

The defendant cannot challenge the jurisdiction of the court to try him solely on the basis of an illegal arrest.[64] Three reasons justify challenging an arrest warrant. First, when the warrant is invalid, the defendant held is illegally restrained of liberty. Second, absent exigent circumstances, an arrest warrant is required to arrest a person in his own home.[65]

> It is true that an arrest warrant requirement may afford less protection than a search warrant requirement, but it will suffice to interpose the magistrate's determination of probable cause between the zealous officer and the citizen. If there is sufficient evidence of a citizen's participation in a felony to persuade a judicial officer that his arrest is justified, it is constitutionally responsible to require him to open his doors to the officers of the law. Thus, for Fourth Amendment purposes, an arrest warrant founded on probable cause implicitly carries with it the limited

---

62 *Id.*, at 212–13.

63 See § 1.7, discussing the Fruit of the Poisonous Tree Doctrine.

64 Frisbie v. Collins, 342 U.S. 519 (1952).

65 Payton v. New York, 445 U.S. 573 (1980).

> authority to enter a dwelling in which the suspect lives when there is reason to believe the suspect is within.[66]

In that circumstance, entry into the defendant's home without a lawful arrest warrant makes any seized evidence inadmissible.

The third reason for challenging an arrest warrant is that it serves as an important discovery tool. The affidavit of complaint alerts defense counsel to the prosecution's primary witnesses and to the facts of the offense. This information may be valuable in a preliminary hearing, enabling the defense to call witnesses whom the prosecution has not used. The arrest warrant also triggers speedy trial requirements. Once a warrant issues, even if the defendant is not in custody, the right to a speedy trial commences.[67]

E. Comparing the Validity of an Arrest Warrant to Validity of the Arrest

The validity of the arrest warrant does not affect the validity of the arrest where the arrest would have been proper even without a warrant. The only exception to this rule is an arrest in another person's home which, absent exigent circumstances, requires a valid search warrant. In *Whiteley v. Warden*,[68] the Court stated that a police officer serving the warrant was "entitled to assume" that the arrest warrant was issued upon "the information requisite to support an independent judicial assessment of probable cause."[69] When probable cause exists to make a warrantless arrest, the arrest is not invalid because the warrant is invalid. In *Whiteley*, the Court held that the arrest was unlawful only after findings both that the arrest warrant was defective and that the officer serving the warrant did not have facts independent of the warrant to constitute probable cause.

F. Comparing an Arrest Warrant with a Search Warrant

How is a search warrant different from an arrest warrant? "[T]he categorical detention rule announced in [*Michigan v.*] *Summers* does not apply to arrest warrants, . . . because there were no particular circumstances justifying [the] detention. . . ."[70]

> [T]he interests of law enforcement in detaining occupants during a search (mostly) do not apply to the execution of an

66 *Id.*, at 602–03.
67 United States v. Marion, 404 U.S. 307 (1971).
68 401 U.S. 560, 568 (1971).
69 Whiteley v. Warden, 401 U.S. 560, 568 (1971).
70 Sharp v. County of Orange, 871 F.3d 901, 913 (9th Cir. 2017).

arrest warrant. The *Summers* Court articulated three such interests: (1) "preventing flight in the event that incriminating evidence is found"; (2) facilitating "the orderly completion of the search" as detainees' "self-interest may induce them to open locked doors or locked containers to avoid the use of force"; and (3) "minimizing the risk of harm to the officers." With the exception of the final factor, these considerations simply do not apply with the same force to arrest warrants.[71]

Of the five basic requirements for issuing and executing an arrest warrant and a search warrant, four are parallel with one another: (1) they both require proof of facts to establish probable cause, although the nature of that probable cause differs;[72] (2) the issuance of either type of warrant may rely on information from an informant; (3) each warrant must satisfy Fourth Amendment standards of particularity; an arrest warrant must sufficiently describe the person to be arrested, and a search warrant must satisfactorily define the place or places to be searched and the objects to be seized; and (4) under specific circumstances, police may gain entry to execute either type of warrant by satisfying knock-and-announce standards.

The primary distinction between an arrest warrant and a search warrant is the timing of the warrant's execution. An arrest warrant may be executed anytime; information supporting probable cause for the issuance of the warrant and the person's arrest generally does not become stale. Probable cause for searching a particular place for specific objects depends on "fresh facts." Before issuing a search warrant, a judge should consider whether the affidavit already contains stale information. After the warrant is executed, a person affected by the search may ask whether too much time passed between the signing of the affidavit supporting the warrant and the execution of the warrant. The passage of time may create considerable doubt as to whether probable cause to find an object would still exist, for example, a month after the affidavit that was presented to the judge for the possible issuance of a search warrant.

G. Comparing an Arrest Warrant with a Material Witness Warrant

An arrest warrant for a material witness may issue in the federal system if "it appears from an affidavit filed by a party that the testimony of a person is material in a criminal proceeding, and if it shown that it may become impracticable to secure the presence of

---

71 *Id.*, at 914.

72 See Chapter 3, discussing Probable Cause.

the person by subpoena."[73] In *Ashcroft v. al-Kidd*,[74] the Court held that a material witness warrant issues "based on individualized suspicion."

> [I]t is important to bear in mind that the material witness statute might not provide for the issuance of warrants within the meaning of the Fourth Amendment's Warrant Clause. The typical arrest warrant is based on probable cause that the arrestee has committed a crime; but that is not the standard for the issuance of warrants under the material-witness statute. . . If material witness warrants do not qualify as "Warrants" under the Fourth Amendment, then material witness arrests might still be governed by the Fourth Amendment's separate reasonableness requirement for seizures of the person.[75]

---

73 18 U.S.C. § 3144.

74 563 U.S. 731 (2011).

75 Ashcroft v. al-Kidd, 563 U.S. 731, 745 (2011) (Kennedy, J., concurring).

Chapter 6

SEARCH INCIDENT TO ARREST

Table of Sections

§ 6.1 Introduction

In the context of making an arrest, the police may conduct a warrantless search of the suspect's person[1] without probable cause or reasonable suspicion to believe that the person arrested possesses either weapons or evidence.[2] Because this authority derives from an officer's need to disarm the suspect, prevent his escape, and to discover evidence,[3] the likelihood that a particular arrestee is armed or concealing evidence is irrelevant to the legality of the search.[4] A search of the defendant's pockets[5] or clothing[6] is permissible

1 See, e.g., Michigan v. DeFillippo, 443 U.S. 31 (1979); United States v. Santana, 427 U.S. 38 (1976); United States v. Robinson, 414 U.S. 218 (1973).

2 Michigan v. DeFillippo, 443 U.S. 31 (1979); United States v. Robinson, 414 U.S. 218 (1973).

3 United States v. Robinson, 414 U.S. 218 (1973).

4 *Id.*

5 *Id.*

6 See United States v. Edwards, 415 U.S. 800 (1974).

regardless of the fact that the search is for items that may not directly relate to the reason for the arrest. A search incident to an arrest for digital information generally is prohibited.[7] This Chapter discusses searches of persons and containers incident to an arrest.

§ 6.2 Requirements of a Search Incident to an Arrest

A. The *Chimel* Principle

Three police officers went to Chimel's home with an arrest warrant for the owner based on probable cause that he had burglarized a coin shop. Chimel's wife consented to the officers' presence in the house where they waited for Chimel to return from his job. When he entered his home, an officer handed him the arrest warrant and asked him if they could "look around." Although he objected, the officers told him that they could search based "on the basis of the lawful arrest." During the search, the officers ordered Chimel's wife to open drawers and move the contents around in those drawers so that they could look for items taken during the burglary. The officers seized coins and other objects.

Chimel's appeals affirmed his burglary conviction until the case reached the Supreme Court. Although the history of the case law addressing searches incident to arrest had not been consistent, the applicable precedent was that "a warrantless search 'incident to a lawful arrest' may generally extend to the area that is considered to be in the 'possession' or under the 'control' of the person arrested."[8]

Prior to *Chimel*, case precedent had permitted a search of the entire interior of a defendant's residence because it was in the defendant's control or possession. With an unlimited search area, the Court's opinions suggested the advantage of arresting a suspect indoors rather than on the front lawn outside his residence. By contrast to the earlier decisions, the Court in *Chimel* decided that a limited search of the area within the defendant's immediate control was a reasonable method to limit the scope of a search incident to an arrest. In reversing Chimel's conviction, the Court held that the search of his entire home exceeded the reasonable scope of the area within his immediate control.

> The only reasoned distinction is one between a search of the person arrested and the area within his reach on the one hand, and more extensive searches on the other. . . . The search here went far beyond the petitioner's person and the

---

[7] Riley v. California, 573 U.S. 373 (2014). See § 6.2(E), Searching the "Area Within Immediate Control."

[8] Chimel v. California, 395 U.S. 752, 760 (1969).

> area from within which he might have obtained either a weapon or something that could have been used as evidence against him. There was no constitutional justification, in the absence of a search warrant, for extending the search beyond that area. The scope of the search was, therefore, "unreasonable" under the Fourth and Fourteenth Amendments and the petitioner's conviction cannot stand.[9]

Chimel noted that the rationale for a reasonable search incident to arrest was threefold, to prevent (1) harm to anyone, (2) the defendant's escape, and (3) concealment and destruction of evidence. Following an arrest, "it is reasonable for the arresting officer to search the person arrested in order to remove any weapons that the latter might seek to use in order to resist arrest or effect his escape" and "to search for and seize any evidence on the arrestee's person in order to prevent its concealment or destruction."[10] Besides the search of the arrested person, *Chimel* endorsed a second feature of a search incident to arrest.

> [T]he area into which an arrestee might reach in order to grab a weapon or evidentiary items must, of course, be governed by a like rule. A gun on a table or in a drawer in front of one who is arrested can be as dangerous to the arresting office as one concealed in the clothing of the person arrested. There is ample justification, therefore, for a search of the arrestee's person and the area "within his immediate control"—construing that phrase to mean the area from within which he might gain possession of a weapon or destructible evidence.
>
> There is no comparable justification, however, for routinely searching any room other than that in which an arrest occurs—or, for that matter, for searching through all the desk drawers or other closed or concealed areas in that room itself. Such searches, in the absence of well-recognized exceptions, may be made only under the authority of a search warrant. The "adherence to judicial processes" mandated by the Fourth Amendment requires no less.[11]

After *Chimel*, following an arrest, the police automatically and immediately can conduct a full search of the person, plus the area within that person's immediate control. The holding is to assure the arresting officer that he can secure custody of the person by removing from him anything that reasonably could be used to effect an escape

---

9 *Id.*, at 766, 768.

10 *Id.*, at 763.

11 *Id.*

or destroy evidence. The search incident to arrest may be conducted, regardless of whether any of the rationales exist.

During a search incident to an arrest, the police may seize weapons that could be used to injure the officer or effect an escape, fruits of the crime for which the arrest was made, instrumentalities used to commit a crime, contraband the possession of which constitutes a crime, any evidence that the arrestee committed the crime for which he was arrested, and evidence that he had committed any other offense. *Robinson* later entitled the officer who legally arrests a person to conduct a search of that person even for evidence unconnected with the arrest or evidence of a concealed weapon to be used in a criminal prosecution.

Chimel may suggest a strategy for a smart police officer who has an arrest warrant to arrest a person anytime. The officer also should consider seeking a search warrant for the entire building where the arrest is likely to occur. Once inside a building, the officer would not be limited by the *Chimel* holding to searching the person or the area of immediate control. After *Maryland v. Buie*,[12] with a search warrant the officer would not be limited by the qualifying language that restricts the officer's ability to search an entire residence as well as the grounds and vehicles there.

B. Lawful Arrest

A search incident to a lawful arrest is a major exception to the requirement of a search warrant. The constitutional validity of the search incident to arrest is wholly dependent upon the legality of the arrest. When the police officer does not make a custodial arrest, as in the case of a traffic citation, a search is limited to areas where a frisk would otherwise be permissible.[13] In *Knowles v. Iowa*,[14] a police officer stopped the defendant for speeding and issued a citation, pursuant to a statute that authorized but did not require issuance of a citation instead of an arrest. The officer then made a full search of the vehicle and found a bag of marijuana. The Court held that the issuance of a citation for the traffic violation did not justify a warrantless search of the passenger compartment, because issuance of a citation does not subject the police officer to the continuing exposure of an arrest situation.[15]

With a citation, the rationale of disarming the suspect is not as relevant as during a custodial arrest. "The threat to officer safety

---

[12] See § 6.4, discussing the "Protective Sweep" Beyond the Area Within Immediate Control.

[13] See Chapter 9, discussing Stop and Frisk.

[14] 525 U.S. 113 (1998).

[15] See Chapter 9, discussing Stop and Frisk.

from issuing a traffic citation . . . is a good deal less than in the case of a custodial arrest." A custodial arrest

> involves "danger to an officer" because of "the extended exposure which follows the taking of a suspect into custody and transporting him to the police station." We recognized that "[t]he danger to the police officer flows from the fact of the arrest, and its attendant proximity, stress, and uncertainty, and not from the grounds for the arrest." A routine traffic stop, on the other hand, is a relatively brief encounter and "is more analogous to a so-called '*Terry* stop' . . . than to a formal arrest."[16]

A police officer has other options when he has issued a citation, but also has concerns for his personal safety before ending the encounter. The officer may order the driver and passenger out of the vehicle,[17] patdown the driver or passengers if he has reasonable suspicion that anyone in the vehicle is armed and dangerous, or patdown the passenger compartment, again based upon reasonable suspicion about a person's danger and access to a weapon. Once any of those options provides the officer with probable cause to arrest the driver or passenger, he may be able to conduct a full search of the passenger compartment incident to that arrest.[18]

As for the search incident to arrest rationale of preserving evidence, the *Knowles* Court observed that "no further evidence of excessive speed was going to be found" on the defendant's person or in the vehicle. Further, no risk existed that the suspect would destroy "evidence relating to identity," because a driver who is unable to produce a driver's license would be arrested instead of receiving another traffic citation.[19]

In *Virginia v. Moore*,[20] the police officer arrested the defendant even though the applicable law required the use of a citation for driving on a suspended license. The Court held that *Knowles* was inapplicable because the defendant in *Moore* was arrested rather than issued a citation, and upheld the search incident to arrest as constitutional. When the officer's search incident to an arrest yielded cocaine, the officer "faced the risks that are 'an adequate basis for

---

16 United States v. Robinson, 414 U.S. 218, 234–35 (1973); Berkemer v. McCarty, 468 U.S. 420, 439 (1984).

17 A driver and any passengers may be ordered out of a car without the officer showing any grounds. Maryland v. Wilson, 519 U.S. 408 (1997); Pennsylvania v. Mimms, 434 U.S. 106 (1977). In the stop of a vehicle with multiple passengers, all occupants are seized. See Brendlin v. California, 551 U.S. 249 (2007).

18 Knowles v. Iowa, 525 U.S. 113, 118 (1998).

19 *Id.*

20 553 U.S. 164 (2008).

treating all custodial arrests alike for purposes of search justification.' "[21]

C. The Meaning of "Incident to Arrest"

The arrest ordinarily precedes the search in order to "fit" within the "search incident" warrantless search exception. However, the Court has recognized rare circumstances when the search may precede the arrest. For example, in *Rawlings v. Kentucky*,[22] after the suspect admitted ownership of a sizable quantity of drugs, a search of his person revealed money and a knife. Only then did the police place him under arrest. The Court characterized the search as "incident to arrest" even though the search preceded the arrest. After the suspect admitted ownership of the drugs found in his friend's purse, the police clearly already had probable cause to arrest him. "Where the formal arrest followed quickly on the heels of the challenged search of [defendant's] person, we do not believe it particularly important that the search preceded the arrest rather than vice versa."[23] While the arrest need not precede the search, it is clear that the probable cause to make the arrest cannot come from the search.

D. Searching the Arrestee

While *Chimel* narrowed the scope of the area within the arrestee's immediate control for a proper search incident to arrest, it recited the Court's longstanding views about the scope of searching the person following his custodial arrest. Four years later, in *United States v. Robinson*, the Court decided that a search incident to arrest automatically flows from a lawful arrest, which then opens the possibility for the search to produce a seizure of evidence that is even unrelated to the offense for which he was initially arrested.

In *Robinson*, based on a prior investigation of the suspect, a police officer arrested Robinson for driving on a revoked license and immediately searched him, even though the officer had no reason to believe and did not in fact believe that Robinson was armed and dangerous. The danger in a traffic arrest is believed to be more serious than a traffic stop, and the case law therefore authorizes a full search of the suspect.

Following departmental policy, the officer conducted a patdown of Robinson during which he felt a hard object in the suspect's jacket pocket. He reached into the suspect's pocket and pulled out a

---

[21] Virginia v. Moore, 553 U.S. 164, 168 (2008), quoting *United States v. Robinson*, 414 U.S. at 235.

[22] 448 U.S. 98 (1980).

[23] Rawlings v. Kentucky, 448 U.S. 98, 111 (1980).

crumpled cigarette package. Because he could not feel any cigarettes in the package, he opened it and found numerous capsules of what turned out to be heroin. The defendant was charged with and later was convicted of drug possession. Most of the Court's opinion focused on the search of Robinson, when the real issue was whether the officer could constitutionally open the cigarette pack to learn its contents, instead of seizing the pack and later applying for a search warrant.

Robinson sought to rebut the District of Columbia Circuit's holding that a *Terry* frisk instead of a full search should first be used for any person arrested for driving with a revoked license. The Court first quoted its *Chimel* statements about the scope of the search of a person during a search incident to arrest.

> When an arrest is made, it is reasonable for the arresting officer to search the person arrested in order to remove any weapons that the latter might seek to use in order to resist arrest or effect his escape. Otherwise, the officer's safety might well be endangered, and the arrest itself frustrated. In addition, it is entirely reasonable for the arresting officer to search for and seize any evidence on the arrestee's person in order to prevent its concealment or destruction.[24]

Tracing judicial opinions since 1848, the Court found that "the validity of the search of a person incidental to a lawful arrest has been regarded as settled from its first enunciation, and has remained virtually unchallenged until the present case."[25] The Court then turned its attention to the lower court's "suggestion that there must be litigated in each case the issue of whether or not there was present one of the reasons supporting the authority for a search of the person." Rejecting a case-by-case approach, the Court noted the necessarily quick *ad hoc* judgment about how and where to search the person of each suspect.

> A police officer's determination as to how and where to search the person of a suspect whom he has arrested is necessarily a quick ad hoc judgment which the Fourth Amendment does not require to be broken down in each instance into an analysis of each step in the search. The authority to search the person incident to a lawful custodial arrest, while based upon the need to disarm and to discover evidence, does not depend on what a court may later decide

[24] United States v. Robinson, 414 U.S. 218, 226 (1973), quoting *Chimel v. California*, 395 U.S. at 762–63.

[25] *United States v. Robinson*, 414 U.S. at 224.

> was the probability in a particular arrest situation that weapons or evidence would in fact be found upon the person of the suspect. A custodial arrest of a suspect based on probable cause . . . requires no additional justification. It is the fact of the lawful arrest which establishes the authority to search, and we hold that in the case of a lawful custodial arrest a full search of the person is not only an exception to the warrant requirement of the Fourth Amendment, but also a "reasonable" search under that Amendment.[26]

Because the source of the authority to search is the custodial arrest, it was irrelevant whether the officer feared the suspect or thought he was armed. When the officer found the crumpled cigarette package, he "was entitled to inspect it" and to seize the contents of heroin as " 'fruits, instrumentalities, or contraband' probative of criminal conduct."[27]

Robinson teaches that a search incident to a lawful arrest may always follow a custodial arrest. Coupled with the Court's statements that no matter what the initial reason is for the arrest, any search that produces fruits, instrumentalities, or contraband related to criminal conduct may be seized and be admitted even for proof of crimes unrelated to the subject of the initial arrest. As the Court had previously stated, law enforcement personnel who have just made an arrest do not have to "impotently stand aside" and ignore crimes that are being committed in their presence, merely because they are not connected to the original arrest or were unknown when the search began.

Even if the arrest is a "sham" or "pretext" to allow the police to search, as long as that arrest is supported by probable cause, the police who arrest the suspect may conduct a search incident to that arrest. In *Whren v. United States*, the Court noted that individual officers' "[s]ubjective intentions play no role in ordinary probable cause Fourth Amendment analysis,"[28] and referred to *Robinson* in stating that "a traffic arrest . . . [will] not be rendered invalid by the fact that it was 'a mere pretext for a narcotics search.' "[29]

E. Searching the "Area Within Immediate Control"

Even though a search incident to arrest begins in the context of making a lawful custodial arrest (with or without an arrest warrant)

---

[26] *Id.*, at 235.

[27] *Id.*, at 236, quoting Harris v. United States, 331 U.S. 145, 154–55 (1947).

[28] 517 U.S. 806, 813 (1996).

[29] Whren v. United States, 517 U.S. 806, 813 (1995). See *United States v. Robinson*, 414 U.S. at 221, n.1.

as a matter of routine and without particular grounds, what is found may be seized immediately and retained by the police if probable cause exists that the object is a fruit, instrumentality or evidence of crime.

When the arrest takes place in a premises, as opposed to a vehicle,[30] the police may search not only the person but also areas within the defendant's "immediate control,"[31] i.e., "the area from within which [the defendant] might gain possession of a weapon or destructible evidence."[32] The interpretation of this rule has allowed for the seizure of various items without an extended analysis of exactly how far the defendant was from the item when the seizure occurred.

There are numerous reasons for a search incident to arrest to include the area within the arrestee's control. Five of those reasons are to search for and seize: (1) weapons that the suspect may use to injure the arresting officer or others, or to effect an escape; (2) fruits of the crime for which the arrest was made, such as objects taken during a burglary; (3) instrumentalities used to commit the crime, such as the tools used to break a lock and enter a building; (4) contraband, the possession of which constitutes a crime, such as narcotics that are illegal to possess; and (5) evidence that the person arrested committed the charged or some other crime, e.g., bloody clothes.

What areas are considered to be within a suspect's "area of immediate control"? Should the concept be applied literally or more mechanically? As Professor LaFave has observed, lower courts may have a tendency to view every arrestee as a combination acrobat and magician who can free himself from restraints and suddenly gain access to a near or distant place.

To assess whether a search incident to arrest was within or beyond the scope of *Chimel*'s description, several factors are useful for thinking about the scope of the "area of immediate control" after the fact of a search in an area near to or distant from the suspect. Was the suspect restrained at the time of the extended search? If so, what legitimate purpose is served for a search beyond the suspect's person? How many officers were involved in the arrest, and what was their position in relation to the defendant at the time of the extended search? Did the suspect physically move toward a place or thing, and how difficult was it for him to gain access to a place like the interior of a closet or container? By applying these factors, the analysis

---

30 See § 6.3(A), discussing Search of a Vehicle Incident to Arrest.

31 Chimel v. California, 395 U.S. 752 (1969).

32 *Id.*

changes from a bright-line standard supposedly known to all, and instead substitutes a case-by-case determination about whether the specific search that occurred was limited to the "area within immediate control."

A categorical method to describe the "area within immediate control" avoids having to answer the questions posed in the above paragraph as analytical factors. *Robinson* answered the question about whether the police can open containers and seize their contents when they were on the suspect's person. Beyond items on the arrestee's person, it is usually assumed that police can open containers and seize the contents when the container is immediately associated with the arrestee, like a purse or bag that the suspect is holding (or was holding at the time of arrest). Police also may seize containers and their contents that are within the suspect's reach, contemporaneous with the arrest. However, if the police do not search the container immediately, they may seize it but search it only after they later obtain a search warrant.

If police training changed the procedure of handcuffing a suspect, the major rationales for a search incident to arrest, i.e., police protection and preservation of evidence, might disappear or no longer justify an automatic search incident to every arrest. For example, handcuffing a suspect with his hands behind him immediately after the arrest would produce far more difficulty for a suspect to harm the officer, escape the scene, and destroy evidence on his person. Handcuffing suspects differently would likely remove the need for area searches, because handcuffing would substantially restrict the suspect's reach so that nearby areas would be outside his control.

The Supreme Court has decided few "area within immediate control" cases. *Vale v. Louisiana*[33] held that when the police arrest a suspect outside his home, no part of the residence can be searched incident to his arrest. Police could still enter the home and search if they had a search warrant, if someone living there consents, or if exigent circumstances are present, e.g., they are chasing another suspect who ran into the house. A year after *Vale*, in the reverse factual scenario, *Coolidge v. New Hampshire*[34] held that a search incident to arrest theory for a suspect arrested in his home does not support a search of the suspect's vehicle in his driveway. As in *Vale*, the Court possibly could have upheld the search under other warrantless search theories.

---

[33] 399 U.S. 30 (1970).

[34] 403 U.S. 443 (1971).

A dozen years later, the Court decided *Washington v. Chrisman.*[35] A police officer approached a college student who was carrying liquor and appeared too young to possess it. Because the student was not carrying any identification, the officer accompanied him to his dormitory room to look at his student identification card. After entering the dorm room, the officer spotted marijuana in plain view. Without requiring the officer to show any risk of danger to himself or others, the Court approved the officer's authority to maintain custody of the student and to go with him to a different location than the site of the arrest. The student's immediate area of control had changed, and the officer seized the drugs as a search incident to an arrest. The Court held that it was "not 'unreasonable' under the Fourth Amendment for a police officer, as a matter of routine, to monitor the movements of an arrested person, as his judgment dictates, following an arrest."[36]

The Court has discussed the search incident to arrest issue in a digital context. *Riley v. California*[37] found that, because a search for digital information on a cell phone on the suspect's person fails to further any rationale for a warrantless search, police can seize the phone without any suspicion that it contains evidence of a crime. Privacy interests in the cell phone are diminished, because "[t]he sources of potential pertinent information are virtually unlimited."[38] The Court declined to apply *Robinson* to the warrantless search of a cell phone found on an arrestee's person, explaining that

> while *Robinson*'s categorical rule strikes the appropriate balance in the context of physical objects, neither of its rationales has much force with respect to digital content on cell phones. On the government interest side, *Robinson* concluded that the two risks identified in *Chimel*—harm to officers and destruction of evidence—are present in all custodial arrests. There are no comparable risks when the search is of digital data. In addition, *Robinson* regarded any privacy interests retained by an individual after arrest as significantly diminished by the fact of the arrest itself. Cell phones, however, place vast quantities of personal information literally in the hands of individuals. A search of the information on a cell phone bears little resemblance to the type of brief physical search considered in *Robinson*. . . .[39]

---

35 455 U.S. 1 (1982).

36 Washington v. Chrisman, 455 U.S. 1, 7 (1982).

37 573 U.S. 373 (2014).

38 Riley v. California, 573 U.S. 373 (2014).

39 *Id.*, at 386.

> Moreover, even though the search incident to arrest exception does not apply to cell phones, other case-specific exceptions may still justify a warrantless search of a particular phone. "One well-recognized exception applies when " 'the exigencies of the situation" make the needs of law enforcement so compelling that [a] warrantless search is objectively reasonable under the Fourth Amendment.' " Such exigencies could include the need to prevent the imminent destruction of evidence in individual cases, to pursue a fleeing suspect, and to assist persons who are seriously injured or are threatened with imminent injury.[40]

If it is necessary to look at a cell phone to protect themselves or others, police may seek a search warrant or rely on a warrantless search under exigent circumstances.[41] Or, if the police are concerned about the destruction of evidence, they can disable the phone by turning it off or removing the phone battery.[42]

Extending *Riley* to the discovery of the digital information elsewhere and to other digital devices may be reasonable. If a seizure of digital information is off-limits when the cell phone is on the arrestee's person, the same conclusion follows if the phone is within the area of the suspect's immediate control.[43] Whatever prohibition on seizing digital information applies to a cell phone would appear to likewise pertain to larger digital devices like a laptop computer.

F. Time Limits for a Search Incident to Arrest

The Court's decisions have created standards for delayed aspects of a search incident to arrest. As discussed, a search incident to arrest has two primary components: a search of the arrestee and a search of the area within the arrestee's immediate control. The former may occur later, perhaps even removed from the scene of the arrest, while the latter must be contemporaneous with the arrest.

Following arrest, the police usually transfer the suspect to a police detention facility for booking, during which they conduct a full body search. If he has not obtained his release by this point, he may trade his clothing for jail attire and is moved to a jail cell. The initial search of the person is justified as a search incident to arrest. If he is allowed to remain in his own clothing, may the police again search his clothing and any personal effects that were not taken for

---

40 *Id.*, at 401–02.

41 See Chapter 10, discussing Searches Under Exigent Circumstances.

42 *Id.*

43 See § 6.2(E), for a discussion of an object being within the suspect's immediate control.

safekeeping? In *United States v. Edwards*,[44] the defendant was arrested for trying to break into a post office by prying open a wooden window. After being placed in a cell, police retrieved his clothing, conducted a laboratory analysis, and found paint chips from the window. The paint chips were admitted at defendant's trial and led to his conviction. On appeal, the Court extended what the arresting officer could have done at the time of the arrest, instead of searching as a necessity suited only to the special circumstances of jail security and processing.

> [O]nce the accused is lawfully arrested and in custody, the effects in his possession at the place of detention that were subject to search and the time and place of his arrest may lawfully be searched and seized without a warrant even though a substantial period of time has elapsed between the arrest and subsequent administrative processing, on the one hand, and the taking of the property for use as evidence, on the other.[45]

The clothing search was proper regardless of whether the suspect's clothes were immediately seized and kept in the property room of the jail, or were not taken from the suspect until after his confinement. *Edwards* stands for the proposition that a search of the arrestee incident to an arrest may occur either at the time and place of the arrest or perhaps hours after the arrest at the police station, despite the fact that the police have ample time to obtain a search warrant to search the clothing. In either situation, the police have probable cause to seize the incriminating matter when a search of the suspect's effects produces evidence for trial.

Unlike a search of the person, a search of the area within the arrestee's immediate control must occur at or about the same time as the arrest. In *Preston v. United States*,[46] the defendant and his colleagues were arrested while riding in a vehicle, after which they were taken to the police station for booking and their vehicle was towed to a garage. There the police searched the passenger compartment of the vehicle and found two loaded guns. The Court invalidated the vehicle search incident to the arrest because it was "too remote in time or place to have been made as incidental to the arrest." *Chimel*'s rationale about police safety supports *Preston*'s conclusion. A later search of the area that was within the arrestee's immediate control at the time of the arrest is no longer conducted under the same conditions once the suspect is no longer there. The

---

44 415 U.S. 800 (1974).

45 United States v. Edwards, 415 U.S. 800, 807 (1974).

46 376 U.S. 364 (1964).

rationale that the arrestee could reach the area to obtain a weapon or destroy evidence has disappeared.

§ 6.3 Search of Containers Incident to Arrest

A. Search of a Vehicle Incident to Arrest

The scope of a search incident to arrest depends on the nature of the arrest. In noncustodial arrests, the officer can require the driver to exit the vehicle.[47] In custodial arrests, for purposes of safety or evidentiary concerns, "police may search a [passenger compartment of a] vehicle incident to a recent occupant's arrest only if the arrestee is within reaching distance of the passenger compartment at the time of the search or it is reasonable to believe the vehicle contains evidence of the offense of arrest."[48]

A skeptical police officer could do one of the following: (1) remove or order the arrestee from the vehicle, but leave the door open so that the passenger compartment remained within the arrestee's area of immediate control at the time of the search, or (2) "time" the arrest, so that the suspect is arrested immediately as he has opened the trunk of the vehicle.

In *New York v. Belton,*[49] the Court applied the warrantless search incident to arrest theory to a container taken by police from a vehicle, described as a "particular and problematic context" for applying the *Chimel* principle. The police stopped the vehicle, arrested the driver and passengers, and then searched a jacket and found drugs. The Court held that "when a policeman has made a lawful custodial arrest of the occupant of an automobile, he may, as a contemporaneous incident of that arrest, search the passenger compartment of that automobile." Using the *Belton* facts, the Court explained its holding.

> [T]he police may also examine the contents of any containers found within the passenger compartment, for if the passenger compartment is within reach of the arrestee, so also will containers in it be within his reach. . . Such a container may, of course, be searched whether it is open or closed.[50]

Almost thirty years later, the Court in *Arizona v. Gant* took note of an assumption in *Belton* "that articles inside the relatively narrow compass of the passenger compartment of an automobile are in fact

---

47 See § 6.2(B), Lawful Arrest.

48 Arizona v. Gant, 556 U.S. 332, 351 (2009).

49 453 U.S. 454 (1981).

50 New York v. Belton, 453 U.S. 454, 460–61 (1981).

generally, even if not inevitably, within 'the area into which an arrestee might reach.' "[51]

In *Thornton v. United States*,[52] the police approached the defendant shortly after he had exited his car, because the car's tags were for a different vehicle. When illegal drugs were found on his person, he was arrested, and a search of his nearby car produced a weapon. Looking back, the Court held that *Belton* applies "even when an officer does not make contact until the person has left the vehicle."[53] *Thornton* explicitly expanded *Belton* to permit a search of the passenger compartment for either a person still in the car or a person who *recently* was there.

> [W]hile an arrestee's status as a "recent occupant" may turn on his temporal or spatial relationship to the car at the time of the arrest and search, it certainly does not turn on whether he was inside or outside the car at the moment that the officer first initiated contact with him.[54]

The reference to "temporal or spatial relationship" suggests that a person is a "recent" occupant of the car when the officer contacts him either soon after he exits the car or while he remains physically close to the vehicle.

Five years later in *Gant*, the police were investigating the defendant for drug trafficking when they saw him return to a residence where he had been on the same day. As he left his car, one officer approached him while he was 10–12 feet from his car, arrested and handcuffed him, and put him in the backseat of the police car. With the suspect in the patrol car, police searched Gant's car and found a gun and a bag of drugs.

Instead of maintaining *Belton*'s scope of a search incident to arrest in a vehicle, *Gant* narrowed its applicability to two circumstances: First, "*Chimel*'s rationale authorizes police to search a vehicle incident to a recent occupant's arrest only when the arrestee is unsecured and within reaching distance of the passenger compartment at the time of the search,"[55] i.e., there is a "possibility of access" to an object inside the vehicle. Second, "circumstances unique to the vehicle context justify a search incident to a lawful arrest when it is 'reasonable to believe evidence relevant to the crime of arrest might be found in the vehicle.' "[56] Therefore, a vehicle is

---

51 *Arizona v. Gant*, 556 U.S. at 341, quoting *New York v. Belton*, 453 U.S. at 460.

52 541 U.S. 615 (2004).

53 Thornton v. United States, 541 U.S. 615, 617 (2004).

54 *Id.*, at 622.

55 *Arizona v. Gant*, 556 U.S. at 343.

56 *Id.*

subject to a search incident to a lawful arrest even though probable cause to search is lacking, and there is no risk of evidence destruction by the defendant.[57]

Gant offered some assistance about the meaning of "possibility of access." The "possibility" is determined as of "the time of the search," rather than an earlier time such as the time of his arrest or a traffic stop. Regardless of the timing of access, the arrestee's access to the contents of a locked container in the passenger compartment, such as the glove compartment, would not be possible. Equally important, *Gant*'s meaning of "access" for a recent occupant of the vehicle is possible only under the first circumstance, described above: "when the arrestee is unsecured and within reaching distance"[58] of the object. Even if an arrestee is not handcuffed, the search of the interior of the vehicle cannot occur unless he also has access to that area.

> Because officers have many means of ensuring the safe arrest of vehicle occupants, it will be the rare case in which an officer is unable to fully effectuate an arrest so that a real possibility of access to the arrestee's vehicle remains.[59]

If it is indeed a rare situation, a police officer could use a pretext arrest to search a person[60] immediately after the arrest, but not the area within his immediate control, i.e., the passenger compartment. By narrowing the scope of *Belton*, the Court ruled that the search of Gant's vehicle's passenger compartment after he was arrested, handcuffed, and secured in a patrol car was unreasonable.

Besides the "possibility of access" concept, the *Gant* also narrowed *Belton* to permit a search of a vehicle incident to arrest only when "the offense of arrest will supply a basis for searching the passenger compartment of an arrestee's vehicle and any containers therein." *Gant* permitted a search when "it is reasonable to believe evidence relevant to the crime of arrest might be found in the vehicle."[61]

This prong is narrower than "possibility of access," because it relates to information that will assist in proving only the crime for which the person is now under arrest. The Court offered no support for this *Gant* standard. Except in a case like *Gant* where there is no evidence (given that the arrest was for driving on a suspended license), the second prong appears to relate to a case when evidence

---

57 *Id.*, at 344.

58 *Id.*, at 343.

59 *Id.*, at 343 n.4.

60 See § 6.2(D), discussing the search of the arrestee's person, incident to arrest.

61 *Arizona v. Gant*, 556 U.S. at 344, 346.

of the offense is not in the vehicle or there is no risk of evidence destruction.

Does "reasonable to believe" mean the same thing as probable cause? If so, it is the same standard as for vehicle searches. If not, is it a lower or higher standard than probable cause? Is "reasonable to believe" a standard only for the crime of arrest? If so, what justifies the difference between *Gant* and *Robinson*, where the search of the person can be for evidence of any criminal behavior?

B. Search of Other Containers Incident to Arrest

While the interior of a vehicle may be searched as a warrantless search incident to arrest, the trunk of the vehicle cannot.[62] Of course, the search of the interior may produce evidence that creates the probable cause to search the trunk or other parts of the vehicle.[63] As mentioned, when the defendant is arrested as he is placing an object in an open trunk, a search of the trunk area incident to the arrest is proper.[64]

When the driver of a vehicle is arrested and the passenger compartment is being lawfully searched incident to that arrest, the police automatically may order any passenger to exit the vehicle.[65] Generally, for their safety, the police then may conduct a patdown search of that passenger, despite having no independent suspicion that the passenger has engaged in criminal conduct.

As discussed, the police may search the defendant's person and clothing incident to arrest. Some restrictions, however, apply to the search of possessions like containers and other personal effects. Any container may be searched contemporaneous with the arrest if it is within the defendant's immediate control. When a search incident to an arrest turns up a container in a vehicle, the police may search the container without a warrant even though they may lack probable cause to search the entire vehicle.[66]

Beyond the context of an arrest made while the arrestee is in a vehicle or adjacent to it, incident to the arrest a container on the arrestee's person can be opened and searched, as is true of a container that the arrestee is holding or is within the area of the arrestee's immediate control. In each of the foregoing situations, the arrestee had access to the container's contents.

---

62 New York v. Belton, 453 U.S. 454 (1981).

63 See Chapter 7, discussing Vehicle Searches.

64 See § 6.3(A), discussing searches of vehicles incident to arrest.

65 Maryland v. Wilson, 519 U.S. 408 (1997).

66 California v. Acevedo, 500 U.S. 565 (1991).

§ 6.4 "Protective Sweep" Beyond the Area Within Immediate Control

What happens if the police see another person or a container that is beyond the arrestee's area of immediate control? When the police make an arrest or execute a search warrant, they may find other persons present, causing the police to fear for their safety, or for the disappearance or destruction of evidence. A protective sweep is a quick and limited search of premises incident to an arrest. During the protective sweep, the police may seize evidence in plain view, even if they find no other persons to arrest or detain.

In *Maryland v. Buie*,[67] the police arrested defendant as he emerged from the basement of his home, and an officer went to the basement to make sure that no one else was there. In the basement, the officer found a red running suit in plain view that implicated the defendant. The Court held that the officer acted properly in entering the basement, because the police are entitled "in such circumstances to take reasonable steps to ensure their safety after, and while making, the arrest."[68]

Buie gives the police investigative powers beyond *Chimel*'s area of immediate control. The Court described two types of protective sweeps incident to an arrest. The first type allows officers, "as a precautionary matter and without probable cause or reasonable suspicion, [to] look in closets and other spaces immediately adjoining the place of arrest from which an attack could be immediately launched."[69] The second type allows officers to undertake a broader search of places beyond spaces immediately adjoining the place of arrest, but only if they have a "reasonable suspicion" to search further in a building.

Although the Court did not define the phrase "immediately adjoining," it did offer a general description of "reasonable suspicion" that exists for the second type of protective sweep: if there are "articulable facts which, taken together with the rational inferences from those facts, would warrant a reasonably prudent officer in believing that the area to be swept harbors an individual posing a danger to those on the arrest scene."[70] Factually, a reasonable

---

[67] 494 U.S. 325 (1990).

[68] Maryland v. Buie, 494 U.S. 325, 334 (1990). In a similar case, police arrested defendant at the bottom of the basement stairs, and ordered him to come up the stairs where he was searched and handcuffed. Because he first submitted to police authority at the bottom of the basement stairs, police performed a valid protective sweep of the room immediately adjoining the area at the bottom of the stairs. United States v. Ackerman, 87 F.4th 925 (8th Cir. 2023).

[69] *Id.*, at 330.

[70] *Id.*, at 334.

suspicion may exist if police think that other persons are involved in the crime of arrest, or if they hear a strange noise suggesting that others are waiting nearby to attack them.

One way to think about a protective sweep is to imagine concentric circles around the place of the arrest, where *Robinson* permits a full search of the arrestee. The first small circle around the arrestee represents the area within the arrestee's immediate control where *Chimel* permits seizure of anything. A somewhat larger circle away from the arrestee represents a second area—immediately adjacent to the place of arrest for the first type of protective sweep; after *Buie,* a search of that area is automatic. The last and potentially largest area is beyond the area of the first protective sweep where the police can conduct a second protective sweep for persons, weapons, or evidence, but only if they have reasonable suspicion. Presumably, the police may seize anything they see in plain view.

The *Chimel* principle does not apply to protective sweeps for two reasons. First, the facts of *Chimel* were "concerned with a full-blown search of the entire house for evidence of the crime for which the arrest was made, . . . not the more limited intrusion contemplated by a protective sweep." Second, "the justification for the search incident to arrest [in *Chimel*] was the threat posed by . . . unseen third parties in the house."[71] Because *Buie* also rejected a bright-line rule that would apply in all indoor arrests,[72] the legality of protective sweeps is examined case-by-case.

What legal standard allows the police to sweep? What is the nature of that sweep? For the first type, the police do not need any information beyond the probable cause used to arrest the person. The second type of protective sweep requires the same type of reasonable suspicion used to evaluate a stop-and frisk. The reasonable suspicion standard, discussed above, is "no more and no less than was required in *Terry*."[73] In court, police must explain why they suspected that another person was there and posed a danger to them, even if they did not find anyone but did seize incriminating objects in plain view.

Once reasonable suspicion exists, the sweep "may extend only to a cursory inspection of those spaces where a person may be found"[74] and includes a weapon search in the grab area of a person deemed by agents to be dangerous. The sweep lasts only until the standard no

---

71 *Id.*, at 336.

72 *Id.*, at 330.

73 *Id.*, at 334. See Chapter 9, discussing Stop and Frisk.

74 *Id.*, at 335.

longer exists or "no longer than it takes to complete the arrest and depart the premises."[75]

§ 6.5 Search of and into the Defendant's Body

In addition to the search of a defendant's clothing for evidence, police have the authority to inspect the defendant's body incident to arrest and, to a more limited extent, intrude into the body. The privilege against self-incrimination offers no protection against compulsion to submit to fingerprinting, photographing, to write or speak for identification, or to take a sobriety test. While such procedures may not violate the Fifth Amendment,[76] they may violate the Fourth Amendment. However, tests conducted by private persons for diagnostic purposes do not involve Fourth Amendment considerations.[77]

A. Inspection of Defendant's Body

Incident to a lawful arrest, the police may conduct inspections *of* the body as part of the general authority to search. This includes fingerprinting, fingernail scrapings, or taking a sample of pubic and cranial hair.[78] At the trial itself, an accused may be required to take the stand so that he may be observed, e.g., to remove a veil, visor, mask, glasses; to exhibit hands; to roll up a sleeve to show a tattoo; to submit to the taking of fingerprints; to remove a coat and shirt to show scars; to allow inspection of his face for identifying marks; to move his feet into view; or to put on a garment, hat, or cap.

B. Intrusion into Defendant's Body

Intrusions *into* the body require not only a showing of probable cause but also require the police to establish the necessity of obtaining the evidence without a warrant. Blood tests are obviously an intrusive type of search. Such tests are allowed if: (1) the process is reasonable and is performed in a reasonable manner; (2) there is a clear indication that in fact the evidence will be found; and (3) exigent circumstances existed, making it impractical to obtain a search warrant.[79] These requirements might exist, for example, following a lawful arrest where the test of the blood is for alcohol which rapidly diminishes over time.[80]

---

75 *Id.*, at 336.

76 See, e.g., Pennsylvania v. Muniz, 496 U.S. 582 (1990) (lack of muscular coordination via slurring words); United States v. Dionisio, 410 U.S. 1 (1973) (voice sample); Gilbert v. California, 388 U.S. 263 (1967) (handwriting sample).

77 See § 1.3(A), discussing Private Actors.

78 See § 7.4(C), discussing DNA Testing.

79 Schmerber v. California, 384 U.S. 757, 765 n.9, 770, 771 (1966).

80 *Id.*, at 770.

However, the police cannot take a blood sample in every case from a drunk driving suspect, without first asking a judge to sign off on the procedure. The Court in *Missouri v. McNeely*[81] held that the "natural dissipation of alcohol in the [suspect's] bloodstream does not constitute an exigency in every case sufficient to justify conducting a blood test without a warrant."[82]

> BAC evidence from a drunk-driving suspect naturally dissipates over time in a gradual and relatively predictable manner. Moreover, because a police officer must typically transport a drunk-driving suspect to a medical facility and obtain the assistance of someone with appropriate medical training before conducting a blood test, some delay between the time of the arrest or accident and the time of the test is inevitable regardless of whether police officers are required to obtain a warrant.[83]

Most States have statutorily adopted means by which police can obtain a warrant much quicker using electronic communications.[84] The Court recognized that the reasonableness of the procedure is also a consideration which obviously varies with the circumstances, e.g., pumping the stomach.[85]

A State may not criminalize a person's refusal to take to a blood test in the absence of a warrant, because warrantless *blood* tests incident to an arrest violate the Fourth Amendment. Blood tests implicate privacy interests because they are both invasive and produce a sample that can be preserved to obtain further information. The penalty for refusing to submit to such testing is the possible revocation of the operator's license and the ability of the State to prove lack of consent at a hearing.[86]

By contrast, in *Birchfield v. North Dakota*,[87] the Court discussed how warrantless *breath* tests are far less invasive than blood tests and seek information that is routinely exposed to the public.[88]

> Blood tests are a different matter. They "require piercing the skin" and extract a part of the subject's body. . . or many, the process is not one they relish. It is significantly more intrusive than blowing into a tube. Perhaps that is

81 569 U.S. 141 (2013).

82 Missouri v. McNeely, 569 U.S. 141, 165 (2013).

83 *Id.*, at 153.

84 *Id.*, at 154–55.

85 Rochin v. California, 342 U.S. 165 (1952).

86 South Dakota v. Neville, 459 U.S. 553 (1983).

87 579 U.S. 438 (2016).

88 Birchfield v. North Dakota, 579 U.S. 438 (2016).

> why many States' implied consent laws, including Minnesota's, specifically prescribe that breath tests be administered in the usual drunk-driving case instead of blood tests or give motorists a measure of choice over which test to take. . . .
>
> In addition, a blood test, unlike a breath test, places in the hands of law enforcement authorities a sample that can be preserved and from which it is possible to extract information beyond a simple BAC reading. Even if the law enforcement agency is precluded from testing the blood for any purpose other than to measure BAC, the potential remains and may result in anxiety for the person tested.[89]

The Court further observed that the State had "offered no satisfactory justification for demanding the more intrusive" blood test alternative without a warrant.

Generally, intrusions of the body to extract evidence depend on a case-by-case approach, in which the individual's interests in privacy and security are weighed against society's interests in conducting the procedure.[90] Whether surgical removal of evidence is reasonable requires consideration of the medical procedures and risks related to the surgery as well as the existence of a compelling need for the evidence, e.g., the existence of significant other evidence connecting the defendant with a crime.[91]

---

89 *Id.*, at 464.

90 Winston v. Lee, 470 U.S. 753 (1985).

91 *Id.*

Chapter 7

VEHICLE AND INVENTORY SEARCHES

Table of Sections

§ 7.1 Introduction

Police may search a vehicle if they have probable cause to believe that a vehicle contains contraband or evidence of other criminal activity. Generally, they do not need a warrant.[1] (Recall that the probable cause to search may be shown from a variety of sources, including police observations or informants' tips.) A vehicle search may also occur incident to arrest. The lawfulness of a search incident

1 California v. Acevedo, 500 U.S. 565 (1991). See Maryland v. Dyson, 527 U.S. 465 (1999) (no separate finding of exigency necessary to invoke vehicle exception; probable cause is sufficient).

to arrest depends on the lawfulness of the arrest.[2] In addition, searches may be conducted where the vehicle is subject to forfeiture or impoundment.

The following sections treat the various aspects relating to vehicle searches. Thereafter, there is a discussion of inventory searches, first of a vehicle and then of arrested and detained persons.

§ 7.2 Requirements for a Vehicle Search

A. What Is a Vehicle?

In *California v. Carney*,[3] a mobile home was parked in a public parking lot with the engine off. The curtains were closed to block any outside view of the interior, and there was no indication that it was about to depart prior to a drug agent's entry where he found evidence of drug activity. The Court treated the mobile home like an automobile, concluding that its mobility is similar to an automobile and therefore is subject to the diminished expectation of privacy associated with automobiles. That the mobile home "possessed some, if not many of the attributes of a home" made no difference, as it was still "readily available" and subject to regulations and inspections as a vehicle usable on the public streets. It does not matter whether a vehicle is being driven at the time of a stop and subsequent search, as long as the vehicle is capable of moving and therefore has "ready mobility." An objective observer would conclude that it was being used not as a residence, but as a vehicle.[4]

> We need not pass on the application of the vehicle exception to a motor home that is situated in a way or place that objectively indicates that it is being used as a residence. Among the factors that might be relevant in determining whether a warrant would be required in such a circumstance is its location, whether the vehicle is readily mobile or instead, for instance, elevated on blocks, whether the vehicle is licensed, whether it is connected to utilities, and whether it has convenient access to a public road.[5]

Carney demonstrated that the vehicle exception is grounded in a hypothetical, but not real, exigency. A motor home is a vehicle as long as it is theoretically and presumptively mobile; it may be searched even when the police have arrested the driver, taken the key, and possessed the parking lot ticket necessary to relocate the vehicle. "[T]he pervasive schemes of regulation, which necessarily lead to

---

2 See Chapter 6, discussing Search Incident to Arrest.

3 471 U.S. 386 (1985).

4 California v. Carney, 471 U.S. 386, 393 (1985).

5 *Id.*, at 394 n.3.

reduced expectations of privacy, and the exigencies attendant to ready mobility justify searches without prior recourse to the authority of a magistrate so long as the overriding standard of probable cause is met."[6]

B. Rationales Supporting the Vehicle Exception

Two rationales support the vehicle exception to obtaining a search warrant. The Court in *Chambers v. Maroney*[7] described how and why vehicle searches differ from the other search warrant exceptions.

> Neither *Carroll* [*v. United States*] nor other cases in this Court require or suggest that in every conceivable circumstance the search of an auto even with probable cause may be made without the extra protection for privacy that a warrant affords. But the circumstances that furnish probable cause to search a particular auto for particular articles are most often unforeseeable; moreover, the opportunity to search is fleeting since a car is readily movable. Where this is true, as in *Carroll* and the case before us now, if an effective search is to be made at any time, either the search must be made immediately without a warrant or the car itself must be seized and held without a warrant for whatever period is necessary to obtain a warrant for the search. . . .
>
> Arguably, because of the preference for a magistrate's judgment, only the immobilization of the car should be permitted until a search warrant is obtained; arguably, only the "lesser" intrusion is permissible until the magistrate authorizes the "greater." But which is the "greater" and which the "lesser" intrusion is itself a debatable question and the answer may depend on a variety of circumstances. For constitutional purposes, we see no difference between on the one hand seizing and holding a car before presenting the probable cause issue to a magistrate and on the other hand carrying out an immediate search without a warrant. Given probable cause to search, either course is reasonable under the Fourth Amendment.
>
> On the facts before us, the blue station wagon could have been searched on the spot when it was stopped since there was probable cause to search and it was a fleeting target for a search. The probable cause factor still obtained

---

6 *Id.*, at 392.

7 399 U.S. 42 (1970).

> at the station house and so did the mobility of the car unless the Fourth Amendment permits a warrantless seizure of the car and the denial of its use to anyone until a warrant is secured. . . The same consequences may not follow where there is unforeseeable cause to search a house. But as *Carroll* held, for the purposes of the Fourth Amendment there is a constitutional difference between houses and cars.[8]

For the Court, the inherent, ready mobility of vehicles was persuasive to its conclusion that a warrantless exception was necessary for vehicle searches. The nature of vehicles provides the exigent circumstances, i.e., generally being readily mobile, the process of obtaining a search warrant is impractical.

The Court also recognizes that a vehicle is subject to less rigorous warrant requirements "because the expectation of privacy with respect to one's automobile is significantly less than that relating to one's home or office" due to the "pervasive regulation" of vehicles on the highways.[9]

> All States require vehicles to be registered and operators to be licensed. States and localities have enacted extensive and detailed codes regulating the condition and manner in which motor vehicles may be operated on public streets and highways. Automobiles periodically undergo official inspection, and they are often taken into police custody in the interests of public safety.[10]

"Pervasive regulation" includes not only the possibility of periodic inspections, but also licensing requirements, e.g., police stop and examine vehicles when license plates or inspection stickers have expired.

Several cases illustrate the Court's consistency regarding a defendant's reduced expectation of privacy while his vehicle is stopped and searched. Given the mobility and diminished expectation of privacy in a vehicle, the existence of probable cause alone justifies an immediate warrantless search "before the vehicle and its occupants become unavailable."[11] This rationale rarely invalidates a vehicle search, even though it is apparent in hindsight that a vehicle's mobility was restricted. For example, in *Chambers*,[12]

---

8 Chambers v. Maroney, 399 U.S. 42, 50–52 (1970).

9 South Dakota v. Opperman, 428 U.S. 364, 367 (1976).

10 United States v. Chadwick, 433 U.S. 1, 13 (1977), abrogated by California v. Acevedo, 500 U.S. 565 (1991) (citations omitted).

11 *California v. Carney*, 471 U.S. at 393.

12 399 U.S. 42 (1970).

a vehicle was taken to the police station after the driver was arrested and jailed. The Court upheld that delayed search of the car at the police station even though, while it was detained, neither the defendant nor anyone else had access to it.

A warrantless but limited intrusion into a vehicle is also possible without probable cause under the Fourth Amendment when important government interests are at stake, i.e., some examinations of the exterior of vehicles do not qualify as traditional searches, even where additional illumination is used to assist the police in looking at the vehicle's exterior. In *Cardwell v. Lewis*,[13] as part of an ongoing murder investigation, the suspect responded to a police request that he return to the police station. There, police interrogated him further and subsequently arrested him that day on the basis of probable cause previously established.

A day later, police removed Lewis's vehicle from a commercial parking lot to an impoundment lot. A technician examined only the exterior of Lewis's car where he removed paint chips that matched the paint from the victim's vehicle and examined the tread of Lewis's tires. Police conducted these searches to strengthen their theory that Lewis had used his vehicle to push the deceased's car over an embankment. Responding to Lewis's argument that no exigent circumstances existed for the search because probable cause to search had existed for weeks, the Court upheld the seizure of evidence because Lewis had no expectation of privacy in his vehicle.

> One has a lesser expectation of privacy in a motor vehicle because its function is transportation and it seldom serves as one's residence or as the repository of personal effects. A car has little capacity for escaping public scrutiny. It travels public thoroughfares where its occupants and its contents are in plain view.[14]

Later language from the Court reinforced the importance of the inherent exigent circumstances associated with a vehicle search, as well as the reduced expectation of privacy. "[T]he justification to conduct such a warrantless search does not vanish once the car has been immobilized; nor does it depend upon a reviewing court's assessment of the likelihood in each particular case that the car would have been driven away, or that its contents would have been tampered with, during the period required for the police to obtain a warrant."[15]

---

13 417 U.S. 583 (1974).

14 Cardwell v. Lewis, 417 U.S. 583, 590 (1974).

15 Michigan v. Thomas, 458 U.S. 259, 261 (1982).

> [I]f an immediate search on the scene could be conducted, but not one at the station if the vehicle is impounded, police often simply would search the vehicle on the street—at no advantage to the occupants, yet possibly at certain costs to the police.[16]

Similar to *Cardwell*, a dozen years later the Court found that there is no reasonable expectation of privacy in viewing a dashboard vehicle identification number (VIN). In *New York v. Class*,[17] police stopped the defendant after observing him commit two traffic offenses, driving in excess of the speed limit, and driving with a cracked windshield. When one of the officers opened the car door, he "intruded" into the passenger compartment, and moved some papers on the dashboard to look at the VIN. After he noticed a gun handle under the driver's seat, the officer seized the gun and arrested Class for criminal possession of a weapon. The defendant had no reasonable expectation of privacy in the VIN, which is an important part of the government's "pervasive regulation" of vehicles that includes federal and State laws that the VIN be visible in plain view.

> [I]t is unreasonable to have an expectation of privacy in an object required by law to be located in a place ordinarily in plain view from the exterior of the automobile. The VIN's mandated visibility makes it more similar to the exterior of the car than to the trunk or glove compartment. The exterior of a car, of course, is thrust into the public eye, and thus to examine it does not constitute a "search."[18]

The Court brushed aside the officer's act of moving the papers that covered the VIN, because "efforts to restrict access to an area do not generate a reasonable expectation of privacy where none would otherwise exist."[19]

While an officer usually would not ask a driver to exit the vehicle for these traffic offenses, the Court recognized the necessary discretion for officers to remove suspects from the vehicle even in the absence of any suspicion about weapons being within reach. (In *Pennsylvania v. Mimms*,[20] the defendant voluntarily exited his vehicle.) A concern for the officer's safety justified the limited police entry into the car to uncover the VIN on the dashboard, instead of having the driver reenter the car to do so. Because the intrusion was not considered a search, the gun found while looking at the VIN was

---

16 United States v. Ross, 456 U.S. 798, 807 n.9 (1982).

17 475 U.S. 106 (1986).

18 New York v. Class, 475 U.S. 106, 114 (1986).

19 *Id.*

20 434 U.S. 106 (1977).

admissible. The officer's search for the gun was "sufficiently unintrusive"[21] after seeing the suspect commit two traffic offenses, as the Court expressed justifiable concerns for the officers' safety.

Because of the reduced expectation of privacy, attaching a beeper to an item which is then placed in a car does not constitute a search or a seizure where the beeper is used merely to monitor the car's progress. In *United States v. Knotts,*[22] after a corporate executive expressed concern that one of its former employees was stealing chemicals from a different company, the latter company installed a beeper inside a five gallon container of a precursor chemical used to manufacture illicit drugs. Information from the beeper as the container traveled around the area led to the issuance of a search warrant.

Executing the warrant produced component chemicals, a laboratory to manufacture amphetamine, and methamphetamine, along with the five-gallon container that held the beeper. The use of the beeper to monitor the movement of the car made *Knotts* an easy case, because like a flashlight, the beeper simply augmented "the sensory faculties bestowed upon" the police "at birth with such enhancement as science and technology afforded them in this case."[23] Because monitoring the beeper signals did not invade any legitimate expectation of privacy that the defendant had, no search or seizure occurred.[24]

Recently, in *Byrd v. United States*[25], the defendant's girlfriend rented a vehicle and turned it over to the defendant who began a trip of several hundred miles. Following a traffic stop, the police searched the trunk of the rented vehicle and found a substantial amount of heroin. The trial court denied his motion to suppress, ruling that he had no expectation of privacy in the vehicle because he was not listed as an authorized driver on the rental agreement. The Court held "that, as a general rule, someone in otherwise lawful possession of a rental car has a reasonable expectation of privacy in it even if the rental agreement does not list him or her as an authorized driver."[26] Whether an unauthorized driver's use of the vehicle may void the agreement's insurance coverage "has little to do with whether one would have a reasonable expectation of privacy in the rental car if,

---

21 *New York v. Class*, 475 U.S. at 119.

22 460 U.S. 276 (1983).

23 United States v. Knotts, 460 U.S. 276, 282 (1983).

24 *Id.*, at 285.

25 584 U.S. 395 (2017).

26 Byrd v. United States, 584 U.S. 395 (2017).

for example, he or she otherwise has lawful possession of and control over the car."[27]

The reduced expectation of privacy in vehicles remains a consistent rationale to justify warrantless vehicle searches. However, the exigent circumstance foundation for warrantless vehicle searches disappeared over time, until *United v. Chadwick* noted that warrantless vehicle searches based on probable cause had been accepted "in cases in which the possibilities of the vehicle's being removed or evidence in it destroyed were remote, if not non-existent."[28] Eventually, the Court explicitly stated that warrantless vehicle searches do "not have a separate exigency requirement."[29]

C. Vehicle Search for Evidence Not Incident to Arrest

Probable cause to search a vehicle may involve a search for a specific item instead of a search of the entire vehicle. In *California v. Acevedo*,[30] the Court held that even though the police lack probable cause to search the vehicle as a whole, but do have probable cause to believe that one or more containers holds contraband or evidence, the police may search a container located within a vehicle and need not seize and detain the container pending the issuance of a search warrant.

More frequently, however, finding one piece of evidence in plain view provides probable cause to search the entire vehicle. The right to search in this circumstance is not dependent on the right to arrest; instead the right to search the vehicle is dependent on the probable cause the seizing officer has for believing that the contents of the vehicle offend the law.[31]

D. Scope of Vehicle Search

In *United States v. Ross*,[32] the Court held that "the scope of the warrantless search authorized by that exception is no broader and no narrower than a magistrate could legitimately authorize by warrant. If probable cause justifies the search of a lawfully stopped vehicle, it

---

27 *Id.*, at 1529.

28 United States v. Chadwick, 433 U.S. 1, 12 (1977), *quoting* Cady v. Dombrowski, 413 U.S. 433, 441–42 (1973). In cases between *Chadwick* and *Acevedo*, the Court approved warrantless vehicle searches, without exigent circumstances. See, e.g., Florida v. Meyers, 466 U.S. 380 (1984) (vehicle was stored in secure area); Michigan v. Thomas, 458 U.S. 259 (1982) (warrantless vehicle search, without exigent circumstances).

29 Maryland v. Dyson, 527 U.S. 465, 466 (1999).

30 500 U.S. 565 (1991).

31 Chambers v. Maroney, 399 U.S. 42 (1970).

32 456 U.S. 798 (1982).

justifies the search of every part of the vehicle and its contents that may conceal the object of the search."[33] "Every part" of the vehicle includes the interior of the passenger compartment, as well as the trunk, the engine area, and beneath the surfaces of the upholstery. In a footnote, *Ross* emphasized the practical importance of completing the entire search without an interval to apply for a search warrant, e.g., to open a container. Given the broad scope of a vehicle search, the issue of probable cause to search is crucial.

> The practical considerations that justify a warrantless search of an automobile continue to apply until the entire search of the automobile and its contents has been completed. Arguably, the entire vehicle itself (including its upholstery) could be searched without a warrant, with all wrapped articles and containers found during that search then taken to a magistrate. But prohibiting police from opening immediately a container in which the object of the search is most likely to be found and instead forcing them first to comb the entire vehicle would actually exacerbate the intrusion on privacy interests. Moreover, until the container itself was opened the police could never be certain that the contraband was not secreted in a yet undiscovered portion of the vehicle; thus in every case in which a container was found, the vehicle would need to be secured while a warrant was obtained.[34]

Until *California v. Acevedo*,[35] the Court had grappled with whether containers found in vehicles could be opened immediately because they had been found in a larger container (the vehicle), or whether the contents of any container found in a vehicle could not be revealed until the issuance of a search warrant.

Acevedo went to a drug dealer's apartment and police observed him as he emerged after a brief stay with a large brown paper package of drugs that matched the appearance of packages that had been mailed from Hawaii. After he placed the package in the trunk of his car and started to drive away, local police officers stopped the car because they feared that both Acevedo and the drugs would disappear. Police opened the trunk and then the package and found the drugs.

Charged with drug trafficking, Acevedo's motion to suppress the drugs was denied. Citing *Chadwick*, the State appellate court held that it was permissible to seize the package from the vehicle but a

---

33 United States v. Ross, 456 U.S. 798, 825 (1982).

34 *Id.*, at 821 n.28.

35 500 U.S. 565 (1991).

search warrant was a prerequisite to opening the package. The appellate court recognized the dichotomy of the case law at that time. "[I]f there is probable cause to search a car, then the entire car—including any closed container found therein—may be searched without a warrant, but if there is probable cause only as to a container in the car, the container may be held but not searched until a warrant is obtained."[36] The Court granted certiorari to clarify the mess its prior decisions had created.

In *Ross*, the police had probable cause to search a vehicle trunk for contraband, during which search they unexpectedly discovered a closed paper bag. In *Acevedo*, the police had probable cause to search the trunk but only so they could find the did not the closed paper bag. After reviewing that case law, the Court stated, without elaboration, that the prior decisions had "confused courts and police officers and impeded law enforcement."[37] Previously, the Court had "drawn a curious line between the search of an automobile that coincidentally turns up a container and the search of a container that coincidentally turns up in an automobile."[38] "The discrepancy between the two rules has led to confusion for law enforcement officers."[39] The protections of the Fourth Amendment must not turn on such coincidences."[40] "We conclude that it is better to adopt one clear-cut rule to govern automobile searches and eliminate the warrant requirement for closed containers set forth in [*Arkansas v.*] *Sanders*."[41] The Court saw

> no principled distinction in terms of either the privacy expectation or the exigent circumstances between the paper bag found by the police in *Ross* and the paper bag found by the police here, [and with respect to the latter comment elaborates that] a container found after a general search of the automobile and a container found in a car after a limited search for the container are equally easy for the police to store and for the suspect to hide or destroy.[42]

The Court summarized its holding: "The interpretation of the *Carroll* doctrine set forth in *Ross* now applies to all searches of containers found in an automobile. In other words, the police may search without a warrant if their search is supported by probable

---

[36] California v. Acevedo, 500 U.S. 565, 568 (1991), *citing* People v. Acevedo, 216 Cal.App.3d 586, 592 (1989).

[37] *Id.*, at 577.

[38] *Id.*, at 580.

[39] *Id.*, at 577.

[40] *Id.*, at 580.

[41] *Id.*, at 579.

[42] *Id.*, at 574.

cause."[43] Police may not search the entire vehicle when they have probable cause to search only a specific container inside the vehicle. If there is probable cause to search one or more containers but not search the entire vehicle, the police may search the container without a warrant.[44] Indeed, police officers with probable cause to believe that there is contraband in a vehicle can conduct a warrantless search of all containers in the vehicle that could hold the contraband, regardless of who owns the containers.

However broad the vehicle exception may be, it does not include the right of the police to enter a home or its curtilage (where a vehicle is parked) to access a vehicle without a warrant. In *Collins v. Virginia*,[45] the Court noted that the vehicle exception expands no further than the vehicle. Thus, in *Collins*, the police could not use the vehicle exception to enter the curtilage to search beneath a tarpaulin that covered a motorcycle.

> "Just as an officer must have a lawful right of access to any contraband he discovers in plain view in order to seize it . . . [or] to arrest a person in his home, so, too, an officer must have a lawful right of access to a vehicle in order to search it pursuant to the automobile exception," which therefore "does not justify an intrusion on a person's separate and substantial Fourth Amendment interest in his home and curtilage."[46]

Before *Mapp v. Ohio* brought notoriety to the Warren Court's decisions, the Court had decided that, during a vehicle search, the police do not automatically have the right to search a passenger in the vehicle. *United States v. Di Re*[47] stated that the necessity for searching passengers was not greater than the need "for searching guests of a house for which a search warrant had issued."[48] If the police have probable cause to search a vehicle for items that a passenger can conceal, *Di Re*'s logic is unsound.

A half century later, the Court distinguished *Di Re* and held in *Wyoming v. Houghton*[49] that when probable cause exists to search the vehicle under the vehicle exception, it may extend to a search of the vehicle's occupants. "When there is probable cause to search for contraband in a car, it is reasonable for police officers—like customs officials in the founding era—to examine packages and containers

43 *Id.*, at 579.

44 California v. Acevedo, 500 U.S. 565 (1991).

45 584 U.S. 586 (2018).

46 Collins v. Virginia, 584 U.S. 586 (2018).

47 332 U.S. 581 (1948).

48 United States v. Di Re, 332 U.S. 581, 587 (1948).

49 526 U.S. 295 (1999).

without a showing of individualized probable cause for each one."[50] The search of the passenger may extend to "a passenger's belongings, just like the driver's belongings or containers attached to the car like a glove compartment," even without added information indicating involvement by the passenger in criminal activity. The passenger and his belongings, "are 'in' the car, and the officer has probable cause to search for contraband *in* the car."[51]

> [T]he balancing of the relative interests weighs decidedly in favor of allowing searches of a passenger's belongings. Passengers, no less than drivers, possess a reduced expectation of privacy with regard to the property that they transport in cars, which "trave[l] public thoroughfares," "seldom serv[e] as . . . the repository of personal effects," are subjected to police stop and examination to enforce "pervasive" governmental controls "[a]s an everyday occurrence," and, finally, are exposed to traffic accidents that may render all their contents open to public scrutiny.[52]

The Court summarized its balancing by observing that "our determinations of 'reasonableness' under the Fourth Amendment must take account of these practical realities. We think they militate in favor of the needs of law enforcement, and against a personal-privacy interest that is ordinarily weak."[53]

E. Timing of Vehicle Search

When there is probable cause to search a vehicle, the vehicle search may take place as soon as probable cause exists, or within a reasonable time. In *Chambers v. Maroney*,[54] although the defendant was in a vehicle at the time of his arrest, it was later searched at the police station rather than at the location of the arrest. The Court upheld that search even though the vehicle was immobilized, the occupants or owners were taken into custody, and it would have been relatively easy to obtain a search warrant.

If probable cause is present, what is the effect of a delayed search? For constitutional purposes, there is no difference between seizing and holding a vehicle before presenting the probable cause issue to a judge, on the one hand, and carrying out an immediate search without a warrant, on the other hand. The justification for a warrantless search: (1) does not vanish once the vehicle has been

---

[50] Wyoming v. Houghton, 526 U.S. 295, 302 (1999).

[51] *Id.*

[52] *Id.*, at 303, quoting Cardwell v. Lewis, 417 U.S. 583, 590 (1974) and South Dakota v. Opperman, 428 U.S. 364, 368 (1976).

[53] *Id.*, at 305.

[54] 399 U.S. 42 (1970).

immobilized,[55] and (2) does not depend on the likelihood that either the vehicle would have been driven away, or someone would have tampered with its contents during the period required for the police to obtain a warrant.[56] Likewise, a warrantless search of containers lawfully seized from a vehicle do not have to occur immediately or soon thereafter.[57] Given the appropriate level of probable cause, a delayed search does not require a warrant. However, a defendant can prove that a delay adversely affected legitimate Fourth Amendment interests.[58]

F. Summary of the Law for Vehicle Searches of Containers

The following is a summary of the law of vehicle searches for containers. The assumption is that probable cause exists for a search of a vehicle. Police may open containers inside a vehicle if they are large enough to hold the evidence that the police are seeking and for which there is probable cause. While the police are searching the vehicle, if they see a container, they may open that container without a warrant.

If probable cause exists for the police to search a specific container but not the entire vehicle, they may open that container. Once the police find that specific container, their right to search ends unless the results of *that* search establishes probable cause for a broader search. If, in looking for a specific container, the police see other evidence in plain view, they may seize that evidence. If the police do not initially see the specific container, they can search for it until they find it. In continuing to look for the container, they can open bigger containers large enough to hold the specific smaller container.

For a container that is outside the vehicle, the police need probable cause to seize it, but they need a search warrant to search it. That may suggest that if the police want to avoid having to obtain a search warrant, they may wait until someone else places the container in the vehicle.

G. Comparing a Vehicle Search with a Search Incident to Arrest

Although the two exceptions to the warrant requirement may overlap in a given situation, the two exceptions do not combine. No matter how tangled a set of facts may be, analysis of the facts for a

---

55 Florida v. Meyers, 466 U.S. 380 (1984).

56 See Michigan v. Thomas, 458 U.S. 259 (1982).

57 United States v. Johns, 469 U.S. 478 (1985).

58 *Id.*, at 487.

vehicle search leads to only one concern: was there probable cause to believe that the vehicle (or a container within the vehicle) contained evidence of a crime. The presence of an actual emergency is irrelevant, as is whether a driver or passenger was arrested, let alone lawfully. The location of the driver or passenger at the time of a vehicle search also does not matter; one or both may still be in the vehicle, or they may be shackled in a police cruiser one hundred yards away, or they may be in jail.

By contrast, with the search incident to arrest exception, such questions may become significant. The threshold issue is whether a driver or passenger is under arrest. From there, probable cause to believe that evidence may be on the person or in the vehicle loses its significance, because a search incident to arrest requires no separate probable cause justification. A search incident to arrest follows automatically from the lawful arrest; the question of whether an emergency exists loses all relevance for a seizure of items found.

For a search incident to arrest, the location of the arrestee is vitally important at the time of search, e.g., inside the vehicle, near the vehicle, or away from the vehicle, i.e., the police may search the person of the arrestee, as well as the area within the arrestee's immediate control. For example, if the driver or passenger is in the vehicle, a search incident of an area within the reaching distance of either person is proper.

If the arrestee is not in the vehicle, whether a vehicle door or the trunk is open is relevant to whether the police may search the interior of the vehicle which has become part of the arrestee's area of immediate control. A closed door or trunk renders the interior of the vehicle or trunk beyond the arrestee's immediate control.

Is there an optimal situation for the availability of both theories simultaneously that also protects the safety of the police? After the officer has both probable cause to arrest a person and to search the vehicle, the police should order the suspect from the vehicle and order him to "spread eagle" with his hands on the roof of the vehicle, as he stands by the open vehicle door from which he departed. Then the police may conduct a search of the entire passenger compartment as part of the vehicle search. Because a search incident to arrest likely would include only a portion of the vehicle's interior, a search incident of the arrestee's person may be necessary to rely upon, but relying on the search incident theory is unnecessary unless the officer's probable cause to search the vehicle was weak.

§ 7.3 Inventory Search of Vehicles

A. Vehicles Subject to Forfeiture

The Fourth Amendment does not require that police obtain a warrant before seizing a vehicle from a public place when there is probable cause to believe that the vehicle is forfeitable contraband. In *Florida v. White*,[59] the Court held that officers with probable cause to believe that a vehicle itself is subject to forfeiture can seize the vehicle from a public place *without* a warrant.

> Although the police here lacked probable cause to believe that respondent's car contained contraband, they had probable cause to believe that the vehicle *itself* was contraband under Florida law. A recognition of the need to seize readily movable contraband before it is spirited away undoubtedly underlies the early federal laws relied upon in *Carroll* [*v. United States*]. This need is equally weighty when the *automobile,* as opposed to its contents, is the contraband that the police seek to secure.[60]

The Court also noted that it confers "law enforcement officials greater latitude in exercising their duties in public places."[61] After the seizure, the police may conduct a warrantless inventory of the vehicle. States use statutory provisions to allow for forfeiture of vehicles used in crimes.[62]

B. Impoundment of Vehicles

Generally, under the laws of most States, a vehicle may be impounded without a warrant in only four situations: (1) the owner or permissive user consents to the impoundment; (2) the vehicle, if not removed, constitutes a danger to other persons or property, or the public safety and the owner or permissive user cannot reasonably arrange for alternative means of removal; (3) the police have probable cause to believe both that the vehicle constitutes an instrumentality or fruit of a crime and that absent immediate impoundment, the vehicle will be removed by a third party; or (4) the police have probable cause to believe both that the vehicle contains evidence of a crime and that absent immediate impoundment, the evidence will be lost or destroyed. As long as the only potential danger that might follow from the failure to impound a vehicle is danger to the safety of

---

59 526 U.S. 559 (1999).

60 Florida v. White, 526 U.S. 559, 564–65 (1999).

61 *Id.*, at 565.

62 See Culley v. Marshall, 601 U.S. 377 (2024) (due process permits law enforcement to keep seized property without a prompt post-seizure retention hearing, if the owner has a "timely" forfeiture hearing following the seizure).

the vehicle and its contents, there is no public interest to justify impoundment without consent of the owner or its permissive user.

During criminal or noncriminal investigations, the police may have the need to impound a vehicle. In *Dyke v. Taylor Implement Manufacturing Co.*,[63] the driver was arrested for reckless driving, and was at the courthouse to make bail at the time of the search. The Court ruled that the search was not incident to the impoundment, because

> the police seem to have parked the car near the courthouse merely as a convenience to the owner and to have been willing for some friend or relative to [the defendant] or [the defendant] himself if he were soon released from custody to drive it away.[64]

Thus, Court found that the immediate impoundment of the defendant's vehicle is inappropriate after his arrest for a minor traffic violation. Instead, the police should enable the defendant to obtain pretrial release and reclaim his vehicle.

The "exercise of police discretion is proper so long as "that discretion is exercised according to standard criteria and on the basis of something other than suspicion of evidence of criminal activity."[65] The standard criteria for impoundment referred to "the feasibility and appropriateness of parking and locking a vehicle rather than impounding it" and establish[ing] several conditions that must be met before an officer may pursue the park and lock alternative."[66] The legality of the search is dependent upon the necessity of impoundment, "even though courts might as a matter of hindsight be able to devise equally reasonable rules requiring a different procedure."[67]

C. Inventory Search of Impounded Vehicles

Inventory searches may be conducted without probable cause or a warrant. The police may inventory a lawfully impounded vehicle to protect: (1) the property in the vehicle, (2) the police against claims of lost property, and (3) the police from potential danger. When a vehicle is legally impounded according to local standards that permit police officers to exercise discretion, police may search the entire vehicle and any closed containers to list the contents. Any evidence recovered may be used in a later criminal prosecution.

---

[63] 391 U.S. 216 (1968).

[64] Dyke v. Taylor Implement Mfg. Co., 391 U.S. 216, 221 (1968).

[65] Colorado v. Bertine, 479 U.S. 367, 375 (1987).

[66] *Id.*, at 376 n.7.

[67] *Id.*, at 374.

The impoundment may arise from the necessity to retain the vehicle for safekeeping, because the vehicle violates a parking regulation or the vehicle is unsafe. An inventory search cannot be *solely* used for a criminal investigation; a mixed motive is allowed, but an itemized routine inventory of the contents of the vehicle is permissible both to preserve the property of the accused and to forestall the possibility that the defendant may later claim that some item has not been returned.[68]

In *South Dakota v. Opperman*,[69] Vermillion police towed the defendant's illegally parked vehicle to a city impound lot where an officer saw personal property in the car and conducted an inventory where he found drugs in the glove compartment. The Court upheld the inventory search, because (1) the vehicle was impounded legally for multiple parking violations, (2) the owner was not present to arrange for the safekeeping of the personal property items, (3) the valuables in the vehicle were in plain view, and (4) there was no suggestion that the search was a pretext for an investigatory police motive.[70]

> Automobiles, unlike homes, are subjected to pervasive and continuing governmental regulation and controls, including periodic inspection and licensing requirements. As an everyday occurrence, police stop and examine vehicles when license plates or inspection stickers have expired, or if other violations, such as exhaust fumes or excessive noise, are noted, or if headlights or other safety equipment are not in proper working order.[71]

Following the impoundment, the police may conduct a search of the vehicle without having to offer the driver the "opportunity to make other arrangements" for the vehicle. In this regard, *Colorado v. Bertine*[72] narrowed *Dyke*'s and *Opperman*'s suggestion that the police must offer the vehicle owner a chance to avoid the impoundment lot by making alternative arrangements for the vehicle. In the absence of a showing that the police, who followed standardized procedures, acted in bad faith for the sole purpose of investigation in conducting an inventory search of the defendant's vehicle, *Bertine* held that the search may be necessary and evidence discovered during the search is admissible.

---

68 Illinois v. Lafayette, 462 U.S. 640 (1983).

69 428 U.S. 364 (1976).

70 South Dakota v. Opperman, 428 U.S. 364, 375–76 (1976).

71 *Colorado v. Bertine*, 479 U.S. at 368.

72 479 U.S. 367 (1987).

Opperman addressed the scope of the inventory search to include an unlocked glove compartment, "since it is a customary place for documents of ownership and registration. . . as well as a place for the temporary storge of valuables." *Bertine* possibly went further, because it stated that "the security of the storage facility does not completely eliminate the need for inventorying; the police may still wish to protect themselves or the owners of the lot against false claims of theft or dangerous instrumentalities."[73] Because false claims could include both unlocked and locked areas of the vehicles, Bertine's broader statement appears to promote any and all false claims, not just those based upon items taken from an unlocked glove compartment.

The inventory must be conducted pursuant to routine police policy, and must not be a sham or pretext to search the vehicle. An inventory search without written regulations to govern the search of containers found during inventory searches is unconstitutional. In *Florida v. Wells*,[74] the inventory search was unconstitutional because the state police "had no policy whatever with respect to the opening of closed containers encountered during an inventory search."[75] Written regulations and policies may give police the discretion to decide whether a particular container should be opened in light of the nature of the search and the container's characteristics.

D. Entry of Vehicle for Other Purposes

Police frequently have occasion to examine vehicles in a non-criminal context as part of a "community caretaking function." Thus, examinations of vehicles may occur where there is concern for public safety, determining ownership of the vehicle, where entry is to aid a person in distress, or where the vehicle itself may be in an unsafe condition. The entry of vehicles under these circumstances must be for a real purpose and not for a pretext to search.

§ 7.4 Booking or Inventory Search of Persons

A. Search upon Arrival at Place of Detention

When an arrested person has been delivered to the place of detention, that person may be subjected to a rather complete search of the person. The search is justified: (1) as a search incident to

---

73 *Colorado v. Bertine*, 479 U.S. at 373.

74 495 U.S. 1 (1990).

75 Florida v. Wells, 495 U.S. 1, 4–5 (1990).

arrest;[76] (2) as an inventory conducted to protect the arrestee's effects;[77] and (3) to maintain the security of the detention facility.[78]

A search to inventory containers provides a basis upon which to justify a search into containers possessed by an arrestee, incident to the arrestee's booking and post-arrest detention. When a defendant's suitcase or similar container is properly impounded at the time of the arrest (or otherwise lawfully comes into the custody of the police acting in good faith and not for the sole purpose of investigation), an itemized routine inventory of its contents at the station is permissible both to preserve the property of the accused and to forestall the possibility that the defendant may later claim that some item has not been returned.[79] *Illinois v. Lafayette*[80] permitted "a stationhouse search of every item carried on by a person who has lawfully been taken into custody by police," if conducted pursuant to "standardized inventory procedures," because that "will amply serve the important and legitimate government interests involved."

Police discretion in conducting such inventory searches must be exercised according to standard criteria or established routine. In *Florida v. Wells*,[81] Florida State Police had no policy regarding the opening of closed containers seized during inventory search. Such policies may give police discretion to decide whether a particular container should be opened in light of the nature of the search and the characteristics of the container.

B. Strip Search

Police may conduct routine, suspicionless strip searches of all arrested persons, regardless of the crime charged. *Florence v. Board of Chosen Freeholders of the County of Burlington*,[82] Florence was arrested for failure to appear at a court hearing, after which police officers strip searched him. After the charge was dismissed, Florence brought a civil rights claim for damages based on what he claimed was an improper search.

On appeal from reversal of the trial court's grant of summary judgment, the Court held that even strip searches are permissible for any arrested persons without any reason and regardless of the reason for the arrest. A plurality rejected the plaintiff's argument that strip searches were appropriate only for persons arrested for serious

---

[76] United States v. Edwards, 415 U.S. 800 (1974).

[77] Illinois v. Lafayette, 462 U.S. 640 (1983).

[78] *Id.*

[79] *Id.*; Colorado v. Bertine, 479 U.S. 367 (1987).

[80] 462 U.S. 640 (1982).

[81] 495 U.S. 1 (1990).

[82] 566 U.S. 318 (2012).

crimes, with the Court stating that "[t]he seriousness of an offense is a poor predictor of who has contraband."[83]

C. Delayed Search

Once the defendant is incarcerated and awaiting trial, the police may later seize the defendant's clothing or effects previously placed in safekeeping for the defendant. In *United States v. Edwards*,[84] the Court saw no difference between taking a defendant's clothing for safekeeping and scientific testing at the time he was arrested, arrived at the jail facility, or the morning after his arrival.

> [I]t is difficult to perceive what is unreasonable about the police's examining and holding as evidence those personal effects of the accused that they already have in their lawful custody as the result of a lawful arrest. . . . When the substitute [clothing was] purchased the next morning, the clothing he had been wearing at the time of arrest was taken from him and subjected to laboratory analysis. This was no more than taking from [Edwards] the effects in his immediate possession that constituted evidence of crime. . . . Edwards was no more imposed upon than he could have been at the time and place of the arrest or immediately upon arrival at the place of detention.[85]

D. DNA Testing

In *Maryland v. King*,[86] the Court held that routine warrantless collection and profiling of DNA samples from individuals arrested and taken into custody for serious crimes does not violate the Fourth Amendment. The Court first agreed that "using a buccal swab on the inner tissues of a person's cheek in order to obtain DNA samples is a search. . . The fact than an intrusion is negligible is of central relevance to determining reasonableness, although it is still a search as the law defines that term."[87] Next, it was necessary to determine whether this process required the use of a search warrant procedure. The need for a warrant for DNA testing was low because the testing was standardized and involves "virtually no facts for a neutral magistrate to evaluate."[88]

---

[83] Florence v. Board of Chosen Freeholders of County of Burlington, 566 U.S. 318, 333 (2012).

[84] 415 U.S. 800 (1974).

[85] United States v. Edwards, 415 U.S. 800, 805, 806 (1974).

[86] 569 U.S. 435 (2013).

[87] Maryland v. King, 569 U.S. 435, 446 (2013).

[88] *Id.*, at 447.

Knowing that all warrantless searches must be reasonable, the Court weighed "the promotion of legitimate governmental interests" against "the degree to which [the search] intrudes upon an individual's privacy." The Court concluded that DNA identification promoted several Governmental interests relating to the criminal history of persons awaiting trial, e.g., more accurate identification of persons pending trials, special risks posed by persons who are incarcerated before trial, increased information for making pretrial release decisions, and possibly identifying persons as culprits who committed a past crime for which another person had been wrongly convicted.[89]

Aware that expectations of privacy for persons taken into police custody are "necessarily of a diminished scope," the Court addressed DNA testing's degree of intrusion.

> [A] buccal swab involves a gentle rub along the inside of the cheek [that] does not break the skin, and it "involves virtually no risk, trauma, or pain." [N]othing suggests that a buccal swab poses any physical danger whatsoever. A brief intrusion of an arrestee's person is subject to the Fourth Amendment, but a swab of this nature does not increase the indignity already attendant to normal incidents of arrest.[90]

In addition, the Court observed that the processing of DNA samples do not intrude on prisoners' privacy "in a way that would make his DNA identification unconstitutional." The Court concluded that DNA identification of arrestees is a "reasonable search that can be considered part of a routine booking procedure."

> When officers make an arrest supported by probable cause to hold for a serious offense and they bring the suspect to the station to be detained in custody, taking and analyzing a cheek swab of the arrestee's DNA is, like fingerprinting and photographing, a legitimate police booking procedure that is reasonable under the Fourth Amendment.[91]

---

89 *Id.*, at 450–56.

90 *Id.*, at 463–64.

91 *Id.*, at 465–66.

Chapter 8

CONSENT SEARCHES

Table of Sections

---

§ 8.1 Introduction

Consent searches are another exception to the requirement of a search warrant. Police or other Government officials may conduct a search without a warrant or probable cause based upon an individual's consent only if that consent both was voluntary,[1] and came from a person with authority to consent.[2]

> In a society based on law, the concept of agreement and consent should be given a weight and dignity of its own. Police officers act in full accord with the law when they ask citizens for consent. It reinforces the rule of law for the citizen to advise the police of his or her wishes and for the police to act in reliance on that understanding. When this exchange takes place, it dispels inferences of coercion.[3]

Evidence discovered during a lawful consent search may be seized and admitted at trial.[4]

Consent searches fall into two broad categories. The first type of consent is consent by the defendant. Actual consent may be actual or

1 Schneckloth v. Bustamonte, 412 U.S. 218, 220 (1973).

2 United States v. Matlock, 415 U.S. 164, 170 (1974).

3 United States v. Drayton, 536 U.S. 194, 207 (2002).

4 See, e.g., Florida v. Royer, 460 U.S. 491, 502 (1983).

implied. The second type of consent derives from a third person who has some type of joint authority over the area searched.

§ 8.2 Requirements for a Valid Consent Search

A. Nature of Consent and Burden of Proof

"[T]he question whether a consent to a search was in fact 'voluntary' or was the product of duress or coercion, express or implied, is a question of fact to be determined from the totality of all the circumstances."[5] When the defendant moves to suppress the fruits of a consent search, the prosecutor "has the burden of proving that the consent was, in fact, freely and voluntarily given."[6] Except in implied consent cases, consent is a waiver of the right for the police to proceed by a search warrant. Conversely, a "search conducted in reliance upon a warrant cannot later be justified on the basis of consent if it turns out that the warrant was invalid."[7]

Voluntary consent does not require that the consenting party know (through a police warning or otherwise) that he has the right to refuse to consent to a search. Thus, proof that consent was given and was not the product of coercion is sufficient, unlike a defendant's waiver of rights associated with preserving a fair trial. *Schneckloth v. Bustamonte* tackled the argument that a person should be told that he may refuse to consent to a requested search.

In the middle of the night, an officer stopped a vehicle that had one headlight and its license plate light burned out. The driver had no operator's license and only one other person could produce any identification; the driver stated that the vehicle belonged to his brother. When requested, the six men exited the vehicle. By that time, two other officers arrived, and the man with the license consented to a search of the vehicle's trunk. Under the left rear seat, the officers found three wadded up bank checks that had been stolen from a car wash.

Reviewing its past consent cases, the Court found that "recognition that knowledge of a right to refuse is not a prerequisite of a voluntary consent."[8]

> While knowledge of the right to refuse consent is one factor to be taken into account, the government need not establish such knowledge as the *sine qua non* of an effective consent. As with police questioning, two competing concerns must be

---

5 *Schneckloth v. Bustamonte*, 412 U.S. at 227.

6 Bumper v. North Carolina, 391 U.S. 543, 548 (1968).

7 *Id.*

8 *Schneckloth v. Bustamonte*, 412 U.S. at 234.

> accommodated in determining the meaning of a "voluntary" consent—the legitimate need for such searches and the equally important requirement of assuring the absence of coercion.[9]

"The protections of the Fourth Amendment are of a wholly different order [than the rights protecting a fair trial], and have nothing whatever to do with promoting the fair ascertainment of truth at a criminal trial."[10]

> [I]t would be thoroughly impractical to impose on the normal consent search the detailed requirements of an effective warning. Consent searches are part of the standard investigatory techniques of law enforcement agencies. They normally occur on the highway, or in a person's home or office, and under informal and unstructured conditions. The circumstances that prompt the initial request to search may develop quickly or be a logical extension of investigative police questioning. The police may seek to investigate further suspicious circumstances or to follow up leads developed in questioning persons at the scene of a crime. These situations are a far cry from the structured atmosphere of a trial where, assisted by counsel if he chooses, a defendant is informed of his trial rights. . . And, while surely a closer question, these situations are still immeasurably, far removed from "custodial interrogation" where, in *Miranda v. Arizona*, we found that the Constitution required certain now familiar warnings as a prerequisite to police interrogation.[11]

The defendant had argued that "the failure to require the Government to establish knowledge as a prerequisite to a valid consent, will relegate the Fourth Amendment to the special province of 'the sophisticated, knowledgeable and the privileged.' " The Court responded by declaring that the "traditional definition of voluntariness we accept today has always taken into account evidence of minimal schooling [and] low intelligence."[12]

In *Bustamonte*, because the search happened when the defendant was not in custody, the Court stated that the consent was less coercive on its face. Later inquiry into the circumstances of the

---

9 *Id.*, at 227.

10 *Id.*, at 241.

11 *Id.*, at 232.

12 *Id.*, at 247–48.

consent are an adequate safeguard without the need for pre-search knowledge. The Court held that

> when the subject of a search is not in custody and the State attempts to justify a search on the basis of his consent, the Fourth and Fourteenth Amendments require that it demonstrate that the consent was in fact voluntarily given, and not the result of duress or coercion, express or implied. Voluntariness is a question of fact to be determined from all the circumstances, and while the subject's knowledge of a right to refuse is a factor to be taken into account, the prosecution is not required to demonstrate such knowledge as a prerequisite to establishing voluntary consent.[13]

The Court has followed *Bustamonte* for decades. In *United States v. Watson*,[14] the Court emphasized that the defendant consented while on a public street, and not at a police station. Later, in *Ohio v. Robinette*,[15] the Court added that police do not have to advise a defendant that he is free to go before his consent to search is considered to be voluntary. In that case, the consent to search the vehicle was voluntary after the driver was lawfully stopped for speeding, given a verbal warning, and the police returned his operator's license. In *United States v. Drayton*,[16] police officers conducted a routine, suspicion-free drug investigation of bus passengers. The Court held that the officers did not have to disclose to the passengers that they had the right not to cooperate and to refuse to consent to searches. Thus, consent deals with the voluntariness of the agreement to allow a search.

B. Scope of Consent

Once consent is given, how far does it extend? A consenting person usually does not include limits on where the search must stop or cannot go. On the other hand, there may be express or implied limitations about the permissible scope of the search in terms of time, duration, area or intensity.

The scope of a consent search may not exceed the scope of the consent given. For example, in *Florida v. Jimeno*,[17] the police search of the defendant's vehicle did not exceed the defendant's consent, because the suspect's consent for drugs implicitly included containers within the vehicle and a closed paper bag found on the floorboard.

---

13 *Id.*, at 248–49.

14 423 U.S. 411 (1976).

15 519 U.S. 33, 40 (1996).

16 536 U.S. 194 (2002).

17 500 U.S. 248 (1991).

The scope of consent also is determined by asking how a reasonable person would have understood the conversation between the officer and person who gave the consent at the time consent was given. In *Jimeno*, the Court held that "it was objectively reasonable for the police to conclude that the general consent to search the [defendant's] car included consent to search containers within that car which might bear drugs."[18] In terms of a foreseeable limit on consent, the Court stated that it is very likely unreasonable to think that a suspect, by consenting to the search of his trunk, has agreed to the breaking open of a locked briefcase within the trunk, but it is otherwise with respect to a closed paper bag.[19] *Jimeno* implied that an ambiguity about the scope of consent favors the view of the officer, and the burden is on the consenting party to clarify the scope of consent. That is expecting a lot of citizens, given that the police do not have to disclose their right to refuse a police request to search.

While conditions may be placed on a consent, the consenting party may change his mind and "waive" those conditions later. It is much easier to refuse a broad search area at the inception of the search than it is to terminate an ongoing search when the police are nearing an especially incriminating object. Consent to search may be revoked, i.e., if a person effectively withdraws consent before the search is completed, the police may not continue the search based on the prior consent.

C. Factors Bearing on Consent

Consent is not voluntary if it was the "product of duress or coercion, express or implied."[20] Consent does not depend "on the presence or absence of a single controlling criterion" but rather "all the surrounding circumstances."[21] Verbal and non-verbal conduct by the defendant may indicate consent. Consent of a person in custody may render a consent involuntary.[22] A police request for consent after a suspect is detained does not render a detainee incapable of consenting unless the period of detention becomes especially long prior to the consent.[23] A defendant who consents to a search after admitting his guilt creates a strong implication of a voluntary consent, as does consent given in the context of cooperating with the police, e.g., a person of interest giving his car keys to the police.

---

18 Florida v. Jimeno, 500 U.S. 248, 251 (1991).

19 *Id.*, at 251–52.

20 United States v. Mendenhall, 446 U.S. 544, 557 (1980).

21 *Schneckloth v. Bustamonte*, 412 U.S. at 226.

22 Compare Florida v. Royer, 460 U.S. 491 (1983) with United States v. Watson, 423 U.S. 411 (1976).

23 United States v. Mendenhall, 446 U.S. 544 (1980).

Suppose a police officer arrests a homeowner or threatens to arrest him by using force, i.e., in a manner which suggests authority to conduct a search? Or, what happens if the officer shows a search warrant to the homeowner or represents that he has[24] or can obtain a search warrant? In either situation, consent to search thereafter is nothing more than submission either to the officer's authority[25] or consent to the inevitable, and is therefore involuntary.[26] Under some circumstances, the mere presence of police officers for the stated purpose of conducting a search may constitute implied coercion which renders any consent involuntary.[27]

As previously discussed, even though the police have no general duty to advise a person of the right to refuse to consent to a search, if that person has been advised of the constitutional right to remain silent or the right to refuse a search, either is a strong indication of the voluntariness of the consent.[28] While consent to search need not be in writing, the execution of a written waiver is a factor which has been found to indicate strongly that consent was voluntarily given.

A defendant's age, intelligence, and education are factors relevant to a determination of the voluntariness of consent.[29] Similarly, a person's physical and mental capacity at the time of consent relate to the voluntariness of consent. On the other hand, a person's call for medical assistance is not a consent for responding police to conduct a full scale search of the caller's premises when they arrive.

D. Implied Consent

The preceding sections concern "overt consent" or explicit consent where the police have requested and received permission to search. Some consent cases deal with implied consent and fall into two general areas, i.e., from the defendant's prior conduct, his consent is implicit. The first type is where the police do not conceal their identity or purpose, e.g., where the police are invited by a resident or inhabitant into the premises so that no search is involved. Consent may also be present as a condition either to enter airports, jails, or other public facilities, to board an airplane, or to drive on highways and roads.

Several implied consent situations relate to an attempt by the police to test the defendant's blood or breath in suspected drunk

---

24 Bumper v. North Carolina, 391 U.S. 543, 550–51 (1968).

25 *Florida v. Royer*, 460 U.S. at 497, 501–02.

26 *Bumper v. North Carolina*, 391 U.S. at 550–51.

27 See Amos v. United States, 255 U.S. 313 (1921).

28 United States v. Watson, 423 U.S. 411 (1976) (*Miranda* warnings).

29 United States v. Mendenhall, 446 U.S. 544 (1980).

driving cases. The implied consent relates to the defendant's allegedly impaired condition while he is driving on public roads, i.e., using the roads implicitly constitutes the driver's consent for the police to conduct a test. In *Missouri v. McNeely*,[30] a plurality of four Justices observed that

> all 50 States have adopted implied consent laws that require motorists, as a condition of operating a motor vehicle within the State, to consent to BAC testing if they are arrested or otherwise detained on suspicion of a drunk-driving offense. Such laws impose significant consequences when a motorist withdraws consent; typically the motorist's driver's license is immediately suspended or revoked, and most States allow the motorist's refusal to take a BAC test to be used as evidence against him in a subsequent criminal prosecution.[31]

In *Birchfield v. North Dakota*,[32] the Court held that before a warrantless *blood* test, a defendant must consent; the test cannot be administered or used without his consent,[33] and the State cannot prosecute him for refusing to consent.[34] By contrast, because police can perform a warrantless *breath* test incident to his arrest, a driver has no right to refuse the test and faces prosecution or sanctions for refusing the test.

Mitchell v. Wisconsin[35] involved an unconscious driver suspected of drunk driving. Instead of relying on the State's implied consent law to support a blood draw, the plurality opinion used the exigent circumstance exception to the search warrant requirement to uphold the blood draw.[36] The plurality emphasized that the Court's prior decisions on the subject "have not rested on the idea that these laws do what their popular name might seem to suggest—that is, create actual consent to all the searches they authorized." The dissent "would go further and hold that the state statute, however phrased, cannot itself create the actual and informed consent that the Fourth Amendment requires."[37]

The second type of implied consent occurs when the police use deception by informants or undercover agents to reject claims that, if

---

30 569 U.S. 141 (2013).

31 Missouri v. McNeely, 569 U.S. 141, 161 (2013).

32 579 U.S. 438 (2016).

33 569 U.S. 141 (2013).

34 But the Court stated that "civil penalties" are proper for "motorists who refuse to comply." Birchfield v. North Dakota, 579 U.S. 438, 444 (2016).

35 588 U.S. 840 (2019).

36 See Chapter 10, discussing Exigent Circumstances.

37 Mitchell v. Wisconsin, 588 U.S. 840, 867 (2019) (Sotomayor, J., dissenting).

he had known the other person's identity, a defendant would not have given consent to search. Several Court decisions have looked past the fact that a person's voluntariness to consent is necessarily undermined when the police use trickery, fraud, or misrepresentation to obtain consent. For example, in *On Lee v. United States*,[38] an informant wearing a wire went to the defendant's place of business and recorded his conversation with the defendant who incriminated himself. The Court refused to suppress the statements on the ground that the informant had gained entry to the business by fraud. The Court also rejected the defendant's argument that the informant's entry was a trespass, because the informant had "entered a place of business with the consent, if not by the implied invitation, of the" defendant.

In *Hoffa v. United States*,[39] an informant-friend testified about conversations with the defendant, and the Court dismissed the defendant's objection, because the Fourth Amendment does not protect "a wrongdoer's misplaced belief that a person to whom he voluntarily confides his wrongdoing will not reveal it."[40] "An undercover officer does not violate the Fourth Amendment merely by accepting an offer to do business that is freely made to the public."[41] *Lewis v. United States*[42] involved a federal drug agent who gained access to the defendant's home by misrepresenting his identity and trying to purchase drugs. The Court stressed that the defendant "invited the undercover agent to his home for the specific purpose of executing a felonious sale of narcotics," and concluded that

> when, as here, the home is converted into a commercial center to which outsiders are invited for purposes of transacting unlawful business, that business is entitled to no greater sanctity than if it were carried on in a store, a garage, a car, or on the street. A government agent, in the same manner as a private person, may accept an invitation to do business and may enter upon the premises for the very purposes contemplated by the occupant.[43]

Together, *On Lee*, *Hoffa*, and *Lewis* stand for the principle that, when a person consents for another to enter a place otherwise protected by the Fourth Amendment and but for a misrepresentation, the consent would not have been given that made the consenting person ignorant

---

38 343 U.S. 747 (1952).

39 385 U.S. 293 (1966).

40 Hoffa v. United States, 385 U.S. 293, 303 (1966).

41 Maryland v. Macon, 472 U.S. 463, 470 (1985).

42 385 U.S. 206 (1966).

43 Lewis v. United States, 385 U.S. 206, 211 (1966).

of the other person's identity as a law enforcement officer or undercover agent.

§ 8.3 Requirements for a Valid Third Party Consent Search

A defendant may consent to a search not only of his own premises, but also another person may consent to the search of the defendant's premises under certain circumstances. Third party consent to search is valid if the third party has either actual (or common) authority to consent. For third party searches, the authority issue is added to the voluntariness and scope issues to determine the admissibility of the fruits of the consent search. The authority that justifies consent by a third party rests on mutual use of the property by persons generally having joint access or control. Since *United States v. Matlock*,[44] the third party consent cases inquire into whether (1) the consenting party could permit the search "on his own right," and (2) the defendant has "assumed the risk" that a co-occupant might permit the search. Third party consent obviously looks to the voluntary nature of the third person's consent.[45]

Third party consent does not rest exclusively on the proof of consent and the proper relationship. Additional factors include: (1) any antagonism between the defendant and the third party, (2) the defendant's specific instructions to the third party, (3) the defendant's prior or contemporaneous refusal to consent to search, (4) the officer's prior failure to seek consent from the occupant under suspicion, (5) the fact that exclusive control is maintained as to certain areas or effects within the shared premises, and (6) the reasonable but mistaken belief by the police that the third party has authority over the placed searched.

A. Common Authority of Third Party to Consent

Another person may consent to a search of the defendant's premises. The cases include third-party consent based on either actual authority or apparent authority of a third party to consent.[46] For actual (or common) authority, it is reasonable to recognize that any co-inhabitant of a place has the right to permit the inspection and that others have assumed the risk that one of their number might permit the common area to be searched.[47]

---

[44] 415 U.S. 164 (1974).

[45] See § 8.2(D), discussing Implied Consent.

[46] United States v. Matlock, 415 U.S. 164, 170 (1974).

[47] *Id.*

In *United States v. Matlock,*[48] the defendant's roommate consented to a search of the bedroom they shared. The Court attempted to clarify alternative grounds for third-party consent. The Court thought it "clear that when the prosecution seeks to justify a warrantless search by proof of voluntary consent, it is not limited to proof that consent was given by the defendant, but may show that permission to search was obtained from a third party. . . ."[49] Voluntary consent may be given by either (1) the defendant, or (2) a third person who "possessed common authority over or other sufficient relationship to the premises or effects sought to be inspected."[50]

> Common authority is . . . not to be implied from the mere property interest a third party has in the property. The authority which justifies the third-party consent . . . rests [also] on mutual use of the property by persons generally having joint access or control for most purposes, so that it is reasonable to recognize that any of the co-inhabitants has the right to permit the inspection in his own right and that the others have assumed the risk that one of their number might permit the common area to be searched.[51]

The third-party search cases thus inquire into whether the consenting party could permit the search "in his own right," and whether the defendant had "assumed the risk" that a co-occupant might permit the search.

Most of the Court's third party consent decisions have addressed issues of common authority to consent. Specifically, what is necessary for a third party to have the common authority to consent on behalf of another person to a search? For example, a hotel clerk lacked common authority to a consent search of a hotel guest's room, because the guest had to surrender his rights "directly or through an agent," and the record failed to support the clerk's requisite authority.[52] A defendant's grandmother had the authority to consent to a search,

---

[48] 415 U.S. 164 (1974).

[49] United States v. Matlock, 415 U.S. 164, 171 (1974).

[50] *Id.* In United States v. Perry, 92 F.4th 500 (4th Cir. 2024), the court cited *Matlock* in holding that the defendant's girlfriend had actual authority to consent to the search of the defendant's cell phone, where incriminating photos were found. She had at least joint, if not sole, access and control over the cell phone at the time of the search. For seven months leading to her decision to give the phone to federal agents, she 1) was the only person to use the phone, 2) regularly used the phone for personal purposes, and 3) had access to the contents of the entire phone.

[51] *United States v. Matlock*, 415 U.S. at 171, n.7.

[52] Stoner v. California, 376 U.S. 483, 489 (1964).

because she owned the house and a weapon seized during the search, although her consent was coerced.[53]

In *Frazier v. Cupp*,[54] the defendant and his cousin shared a duffel bag, and the cousin consented to a police search of the bag. The defendant argued that his cousin had permission to use only one compartment of the bag. In response, the Court refused to "engage in such metaphysical subtleties in judging the efficacy of [the cousin's] consent,"[55] and concluded that the defendant had assumed the risk by allowing his cousin to use the bag and by leaving it in his house that his cousin would consent to someone else [here, a police officer] looking in the bag.

In dicta, *Matlock* stated that "the consent of one who possesses common authority over premises or effects is valid as against the *absent*, nonconsenting person with whom that authority is shared."[56] What happens when one occupant consents to the search of a place, while another co-occupant who is present refuses to permit the search? In *Georgia v. Randolph*,[57] a physically present co-occupant's refusal to permit entry rendered a warrantless entry and search unreasonable and invalid as to him, even though another physically present occupant had consented to the search. The Court held "that a warrantless search of a shared dwelling for evidence over the express refusal of consent by a physically present resident cannot be justified as reasonable as to him on the basis of consent given to the police by another resident."[58]

Randolph acknowledged that a cohabitant's consent may be valid even when another present person denies consent, where there is a socially "recognized hierarchy" such as parents and children or different ranking officials at a military barracks.[59] The Court also recognized that the police could attempt to manipulate the situation by removing the objecting person so that the only remaining person with common authority had consented.

> So long as there is no evidence that the police have removed the potentially objecting tenant from the entrance for the sake of avoiding a possible objection, there is practical value in the simple clarity of complimentary rules, one recognizing the co-tenant's permission when there is no fellow on hand, the other according dispositive weight to the

---

53 Bumper v. North Carolina, 391 U.S. 543 (1968).

54 Frazier v. Cupp, 394 U.S. 731 (1969).

55 *Id.*, at 740.

56 *Id.*, at 170 (emphasis in original).

57 547 U.S. 103 (2006).

58 Georgia v. Randolph, 547 U.S. 103, 120 (2006).

59 *Id.*, at 113.

fellow occupant's contrary indication when he expresses it.[60]

In *Fernandez v. California*,[61] the police observed a robbery suspect enter an apartment building; that was followed by screaming from one of the apartments. Police hurried to the apartment where the woman who answered the door permitted them to enter as the suspect walked up and refused to consent. After the police removed him from the premises and arrested him, the police returned. With the woman's renewed consent to enter and search, they found evidence related to the robbery. In response to the defendant's claim that he was improperly removed, the Court characterized *Randolph* as a "narrow exception" to *Matlock*'s normal rule that "police officers may search jointly occupied premises" without a warrant "if one of the occupants consents."[62]

The Court clarified dictum in *Randolph* that when the objecting person is removed by police for "objectively reasonable" reasons and not the subjective intent of the officers, a consenting co-occupant then may provide sufficient authority to search. "We therefore hold that an occupant who is absent due to a lawful detention or arrest stands in the same shoes as an occupant who is absent for any other reason."[63] *Randolph* "applies only where the objector is standing in the door saying 'stay out' when the officers propose to make a consent search."[64]

Fernandez also rejected the defendant's other argument that his objection, made at the threshold of the premises that the police wanted to search, remained effective until he changed his mind and withdrew his objection. Citing the "practical problems" of adopting such a rule, the Court rejected it. "For one thing, there is the question of duration," because it contemplates no end date. The Court then rejected the duration of the defendant's objection as a reasonable time. "[W]hat interval of time would be reasonable in this context? A week? A month? A year? Ten years?"[65]

Defendant's proposed rule "would also require the police and ultimately the courts to determine whether, after the passage of time, an objector still had 'common authority' over the premises, and this would often be a tricky question." If he stopped paying rent, "would he still have 'common authority,' and would his objection retain its

[60] *Id.*, at 121–22.

[61] 571 U.S. 292 (2014).

[62] Fernandez v. California, 571 U.S. 292, 294 (2014).

[63] *Id.*, at 303.

[64] *Id.*, at 306.

[65] *Id.*, at 305.

force?" The Court also questioned "the procedure needed to register a continuing objection."[66]

> Would it be necessary for an occupant to object while police officers are at the door? If presence at the time of consent is not needed, would an occupant have to be present at the premises when the objection was made? Could an objection be made pre-emptively? . . .
>
> [Which police] would be bound by an objection, . . . [J]ust the officers who were present when the objection was made? Would it also apply to other officers working on the same investigation? Would it extend to officers who were unaware of the objection? How about officers assigned to different but arguably related cases? Would it be limited by law enforcement agency?[67]

B. Apparent Authority of Third Party to Consent

The issue of apparent authority addresses the propriety of third party consent when the police had a reasonable but mistaken belief that the third party had the authority to consent. Apparent authority is judged against an objective standard, i.e., whether the facts then available to the police, even if mistaken, would justify a reasonably cautious person into believing that the consenting party *actually* has common authority over the premises. As the Court stated in *Illinois v. Rodriguez*,[68] as long as the police officers reasonably believed that the consenting individual had authority over the premises, their search on the basis of that consent did not violate the Fourth Amendment.

In *Stoner v. California*,[69] the Government's position was that the police were entitled to believe that a hotel clerk had the authority to a search of a hotel guest's room. The Court rejected that approach by asserting that "the rights protected by the Fourth Amendment are not to be eroded . . . by unrealistic doctrines of 'apparent authority.' "[70] When mistakes of law are made, as in *Stoner*, e.g., the

---

66 *Id.*

67 *Id.*, at 305–06.

68 Illinois v. Rodriguez, 497 U.S. 177, 188 (1990). In a child pornography case, defendant's teen-aged daughter had apparent authority to consent to a police officer's reasonable warrantless search of a camera and memory card. The daughter had joint access to and control of a bathroom in the defendant's home where she lived part-time and was the primary user of the bathroom, where she had found the camera and internal memory card. The camera was neither locked nor concealed. Bermel, 88 F.4th 741 (8th Cir. 2023).

69 376 U.S. 483 (1964).

70 *Stoner v. California*, 376 U.S. at 488.

legal authority of a hotel clerk to open a guest room for search, the apparent authority concept discussed in *Rodriguez* is inapplicable.

In *Rodriguez*, the nature of the mistake related to a factual issue about whether the person giving consent for a search had the authority to consent to a search of a place where she had not lived for at least a month. She had taken her clothes and other effects, but still spent nights there. The Court affirmed the lower court's conclusion that the woman had no "common authority" over the apartment, because her name was not on the lease, she did not pay any of the rent, and she never invited friends there.

Having decided that the consenting party had no common authority to consent, the Court remanded the case for the lower court to decide whether she had *apparent* authority to consent. That apparent authority approach could validate a reasonable though mistaken conclusion by the police, based on the circumstances, suggesting that the consenting person could approve a police search. The actions of the police may be reasonable, even though those actions are based upon factual assumptions that turn out to be incorrect.

On the one hand, how can a person consent to the search of another person's premises when she is not even supposed to have access? On the other hand, perhaps it makes little sense to suppress evidence obtained under circumstances in which the reasonable officer would believe that he had obtained valid consent. The Court was careful to explain what it was *not* holding.

> [W]hat we hold today does not suggest that law enforcement officers may always accept a person's invitation to enter premises. Even when the invitation is accompanied by an explicit assertion that the person lives there, the surrounding circumstances could conceivably be such that a reasonable person would doubt its truth and not act upon it without further inquiry. As with other factual determinations bearing upon search and seizure, determination of consent to enter must "be judged against an objective standard: would the facts available to the officer at the moment . . . 'warrant a man of reasonable caution in the belief' " that the consenting party had authority over the premises? If not, then warrantless entry without further inquiry is unlawful unless authority actually exists. But if so, the search is valid.[71]

The reasonableness standard for third party consent searches validates reasonable mistakes of fact that relate to the consenting

[71] *Illinois v. Rodriguez*, 497 U.S. at 188–89.

party's authority to consent, i.e., consent is valid when the facts were as the police reasonably believed them to be. When the facts are unclear, a reasonable officer should inquire to determine whether the consenting person has *actual* authority.

C. Relationship of Third Party to Defendant

The property-assumption of risk test for determining third party consent may suggest a connection between the assumption of risk aspect and the defendant's justified expectation of privacy in the premises or effects searched. Case law places primary emphasis on the common possessory interest of the third person who consents. Among the persons who have been found to have an immediate possessory interest are a resident owner, a primary tenant, a resident co-occupant, a guest in temporary control of the premises, and a babysitter.

Six categories of cases relate to the possessory interest, usually requiring a factual determination of the relationship between the defendant and the third party. In the first category, the third party is the spouse/paramour of the defendant. Generally, where the spouse/paramour and the defendant jointly occupy the premises on a continuing basis, the consent of the spouse/paramour is binding on the defendant.

A second category of cases involves the parents of the defendant. Usually, where the defendant is living at the parents' home, either parent may consent to a search of the defendant's living quarters, based on the parental authority over the family home, even in the child's presence and over the child's objections. Parental authority to search an item in the child's room depends on the parent's access to the item, and an agreement or understanding about the parent opening the item. A child may not, however, consent to a search of the parents' home.

A third category is comprised of persons having limited property rights in the premises searched, such as landlords[72] or motel clerks.[73] While they have a limited right to enter the premises, this authority does not usually include a right to consent to search the defendant's rented premises. Similarly, a lessee cannot consent to a search of the lessor's property in which the lessee has no interest.

A fourth category of cases involves persons who are co-tenants with the defendant. A co-tenant or other joint occupant may consent but usually the consent is not binding on the area of the premises

---

72 Chapman v. United States, 365 U.S. 610 (1961).

73 Stoner v. California, 376 U.S. 483 (1964).

reserved for the private occupancy or use of the defendant. A host or his guest has similar limited rights of consent.

A fifth category relates to bailments. A bailee may give consent for the search of bailed items but usually a bailor may not.

The last category involves employers and employees. Because of the right to privacy, an employer may not bind the employee-defendant by consenting to a search of areas in which the employee is permitted to keep personal items. An employee probably cannot bind the employer-defendant by the employee's consent to a search of the employer's property, unless the employer has delegated considerable authority to the employee.

Chapter 9

STOP AND FRISK

Table of Sections

§ 9.1 Introduction

Prior to the 1960s, it was assumed that, before the police could interfere in any significant way with the liberty of a citizen, they would need the same sort of evidence that would persuade a judge to issue a warrant for the suspect's arrest, i.e., probable cause. During the 1960s, a few events began to weaken the Court's resolve about police-citizen relations. The crime rate rose, aggressive police foot patrols became acceptable, court critics began to demand a more flexible approach to street encounters, and States began to adopt "stop and frisk" statutes that authorized police to briefly detain suspects on the basis of proof lower than probable cause, now known as reasonable suspicion.

Stop and frisk has become another exception to the Fourth Amendment's search warrant requirement. *Terry v. Ohio*[1] freed Fourth Amendment analysis from the rigidity of the probable cause standard, and described a lesser form of Fourth Amendment seizure, known as a "stop." A stop requires that the police have less proof than probable cause, under specific and articulable facts. In addition to a stop, *Terry* allowed a "frisk" for weapons during the stop. The Court has broadened the scope of post-stop police conduct to include limited searches, questioning, and identification. The validity of these actions rests primarily on the lawfulness of the initial stop.

This Chapter discusses the concept of stop and frisk, especially areas of concern since *Terry*: (1) the factual circumstances justifying an encounter on the street, often leading to a legal stop;[2] (2) the distinction between a stop and an arrest;[3] (3) the permissible activities that may occur during a stop;[4] and (4) the length of the stop.[5]

§ 9.2 Standard and Grounds for a Stop

A. Pre-Stop Encounters

When *Terry* in 1968 stated that "street encounters are incredibly rich in diversity"[6] and the Court described the legal requirements for a stop, it became apparent that not all police-citizen contacts qualify as traditional Fourth Amendment "seizures."

> Obviously, not all personal intercourse between policemen and citizens involves "seizures" of persons. Only when the officer, by means of physical force or show of authority, has in some way restrained the liberty of a citizen may we conclude that a 'seizure' has occurred.[7]

A decade later, when federal drug agents approached a suspect and identified themselves in an airport concourse, they asked the suspect for identification and an airline ticket. The Court declared:

> We conclude that a person has been "seized" within the meaning of the Fourth Amendment only if, in view of all of the circumstances surrounding the incident, a reasonable person would have believed that he was not free to leave. Examples of circumstances that might indicate a seizure,

---

1 392 U.S. 1 (1968).

2 See § 9.2, discussing the Standard and Grounds for a Stop.

3 See § 9.2(G), discussing an Arrest Distinguished from a Stop.

4 See § 9.3, discussing Permissible Activities During Detention.

5 See § 9.4, discussing the Duration of Detention.

6 Terry v. Ohio, 392 U.S. 1, 13 (1968).

7 *Id.*, at 19 n.16.

even where the person did not attempt to leave, would be the threatening presence of several officers, the display of a weapon by an officer, some physical touching of the person of the citizen, or the use of language or tone of voice indicating that compliance with the officer's request might be compelled. In the absence of some such evidence, other inoffensive contact between a member of the public and the police cannot, as a matter of law, amount to a seizure of that person.

On the facts of this case, no "seizure" of the respondent occurred. The events took place in the public concourse. The agents wore no uniforms and displayed no weapons. They did not summon the respondent to their presence, but instead approached her and identified themselves as federal agents. They requested, but did not demand to see the respondent's identification and ticket. Such conduct, without more, did not amount to an intrusion upon any constitutionally protected interest. The respondent was not seized simply by reason of the fact that the agents approached her, asked her if she would show them her ticket and identification, and posed to her a few questions. Nor was it enough to establish a seizure that the person asking the questions was a law enforcement official.[8]

B. Terry v. Ohio

Terry v. Ohio was a case from a State which had no stop and frisk statute. In *Terry*, the Court the issue was "whether it is always unreasonable for a policeman to seize a person and subject him to a limited search for weapons unless there is probable cause for an arrest."[9] In response to articulation of the issue, the Court found that an officer may stop and detain a person or a vehicle when the officer concludes based upon a reasonable suspicion that, in light of his experience, criminal activity is afoot,[10] i.e., a reasonable, articulable suspicion that an offense already has been committed, is being committed, or is about to be committed.[11] The reasonable suspicion required for a stop is less evidence than the probable cause required for an arrest.

---

8 United States v. Mendenhall, 446 U.S. 544, 554–55 (1980).

9 *Terry v. Ohio*, 392 U.S. at 15.

10 *Id.*, at 30. See Michigan v. Chesternut, 486 U.S. 567 (1988) (police car driving next to a running pedestrian is not a seizure).

11 United States v. Hensley, 469 U.S. 221 (1985); Terry v. Ohio, 392 U.S. 1 (1968).

In *Terry*, Officer McFadden saw two men standing on a downtown street in the afternoon. One of them walked up the street, looked in a store window, and then continued walking up the street. He returned to the store, peered in the same window, and walked back to his colleague who went through the same ritual. They continued this ritual until they had completed it a dozen times. Was there reasonable suspicion that "criminal" activity is in the planning stage, aka "afoot"? Why could the officer not assume that the two men are "window shopping"?

The facts appeared sufficiently suspicious so that Officer McFadden could reasonably conclude that the individuals were contemplating an armed robbery. Could he also conclude that the two men were "armed and dangerous"? They had not committed an armed robbery, yet, but they may have committed the crime of attempted robbery depending on how that crime is defined. Under the Model Penal Code, the prosecution needed to show only that they took a "substantial step" toward the robbery by "casing the joint."

Based on the facts, it may be debatable whether Officer McFadden had probable cause to believe that the two had committed an "attempted" armed robbery. It also was not clear that he had probable cause to search this pair for the instrumentalities or fruits or evidence of crime. Because a robbery had not occurred, there were no fruits of a crime. Perhaps there was probable cause to believe that the suspects were carrying concealed weapons. Did he have a mere "suspicion" or was there actually probable cause?

If Officer McFadden lacked probable cause to arrest or to search, how could he protect the public, in particular the store and the people there. He could have waited until the robbers began the robbery and then responded, but that approach was dangerous to him and the people in the store, especially if the robbers responded with force. *Terry* held that if an officer concludes, in light of his experience, that criminal activity is afoot and that the suspect is armed and dangerous, he can "stop" the suspect and ask questions. If his suspicions continue after the suspect answers, he may be entitled to conduct a "frisk" of the suspects for weapons.

The *Terry* Court placed great weight on the need for the search and balanced the need for it against the level of intrusion by the search. The Court concluded that the intrusion (not a full scale search, but only a frisk) outweighed the need for it (apprehending the potential robbers prior to commission of the robbery). *Terry* imposes an objective test with subjective components. The test is objective because it focuses on whether the officer reached a reasonable conclusion. It also is subjective because the officer is entitled to rely on his "experience." The focus is not on what a reasonable person would have thought, but on what a reasonable police officer with his level of experience would have thought. A more experienced officer might be able to conduct a frisk even though a novice officer might not. If an officer reasonably concludes in light of his experience that a suspect is engaged in criminal activity, e.g., shoplifting, but does not have grounds for concluding that the suspect is "armed and dangerous," *Terry* implies that the officer still can "stop" the suspect for questioning.

The Court bypassed the "stop" issue and approved a limited frisk of a person's outer clothing after detaining the suspect. For the first time, the Court approved a significant nonconsensual interference with liberty on grounds less than probable cause. If police were forced to live in an "all or nothing world" in which they could stop a person only if they had probable cause, that standard itself likely would have been watered down over time.

For a Court as maligned by police as the Warren Court, *Terry* was an important case for law enforcement, because it was sensitive to the officer working on the street, and was deferential to the decisions that police are required to make in a hurry based on their experience on the street. Even more important, *Terry* produced more police-citizen encounters that are evaluated by a balance of interests that permits evaluation of police stops without a warrant or probable cause.

C. Reasonable Suspicion Examples

Terry mentioned three different types of police-citizen contacts. First, an encounter is a meeting but does not constitute a "seizure" because there is no touching or submission to a show of authority, and thus no Fourth Amendment activity. The police can encounter a person for any reason or no reason—to question, or ask for identification, or request consent to search—as long as the police do not convey the message that compliance is required.

Florida v. Bostick[12] adopted the "reasonable person" standard in the context of "whether a reasonable person feels free to decline the officer's request or other terminate the encounter." Police conducted a "bus sweep" to ask passengers politely for identification as well as their destination. On a common carrier like a bus, circumstances determine whether a person is "free to leave," e.g., whether the police have their guns drawn, or whether the officer's tone of voice indicates that his request really was a command. If the person is free to leave, there is an encounter. If not, there is at least a stop, requiring reasonable suspicion. *Bostick* applied the reasonable person test from

---

12 501 U.S. 429 (1991).

the perspective of a reasonable person looking at what the police officer is doing or saying without the belief that the officer will surely detain him because there is a basis for an arrest.

The fact that the audience on a bus is "captive" was not a problem for the *Bostick* Court. One officer whose work was to have encounters with bus passengers for three months had searched over 4500 bags by "consent." Noting that the reasonable person standard presupposes an innocent person, the Court decided that the free-to-leave test was inapplicable to a bus sweep context in which the police enter a bus and ask the passengers about their identity, their reason for being on the bus, and their bus tickets, before then asking to search their luggage.

In *United States v. Drayton,*[13] the Court applied *Bostick* to another bus sweep. This time, the police did not inform the passengers that they were free not to cooperate with them. The Court again found no seizure, offering many reasons. The questioning officer did not brandish a weapon, made no intimidating movements, left the aisle free, spoke politely and quietly, and did not say anything indicating that the passengers could not leave the bus. If this encounter had been on the street, it would have been constitutional.

> The fact that an encounter takes place on a bus does not on its own transform standard police questioning of citizens into an illegal seizure. Indeed, because many fellow passengers are present to witness officer conduct, a reasonable person may feel even more secure in his or her decision not to cooperate with police on a bus than in other circumstances.[14]

Second, a stop is a temporary seizure of the person short of an arrest. To stop someone, the officer must reasonably conclude in light of his experience and observation that criminal activity may be afoot and that the person is armed and presently dangerous. The purpose of a stop may be to clarify an ambiguous situation. "Only when the officer, by means of physical force or show of authority, has in some way restrained the liberty of a citizen may we conclude that a 'seizure' has occurred."[15]

From the case law, common sense and ordinary human experience must govern over rigid criteria in an officer's decision to stop a person or vehicle.[16] *Kansas v. Glover*[17] held that a police officer

---

13 536 U.S. 194 (2002).

14 United States v. Drayton, 536 U.S. 194, 204 (2002).

15 *Terry v. Ohio*, 392 U.S. at 19 n.16.

16 United States v. Sharpe, 470 U.S. 675 (1985).

17 589 U.S. 376 (2020).

did not violate the Fourth Amendment by initiating an investigative traffic stop after running a vehicle's license plate number through a database and learning that the registered owner had a revoked driver's license. When the officer lacks information negating an inference that the owner is the driver of the vehicle, the stop is reasonable. The reasonable suspicion standard "depends on the factual and practical considerations of everyday life on which reasonable and prudent men, not legal technicians, act."[18] When applying the reasonable suspicion standard, an officer does not need to "rule out the possibility of innocent conduct."[19]

In any factual determination which looks to the totality of the circumstances, like the reasonable suspicion standard, there is a balance between the need to investigate and the invasion which the seizure entails. The limited intrusion on the personal security of the person or property detained is justified by both (1) substantial law enforcement interests in the detection and prevention of crime, and (2) the safety of the officer balanced against the reasons for the intrusion.

For example, in *United States v. Sokolow*,[20] the suspect paid $2100 for two plane tickets from a roll of $20 bills, traveled under a name that did not match the name under which his telephone number was listed, went to Miami as his original destination that is known as a city for illegal drug trafficking, stayed there for only 48 hours even though a round trip flight from there to Hawaii takes twenty hours, appeared nervous during his trip, and checked none of his luggage. The Court found reasonable suspicion of drug activity. Standing alone, while some of those facts are rather common, coupled with others a finding of reasonable suspicion was not difficult.

In *United States v. Hensley*,[21] the arresting officer was reacting to a flyer that the driver of a car was wanted for committing a robbery and should be considered armed and dangerous. When the officer saw the suspect's car, he approached the car "with his service revolver drawn and pointed in the air." The Court described the officer's conduct as "well within the permissible range in the context of suspects who are reported to be armed and dangerous."[22] *Hensley* expanded *Terry* to include both crimes that had not yet been completed and those that had concluded. Specifically, the Court expressly authorized stopping "a person suspected of involvement in

---

[18] Kansas v. Glover, 589 U.S. 376, 381 (2020) quoting Navarette v. California, 572 U.S. 393, 403 (2014).

[19] *Id.*

[20] 490 U.S. 1 (1989).

[21] 469 U.S. 221 (1985).

[22] United States v. Hensley, 469 U.S. 221, 224, 235 (1985).

a past crime," i.e., where "it is in the public interest that the crime be solved and the suspect detained as promptly as possible."[23]

> A stop to investigate an already completed crime does not necessarily promote the interest of crime prevention as directly as a stop to investigate suspected ongoing criminal activity. Similarly, the exigent circumstances which require a police officer to step in before a crime is committed or completed are not necessarily as pressing long afterwards. Public safety may be less threatened by a suspect in a past crime who now appears to be going about his lawful business than it is by a suspect who is currently in the process of violating the law. Finally, officers making a stop to investigate past crimes may have a wider range of opportunity to choose the time and circumstances of the stop.[24]

Thus, *Terry*'s "may be afoot" language is not to be taken literally; stops are allowed when a person has already committed a crime and the police are looking for the perpetrator.

> The justification for a stop did not evaporate when the armed robbery was completed. Hensley was reasonably suspected of involvement in a felony and was at large from the time the suspicion arose until the stop by the Covington police. A brief stop and detention at the earliest opportunity after the suspicion arose is fully consistent with the principles of the Fourth Amendment.[25]

In *Navarette v. California*,[26] police stopped a pickup truck that matched the vehicle description from an anonymous caller who claimed the vehicle had run her off the road only minutes before the call. When the officers approached the stopped vehicle, they smelled marijuana, searched the truck's bed, and found thirty pounds of marijuana. The Court found the anonymous caller reliable, because the caller "claimed eyewitness knowledge" and was making a contemporaneous report. The Court expanded the crimes for which a stop is authorized to include an ongoing crime like drunk driving, i.e., "the 911 caller's report of being run off the roadway created reasonable suspicion of an ongoing crime such as drunk driving as opposed to an isolated episode of past recklessness."[27]

---

[23] *Id.*, at 229.

[24] *Id.*, at 228–29.

[25] *Id.*, at 234.

[26] 572 U.S. 393 (2014).

[27] Navarette v. California, 572 U.S. 393, 401 (2014).

D. Factors for a Stop

Standing alone, a generalized fear of criminal activity or the presence of a suspect in a high crime neighborhood are factors that do not justify a stop. However, courts may use these and other factors to analyze the totality of the circumstances and determine whether there is an objective basis for suspecting the person of criminal activity. Even if each of several factors alone is susceptible to an innocent explanation, the factors together may satisfy the standard of reasonable suspicion for a stop under the totality of circumstances.

In other words, when there are several points of comparison possible as a result of a description, a person may still be stopped even if he does not match on all points. In *United States v. Arvizu*,[28] the Court noted:

> The [lower] court's evaluation and rejection of seven of the listed factors in isolation from each other does not take into account the "totality of the circumstances," as our cases have understood that phrase. The court appeared to believe that each observation by Stoddard that was by itself readily susceptible to an innocent explanation was entitled to "no weight." *Terry*, however, precludes this sort of divide-and-conquer analysis. The officer in *Terry* observed the petitioner and his companions repeatedly walk back and forth, look into a store window, and confer with one another. Although each of the series of acts was "perhaps innocent in itself," we held that, taken together, they "warranted further investigation."[29]

Most stops of individuals are for investigation of property crimes, when the suspect is carrying some object under suspicious circumstances. Frequently, the defendant's reaction to the officers prior to the stop is given considerable weight, i.e., efforts to avoid the police or avoid being seen by them can contribute to or be the grounds for a stop. "[H]eadlong flight . . . is the consummate act of evasion; it not necessarily indicative of wrongdoing, but it is certainly suggestive of such."[30] In *Illinois v. Wardlow*,[31] the Court upheld a stop of a suspect who ran from the police in a heavy drug trafficking area as soon as he saw them. After catching him, police subjected him to a frisk for weapons and felt a hard object they thought was a gun. The officer pulled out a gun and ammunition.

---

28 United States v. Arvizu, 534 U.S. 266 (2002).

29 *Id.*, at 274.

30 Illinois v. Wardlow, 528 U.S. 119, 124 (2000).

31 528 U.S. 119 (2000).

Although the factors known by the stopping officer may be insufficient to constitute probable cause for a full arrest, the information may be sufficient for a stop. A stop may occur when the police observe a suspect near the scene of a recent crime.[32] An officer may act on his knowledge from a specific description of a vehicle or person, the elapsed time since the crime occurred, the number of other persons in the area, the time of day or night or the area in which the suspect is found, whether the defendant is carrying certain types of property, the type of premises that the defendant is near, whether the individual is in a "high crime" area, or the person's prior criminal record.[33]

The Supreme Court's reluctance to identify a specific formula of factors to govern any stop for an individual has produced an *ad hoc* approach to stopping individuals on the street or in buildings. *Ornelas v. United States* supported that hesitancy when the Court held that the

> standard for appellate review of reasonable-suspicion determinations should be *de novo,* rather than for "abuse of discretion." Other benefits of the approach . . . were its tendency to unify precedent and greater capacity to provide law enforcement officers with the tools to reach correct determinations beforehand. Even if in many instances the factual "mosaic" analyzed for a reasonable-suspicion determination would preclude one case from squarely controlling another, "two decisions when viewed together may usefully add to the body of law on the subject."[34]

United States v. Arvizu added:

> "[*D*]*e novo* review would prevent the affirmance of opposite decisions on identical facts from different judicial districts in the same circuit, which would have been possible under the latter standard, and would allow appellate courts to clarify the legal principles."[35]

As with the exigent circumstances[36] exception for a search warrant, a stop may be justified due to the need for emergency aid "to assist persons who are seriously injured or threatened with such injury."[37] The test for whether this exception is whether the officer,

---

32 United States v. Hensley, 469 U.S. 221, 233 (1985).

33 Michigan v. Long, 463 U.S. 1032 (1983).

34 517 U.S. 690, 691 (1996).

35 *United States v. Arvizu,* 534 U.S. at 275.

36 See Chapter 10, discussing Exigent Circumstances.

37 Mincey v. Arizona, 437 U.S. 385, 393–94 (1978).

based on the information available at the time, had an objectively reasonable belief that a person was in need of immediate aid.[38]

A stop of a vehicle obviously requires reasonable grounds to suspect that a crime is or has been committed. Among the factors which determine the existence of reasonable suspicion in vehicular stop cases are the characteristics of the area, the driver's behavior, the aspects of the vehicle itself, as well as the extraordinarily large numbers of passengers and their actions. A vehicle stop is a seizure of the passengers as well as the driver.[39] The seizure of the passengers is lawful even though there is no additional reason to believe that they are "involved in criminal activity."[40] Without any showing that the suspect may be armed, the police have the authority to order both the driver and any passengers from the vehicle to protect themselves.[41]

Suppose that the police are determined to find some reason to stop a suspect. Are they permitted to follow the suspect's vehicle, waiting for him to do something illegal, such as running a stop sign? *Whren v. United States*[42] answered in the affirmative. The reasonableness of a stop is not dependent upon the subjective motives of police officers who make the stop. The *Whren* Court held that even a minor, civil traffic infraction can be the basis for a stop as long as probable cause exists to believe that a law was broken. The Court rejected the argument that pretextual traffic stops violate the Fourth Amendment.[43]

While the officer's personal knowledge and experience are important grounds for the ability to articulate a reasonable suspicion, the grounds for as stop may even be based upon a reasonable mistake of law. For example, in *Heien v. North Carolina*,[44] a proper traffic stop of defendant was based on a reasonable but mistaken belief by officer that state law required that a vehicle have two operating lamps.

As the next two sections discuss, stops may be based either on the officer's own observation, or on information from others which may be supplemented by corroborating information from the officer

---

38 See Missouri v. McNeely, 569 U.S. 141 (2013).

39 Brendlin v. California, 551 U.S. 249 (2007).

40 Arizona v. Johnson, 555 U.S. 323, 327 (2009).

41 Maryland v. Wilson, 519 U.S. 408 (1997); Pennsylvania v. Mimms, 434 U.S. 106 (1977).

42 517 U.S. 806 (1996).

43 See Arkansas v. Sullivan, 532 U.S. 769 (2001) (a traffic arrest is not invalid by being a pretext for search; probable cause is sole standard for a seizure's legality).

44 574 U.S. 54 (2014).

at the scene. Neither area is isolated from the other and factors may be considered which are common to both.

E. Stops Based on Police Observation

The classic *Terry* stop is where the officer detains a defendant based exclusively on the officer's own observations. The observations must produce a particularized and objective basis for suspecting the person stopped of criminal activity. The "objective basis" has received great attention in the "drug courier profile" cases involving airport searches. For example, in *United States v. Sokolow*,[45] the Court held that the reasonable suspicion for an investigative stop of the defendant was based on the totality of circumstances. An officer may rely upon his training and experience, as well as inferences and deductions therefrom that might elude an untrained person.[46] For example, in vehicular stop cases, the behavior of the vehicle's occupants may raise a reasonable suspicion to stop the vehicle.[47]

F. Stops Based on Information from Others

The observation by a police officer following receipt of third party information is similar to the case of exclusive observation for an officer. Courts consider whether the area is a crime area, the suspicious nature of the vehicle, and the lateness of the hour. The actions of the defendant also receive great weight, as well as any prior knowledge of the officer about the defendant.

A stop may also occur when an officer obtains information from known or anonymous third parties.[48] These stops may take place when the information from others is the exclusive basis or the stop, but more frequently they occur when the officer's own observations corroborate the information from others. To be valid, the stop may be based upon information if the tip is supported by indicia of reliability, i.e., by more than entirely innocent behavior.

For example, in *Florida v. J.L.*,[49] an anonymous tipster called the police to say that a young Black male was wearing a plaid shirt while carrying a concealed weapon and standing with others at a bus stop. Apart from the tip, the officers had no reason to believe that any of the persons was engaged in illegal conduct. The officers at the scene immediately frisked the defendant and found a gun in his

---

[45] 490 U.S. 1 (1989).

[46] Florida v. Rodriguez, 469 U.S. 1 (1984).

[47] United States v. Sharpe, 470 U.S. 675 (1985); Michigan v. Long, 463 U.S. 1032 (1983).

[48] See, e.g., Alabama v. White, 496 U.S. 325 (1990); Adams v. Williams, 407 US. 143 (1972).

[49] 529 U.S. 266 (2000).

pocket. The Court reversed the conviction, because of the nature of the information in the tip. "The reasonable suspicion . . . requires that a tip be reliable in its assertion of illegality, not just in its tendency to identify a determinate person."[50] In other words, police action must be based on objective criteria rather than simply a "hunch." Tips about persons with firearms ae not subject to a lower standard of reasonable suspicion than other types of anonymous tips. The Court also noted that reasonable suspicion requires that a tip be reliable in its assertion of illegality, not just in its tendency to identify a specific person.

In *Navarette v. California*,[51] a motorist's anonymous 911 call, reporting that a pickup truck had just run her off the road, was legally sufficient for the police to stop the truck, without having to independently corroborate the tip. Reasonable suspicion derived from the totality of the circumstances showing that the tip was reliable; the phone caller was credible because (1) the tipster claimed eyewitness knowledge of an incident and (2) the call was made almost immediately after the incident.

When it is clear that a crime has occurred within a short time prior to the stop, the third-party information may establish the connection between the crime and the defendant in order to stop the defendant. Suppose officers are investigating an armed robbery and they have a description of the vehicle and the robber. The vehicle is later stopped because of a broken taillight, but that officer made no connection between the robbery and the defendant in the vehicle. Another officer, who learned of the earlier vehicle stop in the particular vehicle, knew the defendant and knew that he was similar in appearance to the robber. The latter officer may stop the vehicle again, which this time disclosed evidence upon which the defendant was arrested. The second stop is lawful as routine police investigation based on the description of the robber and the vehicle from others.

Proximity to a crime also may permit a stop. Suppose officers receive a call about a robbery in progress but by the time they arrive at the store, the robbers have run out the back door. The officers get in their vehicle and observe another vehicle turn on its lights and leave the premises. At the time of that observation, there were no other moving vehicles or pedestrians in the area. Their observation confirmed reasonable suspicion that the vehicle's occupants were responsible for the robbery.

An officer may corroborate information from others about a vehicle's description in order to support a stop. For example, in

---

50 Florida v. J.L., 529 U.S. 266, 272 (2000).

51 572 U.S. 393 (2014).

Alabama v. White,[52] independent police work supplemented an anonymous telephone tip that the defendant would be leaving a specific place at a specific time in possession of a controlled substance and drive to another specific place. By the time of the stop, the police had corroborated the anonymous tip in sufficient detail. The tipster's accurate predictions about the suspect's future conduct, including innocent conduct, demonstrated a basis of knowledge that established the tipster's reliability.

In *United States v. Hensley*,[53] the police relied on the strength of a "wanted flyer" issued by another city for a robbery two weeks earlier. The defendant argued that, while the officers in the other city may have possessed reasonable suspicion that the defendant was involved in the robbery, the officers making the stop did not have enough information to make the stop. However, the Court found that, if the flyer issued on the basis of articulable facts supporting reasonable suspicion, then reliance on that flyer justified a stop to check identification.

> Assuming the police make a *Terry* stop in objective reliance on a flyer or bulletin, we hold that evidence uncovered in the course of the stop is admissible if the police who issued the flyer or bulletin possessed a reasonable suspicion justifying a stop, . . . and if the stop that in fact occurred was not significantly more intrusive than would have been permitted the issuing department.[54]

While the Court upheld the stop that actually occurred, it cautioned that the flyer could not authorize a lengthy or intrusive detention.[55]

G. Arrest Distinguished from a Stop

The traditional distinction between a "stop" and an "arrest" is probable cause. In *Terry*, the Court stressed that an arrest "is a wholly different kind of intrusion upon individual freedom. . . inevitably accompanied by future interference with the individual's freedom of movement."[56] implying that a lawful stop has a limited duration, scope, and location. Suppose the officers use great force in a stop or at the time of the stop, the officers claim arrest authority. If the actions of the police become the attributes of an arrest, the "stop" is converted into an arrest for which probable cause is required.[57] An

---

52 Alabama v. White, 496 U.S. 325 (1990).

53 469 U.S. 221 (1985).

54 United States v. Hensley, 469 U.S. 221, 233 (1985).

55 *Id.*, at 235.

56 *Terry v. Ohio*, 392 U.S. at 26.

57 Florida v. Royer, 460 U.S. 491 (1983).

arrest is based on probable cause; it permits a search incident to that arrest to preserve evidence and to protect the police.

> Each case of this sort will, of course, have to be decided on its own facts. We merely hold today that where a police officer observes unusual conduct which leads him reasonably to conclude in light of his experience that criminal activity may be afoot and that the persons with whom he is dealing may be armed and dangerous, where in the course of investigating this behavior he identifies himself as a policeman and makes reasonable inquiries, and nothing in the initial stages of the encounter serves to dispel his reasonable fear for his own or others' safety, he is entitled for the protection of himself and others in the area to conduct a carefully limited search of the outer clothing of such persons in an attempt to discover weapons which might be used to assault him.
>
> Such a search is a reasonable search under the Fourth Amendment, and any weapons seized may properly be introduced in evidence against the person from whom they were taken.[58]

With the differing legal standards for a stop and an arrest, as well as an arrest being the next permissible police step after a stop, prosecutors and defense counsel may stake out legal positions based upon the facts. For example, suppose that the police claim that they stopped a defendant and therefore did not need probable cause, but yet instead of frisking the suspect, the police immediately searched the suspect's clothing and the surrounding area. Defense counsel will claim that the police arrested the suspect instead of stopping him, and will claim further that the only explanation for doing a search incident to an arrest was for the person to have already been arrested. Generally the most the police could do initially after a stop is to frisk the suspect. Having heard the police describe their actions, defense counsel may argue that probable cause was lacking for an arrest, although reasonable suspicion justified a stop.[59]

In *United States v. Bonilla*,[60] after a drug dog alerted on his suitcase, the defendant agreed to permit the police to search it. During the suitcase search, the defendant was calm and cooperative. When another officer began asking questions, the defendant showed

---

58 *Terry v. Ohio*, 392 U.S. at 30–31.

59 See Peters v. New York, 392 U.S. 40 (1968), (if an officer perceives that a suspect's conduct is a stop only, but nevertheless makes a full search of the arrestee rather than a mere frisk, the evidence found is admissible if in fact the officer had grounds to arrest).

60 86 F.4th 1196 (8th Cir. 2023).

signs of nervousness. Before the police completed searching the suitcase, the defendant asked the detective twice if he could visit the bus station restroom to brush his teeth. The detective sensed that the request was an excuse to flee or discard something on his person, or to leave the police presence. After the detective told the defendant that he preferred him to stay and watch while the suitcase was searched, he remained visibly nervous and looked around. After finding nothing in the suitcase, the detective then asked his consent to search the backpack. The defendant refused and the detective pursued the search anyway, because often "when someone [consents] . . . to search one bag but not another, it usually means there is some type of contraband in the other bag that the person does not want [officers] to find."[61] At that point, the detective handcuffed the defendant because he had a legitimate concern that the defendant would try to leave the scene, i.e., a reasonable belief that defendant was armed and dangerous. Less than a minute later, the drug dog alerted on fentanyl located in the backpack.

Soon after a grand jury indicted the defendant, he filed a motion to suppress the drugs found in his backpack. Following the trial court's denial of the motion, the defendant entered a conditional guilty plea to possession with intent to distribute. He appealed, arguing that he had been arrested without probable cause when the officers handcuffed him during the stop and that the evidence in his backpack constituted fruit of an illegal arrest. The Eighth Circuit responded:

> On this record, it was not error to find that the use of handcuffs on Bonilla was necessary for a legitimate purpose and that, as a result, there was no de facto arrest.
>
> Because placing Bonilla in handcuffs did not convert the investigative stop into a de facto arrest, it follows that the seizure of the evidence from his backpack was not the fruit of an unlawful arrest. We affirm the denial of the motion to suppress.[62]

H. Reasonable Suspicion for a Stop Compared to Profiling

Like probable cause, reasonable suspicion is based on an individualized assessment of circumstances. Profiles of defendants have been used for at least fifty years to support stopping certain persons based upon certain characteristics and behavioral traits, e.g., persons taking brief round trips by air, purchasing tickets with cash,

---

61 United States v. Bonilla, 86 F.4th at 1198.

62 *Id.*, at 1200.

no baggage, deplaning last, and nervous or unusual behavior. However, profiles for drug couriers or for pedophiles do not necessarily equate with the reasonable suspicion necessary to justify a stop which must be based on actual facts. Reliance on a profile does not necessarily amount to reasonable suspicion for a stop, because the profile does not address why a particular characteristic is important, how many others have that trait, and how often a person with that trait is not a criminal.

In *United States v. Cortez*,[63] the Court noted that reasonable suspicion must be based on the totality of circumstances, which involves the cumulative effect of facts rather the presence of a fact that happens to match a profile characteristic.

> The idea that an assessment of the whole picture must yield a particularized suspicion contains two elements, each of which must be present before a stop is permissible. First, the assessment must be based upon all the circumstances. The analysis proceeds with various objective observations, information from police reports, if such are available, and consideration of the modes or patterns of operation of certain kinds of lawbreakers. From these data, a trained officer draws inferences and makes deductions—inferences and deductions that might well elude an untrained person.
>
> The process does not deal with hard certainties, but with probabilities. Long before the law of probabilities was articulated as such, practical people formulated certain common sense conclusions about human behavior; jurors as factfinders are permitted to do the same—and so are law enforcement officers. Finally, the evidence thus collected must be seen and weighed not in terms of library analysis by scholars, but as understood by those versed in the field of law enforcement.
>
> The second element contained in the idea that an assessment of the whole picture must yield a particularized suspicion is the concept that the process just described must raise a suspicion that the particular individual being stopped is engaged in wrongdoing.[64]

United States v. Sokolow[65] held that police had a "reasonable basis to suspect that respondent was transporting illegal drugs." The

---

[63] 449 U.S. 411 (1981).

[64] United States v. Cortez, 449 U.S. 411, 418 (1981).

[65] 490 U.S. 1 (1989).

Court compared profiling with the reasonable suspicion standard for a Fourth Amendment stop.

> A court sitting to determine the existence of reasonable suspicion must require the agent to articulate the factors leading to that conclusion, but the fact that these factors may be set forth in a "profile" does not somehow detract from their evidentiary significance as seen by a trained agent.[66]

The Court approved the use of profiling as an investigative reference point, but stated that the actual existence of reasonable suspicion must be based on facts. The fear is that police would use profiling to harass segments of the population. Moreover, a profile can dull the senses and lead to police reciting profile factors rather than looking at whether profile factors are relevant evidence of suspicious activity.

Like *Cortez*, *Sokolow* is a reminder that reasonable suspicion is a case-by-case approach based on the totality of circumstances. By themselves, it is no crime to do certain things like purchase a type of gasoline, have a surge in electrical usage at home, or visit with drug convicts. But explaining away each fact ignores the point that profiling may benefit the police when each fact arose in the same case.

§ 9.3 Permissible Activities During Detention

A. Frisking a Person

After a stop, if police officers still suspect that the person seized is about to or has committed a crime, *Terry* permits them to frisk the suspect if they also have reasonable grounds to believe the person is armed and dangerous. Justice Harlan's *Terry* concurrence directly addressed the issue of danger for the police. "If and when a policeman has a right. . . to disarm such a person for his own protection, he must first have a right not to avoid him but to be in his presence."[67] Even though *Terry* does not call for a frisk to follow every stop, Justice Harlan's opinion indicates that a frisk generally may follow a stop. If the officer is in the presence of the suspect to be frisked, he is endangered if that person is armed. The concern for danger usually flows from the nature of the crime for which reasonable suspicion exists.

> [T]here must be a narrowly drawn authority to permit a reasonable search for weapons for the protection of the police officer, where he has reason to believe that he is

---

66 United States v. Sokolow, 490 U.S. 1, 10 (1989).

67 *Terry v. Ohio*, 392 U.S. at 32 (Harlan, J., concurring).

> dealing with an armed and dangerous individual, regardless of whether he has probable cause to arrest the individual for a crime. The officer need not be absolutely certain that the individual is armed; the issue is whether a reasonably prudent man in the circumstances would be warranted in the belief that his safety or that of others was in danger. And in determining whether the officer acted reasonably in such circumstances, due weight must be given, not to his inchoate and unparticularized suspicion or "hunch," but to the specific reasonable inferences which he is entitled to draw from the facts in light of his experience.[68]

If the stop was legal, reasonable suspicion to frisk a suspect may be satisfied by the nature of the investigation, a bulge in the suspect's clothing, a sudden movement by the suspect toward a pocket or other place where a weapon may be hidden, and police awareness that the suspect was armed on a prior occasion.

A frisk typically begins with a patdown of the suspect's outer clothing. The scope of a patdown is of any part of a suspect from which the suspect may be able to retrieve a weapon that could be used against the officer. During the patdown, if the officer feels what he believes is a weapon, he may reach beneath the surface and retrieve it. If he feels an object that is not a weapon, the frisk should cease; he cannot continue it to ascertain whether the soft object is otherwise incriminating. If the hard object turns out to be a container, the officer may open it if he still believes that a weapon is inside the container. If he finds a weapon in the container, he may have probable cause to arrest the suspect for carrying a concealed weapon.

In *Arizona v. Johnson*,[69] officers stopped a vehicle for a traffic infraction and issued a citation. After learning that a backseat passenger had been in prison and his clothing matched how members of a known gang dressed, she ordered him to exit the vehicle. Because she suspected that he was armed, she patted him down for her safety as he exited the vehicle. She felt the butt of a gun; as the passenger began to struggle she handcuffed him and charged him with illegal possession of a weapon. After his conviction for weapons possession, the defendant appealed successfully to the State appellate court. The Court granted certiorari and reversed, holding that the patdown did not violate the Fourth Amendment.

> [A] traffic stop of a car communicates to a reasonable passenger that he or she is not free to terminate the encounter with the police and move about at will. Nothing

---

68 See *id.*, at 27.

69 555 U.S. 323, 327 (2009).

occurred in this case that would have conveyed to Johnson that, prior to the frisk, the traffic stop had ended or that he was otherwise free "to depart without police permission." Officer Trevizo surely was not constitutionally required to give Johnson an opportunity to depart the scene after he exited the vehicle without first ensuring that, in so doing, she was not permitting a dangerous person to get behind her.[70]

During the patdown, if the officer feels something soft, he should not continue a tactile examination in an effort to determine whether the object is incriminating.[71] If the officer retrieves the soft item from beneath the surface and tries to admit it into evidence, the prosecutor may be forced to argue that an arrest had occurred and that seizure of the soft item was part of a search incident to arrest. In that situation, the prosecutor would have to prove that there was probable cause to have already made an arrest of the suspect before the police retrieved the soft item.

Terry noted that a search *more* invasive than a valid frisk is permissible when an officer's reasonable suspicion ripens into probable cause based on his prior knowledge that the defendant was actively selling drugs, and his frisk of the defendant revealed what he knew to be a prohibited controlled substance.[72] An exception to the frisk protocol developed in *Adams v. Williams*,[73] when the officer was allowed to bypass the patdown and reach beneath the suspect's clothing immediately when an informant had told him the exact location of a weapon and the suspect failed to exit the vehicle when requested.

B. Frisking a Vehicle

In *Michigan v. Long*,[74] the Court expanded the area of "frisking" a vehicle during a *Terry* stop. Given specific facts to believe that a suspect is dangerous and may gain control of weapons in a stopped vehicle, an officer may search the passenger compartment where a weapon may be placed or hidden. After the police saw Long's vehicle swerve into a ditch, they stopped to investigate. Long appeared to be "under the influence of something" and both officers observed a long hunting knife on the floorboard of the driver's side of the vehicle. A

---

[70] *Arizona v. Johnson*, 555 U.S. at 333–34.

[71] Minnesota v. Dickerson, 508 U.S. 366 (1993).

[72] See *Terry v. Ohio*, 392 U.S. at 21–24.

[73] 407 U.S. 143 (1972).

[74] 463 U.S. 1032 (1983). See Knowles v. Iowa, 525 U.S. 113 (1998) (issuance of citation for traffic violation invalidates warrantless search of passenger compartment).

frisk of Long revealed weapons and a vehicle frisk for more weapons yielded illicit drugs.

Long held that an officer may search the passenger compartment of a vehicle limited to those areas where a weapon may be located. Even when the suspect is under the "control" of the police, *Long* authorized the officers to conduct a frisk, because the suspect could "break away" and obtain a weapon, or the suspect could grab the weapon when he re-enters the vehicle. The nature of the risk to the officer is unpredictable.

Even if the police lack the reasonable suspicion to frisk a passenger, the officer is not powerless, because the Court has held that officers can order the driver and all passengers to exit the vehicle for their safety.[75] Most States now recognize by statute that, after a vehicle's driver is arrested, the officer may also conduct a patdown for weapons of any passenger who was in the vehicle that was properly stopped, even if there is no independent suspicion that the passenger is guilty of criminal conduct.

While allowing a search for weapons based on a concept of security, *Terry* also permits a search of containers believed to contain contraband. In *United States v. Place*,[76] the Court held that brief detentions of personal property may be so minimally intrusive of Fourth Amendment interests that countervailing State interests justify a seizure based only on specific articulable facts that the property contains contraband or evidence of crime. However, if the detention is prolonged, the seizure may be illegal.[77]

C. Detention for Questioning or Identification

In addition to a search for objects, an officer may detain a suspect briefly for questioning. *Terry* stops, though somewhat inherently coercive, do not usually involve the type of police-dominated atmosphere which requires *Miranda* warnings.[78] However, *Miranda* warnings may be necessary during a *Terry* stop if the suspect is taken into custody and the questioning occurs in a police-dominated or compelling atmosphere.

A *Terry* stop may also be for the purpose of identification. In *Davis v. Mississippi*,[79] twenty-five Black youths were detained for questioning and fingerprinting in connection with a rape for which

---

[75] Maryland v. Wilson, 519 U.S. 408 (1997); Pennsylvania v. Mimms, 434 U.S. 106 (1977).

[76] 462 U.S. 696 (1983).

[77] See § 9.4, discussing the Duration of Detention.

[78] See, e.g., United States v. Bautista, 684 F.2d 1286 (9th Cir. 1982).

[79] 394 U.S. 721 (1969).

the only leads were a general description and a set of fingerprints. While the defendant's prints should have been excluded as the fruits of a seizure in violation of the Fourth Amendment, the Court intimated that a detention at the station might sometimes be permissible on grounds that are insufficient for an arrest.

> Detentions for the sole purpose of obtaining fingerprints are no less subject to the constraints of the Fourth Amendment. It is arguable, however, that because of the unique nature of the fingerprinting process, such detentions might, under narrowly defined circumstances, be found to comply with the Fourth Amendment even though there is no probable cause in the traditional sense. Detention for fingerprinting may constitute a much less serious intrusion upon personal security than other types of police searches and detentions. Fingerprinting involves none of the probing into an individual's private life and thoughts that marks an interrogation or search. Nor can fingerprint detention be employed repeatedly to harass any individual, since the police need only one set of each person's prints. Furthermore, fingerprinting is an inherently more reliable and effective crime-solving tool than eyewitness identifications or confessions and is not subject to such abuses as the improper lineup and the "third degree." Finally, because there is no danger of destruction of fingerprints, the limited detention need not come unexpectedly or at an inconvenient time. For this same reason, the general requirement that the authorization of a judicial officer be obtained in advance of detention would seem not to admit of any exception in the fingerprinting context.[80]

Detentions also may occur for the purpose of an identification by a witness. "The principles of *Terry* permit a state to require a suspect to disclose his name in the course of a *Terry* stop."[81] In *Hiibel v. Nevada*,[82] the Supreme Court upheld a statute requiring an arrest to be based on *both* a person's failure to identify himself and a reasonable suspicion of criminal activity. The defendant's failure to give his name was insufficient for a stop or an arrest, but the police officer's question about identification was "not an effort to obtain an arrest for failure to identify after a *Terry* stop yielded insufficient evidence."[83]

---

[80] Davis v. Mississippi, 394 U.S. 721, 727–28 (1969).

[81] Hiibel v. Nevada, 542 U.S. 177, 187 (2004).

[82] 542 U.S. 177 (2004).

[83] *Hiibel v. Nevada*, 542 U.S. at 189.

§ 9.4 Duration of Detention

A. Detention of a Person

A *Terry* stop was originally for the purposes of a "brief" investigation. If the person is stopped on suspicion that he has just engaged in criminal activity, but the suspect identifies himself satisfactorily or the investigation establishes that no offense has occurred, there is no basis for further detention and the suspect must be released. However, if further inquiry is required, an investigative stop does not have to end after a couple of minutes. In order for a *Terry* stop's purpose "to be served, the police must under certain circumstances be able to detain the individual longer than the brief time period involved in *Terry*."[84]

Even though police must diligently pursue their investigation during the detention to confirm or dispel their suspicion quickly, the Court has not fixed outer time limits for the duration of a stop,[85]

> [I]f an investigative stop continues indefinitely, at some point it can no longer be justified as an investigative stop. But our cases impose no rigid time limitation on *Terry* stops. While it is clear that "the brevity of the invasion of the individual's Fourth Amendment interests is an important factor in determining whether the seizure is so minimally intrusive as to be justifiable on reasonable suspicion," we have emphasized the need to consider the law enforcement purposes to be served by the stop as well as the time reasonably needed to effectuate those purposes.[86]

Delays in the detention will not convert the situation from a stop to an arrest as long as the delay is not caused by the officer's bad faith or laziness, e.g., because a computer system malfunctions, a check for outstanding warrants cannot occur as quickly.

An extended detention "might well be so lengthy or intrusive as to exceed the permissible limits of a *Terry* stop,"[87] whereby a trial court could treat it as an arrest for which probable cause becomes the

---

[84] Michigan v. Summers, 452 U.S. 692, 700 (1981).

[85] See, e.g., United States v. Place, 462 U.S. 696 (1983) (ninety-minute detention excessive; Court declined to set a time limit for a stop).

[86] United States v. Sharpe, 470 U.S. 675, 685 (1985), quoting United States v. Place, 462 U.S. 696, 709 (1983).

[87] United States v. Hensley, 469 U.S. 221, 235 (1985). See United States v. Sharpe, 470 U.S. 675 (1985) (twenty-minute detention not excessive); United States v. Place, 462 U.S. 696 (1983) (ninety-minute detention was excessive; the Court declined to set a time limit for a stop).

correct legal standard. In *Florida v. Royer*,[88] after the police stopped and questioned a suspected drug courier in an airport, they required him to go with them to an office forty feet away. There, he consented to a suitcase search. From stop to consent, only fifteen minutes elapsed. The Court assumed that moving the suspect was permissible for reasons of security and safety, but the Court's plurality held that the defendant's consent was the fruit of an illegal arrest. Because the officers were primarily interested in the luggage contents, the police could have more promptly asked for the defendant's consent, or in the alternative brought in a drug dog to sniff for the drugs.

A detention may last for so long that the suspect was under arrest, requiring a showing of probable cause.[89] In *Hayes v. Florida*,[90] the Court held that a detention to fingerprint a suspect is lawful only when there is "a reasonable basis for believing that fingerprinting will establish or negate the suspect's connection with" the crime justifying the stop. Police must have probable cause or judicial authorization to remove a suspect involuntarily from his home to a police station for investigative purposes for interrogation or fingerprinting. In *Kaupp v. Texas*,[91] a defendant was illegally removed in handcuffs from his home to a crime scene, and was moved again to the sheriff's office for questioning after which he confessed. The Court remanded the case for a decision about whether the confession was the fruit of an illegal arrest.

B. Detention of a Vehicle

A stop begins when a vehicle is pulled over to investigate a traffic violation. That stop constitutes a seizure of the vehicle, the driver, and all other occupants.[92] Police may seize persons to carry out their duties incident to a traffic stop, such as checking licenses or registration information, and determining whether there are outstanding warrants against the driver.[93] The vehicle stop ends when the police do not have to control the scene any longer, and they inform the driver and his passengers that they are free to go. During a vehicle stop, the driver and passengers are not free to end the encounter with the police or to move about at will. In *Arizona v. Johnson*,[94] the police took no action that would have indicated to

---

88 460 U.S. 491 (1983).

89 Dunaway v. New York, 442 U.S. 200 (1979).

90 470 U.S. 811 (1985).

91 538 U.S. 626 (2003).

92 Brendlin v. California, 551 U.S. 249 (2007).

93 See, e.g., Rodriguez v. United States, 575 U.S. 348 (2015) (extending traffic stop to conduct a dog sniff requires continuing reasonable suspicion).

94 555 U.S. 323 (2009).

defendant that traffic stop had ended or that he was free to go without their permission.

In *Illinois v. Caballes*,[95] the defendant was stopped for a minor traffic offense and was ticketed by a trooper, while another trooper appeared with a drug dog that walked around the vehicle and "alerted." A vehicle search revealed drugs in the trunk. The Court held that using the dog and targeting criminality that was not suspected initially is not a violation "unless the dog sniff itself infringed [Caballes'] constitutionally protected interest in privacy."[96] Because using the drug dog was not a search, "the duration of the stop. . . was entirely justified by the traffic offense and the ordinary inquiries incident to such a stop,"[97] and no Fourth Amendment violation occurred.

Rodriguez v. United States[98] continued the *Caballes* approach. A K-9 officer observed a driver violate state law by moving his vehicle to a highway shoulder. The officer stopped the vehicle, gave the driver a written warning, called for a backup officer, and then walked his dog around the vehicle. When the dog alerted, the officer searched the vehicle and found drugs. The Court held that the non-search dog sniff was illegal because it occurred after the traffic stop procedure had concluded.

> Like a *Terry* stop, the tolerable duration of police inquiries in the traffic-stop context is determined by the seizure's "mission"—to address the traffic violation that warranted the stop, and attend to related safety concerns. Because addressing the infraction is the purpose of the stop, it may "last no longer than is necessary to effectuate the[at] purpose." Authority for the seizure thus ends when tasks tied to the traffic infraction are—or reasonably should have been—completed.[99]

The Court majority considered what the officer *could have* done, i.e., arrest the driver, as well as what the officer did.

> If an officer can complete traffic-based inquiries expeditiously, then that is the amount of "time reasonably required to complete [the stop's] mission." As we said in *Caballes* and reiterate today, a traffic stop "prolonged beyond" that point is "unlawful." The critical question, then, is not whether the dog sniff occurs before or after the officer

---

95 543 U.S. 405 (2005).

96 Illinois v. Caballes, 543 U.S. 405, 408 (2005).

97 *Id.*

98 575 U.S. 348 (2015).

99 Rodriguez v. United States, 575 U.S. 348, 354 (2015).

issues a ticket, . . . [but] whether conducting the sniff "prolongs"—*i.e.*, adds time to—"the stop."[100]

C. Detention of Personal Property

The Court's stop and frisk analysis also includes investigative seizures of property. Containers may be seized while police seek a warrant, because "the risk of the item's disappearance or use for its intended purpose before a warrant may be obtained outweighs the interest in possession."[101] When the police "possess specific and articulable facts warranting a reasonable belief that a traveler's luggage contains narcotics, the governmental interest in seizing the luggage briefly to pursue further investigation is substantial."[102]

In *United States v. Place*,[103] the Court stated that "the limitations applicable to investigative detentions of the person should define the permissible scope of the person's luggage on less than probable cause."[104] The defendant was told that he was free to go but that his luggage would remain with the authorities. The seizure of the defendant's property "can effectively restrain the person since he is subjected to the possible disruption of his travel plans in order to remain with his luggage or to arrange for its return."[105]

The Court also observed that the police gave the suspect inadequate information about the seizure of his luggage. The violation of his rights was

> exacerbated by the failure of the agents to inform [Place] of the place to which they were transporting his luggage of the length of time he might be dispossessed, and of what arrangements would be made for return of the luggage if the investigation dispelled the suspicion.[106]

The detention of Place's luggage became so lengthy that it constituted an "arrest" of the luggage that required probable cause. As with the detention of persons, courts look to the length of the detention as well as whether the police diligently pursued their investigation during the detention. Under the circumstances in *Place*, without probable cause, the police cannot search the detained property.

---

100 *Id.*, at 357.

101 *United States v. Place*, 462 U.S. at 701–02.

102 *Id.*, at 703.

103 462 U.S. 696 (1983).

104 *United States v. Place*, 462 U.S. at 708.

105 *Id.*

106 *Id.*, at 710.

In *United States v. Van Leeuwen*,[107] the Court upheld the use of reasonable suspicion for certain types of temporary detentions of property. The defendant mailed two packages at a post office near the Canadian border. The packages were addressed to post office boxes in California and Tennessee, sent by registered mail, and insured for $10,000. That type of mailing did not subject the packages to a discretionary inspection. The postal clerk at the point of origin relayed his suspicions to law enforcement officials. They notified appropriate customs officials who learned that both addresses were under investigation for trafficking in illegal coins.

After a search warrant issued, the contents of the packages were inspected. The Court upheld the reasonableness of the seizures for the twenty-nine hours between the mailings and the service of the warrant, because the officers conducted their investigation diligently and promptly. While the Government's actions deprived the suspect of his possessory interest in the contents of the packages, he had no liberty interest at stake when the packages were seized. The actual intrusion on the property owner was minimal, when he received his mail a day late, given the imprecise nature of mail delivery. The privacy interest of the mail was not disturbed until the issuance of the warrant.

> No interest protected by the Fourth Amendment was invaded by forwarding the packages the following day rather than the day when they were deposited. The significant Fourth Amendment interest was in the privacy of this first class mail; and that privacy was not disturbed or invaded until the approval of the judge was obtained.[108]

---

107 397 U.S. 249 (1970).

108 United States v. Van Leeuwen, 397 U.S. 249, 253 (1970).

Chapter 10

SEARCHES UNDER EXIGENT CIRCUMSTANCES

Table of Sections

§ 10.1 Introduction

The previous text discussed exigent circumstances to justify a warrantless entry to arrest or a warrantless search, i.e., to show the need for a warrantless (1) entry to arrest due to concerns about the arrestee disappearing, or (2) search incident to a lawful arrest, due to concerns about the destruction or removal of evidence. This Chapter discusses the role of the exigent circumstances exception as a stand-alone alternative to securing a warrant to search for evidence or to seize it, i.e., time constraints make it impracticable for the police officer to seek a warrant. In other words, "the exigencies of the situation make the needs of law enforcement so compelling that [a] warrantless search is objectively reasonable."[1]

The Court has identified several examples of exigencies. For example, an officer may "enter a home without a warrant to render emergency assistance to an injured occupant[,] to protect an occupant

1 Kentucky v. King, 563 U.S. 452, 460 (2011).

from imminent injury," or to ensure his own safety.[2] Another exigency exists to "prevent the imminent destruction of evidence" or to "prevent a suspect's escape."[3] The application of the exigent circumstances is on a case-by-case basis, requiring "a court to examine whether an emergency justified a warrantless search in each particular case."[4] Whether a "now or never situation" actually exists—whether an officer has "no time to secure a warrant"—depends upon the facts.[5]

Probable cause that an emergency situation exists will justify entry into private premises, and the ensuing search is limited to an area where the emergency exists, *or* last no longer than the exigency continues.[6] For example, in a hot pursuit case, the police may search for weapons as they are seeking the suspect, but the exigency ends when the suspect is captured. Of course, a search based on another warrantless justification such as a search incident to arrest would enable the police to continue a search within the scope of that warrant exception.

§ 10.2 Lange v. California

A. Facts

Lange v. California[7] discussed the exigent circumstances exception to the search warrant requirement. A State highway patrol officer began following the defendant's vehicle after it passed him while playing loud music and honking the horn. When the officer displayed his overhead lights to signal the defendant to pull over, the defendant decided to drive the remaining distance of about one hundred feet to his driveway and entered his garage. The patrolman followed, entering the defendant's garage without a warrant. There he questioned the defendant after observing signs of intoxication, and put him through field sobriety tests. The defendant "did not do well, and a later blood test showed that his blood-alcohol content was more than three times the legal limit. The State charged [him] with the misdemeanor of driving under the influence of alcohol, plus a (lower-level) noise infraction."[8]

The defendant moved to suppress the breath and blood evidence, based on the warrantless entry into the garage. The State trial court

2 Brigham City v. Stuart, 547 U.S. 398, 403 (2006).

3 *Id.*; Minnesota v. Olson, 495 U.S. 91, 100 (1990).

4 Riley v. California, 573 U.S. 373, 402 (2014).

5 *Id.*, at 391.

6 Flippo v. West Virginia, 528 U.S. 11 (1999).

7 594 U.S. 295 (2021).

8 Lange v. California, 594 U.S. 295, 299 (2021).

denied the defendant's motion, and two appellate courts affirmed. The defendant's failure to stop when the officer flashed the overhead lights also created probable cause to arrest the defendant for the misdemeanor of failing to comply with a police signal.

B. Court's Holding

For the Court, the issue in *Lange* was whether to apply exigent circumstances as an exception to the warrant requirement *whenever* a suspected misdemeanant flees from police into his home, or to apply the exception on a case-by-case basis when such an exigency exists that there was insufficient time to obtain a search warrant. The Court held that pursuit of a fleeing misdemeanor suspect does not always justify a warrantless entry into a home. The Court's Fourth Amendment case law favors a case-by-case assessment of exigency about whether a suspected misdemeanant's flight justifies a warrantless home entry. An officer may make a warrantless entry when "the exigencies of the situation" create "a compelling need for official action and no time to secure a warrant."[9]

The Court first discussed the sanctity of the home in relation to the application of any warrant exception. "[T]his Court has repeatedly declined to expand the scope" of "exceptions to the warrant requirement to permit warrantless entry into the home."[10] "[W]hen it comes to the Fourth Amendment, the home is first among equals."[11] Freedom in one's own "dwelling is the archetype of the privacy protection secured by the Fourth Amendment"; conversely, "physical entry of the home is the chief evil against which [it] is directed."[12] The scope of any warrant exception permitting home entry is "jealously and carefully drawn," in keeping with the "centuries-old principle" that the "home is entitled to special protection."[13] It would "display[ ] a shocking lack of all sense of proportion" to say that "private homes, even quarters in a tenement, may be indiscriminately invaded at the discretion of any suspicious police officer engaged in following up offenses that involve no violence or threats of it."[14]

Because the issue for the *Lange* Court was the scope of the exigent circumstances exception for a fleeing misdemeanant, the

---

9 Kentucky v. King, 563 U.S. 452, 460 (2012); Missouri v. McNeely, 569 U.S. 141, 149 (2014).

10 Caniglia v. Strom, 593 U.S. 194, 199 (2021). *Caniglia* emphatically declined to extend the community caretaking function for searching vehicles to police entries into residences for search purposes.

11 Florida v. Jardines, 569 U.S. 1, 6 (2013).

12 Payton v. New York, 445 U.S. 573, 585, 587 (1980).

13 Georgia v. Randolph, 547 U.S. 103, 109, 115 (2006).

14 McDonald v. United States, 335 U.S. 451, 459 (1948) (Jackson, J., concurring).

Court's discussion turned to the nature of a misdemeanor. "Key to resolving that issue are two facts about misdemeanors: They vary widely, but they may be (in a word) 'minor.'"[15] Throughout the country, "many perpetrators of domestic violence are charged with misdemeanors," despite "the harmfulness of their conduct."[16] So, "a 'felon' is" not always "more dangerous than a misdemeanant."[17]

> States thus tend to apply that label to less violent and less dangerous crimes. Most States count as misdemeanors such offenses as traffic violations, public intoxication, and disorderly conduct. This Court has held that when a minor offense alone is involved, police officers do not usually face the kind of emergency that can justify a warrantless home entry. In *Welsh*, officers responded to a call about a drunk driver only to discover he had abandoned his vehicle and walked home. So no police pursuit was necessary, hot or otherwise. The officers just went to the driver's house, entered without a warrant, and arrested him for a "nonjailable" offense. "[T]he gravity of the underlying offense," we reasoned, is "an important factor to be considered when determining whether any exigency exists." "[W]hen only a minor offense has been committed" (again, without any flight), there is reason to question whether a compelling law enforcement need is present; so it is "particularly appropriate" to "hesitat[e] in finding exigent circumstances." And we concluded: "[A]pplication of the exigent-circumstances exception in the context of a home entry should rarely be sanctioned when there is probable cause to believe that only a minor offense" is involved.[18]

The Court next considered the issue of flight by a suspected misdemeanant as an important factor for applying the exigent circumstances exception.

> We have no doubt that in a great many cases flight creates a need for police to act swiftly. A suspect may flee, for example, because he is intent on discarding evidence. Or his flight may show a willingness to flee yet again, while the police await a warrant. But no evidence suggests that every case of misdemeanor flight poses such dangers. Recall that misdemeanors can target minor, non-violent conduct. *Welsh* held that when that is so, officers can probably take the

---

15 *Lange v. California*, 594 U.S. 295, 305 (2021), quoting Welsh v. Wisconsin, 466 U.S. 740, 751 (1984).

16 Voisine v. United States, 579 U.S. 686 (2016).

17 Tennessee v. Garner, 471 U.S. 1, 14 (1985).

18 *Lange v. California*, 594 U.S. at 305.

time to get a warrant. And at times that will be true even when a misdemeanant has forced the police to pursue him (especially given that "pursuit" may cover just a few feet of ground). Those suspected of minor offenses may flee for innocuous reasons and in nonthreatening ways.[19]

The Court concluded that "flight of a suspected misdemeanant does not always justify a warrantless entry into a home." Any officer who applies the Court's totality of circumstances test will consider all the conditions to decide whether "there is a law enforcement emergency." On the other hand, "when the officer has time to get a warrant, he must do so—even though the misdemeanant fled."[20] The Court vacated the State judgment and remanded the case, because the State appellate court had incorrectly applied a standard that the Court rejected.

§ 10.3 Categories of Exigent Circumstances

One warrantless exception to the Fourth Amendment warrant requirement occurs when "the 'exigencies of the situation' make the needs of law enforcement so compelling that [a] warrantless search is objectively reasonable."[21] In *Kentucky v. King*,[22] the Court identified "several exigencies that may justify a warrantless search of a home."[23] The Court, however, sought to prevent unlimited expansion of the exception when it stated that the exception "must be strictly circumscribed by the exigencies," and cannot be used merely to make law enforcement more efficient, to safeguard evidence that could be protected in another manner, or simply because a serious crime has been committed.[24]

A. Emergency Assistance

The Court has identified several exigencies to justify a warrantless search of a home. In *Brigham City v. Stuart*,[25] the Court discussed the "emergency aid" exception, by which "officers may enter a home without a warrant to render emergency assistance to an injured occupant or to protect an occupant from imminent injury." In *Stuart*, when the police answered a call about a loud party at 3:00 a.m., they heard shouting inside the house and saw juveniles drinking beer in the backyard. After entering the yard, through a

---

19 *Id.*, at 2021.

20 *Id.*

21 Mincey v. Arizona, 437 U.S. 385, 394 (1978).

22 563 U.S. 452 (2011).

23 Kentucky v. King, 563 U.S. 452, 460 (2011).

24 *Mincey v. Arizona*, 437 U.S. at 393.

25 547 U.S. 398 (2006).

screen door and windows, they saw a physical argument involving five people, one of whom was a juvenile whose punch caused one of the adults to spit blood in a sink. One officer entered the house and announced their presence, but no one noticed. He next went into the kitchen and again announced his presence, at which time the argument subsided slowly. The officers arrested the adults for several offenses, including contributing to the delinquency of a minor.

The State trial court granted the motion to suppress all evidence relating to the officers' observations and actions after they entered the house. While all State appellate courts affirmed, the United States Supreme Court reversed. While the Court justified the police entry under the concern for emergency aid, it nonetheless stressed that "there was no violation of the Fourth Amendment's knock-and-announce rule" because the officer used "the only option that had even a chance of rising above the din"[26] in the house.

The Court stated that the officers' subjective intent upon entering the house was irrelevant as long as their actions were objectively justifiable.[27] In response to defendants' argument that "their conduct [as in *Welsh*] was not serious enough to justify the officers' intrusion into the home," the Court disagreed. In *Welsh*, "the 'only potential emergency' confronting the officers was the need to preserve evidence (i.e., the suspect's blood-alcohol level)—an exigency that we held insufficient under the circumstances to justify entry into the suspect's home. Because the officers were confronted with *ongoing* violence occurring within the home,"[28] "[t]he need to protect or preserve life or avoid serious injury is justification for what would be otherwise illegal absent an exigency or emergency."[29]

> [L]aw enforcement officers may enter a home without a warrant to render emergency assistance to an injured occupant or to protect an occupant from imminent injury. . . . [T]he officers had an objectively reasonable basis for believing both that the injured adult might need help and that the violence in the kitchen was just beginning.[30]

Three years after *Stuart*, in *Michigan v. Fisher*[31] the police received a tip to go to the defendant's home because someone was "going crazy" there; they saw the defendant inside the house with a

---

26 Brigham City v. Stuart, 547 U.S. 398, 407 (2006).

27 *Id.*, at 403.

28 *Id.*, at 405 (emphasis in original).

29 *Mincey v. Arizona*, 437 U.S. at 392.

30 *Brigham City v. Stuart*, 547 U.S. at 403, 406.

31 558 U.S. 45 (2009).

cut on his hand. After he refused their offer of assistance, they pushed open the front door and went inside where the defendant was pointing a gun at them. On appeal from his assault conviction, the Court denied the defendant's argument "that the officers here could not have been motivated by a perceived need to provide medical assistance, since they never summoned emergency medical personnel," by responding that "even if the failure to summon medical personnel conclusively established that [the officer] did not subjectively believe . . . that [the defendant] or someone else was seriously injured . . ., the test, as we have said is not what [the officer] believed, but whether there was 'an objectively reasonable basis for believing' that medical assistance was needed, or persons were in danger."[32]

> Officers do not need ironclad proof of "a likely serious, life-threatening" injury to invoke the emergency aid exception. . . [I]t was reasonable to believe that [the defendant] had hurt himself (albeit nonfatally) and needed treatment that in his rage he was unable to provide, or that [he] was about to hurt, or had already hurt, someone else.[33]

B. Hot Pursuit of a Suspect

A second example of an exigent circumstance occurs when police enter a place in hot pursuit of a suspect and/or his evidence. "Hot pursuit" is the immediate or continuous pursuit of a suspected felon from the scene of a felony or from being first observed in a public place. *Warden v. Hayden*[34] acknowledged the right of police, with probable cause to believe that an armed robber had entered a house a few minutes before, to enter the house without a warrant to arrest the suspect and to search for weapons. Prior to entering the house, the police had received a description of the robber, by height, weight, race, and attire.

> The Fourth Amendment does not require police officers to delay in the course of an investigation if to do so would gravely endanger their lives or the lives of others. Speed here was essential, and only a thorough search of the house for persons and weapons could have insured that [defendant] was the only man present and that the police had control of all weapons which could be used against them or to effect an escape.[35]

---

32 Michigan v. Fisher, 558 U.S. 45, 49 (2009).

33 *Id.*

34 387 U.S. 294 (1967).

35 Warden v. Hayden, 387 U.S. 294, 298–99 (1967).

Based on the robber's description, the Court endorsed the constitutionality of seizing the robber's clothes from a washing machine and weapons from the bathroom and admitting that evidence at trial.

Lange v. California clarified that *Warden v. Hayden* applies only if the police are chasing a person suspected of committing a felony. If the police suspect the fleeing person of committing a misdemeanor, their suspicion alone is insufficient to follow the suspect into a home. As previously discussed,[36] additional factors (e.g., the risk that the suspect might destroy evidence, or that she might continue to flee while the police take the time to get the warrant) will provide the police with a sufficient exigency to enter the home in pursuit of the misdemeanant.[37]

In *United States v. Santana*,[38] the police followed an undercover agent's tip that the defendant was in possession of "marked money" for a drug transaction arranged by the agent. When the defendant saw the police she moved from her doorway into her house but the police quickly caught her. When she tried to escape, drugs fell on the floor as she still possessed some of the marked money.

To justify the pursuit by the police, the Court emphasized that the defendant initially had been visible in a public place where she had no expectation of privacy and that she then retreated into her house. The defendant's "act of retreating into her house" could "not defeat an arrest" that had "been set in motion in a public place."[39] Once the defendant "saw the police, there was likewise a realistic expectation that any delay would result in destruction of evidence."[40] The Court later noted that statement did not establish a flat rule permitting warrantless home entry whenever a police officer pursues a fleeing *misdemeanant*.

The *Santana* Court observed that "the need to act quickly" in hot pursuit of the defendant was "even greater than in" *Hayden* while the intrusion was much less. "The fact that the pursuit here ended almost as soon as it began did not render it any the less a 'hot pursuit' sufficient to justify the warrantless entry into the" defendant's house. Once the defendant "saw the police, there was likewise a realistic expectation that any delay would result in destruction of evidence."[41]

---

36 See § 10.2, *supra*.

37 Lange v. California, 594 U.S. 295 (2021).

38 427 U.S. 38 (1976).

39 United States v. Santana, 427 U.S. 38, 43 (1976).

40 *Id.*, at 42–43.

41 *United States v. Santana*, 427 U.S. at 42, 43.

By contrast, in *Minnesota v. Olson*,[42] a day after a gas station robbery resulted in the death of an employee there, a woman told police that the defendant had admitted his participation in the robbery. Despite the homicide, the Court refused to characterize the circumstances as sufficiently exigent to justify a warrantless entry for arresting the suspect or preventing the destruction of evidence. By the time the police entered, they had retrieved the murder weapon and three or four police squads surrounded the house that reportedly was the defendant's current location. After they entered, they found the defendant hiding in a closet. The Court refrained from questioning the State court's "judgment that these facts do not add up to exigent circumstances."

For an emergency to exist to justify entry into a home, the police must be in hot pursuit of a fleeing felon, or dealing with the imminent destruction of evidence, the need to prevent a suspect's escape, or the risk of danger to the police or to other people. Without hot pursuit, probable cause must exist to believe that one or more of the other factors existed. In *Olson*, the Court found insufficient circumstances for any emergency category, because the police knew that this defendant was not the murderer, and the police already had recovered the murder weapon. In addition, there was no showing that the owner of the home was in danger or that the defendant could escape.

C. Seizing Evidence from Defendant's Body to Prevent Imminent Destruction of Evidence

In *Cupp v. Murphy*,[43] the police already had probable cause to arrest the defendant for strangling his wife to death. After he voluntarily appeared at the police station for questioning, the police released him even though they had noticed a dark spot on his finger that they suspected was his wife's dried blood. When the police asked him for permission to take a small scraping from the area under his fingernails for testing, he refused and began rubbing his fingers together and put his hands in his pocket. The police heard a metallic sound, such as keys or change rattling," further indicating that he was trying to destroy the evidence that connected him to his wife's murder. An officer then forcibly took scrapings from under the defendant's fingernails.

The Court approved the reasonableness of the warrantless search, in view of "the existence of probable cause, the very limited intrusion undertaken. . ., and the ready destructibility of the

---

[42] 495 U.S. 91 (1990).

[43] 412 U.S. 291 (1973).

evidence."[44] The suspect's actions in their presence provided the probable cause to believe that the defendant was destroying criminal evidence to justify the limited warrantless search the police conducted.

In *Schmerber v. California*,[45] the defendant was arrested at a hospital for drunk driving. The arresting officer ordered a physician to take a warrantless blood sample from the defendant to test his blood alcohol content (BAC). The Court discussed three standards necessary to a case-by-case balance when police seek bodily intrusions for evidence: (1) the extraction process is "a reasonable one" that is "performed in a reasonable manner," e.g., the "blood was taken by a physician in a hospital environment according to accepted medical practices"; (2) in advance there was "a clear indication that in fact [the evidence sought] will be found"; and (3) an exigent circumstance existed, e.g., a need to take the test before the percentage of alcohol in the blood diminishes.[46]

Winston v. Lee[47] applied the *Schmerber* balancing test when police sought a court order for the defendant in an attempted robbery case to have surgery to remove a bullet that the robbery victim had fired into his shoulder. The Court held that surgical intrusions require a case-by-case approach "in which the individual's interests in privacy and security are weighed against society's interests in conducting the procedure." The Court affirmed the injunction that prohibited the surgery without the defendant's consent, and discussed the factors that distinguished the case from *Schmerber*: general anesthesia was required, the intrusion would be "extensive," the medical risks of the surgery "although apparently not extremely severe, [were] a subject of considerable dispute," and the government failed to prove that it had a compelling need for the bullet to prove its case.

Missouri v. McNeely[48] continued the discussion about taking evidence from a defendant's body in DUI cases. The Court held that "the natural dissipation of alcohol in the bloodstream" is not "a *per se* exigency that suffices on its own to justify an exception to the warrant requirement for nonconsensual blood testing in drunk-driving investigations." The Court emphasized that a search warrant sometimes is necessary when (1) the evidence dissipates "in a gradual and relatively predictable manner," (2) "some delay" is otherwise "inevitable," because the police often transport the suspect to a

---

[44] Cupp v. Murphy, 412 U.S. 291, 296 (1973).

[45] 384 U.S. 757 (1966). See § 6.5(B), discussing Intrusion into Defendant's Body.

[46] Schmerber v. California, 384 U.S. 757, 770–71 (1966).

[47] 470 U.S. 753 (1985).

[48] 569 U.S. 141, 147 (2013).

medical facility for the blood draw, and (3) most jurisdictions permit police to speedily obtain a warrant via electronic communication.[49]

For post-arrest *breath* tests in DUI cases, *Birchfield v. North Dakota* made no mention of exigent circumstances as necessary to justify a breath test. However, blood tests are a different matter, require piercing the skin, extract a part of the subject's body, and are significantly more intrusive. "[E]xigent circumstances almost always permit[ ] a blood test without a warrant . . .when a driver is unconscious."[50] BAC evidence is dissipating and "pressing health, safety, or law enforcement needs . . . take priority over a warrant application."[51]

D. Entering Premises to Prevent Imminent Destruction of Evidence

The need "to prevent the imminent destruction of evidence" historically has also been a sufficient exigent circumstance for a warrantless entry to arrest or to search. *Ker v. California*[52] required that police ordinarily must give notice of their authority and purpose before entering premises to make an arrest. Notice reduces the potential for violence to both the police officers and the occupants of the house into which entry is sought, guards against the needless destruction of private property, and symbolizes the respect for individual privacy summarized in the adage that "a man's house is his castle."

Before entering, the police in *Ker* approached the defendant's apartment with the landlord's passkey, and the officers already had corroborated their belief that the defendant was possessing drugs that "could be quickly and easily destroyed." The officer with the passkey was "proceeding quietly . . .in order to prevent the destruction of evidence." A plurality of the Court held that "the officers' method of entry . . . was not unreasonable under the standards of the Fourth Amendment."[53]

In *Payton v. New York*,[54] the Court remarked that it had "no occasion to consider the sort of emergency or dangerous situation, described in our cases as 'exigent circumstances,' that would justify a warrantless entry into a home" to make an arrest. *Dorman v.*

---

[49] Missouri v. McNeely, 569 U.S. 141, 153 (2013).

[50] Mitchell v. Wisconsin, 588 U.S. 840 (2019). See further discussion of *Mitchell* in § 8.2D, *supra*.

[51] *Mitchell v. Wisconsin*, 588 U.S. at 854.

[52] 374 U.S. 23 (1963).

[53] *Id.*, at 28, 40.

[54] 445 U.S. 573, 583 (1980).

United States[55] listed several emergency contexts that would excuse a warrantless entry to arrest: whether

> (1) "a grave offense is involved"; (2) "the suspect is reasonably believed to be armed"; (3) there is "a clear showing of probable cause" of the person's guilt; (4) there is "strong reason to believe that the suspect is in the premises"; (5) there is a "likelihood that the suspect will escape if not swiftly apprehended"; (6) the entry is "made peaceably"; and (7) the entry is "made at night."

Courts have noted the importance of additional factors in assessing the imminent risk of the destruction or loss of physical evidence: the degree of urgency v. the amount of time to obtain a warrant, a reasonable belief that evidence is about to be removed or that the suspect is armed, any possible danger to the police or others, whether the suspect is aware that the police are looking for him and the likelihood of his escape, and whether the evidence can easily be destroyed.

As to the concern about evidence destruction, in *Segura v. United States*,[56] the police without a warrant entered an apartment, arrested and removed everyone from the premises, and stayed for nineteen hours until their colleagues obtained and executed a search warrant. The Court held

> that where officers, having probable cause, enter premises, and with probable cause, arrest the occupants who have legitimate possessory interests in its contents and take them into custody and, for no more than the period here involved, secure the premises from within to preserve the status quo while others, in good faith, are in the process of obtaining a warrant, they do not violate the Fourth Amendment's proscription against unreasonable seizures.[57]

The Court added that any police illegality in their initial entry did not mandate suppression of evidence first discovered in the later execution of the search warrant.

Later in *Illinois v. McArthur*,[58] two police officers remained at a residence while the defendant's wife removed her effects. When she left, she told the police that her husband had concealed drugs under the couch. When the husband refused to consent, one officer left to seek a search warrant, while the other officer stayed and told the

---

55 435 F.2d 385, 392–93 (D.C.Cir. 1970).

56 468 U.S. 796 (1984).

57 Segura v. United States, 468 U.S. 796, 798 (1984).

58 531 U.S. 326 (2001).

husband he could not enter the house without being accompanied by the officer. Prior to the issuance and execution of the warrant, the husband had returned to the residence where the officer had observed his conduct.

The Court noted that the restriction against the husband entering the home was reasonable, because "the need to preserve evidence of a 'jailable' offense was sufficiently urgent or pressing to justify" the police action. Specifically, the police conduct was legal: "[1] the police had probable cause to believe that [defendant's] home contained evidence of a crime and contraband, namely, unlawful drugs"; "[2] the police had good reason to fear that, unless restrained, [defendant] would destroy the drugs before they could return with a warrant," they reasonably concluded that the husband knew that his wife had told them about the drugs; "[3] the police made reasonable efforts to reconcile their law enforcement needs with the demands of personal privacy" by using "a significantly less restrict restraint" than a warrantless search of the premises; and "[4] the police imposed the restraint for a limited period of time, namely, two hours."[59]

E. Rejected Categories of Exigent Circumstances

Although courts have identified new exigent circumstances, the list of Court-recognized categories remains static. For example, although States have adopted a murder scene exception to the warrant requirement, the Court has refused three times to acknowledge that exception to the warrant requirement.[60] The facts of *Mincey v. Arizona* lacked all the characteristics that lower courts had relied upon to create such an exception: the cause and perpetrator of the death were known, no occupant of the premises had called the police and implicitly approved the investigation, and the investigation did not occur within narrow time and space limitations. *Mincey* "decline[d] to hold that the seriousness of the offense under investigation itself creates exigent circumstances of the kind that under the Fourth Amendment justify a warrantless search, . . . simply because a homicide had recently occurred there."[61]

G.M. Leasing Corp. v. United States[62] was another unsuccessful attempt to tie law enforcement entry to the type of crime under investigation. IRS agents entered corporate offices without a warrant in order to levy taxes on property subject to seizure. Without a

---

59 Illinois v. McArthur, 531 U.S. 326, 332 (2001).

60 Thompson v. Louisiana, 469 U.S. 17 (1984); Mincey v. Arizona, 437 U.S. 385 (1978); Michigan v. Tyler, 436 U.S. 499 (1978).

61 *Mincey v. Arizona*, 437 U.S. at 394, 395.

62 429 U.S. 338 (1977).

warrant, they also seized automobiles from public streets and lots as part of a levy on the corporation's assets for tax deficiencies. The Court rejected the Government's argument that the Fourth Amendment is inapplicable to an "invasion of privacy in furtherance of tax collection," in the absence of showing legitimate exigent circumstances. The Court held that IRS agents had violated the Fourth Amendment when they entered the premises of the corporation and seized its books.

Finally, plain view seizures of allegedly obscene materials do not necessarily qualify as exigent circumstances. In *Roaden v. Kentucky*,[63] after watching a sexually explicit film, the sheriff made a warrantless seizure of the film incident to the theatre owner's arrest. The Court stated that

> [w]here there are exigent circumstances in which police action literally must be "now or never" to preserve the evidence of the crime, it is reasonable to permit action without [a warrant]. The facts surrounding . . . the seizure of the film [here] presented no such "now or never" circumstances.[64]

§ 10.4 Police-Created Exigency

A "police-created exigency" is an exception to the exigent circumstances rule. As the name suggests, the "police may not rely on the need to prevent destruction of evidence when that exigency was 'created' or 'manufactured' by the conduct of the police."[65] In *Kentucky v. King*,[66] police followed a suspected drug dealer to an apartment where they smelled marijuana outside the apartment door. After they knocked loudly, they heard noises from inside the apartment that were consistent with the destruction of evidence. They declared their intention to enter, after which they kicked in the door where they found the defendant and other persons. During a protective sweep, they observed drugs in plain view and seized other evidence. The trial court denied the defendant's motion to suppress, because exigent circumstances, i.e., the need to prevent the evidence from being destroyed, justified the warrantless entry into the apartment.

The essence of *King* was to consider whether the exigent circumstances rule applies when it is the "police, by knocking on the door of a residence and announcing their presence, cause the

---

63 413 U.S. 496 (1973).

64 Roaden v. Kentucky, 413 U.S. 496, 505–06 (1973).

65 Kentucky v. King, 563 U.S. 452, 461 (2011).

66 563 U.S. 452 (2011).

occupants to attempt to destroy evidence."[67] *King* refused to adopt the lower courts' view that the police "should have foreseen" that their demeanor motivated the defendant and others to attempt destruction of the evidence. Those lower courts all require "something more than mere proof that fear of detection by the police cause the destruction of evidence."[68] The Court reviewed the "something more" additional requirements that "are unsound and we now reject."[69] Those lower court tests were whether:

- law enforcement officers deliberately created the exigent circumstances with the bad faith intent to avoid the warrant requirement. Citing *Whren v. United States*, the Court rejected this test because it had never held that "an officer's motive invalidates objectively justifiable behavior under the Fourth Amendment."[70]
- it was reasonably foreseeable that the investigative tactics employed by the police would create the exigent circumstances. The Court has "rejected the notion that police may seize evidence without a warrant only when they come across the evidence by happenstance."[71] A foreseeability test would "also introduce an unacceptable degree of unpredictability."
- after acquiring evidence that is sufficient to establish probable cause to search particular premises, the officers do not seek a warrant but instead knock on the door and seek either to speak with an occupant or to obtain consent to search. "Law enforcement officers are under no constitutional duty to call a halt to criminal investigation the moment they have the minimum evidence to establish probable cause."[72]
- the course of their investigation was contrary to standard or good law enforcement practices (or to the policies or practices of their jurisdictions). "This approach fails to provide clear guidance for law enforcement officers and authorizes courts to make judgments on matters that are the province of those

---

67 *Kentucky v. King*, 563 U.S. at 455.

68 *Id.*

69 *Id.*, at 464.

70 Whren v. United States, 517 U.S. 806, 812 (1996).

71 Horton v. California, 496 U.S. 128, 138 (1990).

72 Hoffa v. United States, 385 U.S. 293, 310 (1966).

> who are responsible for federal and state law enforcement agencies."[73]

After eliminating each lower court test, the Court stated and discarded the "nebulous and impractical" test offered by the defendant, i.e., "law enforcement officers impermissibly create an exigency when they 'engage in conduct that would cause a reasonable person to believe that entry is imminent and inevitable.' "[74]

Finally, the Court announced its own "interpretation of the police-created exigency doctrine," i.e., "the exigent circumstances rule applies when the police do not gain entry to premises by means of an actual or threatened violation of the Fourth Amendment. This holding provides ample protection for the privacy rights that the Amendment protects."[75]

> When law enforcement officers who are not armed with a warrant knock on a door, they do no more than any private citizen might do. And whether the person who knocks on the door and requests the opportunity to speak is a police officer or a private citizen, the occupant has no obligation to open the door or to speak. When the police knock on a door but the occupants choose not to respond or to speak, the investigation will have reached a conspicuously low point, and the occupants will have the kind of warning that even the most elaborate security system cannot provide. And even if an occupant chooses to open the door and speak with the officers, the occupant need not allow the officers to enter the premises and may refuse to answer any questions at any time.
>
> Occupants who choose not to stand on their constitutional rights but instead elect to attempt to destroy evidence have only themselves to blame for the warrantless exigent circumstances search that may ensue.[76]

Applying *its* test to the facts, the Court concluded that

> [one officer] testified without contradiction that the officers "banged on the door as loud as [they] could" and announced either "Police, police, police" or "This is the police." This conduct was entirely consistent with the Fourth Amendment. . . The officers did not violate or threaten to violate the Fourth Amendment prior to the exigency, we

---

[73] Kentucky v. King, 563 U.S. 452, 468 (2011).

[74] *Id.*

[75] *Id.*, at 469.

[76] *Id.*, at 469–70.

hold that the exigency justified the warrantless search of the apartment.[77]

§ 10.5 Evidence Police May Examine and Remove

If police have legally entered a place to search without a warrant, the issue then becomes what evidentiary items they may examine or remove. As discussed elsewhere,[78] the police may seize items in plain view when there is "a nexus—automatically provided in the case of fruits, instrumentalities or contraband—between the item to be seized and criminal behavior."[79] When the defendant objected to the admission of a bloody shirt from a washing machine in *Hayden*, the Court referred to it as "mere evidence," but stated that any evidence may be seized and admitted that aids a particular apprehension or conviction. "The clothes found in the washing machine matched the description of those worn by the robber and the police therefore could reasonably believe that the items would aid in the identification of the culprit."[80] Courts equate that statement with a probable cause requirement.[81]

In decisions like *United States v. Rubin*,[82] lower courts have articulated another way of thinking about warrantless searches based upon exigent circumstances: the police must conduct the warrantless search *now* because they "reasonably conclude that the evidence will be destroyed or removed before they can secure a search warrant."[83]

> When Government agents, however, have probable cause to believe contraband is present and, in addition, based on the surrounding circumstances of the information at hand, they reasonably conclude that the evidence will be destroyed or removed before they can secure a search warrant, a warrantless search is justified. The emergency circumstances will vary from case to case, and the inherent necessities of the situation at the time must be scrutinized. Circumstances which have seemed relevant to courts include (1) the degree of urgency involved and the amount of time necessary to obtain a warrant; (2) reasonable belief that the contraband is about to be removed; (3) the

---

77 *Id.*, at 471, 472.

78 See § 2.4(A), discussing Plain View.

79 Warden v. Hayden, 387 U.S. 294, 307 (1967).

80 *Id.*

81 See, e.g., Arizona v. Hicks, 480 U.S. 321 (1987) (probable cause necessary to move stereo equipment to learn its serial number).

82 474 F.2d 262 (3d Cir. 1973).

83 United States v. Rubin, 474 F.2d 262, 268 (3d Cir. 1973).

possibility of danger to police officers guarding the site of the contraband while a search warrant is sought; (4) information indicating the possessors of the contraband are aware that the police are on their trail; and (5) the ready destructibility of the contraband and the knowledge "that efforts to dispose of narcotics and to escape are characteristic behavior of persons engaged in the narcotics traffic."[84]

[84] *Id.*, at 268–69.

Chapter 11

ADMINISTRATIVE AND SPECIAL NEEDS SEARCHES

Table of Sections

§ 11.1 Introduction

Administrative search warrants have become a part of search and seizure jurisprudence. These warrants are often required for nonconsensual residential and commercial property inspections. They issue for a lower quantum of probable cause, because courts consider the relevant privacy interests as less strict. Justification for the warrants is based upon evidence of either a specific statutory or regulatory violation, or a reasonable plan supported by a valid public interest. Exigent circumstances or valid consent also may justify a warrantless administrative search.

If an administrative search produces evidence of criminal conduct, it may be seized. But administrative searches for investigating only criminal activity are prohibited. Mixed administrative and investigative purposes are permissible, if the administrative purpose prevails.

Warrantless administrative searches are also allowed for pervasively regulated businesses, if (1) there is a substantial state interest for the regulatory scheme, (2) the warrantless search advances the scheme, and (3) an authorizing statute satisfactorily substitutes for warrants to notify businesses and to control the inspectors' discretion.

In addition to administrative searches for closely regulated industries, the courts have found that limited topics, such as the operation of a school and the supervision of probationers or parolees, are appropriate for "special needs" search principles. This Chapter examines the case law by which several factual contexts have evolved for special needs, governmental inspections, and regulatory searches.

§ 11.2 The *Camara* Balancing Principle

Whether a search is described as a special needs situation, an inspection, or as regulatory, the Court has determined that some contexts or problems should be addressed by different standards than the usual Fourth Amendment rules. For example, a "special need" search is a category of Fourth Amendment activity beyond the normal basics of law enforcement for self-protection; special need searches usually treat the search warrant and/or probable cause requirements as impracticable. When a court evaluates the constitutionality of a special needs search, it balances a legitimate governmental interest to justify the search against the intrusion caused by the search, e.g., drug testing of public employees. The intrusion issue commonly focuses on the disclosure of private information and testing procedures.

A Fourth Amendment balancing test appeared in *Camara v. Municipal Court of City and County of San Francisco*.[1] The city and county wanted to conduct periodic inspections of the interior of all individual housing units for building code and other safety concerns. Camara argued that compliance with Fourth Amendment jurisprudence was necessary before housing inspectors could enter his residence to inspect for code and safety violations. The Court

1 387 U.S. 523 (1967).

responded that satisfying all Fourth Amendment and probable cause standards would impede safety inspections.

The Court held that, except in emergencies or with the owner's consent, a search warrant that issues with less than the typical probable cause is permissible for housing safety inspections. Most warrants would be sought when consent is denied. In a restaurant, for example, no warrant would be necessary for inspecting the open part of the restaurant, but without consent a warrant may be necessary for the kitchen or area of food storage. The passage of time, the nature of the building, or the condition of the general area can provide the probable cause necessary to support the search of an individual building covered by a particular administrative scheme. Housing inspections could be conducted for all structures periodically, depending on the type of structure.

> There can be no ready test for determining [Fourth Amendment] reasonableness other than by balancing the need to search against the invasion which the search entails.[2]

The balancing requires consideration of whether the search practice (1) has "a long history of judicial and public acceptance," (2) is essential to achieve "acceptable results," and (3) involves "a relatively limited invasion of . . . privacy."[3]

The Court applied the balancing test a year later in *Terry v. Ohio*[4] to allow brief seizures for investigations with evidence of reasonable suspicion rather than the probable cause necessary for an arrest. The balancing test used in *Terry* supported searches based upon a reasonable suspicion instead of traditional probable cause, or based upon application of standardized procedures entailing neutral criteria.

§ 11.3 Applying the *Camara* Principle

Two examples of the *Camara* principle offer a glimpse into its application by the Court. One is *Camara* itself and the other involves inspections at fire scenes.

A. The *Camara* Case

Before 1967 when the Court decided *Camara*, the judicial branch was unaccustomed to applying the Fourth Amendment

---

2 Camara v. Municipal Court of City and County of San Francisco, 387 U.S. 523, 536–37 (1967).

3 *Id.*, at 537.

4 392 U.S. 1 (1968). See Chapter 9, discussing Stop and Frisk.

directly to normally civil topics. For example, in *Frank v. Maryland*,[5] the Court held that entering a private premises without a warrant to conduct a health inspection was legal because the inspection would "touch at most upon the periphery" of the interests protected by the Fourth Amendment. In effect, the Court decided in favor of the housing inspectors, because the search for rat infestation would benefit the public more than it would harm Frank's privacy interests.

Eight years later, when *Camara* overruled *Frank*, the Court pointed out that there had been no showing "that fire, health, and housing code inspection programs could not achieve their goals within the confines of a reasonable search warrant requirement."[6] Because housing inspections "are significant intrusions," the Court held that they ordinarily could be conducted only with the use of a search warrant. The Court then described what would be necessary for a search warrant to issue in a primarily civil law context. Prior to issuing a search warrant, a judge would have to decide whether an inspection policy exists for the geopolitical area, and whether the inspection for which the warrant is sought is consistent with that policy.

The *Camara* balancing test, described above, evolved as the Court described "persuasive factors" it used to disallow a claim that the right to an inspection was limited to instances "when the inspector possesses probable cause to believe that a particular dwelling contains violations of the minimum standards prescribed by the code being enforced."[7] Instead, the Court held that applying reasonable standards would suffice.

> First, such [inspection] programs have a long history of judicial and public acceptance.... Second, the public interest demands that all dangerous conditions be prevented or abated, yet it is doubtful that any other canvassing technique would achieve acceptable results. Many such conditions—faulty wiring is an obvious example—are not observable from outside the building and indeed may not be apparent to the inexpert occupant himself. Finally, because the inspections are neither personal in nature nor aimed at the discovery of evidence of crime, they involve a relatively limited invasion of the urban citizen's privacy.[8]

---

5 359 U.S. 360 (1959).

6 *Camara v. Municipal Court of City and County of San Francisco*, 387 U.S. at 533.

7 *Id.*, at 534.

8 *Id.*, at 537.

Because of the Court's recognition of the balancing theory, it could apply the Fourth Amendment as a flexible legal standard capable of adjusting to the particular factual context, e.g., inspection criteria for a housing search may differ from criteria used for health or fire inspections. Even more important, the legal standard for housing inspections could differ from a typical Fourth Amendment search. The public perceives inspections by non-police personnel as less offensive in part because they are conducted during daylight hours and with some advance notice.

B. Inspections at Fire Scenes

In *Michigan v. Tyler*,[9] the defendant was charged with conspiracy to burn real property and insured property, i.e., his own furniture store. The issue was whether the occupant's expectation of privacy remained despite the fire, and whether it was permissible for the fire authorities to inspect the burned building to establish the cause of the fire. The Court stated that a "burning building clearly presents an emergency of sufficient proportions to render a warrantless entry 'reasonable,'" because "it would defy reason to suppose that firemen must secure a warrant or consent before entering a burning structure to put out the blaze."[10] Under *Camara*, the need to search may relate to whether the fire would regenerate, justifying a limited intrusion to examine heating, gas, and electrical systems.

The Court set a three-part standard for inspecting the fire scene. First, after the fire, officials were justified without a warrant "to remain in a building for a reasonable time to investigate the cause of the blaze after it has been extinguished."[11] Because a warrantless entry to put out the fire would be constitutionally permitted, a warrantless seizure of evidence while inspecting the premises to determine the cause likewise would be constitutional. Second, a later entry would first require a showing of administrative probable cause for the issuance of an administrative search warrant. Third, if fire officials find probable cause that arson has occurred, any later entry would require either consent or the issuance of a traditional Fourth Amendment search warrant.

Michigan v. Clifford[12] is an example of when administrative search warrants may be required. The case included consideration of exigent circumstances that may justify a warrantless administrative search, perhaps to address an immediate threat that a fire may

---

9 436 U.S. 499 (1978).

10 Michigan v. Tyler, 436 U.S. 499, 509 (1978).

11 *Id.*, at 510.

12 464 U.S. 287 (1984).

rekindle or to enable authorities to preserve evidence from being destroyed. The defendants were charged with arson in a fire at their residence. A plurality of the Court observed that "[s]ome fires may be so devastating that no reasonable privacy interests remain in the ash and ruins, regardless of the owner's subjective expectations."[13] Although the fire had left the residence uninhabitable, the defendant had arranged to secure it from intrusion, prompting the Court to state that the defendant had "retained reasonable privacy interests" in the residence.

> [T]he interim efforts to secure the burned-out premises and the heightened privacy interests in the home distinguish this case from *Tyler*. At least where a homeowner has made a reasonable effort to secure his fire-damaged home after the blaze has been extinguished and the fire and police units have left the scene, a subsequent post-fire search had to be conducted pursuant to a warrant, consent, or the identification of a new exigency.[14]

As with *Tyler*, the purpose of a search determined the type of warrant required. Because the defendants had retained their expectations of privacy, an administrative warrant applied in order to enter and determine that the cause of the fire was in the basement. Without that warrant, evidence found in the basement was inadmissible.

However, if the primary purpose of the search was to gain evidence of criminal behavior, a criminal search warrant based on traditional probable cause was required. Once the investigators knew the fire's cause and location, they needed a criminal search warrant to search other parts of the burned out residence. Without such a criminal search warrant, evidence seized there was inadmissible.

§ 11.4 Business Inspections

The Court has decided numerous cases where the government is attempting to regulate business practices. Closely regulated businesses may be inspected without search warrants, even by police officers, because many communities lack the resources to hire inspectors to enforce civil regulations. Three inspection conditions are required, because of the important role of periodic inspections in effective enforcement of regulatory schemes and the reduced privacy expectation flowing from pervasive regulation. First, a regulatory scheme must exist prior to the inspection that relates to protecting health and safety. Second, an important governmental interest supports the regulatory scheme. Finally, the scheme is an adequate

---

[13] Michigan v. Clifford, 464 U.S. 287, 292 (1984).

[14] *Id.*, at 297.

substitute for a traditional search warrant because it limits the discretion of inspectors regarding the time, place and scope of the searches.

See v. City of Seattle[15] discussed a defendant's conviction for refusing a warrantless fire inspection of his warehouse. The Court held that *Camara* applied, because a "businessman, like the occupant of a residence, has a constitutional right to go about his business free from unreasonable official entries upon his private commercial property." On the other hand, the Court warned

> that business premises may not reasonably be inspected in many more situations than private homes, nor do we question such accepted regulatory techniques as licensing programs which require inspections prior to operating a business of marketing a product.[16]

Three years later, the Court held that the *See* warrant requirement was inapplicable to an inspection of a liquor business, because of that industry's long history of regulation before adoption of the Fourth Amendment.[17]

United States v. Biswell[18] upheld a warrantless inspection of a firearms dealer, because the statute's purpose in authorizing inspections during business hours was to examine records and the weapons on the premises. Such inspections were a "crucial part of a regulatory scheme" for controlling firearms traffic; essential and flexible unannounced inspections outweighed negligible warrant protections that "could easily frustrate inspection." These inspections also posed a limited threat to the dealer's expectations of privacy, because any federal licensee knows that he is subject to the inspections.[19]

Marshall v. Barlow's, Inc.[20] upheld warrantless OSHA inspections of "any factory, plant, establishment, construction site, or other area, workplace or environment where work is performed by an employee." The Court distinguished *Biswell* because it concerned a "closely regulated industry." The Court's flexible attitude reflected the willingness of businessmen to consent to warrantless searches. For example, a factory owner may consent, if he believes that the factory is in compliance, or the regulations are so strict that an

---

15 387 U.S. 541 (1967).

16 See v. City of Seattle, 387 U.S. 541, 546 (1967).

17 Colonnade Catering Corp. v. United States, 397 U.S. 72 (1970).

18 406 U.S. 311 (1972).

19 United States v. Biswell, 406 U.S. 311, 316 (1972).

20 436 U.S. 307 (1978).

inspection always reveals a violation. The Court also defined when an inspection is necessary by following *Camara*.

> A warrant showing that a specific business has been chosen for an OSHA search on the basis of a general administrative plan for the enforcement of the Act derived from neutral sources such as, for example, dispersion of employees in various types of industries across a given area, and the desired frequency of searches in any of the lesser divisions of the area, would protect an employer's Fourth Amendment rights.[21]

A judge is to decide whether there are reasonable legislative or administrative standards, or a reasonable plan based upon a valid public interest, for satisfying a lower level of probable cause, and whether the proposed inspection would meet those standards.

Unlike the unbridled discretion present with OSHA inspections, *Donovan v. Dewey*[22] upheld warrantless inspections of underground and surface mines, because the statute's inspection program was a "constitutionally adequate substitute for a warrant." The statute defined the frequency of inspections and inspection standards, and also provided a mechanism to accommodate special privacy concerns so that a mine owner could turn away inspectors by showing that a specific search was outside the federal regulatory authority.[23]

New York v. Burger[24] upheld a warrantless inspection program based on a statute for vehicle junkyards, because (1) the business was "closely regulated," i.e., a substantial government interest to prevent auto theft supported the regulatory scheme of which warrantless inspections were a necessary part; and (2) the inspection scheme was a constitutionally adequate substitute for a warrant by defining the discretion of the searching officials, i.e., the time, frequency and scope of the inspections. For example, regulatory goals were met by allowing inspectors to search the inventory and compare it with the records to confirm that records are properly kept.

Burger reduced Fourth Amendment protections for businesses, because almost any form of regulation sufficed to make a business "heavily regulated." By holding that an administrative search may be used to enforce criminal objectives, *Burger* also clouded the distinction between administrative and criminal-based searches. Finally, in the absence of a search warrant, the statute authorizing the administrative search controls the officer's discretion, but the

---

21 Marshall v. Barlow's, Inc., 436 U.S. 307, 321 (1978).

22 452 U.S. 594 (1981).

23 Donovan v. Dewey, 452 U.S. 594, 605 (1981).

24 482 U.S. 691 (1987).

Court held that statutory limits on the frequency of the inspections are unnecessary.

While the Court has not been clear about the constitutionality of warrantless inspection programs, as long as a statute limits the time, place and scope of inspections, the business is deemed to be a "closely regulated industry" and may be subject to inspection without the need for warrants. An industry that needs frequent, unannounced inspections is more likely to proceed without warrants because a warrant requirement is impractical. *City of Los Angeles v. Patel*[25] defined a warrant requirement, unless (1) the business owner gave uncoerced, actual consent, (2) an exception to the warrant requirement like exigent circumstances was applicable, or (3) the case was within a narrow exception for a "closely regulated business." If any of the three conditions was present, a warrantless inspection was necessary to further the regulatory scheme, and the inspection program provided a constitutionally adequate substitute for a warrant.

The cases still are unclear about defining when a warrant is necessary for an inspection. *Biswell* argued against warrants when "unannounced, even frequent, inspections" that are flexible "as to time, scope, and frequency" are available. *Burger* noted that warrants are less important for closely regulated businesses. A business licensee may challenge the constitutionality of a warrantless search statutory scheme as well as the conduct of officials in an individual case.

§ 11.5 Special Needs Searches

The remainder of this Chapter discusses "special needs" searches. Courts evaluate whether the Government interest claimed to support the search is a "special need" beyond the normal need for law enforcement[26] that would be jeopardized by the individualized suspicion usually required for searches. To qualify as a "special need," a Government interest must be a legal, current, important problem that Government can address effectively through the proposed search.[27] Even if a special need is present, it must still be balanced against the privacy interest at stake and the nature of the intrusion, to decide the appropriate level of protection required.[28] At

[25] 576 U.S. 409 (2015).

[26] See Ferguson v. City of Charleston, 532 U.S. 67, 76 n.7 (2001).

[27] Chandler v. Miller, 520 U.S. 305, 318–19 (1997) (Government interest in deterring drug use by public officials was not "sufficiently vital").

[28] Board of Education of Independent School District No. 92 of Pottawatomie County v. Earls, 536 U.S. 822, 838 (2002) (Government interest in preventing student drug use was sufficient to justify suspicionless drug testing).

times, the Court has justified a special need search rule on traditional Fourth Amendment principles.[29]

§ 11.6 Vehicle Checkpoints

A. Vehicle Regulation

The Court has applied the *Camara* formula often to decide what procedures are permissible in order to check drivers' licenses, vehicle registration. and vehicles' operating condition. *Delaware v. Prouse*[30] prohibited random vehicle stops to accomplish these goals. The Court balanced the "intrusion on the individual's Fourth Amendment interests against the promotion of legitimate governmental interests."[31] The intrusive aspect for a random stop is inconvenience, time-consumption, creation of anxiety, and interference with freedom of movement.[32] Stopping vehicles and detaining drivers violate the Fourth Amendment, unless there is a reasonable suspicion about an unlicensed driver or an unregistered vehicle, or that either the driver or the vehicle is subject to seizure for a legal violation. The Court believed that Delaware could devise methods for spot checks that would reduce either intrusion or discretion.

> [W]e hold that except in those situations in which there is at least articulable and reasonable suspicion that a motorist is unlicensed or that an automobile is not registered, or that either the vehicle or an occupant is otherwise subject to seizure for violation of law, stopping an automobile and detaining the driver in order to check his driver's license and the registration of the automobile are unreasonable under the Fourth Amendment. This holding does not preclude the State of Delaware or other States from developing methods for spot checks that involve less intrusion or that do not involve the unconstrained exercise of discretion.[33]

The Court offered roadblock stops of "all oncoming traffic" as a possible alternative to random vehicular stops.

The nature of the discretionary checks did not greatly advance the Government's interests "that licensing, registration, and vehicle inspection requirements are being observed."[34] For drivers' licenses,

---

29 See, e.g., United States v. Knights, 534 U.S. 112 (2001) (search of probationer's residence authorized by reasonable suspicion).

30 440 U.S. 648 (1979).

31 Delaware v. Prouse, 440 U.S. 648, 654 (1979).

32 *Id.*, at 657.

33 *Id.*, at 663.

34 *Id.*, at 658.

the "percentage of all drivers on the road who are driving without a license is very small and . . . the number of licensed drivers who will be stopped in order to find one unlicensed operator will be large indeed."[35] By comparison, checking for drivers who have violated the traffic laws is "much more likely" to find "an unlicensed driver."[36] Vehicle registration can be regulated by observing "license plates indicating current registration,"[37] which does not require vehicle stops. For safety inspections, random stopping would contribute little to highway safety because many violations "are observable" without stopping a vehicle and others are detectable through "annual safety"[38] inspections.

In a footnote, the Court suggested that its ruling was not aimed at casting doubt on the permissibility of roadblock truck weigh stations and inspection checkpoints, where some vehicles may be subject to further detention for safety and regulatory inspection.[39] Certain types of roadblocks possibly could perform multiple functions, e.g., drivers' licenses checks and vehicle registrations. Traffic checkpoints for safety inspections of all commercial trucking in a regulated industry have judicial support in *New York v. Burger*.[40]

B. Sobriety Checkpoints

Police use sobriety checkpoints to stop traffic at temporary locations, in order to observe each driver for possibly being under the influence of alcohol or other drugs. If police spot signs of intoxication, the driver is moved from the line of traffic to undergo possible sobriety tests. In *Michigan Dept. of State Police v. Sitz*,[41] the Court upheld the use of sobriety checkpoints, applying the same balancing test it used in *Prouse*, stressing (1) the strong state interest in removing drunk driving, (2) the minor intrusion on drivers who are subjected to a short stop at a checkpoint where "checkpoints are selected pursuant to guidelines and uniformed officers stop every approaching vehicle", and (3) that "politically accountable officials" decide "which among reasonable alternative law enforcement techniques should be employed."[42]

Since the Court's decision in *Sitz*, sobriety checkpoints are upheld when their timing and location are made by persons other

---

35 *Id.*, at 660.

36 *Id.*

37 *Id.*, at 661.

38 *Id.*, at 660.

39 *Id.*, at 663 n.26.

40 482 U.S. 691 (1987). See § 11.4 of this Chapter, discussing Business Inspections.

41 496 U.S. 444 (1990).

42 Michigan Dept. of State Police v. Sitz, 496 U.S. 444, 453 (1990).

than those "in the field," the checkpoint is conducted in a standardized manner to avoid alarming drivers, either all drivers are checked or neutral criteria govern which drivers to check, application of reasonable suspicion criteria to select drivers for continued investigation, and there is advance publicity about the upcoming use of the sobriety checkpoints.

C. Roadblocks for Detecting and Solving Crimes

In *City of Indianapolis v. Edmond*,[43] the Court viewed a city-operated traffic checkpoint to detect narcotics usage as falling short of meeting a "special need" usually associated with vehicle checkpoints and violative of the Fourth Amendment. The checkpoint included the use of drug dogs, designed to interdict unlawful drugs.

> At each checkpoint location, the police stop a predetermined number of vehicles. Approximately 30 officers are stationed at the checkpoint. Pursuant to written directives issued by the chief of police, at least one officer approaches the vehicle, advises the driver that he or she is being stopped briefly at a drug checkpoint, and asks the driver to produce a license and registration. The officer also looks for signs of impairment and conducts an open-view examination of the vehicle from the outside. A narcotics-detection dog walks around the outside of each stopped vehicle.
>
> The directives instruct the officers that they may conduct a search only by consent or based on the appropriate quantum of particularized suspicion. The officers must conduct each stop in the same manner until particularized suspicion develops, and the officers have no discretion to stop any vehicle out of sequence. The city agreed in the stipulation to operate the checkpoints in such a way as to ensure that the total duration of each stop, absent reasonable suspicion or probable cause, would be five minutes or less.[44]

During a four-month period, the city of Indianapolis stopped 1,161 vehicles and arrested 104 motorists. Fifty-five arrests were for drug-related offenses and forty-nine arrests were for unrelated crimes. "The 'overall' hit rate was . . . approximately nine percent."

In response to the City's attempt to defend its program as promoting "law enforcement activities, [where] law enforcement officers employ arrests and criminal prosecutions in pursuit of these goals." the Court responded that analysis at that "high level of

---

43 531 U.S. 32 (2000).

44 City of Indianapolis v. Edmond, 531 U.S. 32, 35–36 (2000).

generality" would mean there "would be little check on the ability of the authorities to construct roadblocks for almost any conceivable law enforcement purpose."[45]

> We have never approved a checkpoint program whose primary purpose was to detect evidence of ordinary criminal wrongdoing. Rather, our checkpoint cases have recognized only limited exceptions to the general rule that a seizure must be accompanied by some measure of individualized suspicion. [E]ach of the checkpoint programs that we have approved was designed primarily to serve purposes closely related to the problems of policing the border or the necessity of ensuring roadway safety. Because the primary purpose of the Indianapolis narcotics checkpoint program is to uncover evidence of ordinary criminal wrongdoing, the program contravenes the Fourth Amendment.[46]

The Court struck down drug interdiction programs like the Indianapolis checkpoint program, because it was "ultimately indistinguishable from a general interest in crime control."[47] By comparison, if the Court characterized *Sitz* as a "highway safety" case, it would appear that a general interest in drug interdiction would also be sufficiently important to justify the *Edmond* roadblock. Perhaps the Court was concerned about the low likelihood of apprehension compared to a sobriety checkpoint. If the roadblock was used instead on a specific interstate highway that was known for its routine use for transporting illegal drugs across or into the country, the Court's decision might have differed.

In addition to detecting crime, police departments have used vehicular checkpoints to attempt to solve crimes. *Illinois v. Lidster*[48] held that the reasonableness of a particular information checkpoint depends upon "(1) the gravity of the public concerns served by the seizure, (2) the degree to which the seizure advances the public interest, and (3) the severity of the interference with individual liberty."[49] Applying its test, the Court upheld the roadblock. The police "stopped all vehicles systematically." Its "objective was to help find the perpetrator of a specific and known crime," that resulted "in a human death."[50] The police established the checkpoint at a place and time to acquire information from drivers who might have been present at the time of the accident. The "stops interfered only

---

45 *Id.*, at 42.

46 *Id.*, at 41–42.

47 *Id.*, at 44.

48 540 U.S. 419 (2004).

49 Illinois v. Lidster, 540 U.S. 419, 427 (2004).

50 *Id.*

minimally with liberty of the sort the Fourth Amendment seeks to protect," because each stop consisted "simply of a request for information," and involved contact with police for "only a few seconds."[51]

§ 11.7 Special Needs Searches at School

A. School Searches

The Court's school cases began with *New Jersey v. T.L.O.*,[52] involving the search of a high school student's purse. A finding of "special needs" (to maintain school discipline) enabled the Court to balance interests under the Fourth Amendment reasonableness clause and to dispose of the probable cause requirement. A warrantless search under *Camara* was lawful if it was based upon "reasonable grounds for suspecting that the search will turn up evidence that the student has violated or is violating either the law or the rules of the school."[53] The search must be reasonable in scope, or as the Court stated, "the measures adopted are reasonably related to the objectives of the search and not excessively intrusive in light of the age and sex of the student and the nature of the infraction."[54]

The Court also described that *T.L.O.* did *not* address "whether individualized suspicion is an essential element of the reasonableness standard," "whether a schoolchild has a legitimate expectation of privacy in lockers, desks, or other school property provided for storage of school supplies," and what standard was necessary in "assessing the legality of searches conducted by school officials in conjunction with or at the behest of law enforcement agencies."[55]

In *Safford Unified School District # 1 v. Redding*,[56] a student reported to school officials that a classmate had given her banned pain relief pills. The Court concluded that the student's statement provided reasonable suspicion "to justify a search of the [classmate's] backpack and outer clothing," because "[i]f a student is reasonably suspected of giving out contraband pills, she is reasonably suspected of carrying them."[57] Because that search turned up no evidence, school officials strip searched the classmate. A strip search was "categorically distinct, requiring distinct elements of justification"

---

[51] *Id.*, at 427–28.

[52] 469 U.S. 325 (1985).

[53] New Jersey v. T.L.O., 469 U.S. 325, 342 (1985).

[54] *Id.*

[55] *Id.*, at 341 n.7.

[56] 557 U.S. 364 (2009).

[57] Safford Unified School District # 1 v. Redding, 557 U.S. 364, 373–74 (2009).

absent in the instant case because "the content of the suspicion failed to match the degree of intrusion."[58] The pills were "common pain relievers equivalent to two Advil," and were not suspected of being "passed around in large amounts" or received by "individual students in great numbers." The school failed to show any "reason to suppose that [the classmate] was carrying pills in her underwear,"[59] as well as how recently the reporting student received the pills. The "combination of these deficiencies was fatal to finding the search reasonable." The *T.L.O.* scope requirement for a strip search is "reasonable suspicion of danger or of resort to underwear for hiding evidence of wrongdoing."[60]

B. School Drug Testing

In *Vernonia School District v. Acton*,[61] the Court upheld suspicionless drug-testing of high school athletes. The Court relied on several factors to justify the testing. As the Court had stated in *T.L.O.*, all school children are subject to considerable supervision and control, and student athletes' privacy expectations "are even less" because they subject themselves to greater regulation, "somewhat like adults who choose to participate in a 'closely regulated industry.' "[62] In addition, athletes' privacy is reduced, especially athletes because they usually shower and dress in front of others.

The intrusion from the testing upon the students' privacy was limited, because the test conditions were "nearly identical to those typically encountered in public restrooms," and test result disclosure was "only to a limited class of school personnel who have a need to know."[63] The State's interest in preventing drugs in schools was unique, because the students are "committed to the temporary custody of the State as schoolmaster."[64] The school district also produced documentation of a drug problem among athletes there. Finally, testing based on individualistic suspicion might be worse than suspicionless testing, because it might be a "badge of shame" on the tested students.

Board of Education of Independent School District No. 92 of Pottawatomie County v. Earls[65] applied *Acton*'s rationale to a broader policy of requiring random drug testing of all middle and high school

---

58 *Id.*, at 374.

59 *Id.*, at 376–77.

60 *Id.*, at 377.

61 515 U.S. 646 (1995).

62 Vernonia School District v. Acton, 515 U.S. 646, 657 (1995).

63 *Id.*, at 658.

64 *Id.*, at 654.

65 536 U.S. 822 (2002).

students who participate in extracurricular activities like the band and FFA. Unlike *Acton*, there was no documented problem of drug abuse among the affected groups or even the district in general. All students who "voluntarily subject themselves" to the testing requirements by opting for extracurricular activities have "a limited expectation of privacy,"[66] but the Court upheld the program in part because there was no direct observation of the samples being collected. The broad testing regimen was necessary because "the nationwide epidemic makes the war against drugs a pressing concern in every school," and there was "specific evidence of drug use"[67] at the schools. The *Earls* testing was "a reasonably effective means of . . . preventing, deterring, and detecting drug use."[68]

§ 11.8 Border Searches

Border searches are considered "special needs" searches, based on the national interest in protecting the United States' borders, and regulating the goods (and the people) who enter the country. Thus, the role of officials who regulate the borders with Mexico and Canada extends beyond investigative law enforcement. Their duties include protecting the United States from anything harmful such as diseases, narcotics, or explosives from being sent or brought into the United States. Like other special needs topics, the Fourth Amendment Reasonableness Clause governs border search court decisions.

A. Drug Searches

Routine border searches are the norm, without search warrants, probable cause, or any suspicion. Border searches, "pursuant to the long-standing right of the sovereign to protect itself by stopping and examining persons and property crossing into this country, are reasonable simply by virtue of the fact that they occur at the border."[69]

Particular kinds of border searches are more than routine and require case-by-case justification. Drug searches may require a possible strip search to disrobe or worse, i.e., smugglers use their alimentary canal to store drugs. Agents may detain suspects at the border either to wait for the "call of nature," or to ask their consent to an x-ray. No search warrants are required for these non-routine and quite intrusive searches.

66 Board of Education of Independent School District No. 92 of Pottawatomie County v. Earls, 536 U.S. 822, 831–32 (2002).

67 *Id.*, at 834.

68 *Id.*, at 837.

69 United States v. Ramsey, 431 U.S. 606, 616 (1977).

Whatever questions are raised by these intrusive searches do not carry over to vehicles. In *United States v. Flores-Montano*,[70] agents' removal and disassembling of a vehicle's gas tank did not require reasonable suspicion, however destructive the property search seemed. Identifying and apprehending illegal aliens require the use of roving patrols to stop and search vehicles. In *Almeida-Sanchez v. United States*,[71] the Court held that a warrantless search of a vehicle without probable cause violated the Fourth Amendment. Vehicle searches[72] require probable cause, and *Camara*[73] prohibits searches "at the discretion of the official in the field."

In *United States v. Brignoni-Ponce*, the Court's answer was "no" when the issue posed was "whether a roving patrol may stop a vehicle in an area near the border and question its occupants when the only ground for suspicion is that the occupants appear to be of Mexican ancestry."[74] As in *Almeida-Sanchez*, the use of "broad and unlimited discretion" would lead to the stopping of untold innocent people, and this practice likewise could not be brought within the reasoning of *Camara*.

Applying the *Terry v. Ohio* stop-and-frisk rule at the border struck a proper equilibrium, leading to the approval of roving patrols to stop vehicles for questioning when the facts reasonably justify "suspicion that the vehicles contain aliens who may be illegally in the country."[75] The Court helpfully listed a "number of factors in deciding whether there is reasonable suspicion to stop a car in a border area."[76] For example, law enforcement may consider the characteristics of the area in which they encounter a vehicle, its proximity to the border, the usual patterns of traffic on the particular road, and the officers' previous experience with alien traffic.

The driver's behavior may be relevant, because erratic driving or obvious attempts to evade officers can support a reasonable suspicion to stop. Aspects of the vehicle itself also may justify suspicion. For instance, officers claimed that certain station wagons, with large compartments for fold-down seats or spare tires, are frequently used for transporting concealed aliens. The vehicle may appear heavily loaded from an extraordinary number of passengers, or the officers may observe persons trying to hide. Consistent with *Terry v. Ohio*, the Court concluded with a generalized factor—such

---

70 541 U.S. 149 (2004).

71 413 U.S. 266 (1973).

72 See Chapter 7, discussing Vehicle Searches.

73 See § 11.2, discussing The *Camara* Balancing Principle.

74 United States v. Brignoni-Ponce, 422 U.S. 873, 876 (1975).

75 *Id.*, at 884.

76 *Id.*

other facts as are meaningful to the officer "in light of his experience detecting illegal entry and smuggling."[77]

B. Searches for Aliens

The Court has decided cases using fixed checkpoints to discover illegal aliens. *United States v. Ortiz*[78] was a checkpoint decision where all vehicles were required to stop for investigation and possibly for a search. The record showed that a small percentage of vehicles were stopped for questioning or a search, suggesting to the Court that "checkpoint officers exercise a substantial degree of discretion in deciding which cars to search." *Ortiz* held "that at traffic checkpoints removed from the border and its functional equivalents, officers may not search private vehicles without consent or probable cause."[79] The Government prevailed in another checkpoint case, *United States v. Martinez-Fuerte*,[80] when the checkpoint's purpose was to stop and question occupants. The Court reasoned that "the potential interference with legitimate traffic is minimal," and the "checkpoint operations both appear to and actually involve less discretionary enforcement activity."[81]

§ 11.9 Searches of Parolees and Probationers

A. Special Needs Searches

The *Camara* balancing principle applies in searching parolees' and probationers' residences. The Governmental interest is that convicts can be rehabilitated, and close surveillance may reduce recidivism. The Court invoked the special needs of the probation system in *Griffin v. Wisconsin*[82] to uphold a search of Griffin's home without a warrant or probable cause. Because officers "have in mind the welfare of the probationer," they must be able to "intervene before a probationer does damage to himself or society."[83] Probation officers apply a case-by-case evaluation about "what degree of surveillance is necessary." Promoting the rehabilitation goal is maximized by giving the search authority to the probation officers rather than to the police.

---

[77] *Id.*, at 884–85.

[78] 422 U.S. 891 (1975).

[79] United States v. Ortiz, 422 U.S. 891, 896–97 (1975).

[80] 428 U.S. 543 (1976).

[81] United States v. Martinez-Fuerte, 428 U.S. 543, 559 (1976).

[82] 483 U.S. 868 (1987).

[83] Griffin v. Wisconsin, 483 U.S. 868, 879 (1987).

B. Fourth Amendment Interest Balancing

In *United States v. Knights*,[84] the Court took a different approach by balancing a probationer's reduced privacy interests against the Government's interests in monitoring probationers, deterring recidivism, and protecting the public. One of Knights' probation conditions was that he "[s]ubmit his . . . person, property, place of residence, vehicle, personal effects, to search at any time," without even reasonable cause. Several days after release, a sheriff's detective searched Knights' residence on reasonable suspicion of vandalism, without probation officials' knowledge or participation.

The Court unanimously upheld the warrantless search "under [its] general Fourth Amendment approach of 'examining the totality of the circumstances,' "[85] and interest balancing. Knights' probation conditions significantly reduced his reasonable expectation of privacy, and Knights was unambiguously informed of it. Because a probationer "will be more likely to engage in criminal conduct than an ordinary member of the community," the State's "interest in apprehending violators of the criminal law . . . may therefore justifiably focus on probationers in a way that it does not on the ordinary citizen."[86] "[T]he balance of these considerations requires no more than reasonable suspicion to conduct a search of this probationer's house," "render[ing] a warrant requirement unnecessary."[87] Because its holding applied "ordinary Fourth Amendment analysis that considers all the circumstances of a search," the Court did not examine any "official purpose" of the Sheriff's detective in conducting the search. *Knights* did not foreclose any searches lacking suspicion.

Samson v. California[88] upheld a search of a parolee "at any time," under a State statute that included no standardized procedures for searching and required no individualized suspicion to conduct a search. The Court found even fewer expectations of privacy for parolees than for probationers. State officials had informed Samson about the parole search condition, the State had an "overwhelming interest" in supervising parolees given their 68–70% recidivism rate, and any concern about State officials' "unbridled discretion" was belied by the State ban on "arbitrary, capricious or harassing searches."[89]

---

[84] 534 U.S. 112 (2001).

[85] United States v. Knights, 534 U.S. 112, 118 (2001).

[86] *Id.*, at 121.

[87] *Id.*

[88] 547 U.S. 843 (2006).

[89] Samson v. California, 547 U.S. 843, 856 (2006).

§ 11.10 Other Special Needs Searches

For public employees and expectant mothers, the Court has developed additional special needs categories that go beyond the normal need for law enforcement. Using the *Camara* test, the Court balanced the State's interest to justify a search against the intrusion upon the privacy of the individual caused by the search.

A. Drug Testing

In *Skinner v. Railway Labor Executives' Association*,[90] the Court denied a challenge to federal regulations that required blood and urine tests of railroad employees who (1) were involved in "major" train accidents, and (2) violated certain safety rules. In upholding the regulations, the Governmental interest was "ensuring the safety of the traveling public and of the employees themselves." The Court also emphasized the need to (1) restrict drug and alcohol use, and (2) act quickly to take samples after train accidents. The Court ruled that the testing constituted a Fourth Amendment search, although the intrusion on privacy was limited. The private employees worked "in an industry that is regulated pervasively to ensure safety, a goal dependent in substantial part on the health and fitness of covered employees."[91]

The tests were not intrusive, could be "conducted safely outside a hospital environment and with a minimum of inconvenience or embarrassment," and revealed "the level of alcohol in the employee's bloodstream and nothing more."[92] The drug tests could be required as a deterrent to drug use, even in the absence of reasonable suspicion, because the employees' jobs involved "duties fraught with such risks of injury to others that even a momentary lapse of attention can have disastrous consequences."[93] In addition, the testing provided "invaluable information about the causes of major accidents."[94]

For those who were thinking that there are no limits to the proliferation of special needs searches, consider the next two cases. The Court struck down a hospital's policy of drug testing pregnant women suspected of cocaine use in *Ferguson v. City of Charleston*.[95] Unlike prior cases, the Court held that these tests were not "special

---

[90] 489 U.S. 602 (1989).

[91] Skinner v. Railway Labor Executives' Association, 489 U.S. 602, 627 (1989). See National Treasury Employees Union v. Von Raab, 489 U.S. 656 (1989) (Customs Service drug-testing program for applicants for promotion is reasonable).

[92] *Skinner v. Railway Labor Executives' Association*, 489 U.S. at 625.

[93] *Id.*, at 628.

[94] *Id.*, at 630.

[95] 532 U.S. 67 (2001).

needs" searches because their central and indispensable feature was to promote law enforcement goals, i.e., the medical center testing the women had already determined that no testing program would be effective without the threat of criminal sanctions. The drug test results were turned over to the police without the knowledge or consent of the tested women so that they could be prosecuted for child neglect and/or drug offenses. The Court distinguished earlier drug testing cases, because those policies protected against dissemination of the test results to third parties like the police, and the special need in those cases was "divorced from the State's general interest in law enforcement."[96]

Drug testing candidates for public office was successfully challenged in *Chandler v. Miller*.[97] Because no demonstrated drug problem among candidates existed, the State had to prove that a suspicionless plan was necessary to protect against a public hazard. Unlike *Skinner*, where there was a risk that railroad employees could cause serious harm if they were under the influence of drugs, the Court identified no comparable risk for candidates.

B. Public Employees

In *City of Ontario v. Quon*,[98] the city claimed that it had the right to read text messages being sent and received by Government employees on pagers owned and issued by the city to its employees. To reduce the intrusiveness of the search, the city had redacted all messages sent while each employee was off-duty. In addition, the employees had read and signed a statement that they understood the city's computer policy that text message transcripts could be reviewed by supervisors.

The Court held that the Government's warrantless search policy was reasonable if it was "justified at its inception." Here, "there were 'reasonable grounds for suspecting that the search [was] necessary for a noninvestigatory work-related purpose,' "[99] Reading "the transcripts was reasonable because it was an efficient and expedient way to determine whether Quon's overages were the result of work-related messaging or personal use."[100] The search was not excessive in scope, even if it could have been conducted in a less intrusive manner.

---

96 Ferguson v. City of Charleston, 532 U.S. 67, 79 (2001).

97 520 U.S. 305 (1997).

98 560 U.S. 746 (2010).

99 City of Ontario v. Quon, 560 U.S. 746, 761 (2010).

100 *Id.*

Chapter 12

CONFESSIONS STANDARDS UNDER *MIRANDA V. ARIZONA*

Table of Sections

§ 12.1 Introduction

No area of criminal procedure has provoked more debate than police interrogation. The Court has applied four theories by which to assess the admissibility of confessions. First, a court may exclude a confession under its supervisory powers, if the defendant confessed during a period of "unnecessary delay" in taking the defendant before a judge for the first time (referred to as a preliminary arraignment or initial appearance). Every State has a statute or rule about prompt arraignment; in the federal system; 18 U.S.C. § 3501 makes a confession inadmissible if it was given after a six-hour period (plus transportation) following an arrest. The issue under this theory is whether the defendant (1) made an incriminating statement, (2) during a period of unnecessary delay.

The second theory is based on the Fifth Amendment privilege against self-incrimination. *Miranda v. Arizona* established a procedural mechanism of warnings by law enforcement to individuals who are questioned while in custody. The purpose of the warnings is to safeguard the exercise of Fifth Amendment rights against the inherently coercive effects of custodial interrogation. In this area, the key issues are whether the defendant (1) was warned before confessing, (2) was in custody, (3) was interrogated, and (4) waived his Fifth Amendment rights.

Two other confessions theories are discussed in the next Chapter. Once the Sixth Amendment right to counsel attaches at or after adversary proceedings begin, law enforcement officials cannot "deliberately elicit" incriminating statements from the accused without counsel's presence or the defendant's waiver of his right to counsel. The issues are whether (1) the right to counsel has attached, (2) statements were deliberately elicited, and (3) the defendant waived his right to counsel.

The last theory used to challenge the admissibility of a confession is based on Due Process concepts. To be admissible, a confession must be voluntary rather than coerced, examining the totality of circumstances. A confession may be of doubtful reliability because police used offensive police practices suggesting that the defendant's free will was significantly impaired. Even if a confession satisfies the requirement of *Miranda* or the Sixth Amendment, it still may be excludable under the Due Process test.

Using a timeline, a confession may be excluded if it was made (1) during unnecessary delay prior to the defendant's first court appearance, or (2) at or after that first appearance, per the Sixth Amendment. Confessions made at *any* time may be challenged, if they were obtained (1) involuntarily, using Due Process concepts, and/or (2) during custodial interrogation, applying the Fifth Amendment.

§ 12.2 Prompt Arraignment and Confessions

Law enforcement officials are responsible for promptly presenting arrested persons to a judicial officer. When the accused appears, the judge informs him of the pending charges and notifies him of certain statutory and constitutional rights. In *McNabb v. United States*[1] federal agents questioned murder suspects for days before taking them to a judge for an initial appearance, but not before they had confessed. The Court exercised its supervisory powers and invalidated the confessions because of the delay in arraigning them. Shortly after *McNabb*, the legislative and judicial branches consolidated several federal provisions to produce Fed.R.Crim.P. 5(a).[2] A portion of Rule 5(a) reads: "A person making an arrest . . . must take the defendant without unnecessary delay before a magistrate judge. . . ."[3]

The Court applied Rule 5(a) in *Mallory v. United States*,[4] holding that a confession made seven hours after arrest was inadmissible due to the "unnecessary delay" in conducting an initial appearance. The questioning occurred "within the vicinity of numerous" judges. *Mallory* discussed the scope of "unnecessary delay."

> The police may not arrest upon mere suspicion but only on "probable cause." The next step in the proceeding is to arraign the arrested person before a judicial officer as quickly as possible so that he may be advised of his rights and so that the issue of probable cause may be promptly determined. The arrested person may, of course, be "booked" by the police. But he is not to be taken to police headquarters in order to carry out a process of inquiry that lends itself, even if not so designed, to eliciting damaging statements to support the arrest and ultimately his guilt. The duty enjoined upon arresting officers to arraign "without unnecessary delay" indicates that the command does not call for mechanical or automatic obedience.

---

1 318 U.S. 332 (1943).

2 See, e.g., Fed.R.Crim.P. 5(a).

3 Fed.R.Crim.P. 5(a)(1)(A).

4 354 U.S. 449 (1957).

> Circumstances may justify a brief delay between arrest and arraignment, as for instance, where the story volunteered by the accused is susceptible of quick verification through third parties. But the delay must not be of a nature to give opportunity for the extraction of a confession. . . . In every case where the police resort to interrogation of an arrested person and secure a confession, they may well claim, and quite sincerely, that they were merely trying to check on the information given by him.[5]

As part of major criminal justice legislation in 1968, Congress enacted a prompt initial appearance statute, stating in part that a confession "shall not be inadmissible solely because of delay" in the initial appearance if the confession is voluntary and is made within six hours of arrest. 18 U.S.C. § 3501(c) focused on what had become known as the *McNabb-Mallory* rule, providing

> that in any federal prosecution, "a confession made . . . by . . . a defendant therein, while such person was under arrest . . ., shall not be inadmissible solely because of delay in bringing such person before a magistrate judge . . . if such confession is found by the trial judge to have been made voluntarily . . . and if such confession was made . . . within six hours [of arrest]"; the 6-hour time limit is extended when further delay is "reasonable considering the means of transportation and the distance to be traveled to the nearest available [magistrate judge]."

Corley v. United States[6] settled whether § 3501(c) swept "*McNabb-Mallory*'s exclusionary rule aside entirely," or merely immunized "voluntary confessions given within six hours of a suspect's arrest."[7] The defendants were arrested and questioned about a bank robbery in the same building as a magistrate judge for more than nine hours before one defendant orally confessed. The next afternoon, almost twenty hours after his arrest, that suspect was taken before a federal magistrate for his arraignment. The Court posed the issue from the defendant's viewpoint: § 3501(c) "leaves *McNabb-Mallory* inapplicable to confessions given within the six hours, but when a confession comes even later, the exclusionary rule applies and courts have to see whether the delay was unnecessary or unreasonable."[8] The Court held

---

5 Mallory v. United States, 354 U.S. 449, 454–56 (1957).

6 556 U.S. 303, 310 (2009).

7 Corley v. United States, 556 U.S. 303, 311 (2009).

8 *Id.*, at 313–14.

> that § 3501(c) modified *McNabb-Mallory* without supplanting it. Under. . . § 3501(c), a district court with a suppression claim must find whether the defendant confessed within six hours of arrest (unless a longer delay was "reasonable considering the means of transportation and the distance to be traveled to the nearest available [magistrate judge]"). If the confession came within that period, it is admissible, subject to the other Rules of Evidence, so long as it was "made voluntarily and . . . the weight to be given [it] is left to the jury." If the confession occurred before presentment and beyond six hours, however, the court must decide whether delaying that long was unreasonable or unnecessary under the *McNabb-Mallory* cases, and if it was, the confession is to be suppressed.[9]

A confession made during a statutory period of "unnecessary delay" of the initial appearance is inadmissible. If the confession does not violate the statute and is admissible, a defendant may still challenge his confession under *Miranda*'s Fifth Amendment standard, discussed later in this Chapter.

The federal prompt arraignment statute is not binding on the States under the Fourteenth Amendment, but some States have adopted their own version. Most cases indicate that it is not unnecessary delay to hold someone until regular business hours before taking the accused to a judicial officer the first time. If courts are closed for weekends or holidays, that could lead to timed arrests to provide police with an opportunity to interrogate a suspect for as long as possible before the initial appearance.

§ 12.3 The *Miranda* Principle and the Fifth Amendment

A. Miranda v. Arizona

Miranda v. Arizona[10] bars the admission during the prosecution's case-in-chief of any statement elicited from the defendant through official custodial questioning unless the defendant, prior to making the statement, was warned of certain rights and then knowingly waived those rights prior to making the statement. The majority's recitation of the facts follows.

> On March 13, 1963, petitioner, Ernesto Miranda, was arrested at his home and taken in custody to a Phoenix

---

9 *Id.*, at 322.

10 384 U.S. 436 (1966).

> police station. He was there identified by the complaining witness. The police then took him to "Interrogation Room No. 2" of the detective bureau. There he was questioned by two police officers. The officers admitted at trial that Miranda was not advised that he had a right to have an attorney present. Two hours later, the officers emerged from the interrogation room with a written confession signed by Miranda. At the top of the statement was a typed paragraph stating that the confession was made voluntarily, without threats or promises of immunity and "with full knowledge of my legal rights, understanding any statement I make may be used against me."[11]

The dissent's factual report added information about the victim: her age, the charged crimes, Miranda's age, his indigency, education, emotional condition, competency, initial denial of the crime, an oral statement, and finally a written confession.[12] In effect, the dissent's description fit the typical judicial approach leading to a Due Process analysis under the voluntariness test that predated *Miranda.*

The discussion of police interrogation began by referring to "various police manuals and texts, as a "valuable source of information about present police practices."[13] The Court's treatment of the police manuals provided context to fashion a constitutional standard for police interrogation throughout the United States.

> [T]he modern practice of in-custody interrogation is psychologically rather than physically oriented. . . . Interrogation still takes place in privacy. Privacy results in secrecy and this in turn results in a gap in our knowledge as to what in fact goes on in the interrogation rooms. . . .These texts . . . present the most enlightened and effective means presently used to obtain statements through custodial interrogation.
>
> The officers are told by the manuals that the "principal psychological factor contributing to a successful interrogation is privacy—being alone with the person under interrogation."
>
> To highlight the isolation and unfamiliar surroundings, the manuals instruct the police to display an air of confidence in the suspect's guilt and from outward appearance to maintain only an interest in confirming certain details. The guilt of the subject is to be posited as a

---

11 Miranda v. Arizona, 384 U.S. 436, 491 (1966).

12 *Id.*, at 518 (Harlan, J., dissenting).

13 *Id.*, at 448.

> fact. The interrogator should direct his comments toward the reasons why the subject committed the act, . . . The officers are instructed to minimize the moral seriousness of the offense, to cast blame on the victim or on society. These tactics are designed to put the subject in a psychological state where his story is but an elaboration of what the police purport to know already—that he is guilty. Explanations to the contrary are dismissed and discouraged.[14]

Psychological police ploys are intended to take advantage of weak individuals. One bit of trickery misrepresents to the suspect the strength of the case against him. In *Frazier v. Cupp*,[15] the police knew that the main suspect had been with his cousin on the night of a murder. They told the suspect that the cousin had been brought in and had already confessed. The Court concluded that the "fact that the police misrepresented the statements that [the cousin] made is, while relevant, insufficient . . . to make this otherwise voluntary confession inadmissible."[16]

Another deceptive strategy used in the decades before *Miranda* was the "false friend" technique. The interrogator tells the suspect that he is his friend and is acting in the suspect's best interest. In *Leyra v. Denno*,[17] the Court held that a confession was involuntary where a police psychiatrist pretended he was a general practitioner solicited to treat the suspect for a painful sinus attack. In *Spano v. New York*,[18] to extract a confession, a policeman friend of the suspect told him that he (the policeman) would be in trouble if the defendant did not confess.

After noting these psychological strategies, the Court concluded that even without physical brutality "the very fact of custodial interrogation exacts a heavy toll on individual liberty and trades on the weaknesses of individuals."[19] Even though the police used none of the cited techniques in the cases before the *Miranda* Court, the majority concluded that questioning by police is inherently coercive, a concept that became the theme of Fifth Amendment confession cases. In each confession of the cases before the Court, there was a "potentiality for compulsion": police interrogation of an arrested person without advice that he could remain silent. From there, the Court deduced that "[u]nless adequate protective devices are employed to dispel the compulsion inherent in custodial

---

14 *Id.*, at 448–49, 450.

15 394 U.S. 731 (1969).

16 Frazier v. Cupp, 394 U.S. 731, 739 (1964).

17 347 U.S. 556 (1954).

18 360 U.S. 315 (1959).

19 *Miranda v.* Arizona, 384 U.S. at 455.

surroundings, no statement obtained from the defendant can truly be the product of his free choice."[20]

Building on its concerns about coercive, custodial interrogation, the Court stated its premise:

> [W]e cannot say that the Constitution necessarily requires adherence to any particular solution for the inherent compulsions of the interrogation process as it is presently conducted. Our decision in no way creates a constitutional straitjacket which will handicap sound efforts at reform, nor is it intended to have this effect. We encourage Congress and the States to continue their laudable search for increasingly effective ways of protecting the rights of the individual while promoting efficient enforcement of our criminal laws. However, unless we are shown other procedures which are at least as effective in apprising accused persons of their right of silence and in assuring a continuous opportunity to exercise it, the [warnings as] safeguards must be observed.[21]
>
> We have already pointed out that the Constitution does not require any specific code of procedures for protecting the privilege against self-incrimination during custodial interrogation. Congress and the States are free to develop their own safeguards for the privilege, so long as they are fully as effective as those described above in informing accused persons of their right of silence and in affording a continuous opportunity to exercise it.[22]

More than a half century after issuing this request, the Court has not recognized any alternative threshold rules.

Because the Fifth Amendment is so fundamental to overcoming the pressures of the interrogation atmosphere, police must give the warnings even to persons who already know their rights.

> [W]e will not pause to inquire in individual cases whether the defendant was aware of his rights without a warning being given. Assessments of the knowledge the defendant possessed, based on information as to his age, education, intelligence, or prior contact with authorities, can never be more than speculation; a warning is a clear-cut fact. . . . No amount of circumstantial evidence that the persons may have been aware of [his] right will suffice to stand in its

---

20 *Id.*, at 458.

21 *Id.*, at 467–68. See § 12.3(C), discussing Dickerson v. United States, 530 U.S. 428 (2000), as a legislative attempt to "repeal" *Miranda*.

22 *Miranda v. Arizona*, 384 U.S. at 490.

> stead. Only through such a warning is there ascertainable assurance that the accused was aware of this right.[23]

This statement negates Due Process analysis indicating that prior experience with the criminal justice system is an important factor for determining whether a confession was voluntarily made.

Failure to comply with *Miranda* renders a confession inadmissible even if the confession is otherwise wholly voluntary, and regardless of whether the illegally obtained statement is inculpatory or exculpatory. A suspect's exercise of the privilege may not be penalized, and "the prosecution may not, therefore, use at trial the fact that he stood mute or claimed his privilege in the face of accusation."[24]

Estelle v. Smith[25] held that *Miranda* applies in criminal cases at both the guilt phase of a trial and the sentencing phase.

> We can discern no basis to distinguish between the guilt and penalty phases of respondent's capital murder trial so far as the protection of the Fifth Amendment privilege is concerned. . . . Any effort by the State to compel respondent to testify against his will at the sentencing hearing clearly would contravene the Fifth Amendment.[26]

In general, "*Miranda* warnings" are required only where there is: (1) interrogation, (2) by the "Government," and (3) when the defendant is "in custody." Each of these concepts is somewhat complex and the terms "custodial" and "interrogation" have become significant terms of art. Assuming the necessity of the warnings, the question of waiver becomes a major consideration. The prosecution's use of the defendant's assertion of his right to silence, as well as impeachment with *Miranda* statements, are treated under the discussion of the exclusionary rule.[27]

As often occurs with Court decisions announcing important principles, *Miranda* proclaimed a new principle that the defendants and the police had no way of knowing was applicable when the defendants made their incriminating statements. Perhaps such decisions should be prospective only, while reserving a standard about whether to apply the new principles to theretofore unsuspecting parties.

---

[23] *Id.*, at 468–69, 471–72.

[24] *Id.*, at 468 n.37.

[25] 451 U.S. 454 (1981).

[26] Estelle v. Smith, 451 U.S. 454, 462–63 (1981).

[27] See Chapter 1, discussing the Exclusionary Rule.

B. Rationales for *Miranda*

Two findings were at the core of the *Miranda* Court's reasoning. First, all custodial interrogations create a "potentiality for compulsion," based on the Court's review of police manual instructions for interrogation techniques which promoted an "atmosphere of domination"[28] by police interrogators. Second, the "human dignity" value of the Fifth Amendment could be protected only if new rules were created to limit the inherent coercion of interrogation so that confessions may be "truly the product of free choice." A "full opportunity to exercise the privilege" could be provided if the accused was "adequately and effectively apprised of his rights and the exercise of those rights . . . [is] fully honored."[29]

The Court offered several justifications for its holding. Before *Miranda*, judges had serious difficulties in making voluntariness determinations. An important challenge was to determine how coercive the police interrogation had been. After all, the only witnesses (usually, the police officers and the suspect) had their own skewed views of the process. The intent of the bright-line *Miranda* rule was to aid judicial review, i.e., if the warnings were not given, the confession was tainted. Even with warnings, a confession may be involuntary, but the hope was that courts would have greater confidence in any confession that was obtained.

If *Miranda* was supposed to improve the task of judicial review, video recording all interrogations with a heavy burden on the prosecution to show voluntariness might have promoted even more effective judicial review. Even with the addition of warnings, however, reviewing courts remain dependent on the testimony of police and suspects to figure out whether the warnings were given, as well as what followed the warnings. Recording all confessions and the accompanying interrogation would provide better perception about what happened, i.e., the sequence of warnings and waiver, as well as who said what and when it was disclosed.

A further justification for *Miranda* was the education of suspects about the real choice they have in the interrogation process. No person should be deemed to confess voluntarily and intelligently, unless that person is aware of both the right to remain silent and that any confessions may be used as evidence against the speaker at a later proceeding. Before *Miranda*, very few people could articulate their constitutional rights to remain silent and refuse to cooperate with police.

---

[28] *Miranda v. Arizona*, 384 U.S. at 451.

[29] *Id.*, at 467.

Educationally, *Miranda* effectively made the Government the teacher of individual rights in custody situations. Two problems existed with the Court's reasoning. First, the Court is depending on the police officers about whom it was concerned to give the warnings. Second, as a set of warnings, *Miranda* is not perfect as an educational tool. Because *Miranda* repeats its holding, there may be subtle differences in different parts of *Miranda*. For example, in one recitation of the holding, the Court refers to the second warning as anything the suspect says "can and will be used" against the suspect. In another portion, that warning was expressed that anything the suspect says "can be used," and in a third place the warning states that anything said "may be used."

If the warnings are educational, the current warnings are not comprehensive, i.e., in overlooking some topics, what have the police *not* told the suspect? First, although later case law may have filled in some initially unstated matters, the *Miranda* warnings require disclosure about the right to remain silent, but they say nothing about what happens if the suspect *does* remain silent. Second, the police do not reveal to the suspect that, even if he initially exercises the right to remain silent, he can change his mind and begin talking to them.

Third, the warnings do not require the police to disclose the charges for which an arrest was made, or any other charges that the police contemplate bringing against the suspect. Fourth, the warnings do not describe the legal consequences if the suspect asserts the right to remain silent or the right to have a lawyer present. *Colorado v. Spring*[30] held that a suspect does not have to be told about all the possible subjects or questioning prior to interrogation. *Michigan v. Mosley*[31] and *Edwards v. Arizona*[32] later described the consequences of the suspect's assertion of his rights to silence and counsel, respectively. Fifth, the warnings do not invite persons to ask questions to assure an understanding of the warnings. A suspect might want to clarify his rights, after which the police may issue the same warnings because they do not know the answer to the clarifying question.

C. "Repealing" *Miranda*

In the Crime Control Act of 1968, Congress purported to "repeal" *Miranda* in federal prosecutions. The statute provided that in the

---

30 479 U.S. 564 (1987).

31 423 U.S. 96 (1975). See § 12.7(E), discussing a defendant's invocation of the right to silence.

32 451 U.S. 477 (1981). See § 12.7(F), discussing a defendant's invocation of the right to counsel.

federal courts a confession "shall be admissible in evidence if it is voluntarily given,"[33] and thereafter listed factors to be taken into account on the voluntariness issue. In *Dickerson v. United States*,[34] despite *Miranda*'s "invitation for legislative action," the Court concluded that the federal statute could not be upheld given that invitation's "requirement that a legislative alternative to *Miranda* be equally as effective in preventing coerced confessions."[35] The statute merely "reinstate[d] the totality test as sufficient," while *Miranda* had "concluded that something more than the totality test was necessary."[36]

"Congress intended by its enactment to overrule *Miranda*," and the Court deemed it necessary to focus on "whether Congress has constitutional authority" to do so. Congress "retains the ultimate authority to modify or set aside any judicially created rules of evidence and procedure that are not required by the Constitution" but it "may not legislatively supersede our decisions interpreting and applying the Constitution." The case consequently turned "on whether the *Miranda* Court announced a constitutional rule or merely exercised its supervisory authority to regulate evidence in the absence of congressional direction."[37]

The Court then refused to overrule *Miranda*, because "principles of *stare decisis* weigh heavily against overruling it now." It "has become embedded in routine police practice to the point where the warnings have become part of our national culture." While under *Miranda* it may sometimes be the case that "a guilty defendant go[es] free," the Court declared that situation to be a lesser disadvantage than operating exclusively under a totality-of-the-circumstances test, i.e., it "is more difficult than *Miranda* for law enforcement officers to conform to, and for courts to apply in a consistent manner."[38] Thus, the Court held that the Congress cannot legislatively overrule *Miranda*.[39]

---

33 18 U.S.C. § 3501.

34 530 U.S. 428 (2000).

35 Dickerson v. United States, 530 U.S. 428, 441 (2000).

36 *Id.*, at 442–43.

37 *Id.*, at 437.

38 *Id.*, at 444.

39 See Vega v. Tekoh, 597 U.S. 134 (2022), the Court held that a *Miranda* violation alone is insufficient to justify a civil § 1983 remedy. Although *Miranda* warnings are "constitutionally based" prophylactic rules to protect the Fifth Amendment, they are not constitutionally compelled.

§ 12.4 *Miranda* Warnings

A. Warnings Required

Miranda held that a suspect

> must be warned prior to any questioning that he has the right to remain silent, that anything he says can be used against him in a court of law, that he has the right to the presence of an attorney, and that if he cannot afford an attorney one will be appointed for him prior to any questioning if he so desires. Opportunity to exercise these rights must be afforded to him throughout the interrogation. After such warnings have been given, and such opportunity afforded him, the individual may knowingly and intelligently waive these rights and agree to answer questions or make a statement. But unless and until such warnings and waiver are demonstrated by the prosecution at trial, no evidence obtained as a result of interrogation can be used against him.[40]

Miranda's warnings were "protective devices" to replace a "totality of circumstances" approach begun only two years earlier in *Escobedo v. Illinois*.[41] The warnings' purpose was to safeguard against the coercive police questioning that could threaten a suspect's exercise of the Fifth Amendment privilege. Assuming that a defendant is subject to "custodial interrogation," the defendant must be given his "rights" pursuant to *Miranda*.

The first warning: a defendant, without regard to any prior awareness of his rights, "must first be informed in clear and unequivocal terms that he has the right to remain silent." The purpose of this warning is to educate the ignorant person about this right, and to overcome the pressures of the interrogation atmosphere for persons previously aware of the right.

The second warning: "anything said can and will be used against the individual in court." The intent of this warning is to ensure that the suspect fully understands the consequences of foregoing the privilege against self-incrimination.

The third warning: the individual "must be clearly informed that he has the right to consult with a lawyer and to have the lawyer with him during interrogation." The reason for this warning is to inform the suspect of this right, without regard to whether it appears that

---

40 *Id.*, at 479.

41 378 U.S. 478 (1964).

he is already aware of this right. *Florida v. Powell*[42] held that police do not have to explicitly tell suspects they have a right to a lawyer during an interrogation. The combination of (1) informing a defendant about the right to talk to a lawyer before answering police questions, and (2) telling him that he could use any of his rights during the interview "reasonably conveyed" the right to have an attorney present during an interrogation.

> If the accused decides to talk to his interrogators, the assistance of counsel can mitigate the dangers of untrustworthiness. With a lawyer present the likelihood that the police will practice coercion is reduced, and if coercion is nevertheless exercised the lawyer can testify to it in court. The presence of a lawyer can also help to guarantee that the accused gives a fully accurate statement to the police and that the statement is rightly reported by the prosecution at trial.[43]

The fourth warning: not only does the suspect have the "right to consult with an attorney, but, also, that if he is indigent, a lawyer will be appointed to represent him." Without this warning, a suspect might understand the third warning as meaning only that an individual may consult a lawyer *if* he has the funds to obtain one.

B. Rejected Warnings and Warning Alternatives

Since *Miranda*, other warnings have been proposed on the theory that they would result in a more intelligent waiver. However, the courts have held that law enforcement officers need not inform a suspect either that a lawyer retained on his behalf has tried to contact him,[44] or about the possible subjects of interrogation.[45] As to the latter right, a suspect's awareness of all the crimes about which he could be questioned was not relevant to determining the validity of his decision to waive the privilege against self-incrimination. Is that true? The Court also declared that warnings about the subject of the interrogation would change the balance of power between the police interest in truth-finding and the defendant's interest in understanding the Fifth Amendment privilege.[46]

No warning is necessary that, if the suspect invokes his constitutional right to silence or to counsel, questioning must stop. Nor does the suspect have to be told that he has (1) no right to contact

---

[42] 559 U.S. 50 (2010).

[43] *Miranda v. Arizona*, 384 U.S. at 470.

[44] Moran v. Burbine, 475 U.S. 412 (1986).

[45] Colorado v. Spring, 479 U.S. 564 (1987).

[46] *Miranda v. Arizona*, 384 U.S. at 469.

anyone outside the place of interrogation, or (2) no right of his counsel to have access to him during interrogation.

C. How *Miranda* Warnings Are Delivered

The four warnings are the minimum required. There is no requirement that they be given in the exact order as set forth by the Court, nor is there a necessity for the warnings to be a virtual incantation of the precise language contained in *Miranda*.[47] Police officers who used "*Miranda* cards" immediately after *Miranda* was decided occasionally incorporated a fifth warning to the effect that a defendant must be permitted the "opportunity to exercise these rights . . . throughout the interrogation."[48]

The prosecution must prove that the warnings were given. Police departments often provided written warning forms as well as oral warnings, and asked arrestees to sign a form to acknowledge that they received and understood them. The receipt of the warnings is the first step toward a valid *Miranda* waiver. The cases have focused on either incomplete or misleading warnings, or a recent development (discussed in *Missouri v. Seibert* later in this subsection) referred to as "question first, warn later."

The Court has tolerated ambiguity in the *Miranda* warnings. The warnings need not duplicate *Miranda*'s language, but they must convey the essential message. Some arrestees may not understand the legal concepts included in the warnings. In *California v. Prysock*,[49] the police officer's language was as follows:

> You have the right to talk to a lawyer before you are questioned, have him present with you while you are being questioned, and all during the questioning. Do you understand this? . . . You also, being a juvenile, you have the right to have your parents present, which they are. Do you understand this? . . . You have the right to have a lawyer appointed to represent you at no cost to yourself. Do you understand this?[50]

The defendant argued that the warnings failed to connect the right to consult counsel before questioning with the right to appointed counsel. The defendant did not realize that the "lawyer appointed to represent" him "at no cost" would be appointed before any questioning began. The defendant assumed instead that any

---

47 Duckworth v. Eagan, 492 U.S. 195 (1989); California v. Prysock, 453 U.S. 355 (1981).

48 Miranda v. Arizona, 384 U.S. 436, 479 (1966).

49 453 U.S. 355 (1981). *Prysock* also settled that *verbatim* recitation of the *Miranda* warnings is unnecessary.

50 California v. Prysock, 453 U.S. 355, 357 (1981).

"appointed lawyer" would be appointed after the interrogation, presumably by a judge at some proceeding in the future.

The Court ruled that separate references to the right to consult counsel before questioning and the abstract right to appointed counsel sufficiently conveyed the meaning of the *Miranda* rights. What saved the *Prysock* warnings was the clarity with which the right to consult counsel was attached to the time period "prior to and during interrogation." The Court did recognize, however, that the "right to counsel" warnings would be constitutionally inadequate if they expressly suggested "any limitation on the right to the presence of appointed counsel" that was different from the "rights to a lawyer in general."[51]

In *Duckworth v. Eagan*,[52] the police told the suspect that he had a right to an attorney during interrogation and to an appointed attorney. In addition, they told him that an attorney would be appointed for him if and when he went to court. The Court again found that the warning was sufficient, because it "simply anticipated" a question the suspect might be expected to ask after receiving *Miranda* warnings, i.e., "When will I have an attorney?"

The Court stated in *Florida v. Powell*[53] that it had "not dictated the words in which the essential [*Miranda*] information must be conveyed." When police officers arrested the defendant, they warned him about his "right to talk to a lawyer before answering any . . . questions." They also told him that he had "the use of these [*Miranda*] rights at any time [he] want[ed] during th[e] interview." The State court

> found that the advice . . . received was misleading because it suggested that [defendant] could "only consult with an attorney before questioning" and did not convey [his] entitlement to counsel's presence throughout the interrogation. . . . [T]he final catchall warning [did not] cure the defect the court perceived in the right-to-counsel advice.[54]

The lower court questioned how the defendant knew which statement to believe—that an attorney could talk to him before any questioning, or that he could talk to the attorney during the questioning. Similar to *Eagan*, the defendant in *Powell* was left to wonder, "When will I have a lawyer to consult?" *Powell* upheld the warnings, which "reasonably conveyed [defendant's] right to have an attorney present

---

51 *Id.*, at 361.

52 492 U.S. 195 (1989).

53 559 U.S. 50 (2010).

54 Florida v. Powell, 559 U.S. 50, 55 (2010).

not only at the outset of interrogation but at all times."[55] *Powell* and *Prysock* changed the *Miranda* emphasis that the delivery of the warnings must be "fully effective" to whether the warnings recited by the police "reasonably conveyed" the rights required.

A police technique known as "question first and warn later" developed in the wake of *Miranda*, and became the subject of *Missouri v. Seibert*.[56] Police would question the suspect without warnings, obtain a confession, and then administer the warnings and ask the suspect to repeat the confession. *Seibert* held that the strategy did not "reasonably convey" the *Miranda* rights when the warnings were given "midstream" between two interrogations that were "close in time and similar in content." This technique likely misleads the suspect about "the nature of his rights and the consequences of abandoning them." "[A] suspect would hardly think he had a genuine right to remain silent, let alone persist in so believing once the police began to lead him over the same ground again."[57]

Seibert did note that midstream warnings may be adequate in some circumstances, as in *Oregon v. Elstad*,[58] where police made a "good faith" mistake in failing to give warnings before a single comment by an officer prompted an unwarned admission by the defendant during his arrest in his home. Because the later warnings to Elstad at the police station were "adequate" (according to the *Seibert* Court), the station house interrogation was deemed to be a "new and distinct experience" for the defendant, and thus his stationhouse confession was admissible.

D. Who Gives the Warnings

Miranda applies to custodial interrogation conducted by any State agent involved in the adversarial process. Like the application of the Fourth Amendment,[59] *Miranda* does not apply to interrogation by private persons, including undercover police officers whose true identity is not known to the suspect at the time he makes incriminating remarks. *Illinois v. Perkins*[60] held that an undercover officer is not required to give warnings to an incarcerated suspect before interrogating him, because the suspect did not know that the person with whom he was talking was an undercover officer.

---

[55] *Id.*, at 62.

[56] 542 U.S. 600 (2004).

[57] Missouri v. Seibert, 542 U.S. 600, 613 (2010).

[58] 470 U.S. 298 (1985).

[59] See Chapter 1, discussing the Exclusionary Rule.

[60] 496 U.S. 292 (1990).

> Conversations between suspects and undercover agents do not implicate the concerns underlying *Miranda*. The essential ingredients of a "police-dominated atmosphere" and compulsion are not present when an incarcerated person speaks freely to someone that he believes to be a fellow inmate. Coercion is determined from the perspective of the suspect. When a suspect considers himself in the company of cellmates and not officers, the coercive atmosphere is lacking.
>
> It is the premise of *Miranda* that the danger of coercion results from the interaction of custody and official interrogation. We reject the argument that *Miranda* warnings are required whenever a suspect is in custody in a technical sense and converses with someone who happens to be a government agent. Questioning by captors, who appear to control the suspect's fate, may create mutually reinforcing pressures that the Court has assumed will weaken the suspect's will, but where a suspect does not know that he is conversing with a government agent, these pressures do not exist.[61]

Therefore, the defendant did not experience the coercion associated with police questioning. In effect, *Perkins* permits law enforcement to ignore the *Miranda* mandate, allowing police to do indirectly what would be forbidden if they were in uniform.

E. When Warnings Are Unnecessary

The post-*Miranda* decisions have not required the warnings in all custodial interrogations. First, the warnings may be excused when interrogation is reasonably prompted by concern for the officer's or the public's safety. In *New York v. Quarles*[62] the police were chasing a rape suspect through a grocery when they found and arrested him. During the frisk of the suspect, an officer felt a shoulder holster that was empty. They quickly asked, "Where's the gun?" The suspect pointed toward some boxes and said, "Over there." On these facts, the Court condoned the police questions about a weapon that he may have abandoned or hidden in a public area near the scene of the arrest.

> [T]he need for answers to questions in a situation posing a threat to the public safety outweighs the need for the prophylactic rule protecting the Fifth Amendment's privilege against self-incrimination. We decline to place

---

61 Illinois v. Perkins, 496 U.S. 292, 296–97 (1990).

62 467 U.S. 649 (1984).

> officers . . . in the untenable position of having to consider, often in a matter of seconds, whether it best serves society for them to ask the necessary questions without the *Miranda* warnings and render whatever probative evidence they uncover inadmissible, or for them to give the warnings in order to preserve the admissibility of evidence they might uncover but possibly damage or destroy their ability to obtain that evidence and neutralize the volatile situation confronting them.[63]

These questions may be asked without first providing *Miranda* warnings that could prompt the arrestee to refuse to disclose any information about the weapon. The police in *Quarles* asked "only the question necessary to locate the missing gun" before providing the defendant with *Miranda* warnings. If a question about a weapon was "reasonably prompted by a concern for public safety" under the circumstances of the arrest, the arrestee's answer to the question is admissible evidence, as well as any weapon that is located. The contrast between *Miranda* and *Quarles* is striking. The former imagines a victim in need of warnings and an officer in need of restraint, while the latter anticipates an officer acting in good faith and a suspect who has not been coerced until he convinces the court otherwise.

Second, a suspect also had no right to receive the warnings when he is questioned by an undercover agent of the police, perhaps posing as a fellow inmate.[64] Interrogation by a person not known to be a police officer does not carry the inherently coercive atmosphere associated with questioning by a law enforcement officer. Third, suspects also do not have to receive *Miranda* warnings during routine "booking" procedures at a police station where the questioning seeks biographical data rather than incriminating statements.[65] The presence of the defendant's attorney also removes the necessity for *Miranda* warnings.[66]

F. Cutting off Warnings Before They're Delivered

Sometimes, after the officer has begun to read the *Miranda* warnings, the officer never completes his task of warning, because the suspect cuts him off by confessing or by saying the warnings are unnecessary. Perhaps the officer knows that the suspect has been questioned before and is fully experienced with the criminal justice process. *Miranda* emphasized that the giving of the warnings is so

---

63 New York v. Quarles, 467 U.S. 649, 657–58 (1984).

64 Illinois v. Perkins, 496 U.S. 292 (1990).

65 Pennsylvania v. Muniz, 496 U.S. 582 (1990).

66 *Miranda v. Arizona*, 384 U.S. at 466.

simple that no amount of proof that the suspect's awareness of constitutional rights not yet given will suffice to stand in place of the giving of the *Miranda* warnings,[67] i.e., there is no excuse for failing to complete the warnings. The use of warnings was in part intended to function as a bright-line, in order to reduce the case-by-case analysis that is inherent with the Due Process analysis.

G. Necessity for Repeating the Warnings

Where a defendant has been fully advised of his rights under *Miranda*, it is not necessary to repeat them on a subsequent day prior to a new interrogation. However, if there has been some intervening illegality, the giving of new warnings will aid in establishing the absence of a "taint."[68] Also, if a defendant requests counsel, new warnings are required before a valid waiver may be obtained.[69]

§ 12.5 When Is Questioning Custodial?

A. Custody Defined

While police questioning anywhere generates some pressures and anxieties, *Miranda* does not require a police officer to give warnings to everyone approached for information concerning a crime. *Miranda* refers to "custodial interrogation," defined as "questioning initiated by law enforcement officers after a person has been taken into custody or otherwise deprived of his freedom of action in any significant way."[70] *Miranda*'s infamous footnote 4 stated that the definition of custody was intended to be identical to what the Court had stated two years earlier in *Escobedo v. Illinois*[71] when the Court referred to an investigation that had focused on an accused. Despite that reference, a decade after *Miranda*, the Court in *Beckwith v. United States*[72] rejected the interpretation that custody and focus are alternative grounds for requiring the warnings.

> An interview with Government agents in a situation such as the one shown by this record simply does not present the elements which the *Miranda* Court found so inherently coercive as to require its holding. Although the "focus" of an investigation may indeed have been on Beckwith at the time of the interview in the sense that it was his tax liability which was under scrutiny, he hardly found himself in the

---

67 See § 12.3(A), discussing warnings to persons who know their rights.

68 See Chapter 1, discussing Fruit of the Poisonous Tree.

69 See Oregon v. Bradshaw, 462 U.S. 1039 (1983).

70 *Id.*, at 444. On appeal, the standard of review for whether a defendant was in custody is *de novo*.

71 378 U.S. 478 (1964).

72 425 U.S. 341 (1976).

> custodial situation described by the *Miranda* Court as the basis for its holding. Miranda implicitly defined "focus," for its purposes, as "questioning initiated by law enforcement officers After a person has been taken into custody or otherwise deprived of his freedom of action in any significant way."[73]

Beckwith also was significant for its holding that police questioning in the suspect's home was not custodial. The inherently coercive pressures of a police-dominated atmosphere dissipated when the suspect was in familiar surroundings.

More generally, *Miranda* is inapplicable to the interrogation of jail and prison inmates. *Maryland v. Shatzer*[74] held that whether a person in prison is in custody for purposes of receiving the *Miranda* warnings depends on whether "lawful imprisonment" creates the coercive pressures identified in *Miranda*.[75] *Howes v. Fields*[76] refused to adopt a categorical rule that the questioning of a prisoner is always custodial when the prisoner is removed from the general prison population and questioned about events that occurred outside the prison. "[A] prison environment does not present the same inherently coercive pressures as the type of station house questioning at issue in *Miranda*."[77]

To support its holding, the Court cited three grounds: (1) questioning a person who is already serving a prison term does not generally involve the shock that often accompanies arrest; (2) unlike a person who has not been sentenced to a term of incarceration, a prisoner is unlikely to be lured into speaking by a longing for prompt release; and (3) a prisoner, unlike a person who has not been convicted and sentenced, knows that the law enforcement officers who question him probably lack the authority to affect the duration of his sentence.[78]

If the defendant is "in custody" on one charge, *Miranda* is still required even when the police questioning is about a different charge. In *Mathis v. United States*,[79] an IRS agent did not warn a taxpayer (who was then serving a State sentence) who was questioned about tax returns for prior years. The Government argued that *Miranda* did not apply because the IRS did not incarcerate the defendant; he was imprisoned for a different crime. The Court described that

---

73 Beckwith v. United States, 425 U.S. 341, 347 (1976).

74 559 U.S. 98 (2010).

75 Maryland v. Shatzer, 559 U.S. 98, 113 (2010).

76 565 U.S. 499 (2012).

77 Howes v. Fields, 565 U.S. 499, 509 (2012).

78 *Id.*, at 511–12.

79 Mathis v. United States, 391 U.S. 1 (1968).

distinction as "too minor and shadowy to justify a departure from the well-considered conclusion of *Miranda* with reference to warnings to be given to a person held in custody."[80]

> *Miranda* rested not on the mere fact of physical restriction but on a conclusion that coercion—pressure to answer questions—usually flows from a certain type of custody, police station interrogation of someone charged with or suspected of a crime. Although petitioner was confined, he was at the time of interrogation in familiar surroundings. . . . The rationale of *Miranda* has no relevance to inquiries conducted outside the allegedly hostile and forbidding atmosphere surrounding police station interrogation of a criminal suspect.[81]

B. Significance of Custody

Miranda warnings are required only for someone who is in custody. A suspect's ability to invoke the right to silence or the right to counsel also depends on being in custody, i.e., an invocation of rights has no legal effect unless the suspect is in custody at the time such rights are invoked.[82] "Custody" questions first come into play when the police begin an investigation. This initial investigative inquiry by police may be "general on-the-scene questioning as to facts surrounding a crime or other general questioning of citizens in the fact-finding process" which does not require warnings because "the compelling atmosphere inherent in the process of in-custody interrogation is not necessarily present."[83] This is not to suggest, however, that all "on-the-scene" questioning falls outside *Miranda* even if the person questioned is under arrest. The "ultimate inquiry is simply whether there is a 'formal arrest or restraint on freedom of movement' of the degree associated with a formal arrest."[84]

C. Objective "Reasonable Person" Standard

The current legal standard for custody is objective: how a reasonable person in the suspect's position would have understood the situation. Any questioning anywhere generates some pressure and anxiety, even for on-the-scene questioning or police visits to a

---

[80] *Id.*, at 4.

[81] *Id.*, at 7 (White, J., dissenting).

[82] See §§ 12.7(E)–(F), discussing the invocation of the right to remain silent and invocation of the right to counsel.

[83] *Miranda v. Arizona*, 384 U.S. at 478.

[84] *New York v. Quarles*, 467 U.S. at 655 (quoting California v. Beheler, 463 U.S. 1121, 1125 (1983)).

suspect's home or place of business. However, the warnings need not be given unless the suspect is in custody, as defined by the Court.

Soon after *Miranda*, though, the Court followed the subjective view of the police in two cases. In *Orozco v. Texas*,[85] the Court held that the police officer's uncommunicated intent that the suspect "was under arrest and not free to leave when was questioned" determined *Miranda*'s applicability, even when several police officers entered defendant's bedroom at 4:00 a.m. to question him about a shooting. The "potentiality for compulsion" paralleled a station house interrogation.

Then, in *Oregon v. Mathiason*,[86] a police officer left a note at the defendant's apartment that he wanted to talk to him. The defendant, who was a parolee, called the officer and arranged to meet him a few blocks away at a State patrol office. At their meeting, the officer told the defendant that he wanted to speak to him about a burglary but that he was not under arrest. When the officer later falsely told him that his fingerprints were present at the crime scene, the defendant confessed and was permitted to leave the office. The Court held that the police did not believe that the defendant was in custody, and the falsity was irrelevant to the custody issue.[87] If the Court's test had been from the standpoint of the reasonable person, would a parolee who just confessed to committing another crime have felt free to leave? Even applying the then subjective test, could a police officer believe that what was a noncustodial situation had not become custodial after the parolee confessed?

In *Berkemer v. McCarty*,[88] the Court held that *Miranda* did not apply to an interrogation that accompanied a traffic stop. A motorist is not entitled to *Miranda* warnings, the Court said, because the situation does not resemble the setting of custodial interrogation, as long as the stop is routine, occurs in public, and is expected to be brief. As in *Orozco*, the officer did not tell the defendant that he would be arrested, charged, and questioned, but in *Berkemer* the Court said that a "policeman's unarticulated plan has no bearing on . . . whether a suspect was 'in custody' at a particular time; the only relevant inquiry was how a reasonable man in the suspect's position would have understood his situation."[89] *Berkemer* also confirmed that *Miranda* applies without more once the suspect is arrested.

---

85 394 U.S. 324 (1969).

86 429 U.S. 492 (1977).

87 Oregon v. Mathiason, 429 U.S. 492, 495–96 (1977).

88 468 U.S. 420 (1984).

89 Berkemer v. McCarty, 468 U.S. 420, 442 (1984).

In *Stansbury v. California*,[90] the Court laid to rest the notion that an officer's subjective view of whether a person is a suspect, if undisclosed, is relevant to whether the person is in custody for *Miranda* purposes. "[T]he initial determination of custody depends on the objective circumstances of the interrogation, not on the subjective views harbored by either the interrogating officers or the person being questioned."[91] Later in *Stansbury*, the Court stated that the age of a child sometimes "would have affected how a reasonable person" in the suspect's position "would perceive his or her freedom to leave."[92]

The *Stansbury* standard puts a burden on the police to know the facts as they reasonably appear to the suspect, but this suspect may unreasonably believe that he is not free to leave. By contrast, the problem with the subjective viewpoint of the police on custody was that the uncommunicated intent of the officer does not change the situation from the suspect's view. Looking at the custody issue from the defendant's subjective perspective places the burden on the police to anticipate the personality of every person they question.

In *J.D.B. v. North Carolina*,[93] the Court discussed the age of a suspect.

> By limiting analysis to the objective circumstances of the interrogation, and asking how a reasonable person in the suspect's position would understand his freedom to terminate questioning and leave, the objective test avoids burdening police with the task of anticipating the idiosyncrasies of every individual suspect and divining how those particular traits affect each person's subjective state of mind.[94]

A "reasonable child subjected to police questioning will sometimes feel pressured to submit when a reasonable adult would feel free to go. We think it clear that courts can account for that reality without doing any damage to the objective nature of the custody analysis."[95] If a suspect's age was known at the time of the interrogation or if it would have been apparent to a reasonable officer, then a juvenile's age is relevant to the analysis of whether the suspect is in custody.[96]

---

90 Stansbury v. California, 511 U.S. 318, 323 (1994).

91 *Id.*

92 *Id.*, at 325.

93 564 U.S. 261 (2011).

94 J.D.B. v. North Carolina, 564 U.S. 261, 271 (2011).

95 *Id.*, at 272.

96 *Id.*, at 274.

By contrast, the suspect's inexperience with law enforcement is irrelevant when making a custody determination.[97]

Even with a reasonable person standard, certain factors are relevant to deciding whether the suspect was in custody at the time of interrogation: (1) whether the suspect was free to leave the scene, (2) the purpose, place and length of the interrogation, (3) whether the suspect initiated the contact with police or voluntarily agreed to an official request to answer questions, (4) whether the suspect was informed that the questioning was voluntary, (5) whether the suspect had unrestrained freedom of movement during the questioning, (6) whether strong arm or deceptive strategies were used, (7) whether the atmosphere was police-dominated, and (8) whether the suspect was placed under arrest at the termination of the questioning.

State v. Marquis[98] is an attempt to apply multiple custody factors when it held that a suspect was in custody, even though he voluntarily came to the station, signed in as a visitor, and was told by police that he could terminate the conversation. However, the court pointed out that the 1) police had requested that he come to the station, 2) nature of the questioning was "increasingly accusatory" over a 90-minute period, and 3) questioning was done in a small room at the police station that limited the suspect's freedom of movement). The court noted that "boilerplate assurances that a defendant is free to leave do not necessarily negate confrontational and accusatory questioning."[99]

Miranda intended to create an environment where everyone who was in custody is given warnings prior to interrogation. If an objective test is unlikely to lead to a consistent, standard application of custody, litigation about custody may be avoidable by over-warning, i.e., when in doubt about the custody issue, warn a suspect.

D. California v. Beheler

In *California v. Beheler*,[100] the defendant was implicated in a murder and voluntarily agreed to accompany the police to the stationhouse although the police specifically told him that he was not under arrest. The defendant gave a statement to the police, but was not given *Miranda* warnings. After the interview, the defendant was allowed to leave. The State court found the statement inadmissible, because the interview took place in the stationhouse and was designed to produce incriminating evidence. The Court reversed, finding that the defendant was neither taken into custody nor

---

[97] Yarborough v. Alvarado, 541 U.S. 652 (2004).

[98] 301 A.3d 812 (N.H. 2023).

[99] *State v. Marquis*, 812 A.3d at 821.

[100] 463 U.S. 1121 (1983).

significantly deprived of his freedom of action. Relying upon its earlier opinion in *Mathiason*,[101] the *Beheler* Court found it insufficient that the defendant was questioned at the police station:

> Although the circumstances of each case must certainly influence a determination of whether a suspect is "in custody" for purposes of receiving *Miranda* protection, the ultimate inquiry is simply whether there is a "formal arrest or restraint of freedom of movement" of the degree associated with a formal arrest. In the present case, the "totality of circumstances" on which the [California] court focused primarily were that the interview took place in a station house, and that Beheler was a suspect because he had spoken to police earlier. But we have explicitly recognized that *Miranda* warnings are not required "simply because the questioning takes place in the station house, or because the questioned person is one whom the police suspect." That the police knew more about Beheler before his interview than they did about Mathiason before his is irrelevant, especially because it was Beheler himself who had initiated the earlier communication with police. Moreover, the length of time that elapsed between the commission of the crime and the police interview has no relevance to the inquiry.[102]

E. Routine Traffic Stops Are Not Custodial

A person detained pursuant to a routine traffic stop is not "in custody" for *Miranda* purposes.[103] In the typical traffic stop, a driver expects to be detained only briefly and to be questioned by no more than one or two police officers in the comparative safety of the public eye. A temporary detention to receive a traffic citation does not compare to the "police-dominated" atmosphere of a station house interrogation. However, an *arrest* for even a minor traffic offense requires *Miranda* warnings prior to questioning.[104]

F. Probation Officer Questioning Is Not Custodial

In *Minnesota v. Murphy*,[105] a probationer who met with his probation officer at the latter's office made incriminating statements to the probation officer about a rape and murder he had committed years earlier. The Court held that the probationer was not in custody.

---

101 429 U.S. 492 (1977).

102 California v. Beheler, 463 U.S. 1121, 1125 (1983).

103 Pennsylvania v. Bruder, 488 U.S. 9 (1988); Berkemer v. McCarty, 468 U.S. 420 (1984).

104 Stansbury v. California, 511 U.S. 318, 325 (1994).

105 465 U.S. 420 (1984).

Although the probation officer had ordered the probationer's attendance, that alone did not transform a routine interview into an inherently coercive setting.

> Custodial arrest is said to convey to the suspect a message that he has no choice but to submit to the officers' will and to confess. . . . It is unlikely that a probation interview, arranged by appointment at a mutually convenient time, would give rise to a similar impression. . . . Many of the psychological ploys discussed in *Miranda* capitalize on the suspect's unfamiliarity with the officers and the environment. Murphy's regular meetings with his probation officer should have served to familiarize him with her and her office and to insulate him from psychological intimidation that might overbear his desire to claim the privilege. Finally, the coercion inherent in custodial interrogation derives in large measure from an interrogator's insinuations that the interrogation will continue until a confession is obtained. . . . Since Murphy was not physically restrained and could have left the office, any compulsion he might have felt from the possibility that terminating the meeting would have led to revocation of probation was not comparable to the pressure on a suspect who is painfully aware that he literally cannot escape a persistent custodial interrogator.[106]

§ 12.6 What Is Interrogation?

A. Interrogation Defined

In addition to the custody requirement, the police must be interrogating the suspect before there is a need for *Miranda* warnings. Thus, volunteered statements, e.g., where a suspect blurts a confession during the booking process, are admissible even if they were not preceded by the warnings. Because of the possibility of a spontaneous confession, cautious police often give the warnings before pursuing follow-up questions to a blurted statement. One difficulty with a blurted statement is whether the police have to give the suspect the warnings in order to clarify what he just said. The suspect exclaims, "I did it" and the police without warning him then ask, "Did what?" The clarifying question may be characterized as part of the original volunteered statement and not as interrogation.

As discussed previously, warnings are unnecessary before general on-the-scene questioning or before routine "booking" questions, i.e., questions "attendant to custody." In *Pennsylvania v.*

---

[106] *Id.*, at 433.

Muniz,[107] the defendant was arrested for driving under the influence. Police officers asked him a series of questions about his name, address, birthday, and age. Although his answers were incriminating because his slurred speech showed his drunkenness, the failure to give him *Miranda* warnings did not require suppression. The Court distinguished between "booking" questions and answers (without *Miranda* warnings, and not testimonial) after a DUI arrest, and a question about the arrestee's birthday requiring him to disclose whether he could recall that information (testimonial). The burden of proof is on the prosecution to show the impromptu nature of the statement. The Court concluded that

> any slurring of speech and other evidence of lack of muscular coordination revealed by Muniz's responses to [the officer's] direct questions constitute nontestimonial components of those responses. Requiring a suspect to reveal the physical manner in which he articulates words, like requiring him to reveal the physical properties of the sound produced by his voice, . . . does not, without more, compel him to provide a "testimonial" response for purposes of the privilege.[108]

That the defendant did not know the date of his sixth birthday was incriminating, because it created the inference that his mental state was confused.

Courts draw a line between seeking "standard information that turns out to be incidentally (and indirectly) incriminating" and asking a question that constitutes interrogation and knowingly connects a suspect directly to evidence in the case. *Kinney v. United States*[109] is an example of a question that is outside the routine booking exception. An officer asked a robbery suspect about an address that connected him to a car used in the robberies. The seemingly casual conversation "prompted descriptions of difficult circumstances demonstrating a potential motive for the robberies."[110]

B. Rhode Island v. Innis

In *Rhode Island v. Innis*,[111] the defendant was arrested for armed robbery, and was also suspected of a murder five days earlier. After being placed in the backseat of a police cruiser, he overheard officers talking about how they should "continue to search for the weapon," "because a school for handicapped children [was] located

---

107 496 U.S. 582 (1990).

108 Pennsylvania v. Muniz, 496 U.S. 582, 592 (1990).

109 286 A.3d 1027 (D.C. 2022).

110 *Kinney v. United States*, 286 A.3d at 1033.

111 446 U.S. 291 (1980).

nearby," and a little girl might "pick up the gun, maybe kill herself." Innis immediately stated that he would show the officers the location of the gun, and he led them there.

Innis established a test for determining whether a police comment or action qualifies as "interrogation." *Miranda* safeguards "come into play whenever a person in custody is subjected to either express questioning or its functional equivalent,"[112] defined as

> any words or actions on the part of the police (other than those normally attendant to arrest and custody) that the police should know are reasonably likely to elicit an incriminating response from the suspect. The latter portion of this definition focuses primarily upon the perceptions of the suspect, rather than the intent of the police. This focus reflects the fact that the *Miranda* safeguards were designed to vest a suspect in custody with an added measure of protection against coercive police practices, without regard to objective proof of the underlying intent of the police. A practice that the police should know is reasonably likely to evoke an incriminating response from a suspect thus amounts to interrogation. But, since the police surely cannot be held accountable for the unforeseeable results of their words or actions, the definition of interrogation can extend only to words or actions on the part of police officers that they *should have known* were reasonably likely to elicit an incriminating response.[113]

The *Innis* definition is consistent with the *Stansbury* definition of custody; both rules avoid focusing on the police officer's intent or state of mind. The Court also stated that its *Miranda* definition of interrogation was "not necessarily interchangeable"[114] with the *Brewer v. Williams* interrogation standard for Sixth Amendment violations. Unlike *Innis*, *Brewer*'s definition of "deliberately elicited" emphasizes police intent.[115] The Fifth Amendment definition also rejected a narrow definition of questioning that focuses only on direct questioning of the suspect.

Applying its test to the facts, *Innis* emphasized several aspects of the police dialogue that justified its conclusion that interrogation did not occur: The police comments were not directed to Innis but merely "overheard"[116] by him. The police had no knowledge of any

---

112 Rhode Island v. Innis, 446 U.S. 291, 300 (1980).

113 *Id.*, at 301–02 (emphasis in original).

114 *Id.*, at 300 n.4.

115 See Chapter 13, discussing Sixth Amendment issues regarding confessions.

116 *Rhode Island v. Innis*, 446 U.S. at 295.

"peculiar"[117] susceptibility of Innis to an appeal for the safety of handicapped children, and they knew of no disorientation or upset suffered by Innis at the time of arrest, i.e., the incriminating response was "unforeseeable."[118] Finally, the police conversation was "brief," and not "evocative."[119] While the defendant may have been subjected to "subtle coercion," in the sense that the "officers' comments struck a responsive chord,"[120] the defendant's response was not a product of words or conduct that the police should have known were reasonably likely to elicit an incriminating response.

The *Innis* majority believed that an objective observer could possibly conclude that the officers' remarks were made solely to express their genuine concern about the danger posed by the hidden gun. The facts supported that conclusion. The police were patrolmen assigned merely to transport the defendant, not detectives trained in interrogation, and their instructions were not to question the defendant. Is the suspect likely to view the police purpose in the same way?

Because the police are not responsible for the unforeseen results of their words and actions, the *Innis* definition extends only to words and actions that the police should have known were reasonably likely to elicit an incriminating reaction. *Innis* included a hypothetical to illustrate what would not amount to interrogation, when the police do "no more than . . . drive past the site of a concealed weapon while taking the most direct route to the police station."[121] Even if the police were to concede that their "purpose" was to "elicit an incriminating statement," the outcome is the same—no interrogation.

C. Functional Equivalent of Interrogation

"Psychological ploys" designed to elicit incriminating responses may also constitute *Miranda* interrogation. In *Arizona v. Mauro*,[122] the police used a "reverse lineup" where the defendant was identified by coached witnesses as the perpetrator of a fictitious crime, an example of a psychological ploy that is the equivalent of interrogation. The *Mauro* Court stated, however, that taping a conversation between the defendant and his wife was not such a ploy, because an officer was present and the recording machine was in full view.[123] "[T]he weakness of Mauro's claim that he was interrogated

117 *Id.*, at 302.

118 *Id.*

119 *Id.*, at 303 (1980).

120 *Id.*, at 296, 303.

121 *Id.*, at 303 n.10.

122 481 U.S. 520 (1987).

123 Arizona v. Mauro, 481 U.S. 520, 527 n.5 (1987).

is underscored by examining the situation from his perspective. . .We doubt that a suspect, told by officers that his wife will be allowed to speak to him, would feel that he was being coerced to incriminate himself in any way."[124] The defendant "was not subjected to compelling influences, psychological ploys, or direct questioning."[125] The recording was not as likely to lead to an incriminating response that requires *Miranda* warnings. In other words, the police do not interrogate by simply *hoping* that a suspect will incriminate himself, i.e., would an objective observer infer that any police remarks were designed to elicit an incriminating response?

Examples of other circumstances when a judicial finding of no interrogation include: (1) an officer's reading from scripted booking instructions to a defendant about whether the defendant understands instructions about physical sobriety tests,[126] or (2) when the police or their agents eavesdrop on a defendant's conversations with others. In either case, *Miranda* does not apply because there was no interrogation. Consider whether interrogation has occurred in the following situations:

- Police show a search warrant to a suspect and explain its purpose.
- Police seize incriminating physical evidence in the suspect's presence.
- After seizing evidence, the police stare at the defendant.
- At the scene of a shooting, the police ask a crying girl who shot the person on the floor and she points at the suspect.
- Police accuse the suspect, saying, "You're a liar. You were there. You did it."
- Police say to the suspect, "You look down in the dumps. If you want to talk, talk."
- The suspect says, "What can I do help myself?" and the officer replies, "You don't have to talk to me at all."
- The suspect says that he had never done anything like this before, and the police respond, "What have you done?"

---

124 *Id.*, at 528.

125 *Id.*, at 529.

126 Pennsylvania v. Muniz, 496 U.S. 582 (1990).

D. Requests for Identification

Requiring a person to identify himself other than as part of the booking process presents problems for defining the meaning of interrogation. Without warning the suspect, may the police ask a person to identify himself? *California v. Byers*[127] held that a statute requiring a driver of a car involved in an accident to give the driver of the other car his name and address does not violate the privilege against self-incrimination. The statutory requirement does not entail a "substantial risk of self-incrimination." "A name, linked with a motor vehicle, is no more incriminating than the tax return, linked with the disclosure of income. . . It identifies but does not by itself implicate anyone in criminal conduct."[128]

In *Hiibel v. Nevada*,[129] the Supreme Court upheld a statute requiring an arrest to be based on *both* a person's failure to identify himself and a reasonable suspicion of criminal activity. The defendant refused to provide his name "only because he thought his name was none of the officer's business" and did "not explain how the disclosure of his name could have been used against him in a criminal case."[130] The Court thus rejected the defendant's self-incrimination challenge, indicating this would be the proper result in most other cases, because "[a]nswering a request to disclose a name is likely to be so insignificant in the scheme of things as to be incriminating only in unusual circumstances."[131]

E. Inherently Coercive Atmosphere

A suspect does not have to be advised of his *Miranda* warnings immediately upon his arrest, as long as he is advised prior to the commencement of interrogation. The warnings "are not required when the suspect is unaware that he is speaking to a law enforcement officer and gives a voluntary statement."[132] Volunteered statements are admissible even if the defendant is in custody when the statement was made and no *Miranda* warnings had been given. "There is no requirement that police stop a person who enters a police station and states that he wishes to confess to a crime, or a person who calls the police to offer a confession or any other statement he desires to make."[133]

---

127 402 U.S. 424 (1971).

128 California v. Byers, 402 U.S. 424, 433–34 (1971).

129 542 U.S. 177 (2004).

130 Hiibel v. Nevada, 542 U.S. 177, 190 (2004).

131 *Id.*, at 190, 191.

132 Illinois v. Perkins, 496 U.S. 292, 294 (1990).

133 *Miranda v. Arizona*, 384 U.S. at 478.

§ 12.7 What Constitutes a Waiver of Rights?

A. Legal Standard for Waiver

In order for any statement obtained during custodial interrogation to be admissible at a criminal trial, the prosecution must prove both that the police administered the warnings and that the person waived his *Miranda* rights. *Miranda* provided only one example of a hypothetical case where a waiver could be found—an express statement that the arrestee "is willing" to make a statement and does not want an attorney, followed closely by a statement could constitute a waiver."[134]

> Whatever the testimony of the authorities as to waiver of rights by an accused, the fact of lengthy interrogation or incommunicado incarceration before a statement is made is strong evidence that the accused did not validly waive his rights. In these circumstances the fact that the individual eventually made a statement is consistent with the conclusion that the compelling influence of the interrogation finally forced him to do so. It is inconsistent with any notion of a voluntary relinquishment of the privilege.[135]

Because the Court's waiver standard looks to the totality of the circumstances, all the facts surrounding a confession and waiver must be viewed together. A similar analysis is conducted to determine if a confession is voluntary.[136] The prosecution must prove by a preponderance of the evidence that the defendant made an uncoerced choice to forego his constitutional rights, fully aware of both the nature of the right being waived and the consequences of waiving it, i.e., a voluntary, knowing and intelligent waiver.

The strength of a waiver is a question of fact in the particular case. *Moran v. Burbine*[137] stated the requirements for a valid waiver.

> Relinquishment of the right must have been voluntary in the sense that it was the product of a free and deliberate choice rather than intimidation, coercion, or deception. . . [T]he waiver must have been made with full awareness of both of the nature of the right being abandoned and the consequences of the decision to abandon it. Only if the "totality of the circumstances surrounding the

---

134 *Id.*, at 475.

135 *Id.*, at 476.

136 See Chapter 13, discussing Confession Standards for Sixth Amendment and Due Process.

137 475 U.S. 412 (1986).

interrogation" reveal both an uncoerced choice and the requisite level of comprehension may a court properly conclude that the *Miranda* rights have been waived.[138]

A valid waiver will not be assumed from the silence of the accused after the warnings are given, nor from the fact that a confession is eventually obtained. However, the Court in *North Carolina v. Butler*[139] held that neither an express statement of waiver nor a written waiver is required. The refusal to sign a waiver form also does not preclude a finding of a later waiver.

B. Voluntary Waiver

The first key component of a waiver is its "voluntary" nature. A totality of the circumstances test includes "the duration and conditions of [detention]," the "manifest attitude of the police" toward the defendant, the "physical and mental state" of the defendant, [and] the "diverse pressures which sap or sustain" the defendant's "powers of resistance and self-control."[140] A defendant trying to negate the voluntariness element will try to demonstrate that coercive police conduct caused the waiver to be the product of intimidation, coercion, or deception.

The Court in *Colorado v. Spring* was unsympathetic to claims that silence by the police constitutes a form of coercion. Although any indication that the suspect was threatened, tricked, or cajoled by police overreaching will render a confession involuntary, the failure to inform a suspect of the topics of interrogation is not trickery or deception.[141] Because the defendant had been affirmatively warned that anything he said could be used against him, he should have inferred that he was giving the police an unlimited waiver for interrogation about *all* his crimes. The *Spring* Court reserved the issue of whether sufficient "coercion" invalidates a waiver if police affirmatively misrepresent the scope of the interrogation. Absent police overreaching, a defendant has the right to choose between speech and silence.[142]

A more difficult case occurs when law enforcement read administrative warnings together with *Miranda* warnings. A border patrol agent found a suspect attempting to illegally cross the border

---

138 Moran v. Burbine, 475 U.S. 412, 421 (1986).

139 441 U.S. 369 (1979).

140 Colorado v. Spring, 479 U.S. 564, 574 (1987).

141 *Id.*, at 576.

142 Connecticut v. Barrett, 479 U.S. 523, 529 (1987). See People v. Smiley, 530 P.3d 639 (Colo. 2023), in which the officer deceptively told a murder suspect immediately after reading the *Miranda* warnings that he was "not in trouble and would be leaving the police station that day." That falsehood undermined the voluntariness of the suspect's *Miranda* waiver.

from Mexico into California. The agent brought the suspect in for questioning, read him the *Miranda* warnings, and then also warned him that this "post-arrest interview may be his only chance to seek asylum."[143] The Ninth Circuit Court rejected the defendant's argument that the additional administrative immigration warning contradicted or undermined his *Miranda* right to remain silent. The Court recognized that "there may be some tension between those rights," but held that it "reflects the difficult trade-off that immigration defendants must sometimes make."[144]

C. Knowing and Intelligent Waiver

The second component of a valid waiver is its "knowing and intelligent" quality, i.e., when the defendant is aware of his right to remain silent and a decision to forego that right. A knowing and intelligent waiver has nothing to do with whether waiver is a wise choice. In *Spring*, the Court rejected defendant's argument that more information about the subject of the interrogation was necessary for a knowing waiver. The *Miranda* warnings supplied all the information necessary for a "knowing and intelligent" waiver. Moreover, an "extension of *Miranda* would spawn numerous problems of interpretation because any number of factors could affect a suspect's decision to waive *Miranda* rights."[145]

Whether a person has intelligently waived his rights depends on his ability to understand and act upon the warnings. One competence factor is an assessment of a suspect's age. In *Fare v. Michael C.*,[146] the Court held that the "totality of circumstances" approach determines whether a juvenile has waived his rights. The totality of circumstances standard for a juvenile must include

> evaluation of the juvenile's age, experience, education, background, and intelligence, and into whether he has the capacity to understand the warnings given him, the nature of his Fifth Amendment rights, and the consequence of waiving those rights. . . There is no reason to assume that such courts—especially juvenile courts, with their special expertise in this area—will be unable to apply the totality-of-the-circumstances analysis so as to take into account those special concerns that are present when young persons, often with limited experience and education and with immature judgment, are involved.[147]

---

143 United States v. Gonzalez-Godinez, 89 F.4th 1205 (9th Cir. 2024).

144 *Id.*, at 1209,

145 *Colorado v. Spring*, 479 U.S. at 577 n.9.

146 442 U.S. 707 (1979).

147 Fare v. Michael C., 442 U.S. 707, 725 (1979).

Similarly, if a defendant appears to be mentally retarded, intoxicated, or unable to understand English, the police must exercise extra care to as they attempt to secure from the suspect a proper waiver of rights.

The Court has permitted a conditional waiver of rights, and the resulting confession is admissible if the police comply with the imposed condition. In *Connecticut v. Barrett,*[148] the defendant told the police that he had "no problem" *speaking* to them, but he would not make a written statement without the presence of his attorney. He then made incriminating oral admissions without the police asking him for a written statement. The defendant repeatedly said that he understood his rights and later testified about knowing that he did not have to talk without a lawyer present.

The Court ruled that his waiver was limited by its terms to not making a written statement, but did not prohibit all further oral discussions with the police. Even though the defendant's oral confession while refusing to give a written statement, seemed illogical, the Court stated that "we have never embraced the theory that a defendant's ignorance of the full consequences of his decisions vitiates their voluntariness."[149] The Court then approved his conditional waiver of the right to silence as being voluntarily, knowingly and intelligently made.

D. Express and Implied Waivers

Miranda permits waivers to be either express or implied. An express waiver ideally is an explicit written or oral waiver by a suspect, consisting of a statement like "I'm ready to talk," or "I do not need an attorney."

> [A] valid waiver will not be presumed simply from the silence of the accused after warnings are given or simply from the fact that a confession was in fact eventually obtained. A statement we made in *Carnley v. Cochran,* is applicable here:
>
> > "Presuming waiver from a silent record is impermissible. The record must show, or there must be an allegation and evidence which show, that an accused was offered counsel but intelligently and understandingly rejected the offer. Anything less is not waiver."

---

148 479 U.S. 523 (1987).

149 Connecticut v. Barrett, 479 U.S. 523, 530 (1987), quoting Oregon v. Elstad, 470 U.S. 298, 308 (1985).

> Moreover, where in-custody interrogation is involved, there is no room for the contention that the privilege is waived if the individual answers some questions or gives some information on his own prior to invoking his right to remain silent when interrogated.[150]

If waivers could be explicit only, perhaps through a written or recorded waiver, swearing contests between the suspect and the police about who said what and when could be eliminated or at least reduced. The government's "heavy burden" of proving a waiver would also be clarified if express waivers were the only type of waiver recognized by the courts.

North Carolina v. Butler indicated that a waiver may be inferred from the circumstances,[151] e.g., from the fact that the suspect eventually makes statements to the police.[152]

> An express written or oral statement of waiver of the right to remain silent or of the right to counsel is usually strong proof of the validity of that waiver, but is not inevitably either necessary or sufficient to establish waiver. The question is not one of form, but rather whether the defendant in fact knowingly and voluntarily waived the rights delineated in the *Miranda* case. As was unequivocally said in *Miranda*, mere silence is not enough. That does not mean that the defendant's silence, coupled with an understanding of his rights and a course of conduct indicating waiver, may never support a conclusion that a defendant has waived his rights. The courts must presume that a defendant did not waive his rights; the prosecution's burden is great; but in at least some cases waiver can be clearly inferred from the actions and words of the person interrogated.[153]

In *Berghuis v. Thompkins*,[154] the police read the defendant his *Miranda* rights but he then declined to sign a form indicating that he understood his rights. After three hours of questioning during which he said very little, he answered "yes" when asked if he prayed to God to forgive him for the shooting. "Where the prosecution shows that a *Miranda* warning was given and that it was understood by the accused, an accused's uncoerced statement establishes an implied

---

[150] *Miranda v. Arizona*, 384 U.S. at 475, 476, quoting Carnley v. Cochran, 369 U.S. 506, 516 (1962).

[151] North Carolina v. Butler, 441 U.S. 369, 373 (1979).

[152] Berghuis v. Thompkins, 560 U.S. 370 (2010).

[153] *North Carolina v. Butler*, 441 U.S. at 373.

[154] 560 U.S. 370 (2010).

waiver of the right to remain silent."[155] The Court concluded that there was an "implied" waiver in *Berghuis*, because (1) there was "no contention" that he "did not understand his rights"; (2) his "statement about three hours after receiving a *Miranda* warning does not overcome the fact that he engaged in a course of conduct indicating waiver"; and (3) the defense introduced "no evidence"[156] that the defendant's statement was coerced.

An implied waiver requires that the court look at the defendant's words and actions, i.e., whether the defendant in fact waived his *Miranda* rights. An understanding of rights and the waiver of those rights are separate. Although the latter cannot be inferred merely because the former is clear, the inference is easier to make. A waiver by implication is easier to show if the defendant is the one who initiated either contact or conversation with the police. Likewise, a court will imply a waiver when a defendant declines to confess, but immediately makes other statements indicating guilt. Although a confession does not have to be written, a written confession is a strong factor indicating the voluntariness of a disputed claim of waiver.[157]

While the right to have counsel present during custodial interrogation may be waived, a waiver is invalidated by police deception of the lawyer, e.g., giving counsel misleading information about when the suspect is going to be questioned.[158] After a valid waiver, a suspect's reaffirmation of an initial voluntary statement, which was inadmissible because it was made without the benefit of *Miranda* warnings, is admissible.[159]

E. Waiver After Defendant Invokes Right to Remain Silent

As discussed previously, prior to custodial interrogation, *Miranda* required that the police warn a defendant about the right to remain silent and the right to counsel. At some time during interrogation, if a defendant unambiguously and affirmatively invokes his right to silence, police interrogation must stop. The invocation of the right to remain silent is a critical first step. *Miranda*'s view on the invocation of the right to silence follows.

---

155 *Berghuis v. Thompkins*, 560 U.S. at 384.

156 *Id.*, at 385, 386.

157 See Connecticut v. Barrett, 479 U.S. 523, 530 (1987) (no distinction between oral and written statements on the issue of waiver).

158 Moran v. Burbine, 475 U.S. 412 (1986) (Court refused to require the police to inform a suspect about whether legal counsel had been retained for the suspect).

159 Oregon v. Elstad, 470 U.S. 298, 306 (1985).

> Once warnings have been given, the subsequent procedure is clear. If the individual indicates in any manner, at any time prior to or during questioning, that he wishes to remain silent, the interrogation must cease. At this point he has shown that he intends to exercise his Fifth Amendment privilege; any statement taken after the person invokes his privilege cannot be other than the product of compulsion, subtle or otherwise. Without the right to cut off questioning, the setting of in-custody interrogation operates on the individual to overcome free choice in producing a statement after the privilege has been once invoked.[160]

In *Berghuis v. Thompkins*,[161] the defendant refused to sign a form attesting that he understood his rights. During three hours of interrogation, he was silent most of the time but gave a limited number of verbal responses such as "yeah," "no," and "I don't know." The Court ruled that he did not invoke his right to remain silent, because he never said that "he wanted to remain silent or that he did not want to talk to the police." "Had he made either of these simple, unambiguous statements, he would have invoked his 'right to cut off questioning.' "[162] Never having invoked his right to silence, he waived his rights when he knowingly and voluntarily made a statement to police.

In *Michigan v. Mosley*,[163] the Court explained what *Miranda* intended by its declaration about what happens *after* a suspect invokes his right to silence. The Court rejected any requirement that the suspect's invocation creates either: (1) a *per se* proscription of indefinite duration upon any further police questioning, (2) a blanket prohibition against the taking or admission of voluntary statements, or (3) a prohibition against a resumption of police interrogation after a momentary cessation. *Mosley* held:

> The critical safeguard identified in the passage at issue is a person's "right to cut off questioning." Through the exercise of his option to terminate questioning he can control the time at which questioning occurs, the subjects discussed, and the duration of the interrogation. The requirement that law enforcement authorities must respect a person's exercise of that option counteracts the coercive pressures of the custodial setting. We therefore conclude that the admissibility of statements obtained after the person in

---

160 *Miranda v. Arizona*, 384 U.S. at 474. See § 12.7(F), for a discussion of what constitutes an unambiguous invocation of rights.

161 560 U.S. 370 (2010).

162 Berghuis v. Thompkins, 560 U.S. 370, 382 (2010).

163 423 U.S. 96 (1975).

> custody has decided to remain silent depends under Miranda on whether his "right to cut off questioning" was "scrupulously honored."[164]

In other words, the only sensible reading of *Miranda* was not that the suspect could never again be interrogated, but that the suspect's right to cut off questioning must be carefully respected. The Court seemed capable of finding two distinct interrogation sessions in order for the police to show that they had complied with the defendant's request.

Whether a defendant's invocation of the right to silence was scrupulously honored depends on: (1) whether the suspect was informed of his *Miranda* rights before the initial interrogation; (2) after the invocation, whether the officer "immediately ceased" the interrogation and did not try either to resume the questioning or in any way to persuade [the suspect] to reconsider his position; (3) the differences in the circumstances between the original and subsequent interrogation, e.g., whether the subsequent interrogation session was about the same or a different offense, the length of time between the two interrogations, whether the subsequent session was conducted in a different location, and whether it was conducted by a different officer; and (4) whether the suspect was re-informed of the *Miranda* rights prior to the second interrogation session.[165]

The confession in *Mosley* was admissible because, when the defendant exercised the right to remain silent, the officer ceased questioning, fresh *Miranda* warnings were given by a different detective, and the topic of questioning related to a different crime.[166] The Court has not explained the scope of its multi-factor holding since *Mosley*.

F. Waiver After Defendant Invokes Right to Counsel

The Court treats the invocation of counsel differently than the invocation of silence, because requesting counsel may present a more serious situation than *Mosley*. There are many reasons why a person might change his mind about not speaking, but by requesting counsel, the suspect indicates that he does not want to talk to the police, *and* that he is unable to talk to them on his own. Thus, it may be unlikely that he will change his mind for reasons other than police pressure.

---

164 Michigan v. Mosley, 423 U.S. 96, 103–04 (1975).

165 *Id.*, at 105–06.

166 *Id.*, at 106.

If the individual states that he wants an attorney, the interrogation must cease until an attorney is present during any subsequent questioning.[167] "If the interrogation continues without the presence of an attorney and a statement is taken, a heavy burden rests on the government to demonstrate that the defendant knowingly and intelligently waived both his privilege against self-incrimination and his right to retained or appointed counsel."[168] A waiver may not be presumed from the suspect's silence after the warnings or from the fact that a confession was eventually obtained.

> At that time, the individual must have an opportunity to confer with the attorney and to have him present during any subsequent questioning. If the individual cannot obtain an attorney and he indicates that he wants one before speaking to police, they must respect his decision to remain silent. . . . If authorities conclude that they will not provide counsel during a reasonable period of time in which investigation in the field is carried out, they may refrain from doing so without violating the person's Fifth Amendment privilege so long as they do not question him during that time.[169]

An invocation of the presence of counsel must be unambiguous and unequivocal. A defendant "must articulate his desire to have counsel present sufficiently clearly that a reasonable police officer in the circumstances would understand the statement to be a request for an attorney." The police do not have to ask clarifying questions when the request is equivocal,[170] and an officer can ignore an invocation that is "ambiguous or equivocal in that a reasonable officer in light of the circumstances would have understood only that the suspect might be invoking the right to counsel."[171]

In *Davis v. United States*,[172] the suspect had waived his rights and answered police questions for ninety minutes before saying, "Maybe I should have a lawyer." When asked to clarify his statement, he said that he "was not asking for a lawyer," and added, "No, I don't want a lawyer." The Court held that the initial "maybe" request for

---

[167] Minnick v. Mississippi, 498 U.S. 146, 152 (1990); Miranda v. Arizona, 384 U.S. 436, 474 (1966). See Arizona v. Mauro, 481 U.S. 520 (1987) (not improper for the defendant's wife to speak with him and record their conversation, even after the defendant declined to speak with police and requested an attorney).

[168] *Miranda v. Arizona*, 384 U.S. at 475.

[169] *Id.*, at 474. Invocation of the right to counsel during a judicial proceeding does not constitute a request for counsel under *Miranda*. McNeil v. Wisconsin, 501 U.S. 171 (1991).

[170] Davis v. United States, 512 U.S. 452, 459 (1994).

[171] *Id.*

[172] 512 U.S. 452 (1994).

counsel did not "meet the requisite level of clarity," and the police did not have to stop questioning. Requiring an "unambiguous" invocation ensured that police officers would not "be forced to make difficult judgment calls" about ambiguous invocations, and not be faced with "the threat of suppression if they guess wrong."[173] Other examples of ambiguous requests include: "Should I have somebody here?", and "Do I need to get an attorney for this because I'm really concerned?", or "I don't think I need one but you know. . . ."

Davis refused to "require law enforcement officers to cease questioning immediately upon the making of an ambiguous or equivocal reference to an attorney." While an unclear invocation "might disadvantage some suspects who, because of fear, intimidation, lack of linguistic skills, or a variety of other reasons, will not clearly articulate their right to counsel although they actually want to have a lawyer present," that perspective is outweighed by the fact that the "clarity and ease of application" of *Edwards* "would be lost" if "we were to require questioning to cease if a suspect makes a statement that might be a request for an attorney."[174]

After a definitive request for counsel, is there any time limit on the resumption of police interrogation? In *Maryland v. Shatzer*,[175] the Court specified that a suspect's request for a lawyer is good for only fourteen days after the defendant's release from custodial interrogation (that follows the request) back to the general prison population. After fourteen days of being back in the general prison population, i.e., released from the coercive questioning process, the police may interrogate the suspect.

In *Edwards v. Arizona*,[176] the defendant stated, "I want an attorney before making a deal." The police stopped questioning him, but returned the next morning telling him that he "had to" talk to them. The Court held that the defendant's waiver was invalid because the police initiated the second interrogation. After a proper invocation of counsel, the only proper scenario for the police to follow in order to secure a valid waiver is for the *suspect* (not the police) to initiate "further communication, exchanges, or conversations with the police"[177] about the same or a different criminal investigation.[178] Two policies support *Edwards*: a need for uniformity and

---

173 *Davis v. United States*, 512 U.S. at 461.

174 *Id.*, at 460–61. Still, the Court commended the officers for "good police practice" by seeking to clarify the defendant's initial ambiguous statement.

175 559 U.S. 98 (2010).

176 451 U.S. 477 (1981).

177 Edwards v. Arizona, 451 U.S. 477, 485 (1981).

178 Arizona v. Roberson, 486 U.S. 675, 684 (1988).

predictability in applying *Miranda*, and the need to deter the police coercion of badgering suspects to give up their requests and instead waive their rights.[179]

Following an invocation of the right to counsel, the prohibition against further questioning by the police includes *any* form of "interrogation" which as discussed[180] is questioning or its functional equivalent. Merely giving another set of *Miranda* warnings and obtaining a waiver is insufficient. An accused's post-request responses to further interrogation may not be used to cast retrospective doubt on the clarity of the initial request itself.[181]

What happens if the defendant has invoked his right to counsel but later initiates a further discussion with the police? The Government is allowed to resume questioning, if the circumstances show that the accused by initiating conversation with the police voluntarily and knowingly waived the right to counsel.[182] In *Oregon v. Bradshaw*,[183] a plurality of the Court examined *Edwards* as to what defendant conduct constitutes "initiation" of further communication with the police. After making several statements, the defendant requested counsel and the officer stopped the questioning. However, while being taken to jail the defendant asked, "Well, what is going to happen to me now?" After fresh *Miranda* rights and a new waiver, the defendant confessed. The Court found the confession admissible.

> There can be no doubt in this case that . . . [Bradshaw] "initiated" further conversation in the ordinary dictionary sense of that word. . . . There are some inquiries, such as a request for a drink of water or a request to use a telephone that are so routine that they cannot be fairly said to represent a desire on the part of an accused to open up a more generalized discussion relating directly or indirectly to the investigation. Such inquiries or statements, by either an accused or a police officer, relating to routine incidents of the custodial relationship, will not generally "initiate" a conversation in the sense in which that word was used in *Edwards*. Although ambiguous, the . . . question in this case as to what was going to happen to him evinced a willingness and a desire for a generalized discussion about the

---

179 *Id.*, at 686.

180 See § 12.6, discussing What Is Interrogation?

181 Smith v. Illinois, 469 U.S. 91 (1984).

182 Oregon v. Bradshaw, 462 U.S. 1039 (1983).

183 462 U.S. 1039 (1983).

> investigation; it was not merely a necessary inquiry arising out of the incidents of the custodial relationship.[184]

The issue of waiver, however, is conceptually a separate issue from whether the defendant "initiated" further conversations with the police.[185] Moreover, the totality of the circumstances must include the necessary fact that the accused, not the police, reopened the dialogue with law enforcement authorities.[186] When an accused has invoked his right to have counsel present during custodial interrogation, a valid waiver of that right cannot be established by showing only that he responded to further police-initiated custodial interrogation even if the police again advise him of his rights.[187] Once a valid waiver is made, questioning may continue until circumstances change so seriously that the defendant's responses are no longer voluntary or when he revokes the waiver.[188]

The preceding discussion has assumed that the invocation of rights by the suspect was to request the presence of counsel. What happens if the suspect invokes his right to consult with someone other than *an* attorney or *his* attorney? In *Fare v. Michael C.*, the suspect who was a juvenile asked to see his probation officer. The Court responded.

> The *per se* aspect of *Miranda* was. . . based on the unique role the lawyer plays in the adversary system of criminal justice in this country. Whether it is a minor or an adult who stands accused, the lawyer is the one person to whom society as a whole looks as the protector of the legal rights of that person in his dealings with the police and the courts. For this reason, the Court fashioned in *Miranda* the rigid rule that an accused's request for an attorney is *per se* an invocation of his Fifth Amendment rights, requiring that all interrogation cease.[189]

The minor's request to see his probation officer was not an invocation of *Miranda* rights, but instead was one factor to consider in the totality of circumstances evaluation of whether the defendant voluntarily waived his constitutional rights.

---

184 *Oregon v. Bradshaw*, 462 U.S. at 1045–46.

185 Smith v. Illinois, 469 U.S. 91, 98 (1984).

186 Edwards v. Arizona, 451 U.S. 477, 486 n.9 (1981).

187 *Id.*

188 Wyrick v. Fields, 459 U.S. 42, 47 (1982).

189 Fare v. Michael C., 442 U.S. 707, 719 (1979).

Chapter 13

CONFESSION STANDARDS FOR SIXTH AMENDMENT AND DUE PROCESS

Table of Sections

§ 13.1 Introduction

The Fifth Amendment is not the only constitutional provision that applies to the admissibility of confessions. The Court uses two other constitutional grounds to evaluate confessions. The Sixth Amendment right to counsel governs the admissibility of confessions made at or after the commencement of adversary judicial proceedings, "whether by way of formal charge, preliminary hearing, indictment, information, or arraignment."[1] Due Process is the other basis for challenging the voluntariness of confessions. This Chapter will discuss both the Sixth Amendment and Due Process grounds for admitting confessions against criminal defendants.

§ 13.2 Sixth Amendment Confession Challenges

A. To Which Confessions Does the Sixth Amendment Apply?

Rothgery v. Gillespie County, Tex. held that the Sixth Amendment right to counsel attaches at or after the defendant is formally charged, has a preliminary hearing, is prosecuted by indictment or information, or is arraigned, whichever occurs first. While Supreme Court case law has included cases where a defendant has moved to suppress a confession *after* indictment, though *before* arraignment,[2] most Sixth Amendment cases have arisen in the typical context of a defendant who has had an initial appearance soon after his arrest.

After arrest, the first court appearance made by a defendant in most jurisdictions is called an initial appearance or preliminary arraignment. At that proceeding, rules of criminal procedure or statutory provisions require that a judge inform the accused about several matters, such as the charges against him, as well as the right to remain silent and to a preliminary hearing.[3] The initial appearance or arraignment also marks the initiation of adversary judicial proceedings that trigger attachment of the Sixth Amendment right to counsel.

Just as the Sixth Amendment right to counsel applies at or after the initiation of adversary criminal proceedings against a defendant, so too does the ability of a defendant to challenge a confession made in that same time frame without the presence of constitutionally required counsel. At the initial appearance, the "Government's commitment to prosecute" is "sufficiently concrete" because the accusation "prompts arraignment and restrictions on the accused's liberty to facilitate the prosecution."[4] Once adversary proceedings are instituted, law enforcement officials or their agents[5] may not

---

1 Rothgery v. Gillespie County, Tex., 554 U.S. 191, 198 (2008), quoting Kirby v. Illinois, 406 U.S. 682, 689 (1972).

2 See, e.g., Fellers v. United States, 540 U.S. 519 (2004); Massiah v. United States, 377 U.S. 201 (1964).

3 See Fed.R.Crim.P. 5(d).

4 *Rothgery v. Gillespie County, Tex.*, 554 U.S. at 207.

5 See Estelle v. Smith, 451 U.S. 454 (1981) (Stewart, J., concurring) (psychiatric interview).

interrogate the accused in the absence of counsel,[6] unless the accused has validly waived that right.[7]

While Fifth Amendment *Miranda* rights are concerned with the inherently coercive pressure of custodial interrogation on suspects, the purpose of a suspect's Sixth Amendment rights is to prevent Government officials from engaging in activity that intrudes on the attorney-client relationship once formal litigation has begun. It is a fundamental ethical principle that once adversary proceedings have begun, one party (e.g., a prosecutor or his agents) cannot contact the adversary party (e.g., a criminal defendant) in the absence of the adversary counsel's consent.[8] The case law, though, indicates that an ethical violation does not always translate to a Sixth Amendment violation.

When a court refers to the Sixth Amendment right to counsel as "offense specific," it prohibits interrogation only for the offenses with which a suspect is currently charged. However, interrogation is permitted for uncharged offenses that merely are "closely related factually," unless they are considered to be the "same offense" as the charged offenses under the Fifth Amendment Double Jeopardy Clause.[9]

In *Massiah v. United States*,[10] the Court examined the case of an indicted defendant on pretrial release, who was pulled into an incriminating conversation by an acquaintance who as a Government informer was equipped with a portable transmitter. The Court viewed the situation as a form of interrogation, holding that no indicted defendant can be interrogated under any circumstances without counsel's presence—even if the accused is not in custody at the time of the interrogation. The Court held that Massiah

> was denied the basic protections of that guarantee when there was used against him at his trial evidence of his own incriminating words, which federal agents had deliberately elicited from him after he had been indicted and in the absence of his counsel. It is true that in the *Spano* case [a voluntariness case] the defendant was interrogated in a police station, while here the damaging testimony was elicited from the defendant without his knowledge while he was free on bail. But, as Judge Hays pointed out in his

6 Brewer v. Williams, 430 U.S. 387 (1977); Massiah v. United States, 377 U.S. 201 (1964).

7 See Brewer v. Williams, 430 U.S. 387 (1977); Powell v. Texas, 492 U.S. 680 (1989).

8 See American Bar Association Model Rules of Professional Conduct, Rule 4.2.

9 Texas v. Cobb, 532 U.S. 162 (2001).

10 377 U.S. 201 (1964).

dissent in the Court of Appeals, "if such a rule is to have any efficacy it must apply to indirect and surreptitious interrogations as well as those conducted in the jailhouse. In this case, Massiah was more seriously imposed upon. . . because he did not even know that he was under interrogation by a government agent."[11]

The constitutional basis for *Massiah* was the Sixth Amendment right to counsel, rather than the Fifth Amendment privilege against self-incrimination. After *Miranda*, it was unclear whether the filing of an indictment or other formal charge, then the *Massiah* test, retained independent constitutional significance. *Massiah* enlarged the function of counsel to assist the defendant at an evidence-gathering stage of the proceeding.

In 1968, as with *Miranda*, the Congress attempted to "repeal" *Massiah* by stating that federal court confessions are "admissible in evidence if it is voluntarily given," and by listing various factors to be considered on the voluntariness issue.[12] Federal courts have disregarded the legislation, and have continued to recognize the right to counsel in confession cases.

B. Rationale for the Sixth Amendment Principle

Massiah described three grounds for requiring counsel for any accused whose criminal court proceedings have begun. Lack of access to counsel during questioning "might deny a defendant effective representation by counsel at the only stage when legal aid and advice would help him."[13] Counsel's investigation and preparation are "vitally important," and defendants are therefore "as much entitled to [the] aid of counsel during that period as at the trial itself." If the Sixth Amendment right to consult counsel is to be meaningful, "it must apply to indirect and surreptitious interrogations as well as those conducted in the jailhouse."[14]

C. Brewer v. Williams

After *Miranda* was decided on Fifth Amendment grounds two years after *Massiah*, there was uncertainty about the continued vitality of the Sixth Amendment as an independent basis for suppressing illegally obtained confessions. Opponents of *Miranda* saw *Brewer v. Williams* as an opportunity for the Court to reverse its Fifth Amendment mandate of warnings to suspects in custody, with a possible return to Due Process as the exclusive constitutional

---

11 Massiah v. United States, 377 U.S. 201, 206 (1964).

12 18 U.S.C. § 3501(a).

13 *Massiah v. United States*, 377 U.S. at 204.

14 *Id.*, at 206.

source of a motion to suppress. However, instead of repealing *Miranda*, *Williams* reaffirmed that, after *Miranda*, a defendant may challenge the admissibility of a confession on the basis of the Fifth Amendment, the Sixth Amendment, *and* Due Process.

In *Williams*, on the advice of his Des Moines, Iowa, lawyer, the defendant surrendered to police and was arraigned on an abduction charge in Davenport, Iowa, while two officers traveled by car from Des Moines to retrieve the defendant and escort him back for "booking" in Des Moines on suspicion of murdering the victim of the abduction. His lawyer obtained the agreement of police officials that they would not question him in transit, and he would be allowed to consult with the lawyer in Des Moines before questioning. Defendant received *Miranda* warnings from the Davenport police, the Davenport judge, and a Des Moines detective. Both of his lawyers warned him against making any statements.

Soon after the police car left Davenport, the detective delivered the so-called "Christian burial speech." He told the defendant that they probably would be driving past the area where the victim's body was hidden, and that the defendant might be unable to find it because "[t]hey are predicting several inches of snow for tonight." The detective reminded the defendant that, "you yourself are the only person that knows where this little girl's body is. . . . [T]he parents of this little girl should be entitled to a Christian burial for the little girl who was snatched away from them on Christmas Eve and murdered." Finally, the detective said, "I do not want you to answer me. I don't want to discuss it any further. Just think about it as we're riding down the road."[15] The defendant soon made incriminating statements and ultimately led the police to the body.

The Court reversed the murder conviction, holding that a violation of the Sixth Amendment requires three elements: the attachment of the right to counsel, the failure of police to obtain a waiver of Sixth Amendment rights, and the prohibited act of "deliberate elicitation" (equivalent to improper "interrogation") by police that produced incriminating statements. It compared the *Massiah* facts to the *Williams* circumstances to show that they were constitutionally indistinguishable.

> [T]he incriminating statements were elicited surreptitiously in [*Massiah*], and otherwise here, is constitutionally irrelevant. Rather, the clear rule of *Massiah* is that once adversary proceedings had commenced against an individual, he has a right to legal representation when the government interrogates him. It

15 *Brewer v. Williams*, 430 U.S. at 392–93.

thus requires no wooden or technical application of the *Massiah* doctrine to conclude that Williams was entitled to the assistance of counsel guaranteed to him by the Sixth and Fourteenth Amendments.[16]

The Sixth Amendment right to counsel had attached, because the Davenport arraignment qualified as the commencement of "adversarial judicial proceedings." The detective engaged in "deliberate elicitation" by making the "Christian burial speech," which was viewed as "tantamount to interrogation." *Williams* implicitly recognized that express questioning was unnecessary for a finding of "deliberate elicitation."[17] There was no affirmative evidence of waiver before the "Christian burial speech" was delivered. Instead, the defendant stated several times that he would talk to police only after seeing his lawyer in Des Moines. Evidence also negated a waiver of Williams' rights, namely the defendant's "consistent reliance on the advice of counsel in dealing with the authorities," and his "express and implicit assertions of his right to counsel."[18]

The detective interposed himself between the attorneys and the defendant, rendered the attorneys' advice meaningless, and impaired their effectiveness at trial. Despite the unsympathetic facts of the crime, what was the defendant trying to do by obtaining counsel, and what were counsel trying to do in their instructions to the police? The police did exactly what the defendant and counsel had tried to prevent. Was the Court suggesting that a suspect has a right to be protected against his own weakness? If he had such a claim, did this defendant knowingly and voluntarily give up the protections that he had sought by obtaining counsel? Because the defendant's counsel warned him several times not to talk to the police, did this defendant not realize that he had a right to an attorney and to say nothing? Would additional warnings have made a factual difference?

With a view toward Williams' invocation of his right to counsel and a subsequent waiver,[19] Williams was told by counsel in Davenport that the police would not question him during the trip to Des Moines. An argument is plausible that he invoked his right to counsel under *Edwards v. Arizona* *before* the drive began, and that it was still in effect during the ride. If so, the police should not have spoken to him at all. The prosecutor might respond by saying that the police had no duty to cut-off questioning unless Williams invoked his right to counsel's presence *during* the drive. Defense counsel

---

16 *Id.*, at 401.

17 *Id.*, at 400.

18 *Id.*, at 405.

19 See § 13.4(B), discussing Waiver After Invocation of Right to Counsel.

would reply by saying that his earlier invocation was clear and unambiguous and that he never initiated a conversation or expressed a willingness to speak with the police. The prosecutor would say that Detective Leaming's comment following the Christian burial speech that Williams should not speak but just "think about" the situation, and his subsequent incriminating statements waived his Sixth Amendment rights.

§ 13.3 Sixth Amendment Interrogation

A. Deliberate Elicitation

Rhode Island v. Innis observed that the concepts of "deliberate elicitation" under the Sixth Amendment and "interrogation" under the Fifth Amendment are "not necessarily interchangeable, because the policies underlying the two constitutional protections are quite distinct."[20] However, the Court did not identify any differences between *Miranda* "interrogation" and "deliberate elicitation" when police question defendants. If there is no deliberate elicitation by the police or police agents, there is no Sixth Amendment violation.

Unconstitutional interrogation occurs for Sixth Amendment purposes when police deliberately elicit incriminating statements from the accused in the absence of counsel.[21] In *Fellers v. United States*,[22] after the grand jury indicted the defendant for conspiracy to traffic in drugs, law enforcement personnel went to his home to arrest him. After a brief conversation, they took him to the local jail where they read him his *Miranda* warnings; he then signed a waiver form and repeated the incriminating statements he had made at home. The Court held that the police deliberately elicited defendant's statements at his home illegally, because at that time he was already under indictment, no defense counsel was present, and he had not waived his constitutional rights there.

B. Using Known Persons

Interrogation, however, is not limited to direct questioning by known law enforcement officials. When the prosecution obtains incriminating statements by knowingly circumventing the accused's right to have counsel present in a confrontation between the accused and the prosecution's agent, a Sixth Amendment violation occurs. For example, in *Maine v. Moulton*,[23] the police exploited an opportunity for a codefendant to record a conversation with a suspect. The

---

[20] Rhode Island v. Innis, 446 U.S. 291, 300 n.4 (1980).

[21] Fellers v. United States, 540 U.S. 519, 523 (2004).

[22] 540 U.S. 519 (2004).

[23] Maine v. Moulton, 474 U.S. 159 (1985).

defendant had pleaded not guilty to theft charges after his indictment. His codefendant told the police that he had received anonymous threatening telephone calls about the pending charge.

Before meeting with the police, the codefendant met with the defendant, who discussed killing a State's witness. The codefendant then met with police and consented to wear a wire to record any other meetings with the defendant. Although the codefendant was told not to question the defendant, his remarks caused the defendant to make incriminating statements. Some of those recorded incriminating statements were admitted in evidence. The Court held that the police violated the defendant's Sixth Amendment rights because he was denied his right to counsel after he had been indicted. Once the Sixth Amendment right attaches, "the prosecutor and police have an affirmative obligation not to act in a manner that circumvents and thereby dilutes the protection afforded by the right to counsel."[24] The Court also rejected the State's argument that the defendant's rights were not violated because it was the defendant who initiated the meeting where he made the incriminating statements.

> When the police requested that Colson wear a body wire transmitter to the meeting with respondent, the police knew that respondent would make statements that he had a constitutional right not to make to their agent prior to consulting with counsel. By concealing the fact that Colson was an agent of the State, the police denied respondent the opportunity to consult with counsel and thus denied him the assistance of counsel guaranteed by the Sixth Amendment.[25]

The Court also dismissed the State's argument that the police had other, legitimate reasons for listening to the defendant's conversations, i.e., to check the defendant's plan to kill the State's witness and to ensure the codefendant's safety. This argument invites abuse such as fabricated investigations. The Court confirmed the admissibility of statements through deliberate elicitation by undercover agents for any crimes other than the crime to which the Sixth Amendment has attached.[26]

C. Using Undercover Agents

This last point from *Moulton* raises an important difference between Fifth and Sixth Amendment treatment of confessions that relates to the questioning of the suspect by undercover police agents.

---

24 *Id.*, at 171.

25 *Id.*, at 177.

26 *Id.*, at 180.

The *Illinois v. Perkins* exception described in the previous Chapter for allowing interrogation by undercover agents of a person in custody does not apply to the "deliberate elicitation" of statements by undercover agents from suspects whose criminal cases have begun. For the Sixth Amendment, whether the suspect is in jail when undercover questioning occurs does not matter. But whether an undercover agent deliberately elicits information actively or is merely a passive listener is an important distinction in the Sixth Amendment admissibility of statements.[27] As the Court stated in *Kuhlman v. Wilson*, because

> "the primary concern of the *Massiah* line of cases is secret interrogation by investigatory techniques that are the equivalent of direct police interrogation," "a defendant does not make out a violation of that right simply by showing that an informant, either through prior arrangement or voluntarily, reported his incriminating statements to the police."[28]

Using its phrase "deliberate elicitation," the Court has distinguished between active questioning by an unknown agent, i.e., when the defendant's resulting statement is inadmissible, and passive conduct by the agent who merely listens and asks no questions to provoke conversation by the suspect.

In *United States v. Henry*,[29] following the defendant's indictment for bank robbery, he was jailed awaiting trial. The Government contacted an informant who was an inmate in the same jail. The Government instructed the informant to be alert for any statements but not to initiate any conversations with the defendant about the pending charges. *Henry*, then, is the "situation where the 'listening post' is an inanimate electronic device," because "such a device has no capability of leading the conversation into any particular subject or prompting any particular replies."[30] The *Henry* informant reported that the defendant had in fact made incriminating statements about the robbery. The Government paid the informant for his information, and he testified at the defendant's trial.

The Court reversed the bank robbery conviction because of a Sixth Amendment violation, finding that the Government had intentionally created a situation likely to induce the defendant to make incriminating statements without counsel.[31] The Court

---

[27] See, e.g., Kuhlmann v. Wilson, 477 U.S. 436 (1986); United States v. Henry, 447 U.S. 264 (1980).

[28] *Kuhlman v. Wilson*, 477 U.S. at 459.

[29] 447 U.S. 264 (1980).

[30] United States v. Henry, 447 U.S. 264, 271 n.9 (1980).

[31] *Id.*, at 274.

emphasized four facts: the informant was paid, was ostensibly a fellow inmate, was in custody, and was under indictment at the time of the conversations. The Court found that incriminating statements were "deliberately elicited" from the defendant. In addition, because the defendant did not know that he was talking to an informant, he could not have waived his right to counsel.[32] "[T]he concept of a knowing and voluntary waiver of Sixth Amendment rights does not apply in the context of communications with an undisclosed undercover informant acting for the government." Because the defendant was unaware the other person "was a government agent expressly commissioned to secure evidence, [he] cannot be held to have waived his right to the assistance of counsel"[33] by communicating with him.

In *Kuhlmann v. Wilson*,[34] after arraignment on robbery and murder, defendant was in a cell with a prisoner who had agreed to be an informant and reported to the police about the defendant's incriminating statements. Before trial, at a hearing on a motion to suppress the statements, the trial court ruled both that the informant followed police instructions only to listen to the defendant and not to question him, and that the defendant's statements were "spontaneous" and "unsolicited."

The Court stated that its primary concern in *Henry* was secret interrogation techniques that are equivalent to direct police interrogation. The defendant must demonstrate that the police and the informant took action beyond "merely listening" that was devised to deliberately elicit incriminating statements.[35] Although the police in *Kuhlmann* intentionally created an opportunity to obtain a statement from the defendant by assigning a paid jail informant to the same cell as the suspect, the defendant failed to prove that "the police and their informant took some action, beyond merely listening, that was designed deliberately to elicit incriminating remarks" in order to prove a Sixth Amendment violation.[36] Statements are inadmissible if the agent is active and the statements relate to the charges that have already been filed, but they are admissible if no charges have been filed or the agent is passive.

---

32 *Id.*, at 273.

33 *Id.*

34 477 U.S. 436 (1986).

35 *Kuhlmann v. Wilson*, 477 U.S. at 459.

36 *Id.*

§ 13.4 Sixth Amendment Waiver of Counsel

A. Waiver Standard

The preceding sections demonstrate that the police must not violate a defendant's right to counsel. A defendant, though, may still waive the right to counsel for interrogation purposes. *Brewer v. Williams*[37] held that a defendant could waive his rights under the Sixth and Fourteenth Amendments without notice to his counsel.[38]

Williams stressed that "waiver requires not merely comprehension but relinquishment." Thus, although it seemed that Williams "had been informed of and appeared to understand his right to counsel," he relied "upon the advice of counsel in dealing with the authorities," his statements "that he desired the presence of an attorney before any interrogation took place," his awareness of the police-counsel agreement "that no interrogation was to occur during the journey," and the police "made no effort at all to ascertain whether Williams wished to relinquish that right."[39]

The analysis for a Sixth Amendment waiver of counsel is identical to the Fifth Amendment analysis.[40] *Patterson v. Illinois*[41] decided that *Miranda*'s Fifth Amendment waiver requirements would suffice for a Sixth Amendment waiver. The "State's decision to take an additional step and commence formal adversarial proceedings against the accused does not substantially increase the value of counsel to the accused at questioning, or expand the limited purpose that an attorney serves when the accused is questioned by authorities." That is, "because the role of counsel at questioning is relatively simple and limited," as compared to counsel's responsibilities at trial, there is "no problem in having a waiver procedure at that stage which is likewise simple and limited."[42]

The Court interpreted the fundamental inquiry in both "formulations" of waiver to be whether

> the accused, who waived his Sixth Amendment rights during postindictment questioning, [was] made sufficiently aware of his right to have counsel present during the questioning, and of the possible consequences of a decision to forgo the aid of counsel?[43]

---

37 430 U.S. 387 (1977).

38 *Brewer v. Williams*, 430 U.S. at 405–06.

39 *Id.*, at 404–05.

40 *Id.*, at 404.

41 Patterson v. Illinois, 487 U.S. 285 (1988).

42 *Id.*, at 300.

43 *Id.*, at 292–93.

In *Patterson*, after the defendant learned from police that he was indicted for murder, he was given a set of *Miranda* warnings and he then offered to discuss the crime with police. He confessed after the police again read him his rights from a waiver form that he signed. The Government used his statements against him during trial and he was convicted. The Court held that use of his statements did not violate the Sixth Amendment right to counsel. While his indictment entitled him to counsel under the Sixth Amendment, he did not invoke that right. Citing *Edwards v. Arizona*,[44] the Court reiterated that the essence of the Sixth Amendment is "preservation of the integrity of an accused choice to communicate with police only through counsel."[45]

The *Miranda* "right-to-counsel" warnings satisfied the first component of the *Patterson* waiver formulation to make the defendant "sufficiently aware of his right to have counsel present during the questioning."[46] Having counsel would have enabled the defendant to hear (and possibly follow) counsel's likely advice not to make any incriminating statements. The warnings also informed him about the effect of talking to the police, i.e., any statement he made could be used against him at his trial.[47] If Patterson had asked for counsel, police questioning would have ceased until he initiated conversations with police. Despite the warnings, he decided "knowingly and intelligently" to speak to the police without counsel. His subsequent waiver was valid, and his incriminating statements were admissible at trial. Because the effect of the Fifth Amendment *Miranda* warnings was sufficient to make him aware of his *Williams* Sixth Amendment rights, the defendant's waiver was knowing and intelligent, and his statements were admissible at trial.

B. Waiver After Invocation of Right to Counsel

When a defendant is questioned by police after the initiation of "adversary judicial proceedings," he may invoke his Sixth Amendment right to counsel.[48] Like the Fifth Amendment invocation,[49] the Sixth Amendment invocation must be unequivocal and the defendant must reinitiate communications with his police interrogators in order to waive his rights. In *Montejo v. Louisiana*,[50] the defendant was charged with murder and the court appointed counsel for him. That same day, the police read him his *Miranda*

---

44 451 U.S. 477 (1981).

45 Patterson v. Illinois, 487 U.S. 285, 291 (1988).

46 *Id.*, at 292.

47 *Id.*, at 294.

48 Montejo v. Louisiana, 556 U.S. 778 (2009).

49 See § 12.7(F), discussing Waiver After Defendant Invokes Right to Counsel.

50 556 U.S. 728 (2009).

rights and he agreed to accompany them to look for the murder weapon. On the way, he wrote an apology to the victim's widow. After the trip, he met with appointed counsel for the first time. At trial, the prosecution admitted the written apology over the defendant's objection.

Following his conviction, he was sentenced to death and appealed. The State appellate court affirmed the conviction, relying on *Michigan v. Jackson*,[51] which prohibited police interrogation only after an explicit invocation of the right to counsel at an arraignment or similar proceeding. The *Montejo* Court disagreed, and overruled *Jackson*, because *Jackson* provided little added protection beyond what *Edwards* held. The Court disagreed with the defendant's argument to eliminate the invocation requirement. *Jackson*'s purpose was to prevent the police from badgering defendants into changing their minds about counsel after they ask for counsel. A defendant who never asks for counsel has not invoked his right.

The Court applied its cost-benefit analysis and found that the substantial costs of *Jackson* "dwarfed" it "marginal" benefits. Even without *Jackson,* few waivers would be admitted at trial because the Court's other procedures to exclude badgering-induced waivers are sufficient: (1) *Miranda* requires that any suspect must be advised about the right to have a lawyer present;[52] (2) after invocation of the right to counsel, *Edwards* requires interrogation to cease;[53] and (3) *Minnick v. Mississippi* prohibits any subsequent interrogation until counsel is present.[54] Because of those precedents, no procedure to replace *Jackson* was necessary.

A defendant may waive his right to counsel, even if he already has counsel. (A request for or an acceptance of appointed counsel is insufficient to constitute an invocation for the presence of counsel.) The legal consequences of an invocation of counsel depend on whether the suspect is in custody when the invocation occurs. Regardless of whether a suspect has requested or obtained a lawyer, the police may question and seek a waiver from any suspect who is *not* in custody. If the suspect *is* in custody and the police have informed him of his *Miranda* rights, a suspect who asserts his right to counsel is protected by the *Edwards v. Arizona* rules discussed in Chapter 12. If the suspect re-initiates contact with the police following the invocation, the police may seek a waiver and question him.

---

51 475 U.S. 625 (1986).

52 Miranda v. Arizona, 384 U.S. 436, 474 (1966).

53 *Edwards v. Arizona*, 451 U.S. at 484.

54 Minnick v. Mississippi, 498 U.S. 146, 153 (1990).

The invocation of the Sixth Amendment right to counsel applies *only* to the offenses that have been charged. By comparison, the Fifth Amendment rule in *Arizona v. Roberson*[55] prohibits questioning arrestees for *any* crime, once the *Miranda* right to counsel is invoked. The Court refused to extend *Roberson* to the Sixth Amendment context in *McNeil v. Wisconsin*.[56] While awaiting trial for armed robbery, the defendant invoked his right to counsel at a bail hearing. Police nevertheless questioned him later about a murder and related crimes in another part of the State. After police advised him of his *Miranda* rights and he signed a waiver form, he made incriminating statements and was formally charged with the additional crimes.

On appeal from his conviction of the added crimes, he argued that his invocation of Sixth Amendment counsel was equivalent to an invocation under the Fifth Amendment. The Court disagreed, holding that an invocation of his Sixth Amendment right to counsel during a judicial proceeding is not the same as an invocation of the right to counsel under *Miranda*. The Sixth Amendment right to counsel is "offense-specific," i.e., invocation of the *Williams* right to counsel cannot bar questioning for crimes to which the Sixth Amendment has not yet attached—where adversary proceedings have not begun for that charge. The purpose of the Fifth Amendment right is to protect a suspect's "desire to deal with police only through counsel,"[57] while the Sixth Amendment right protects a suspect without counsel in dealing with the Government after the start of criminal proceedings.[58]

Building on *McNeil*, the Court's decision in *Texas v. Cobb*[59] defined the method of determining the difference between charged and uncharged offenses in applying the Sixth Amendment. The defendant was already under arrest for an unrelated offense when he confessed to a burglary, though denying any knowledge about the disappearance of two people who lived in the burgled home. After he was indicted for the burglary and waived his *Miranda* rights, he admitted to police that he had killed the two people. On appeal from his capital murder convictions, he claimed that the police had violated his Sixth Amendment rights that had attached in the burglary prosecution.

The Court disagreed, holding that, because the Sixth Amendment right to counsel is "offense specific," it does not always

---

55 Arizona v. Roberson, 486 U.S. 675 (1988).

56 501 U.S. 171 (1991).

57 McNeil v. Wisconsin, 501 U.S. 171, 178 (1991), quoting Edwards v. Arizona, 451 U.S. 477, 484 (1981).

58 See United States v. Gouveia, 467 U.S. 180, 189 (1984).

59 Texas v. Cobb, 532 U.S. 162 (2001).

include offenses that are "factually related" to crimes that have already charged. Although the Sixth Amendment attaches only to charged offenses, the definition of an "offense" is not necessarily limited to the content of an indictment.[60] The Court formally adopted the *Blockburger* definition of "offense" from the Fifth Amendment Double Jeopardy context, i.e., "where the same act or transaction constitutes a violation of two distinct statutory provisions, the test to be applied to determine whether there are two offenses or only one, is whether each provision requires proof of a fact which the other does not."[61]

Because there is no difference between an "offense" in the right to counsel and the Double Jeopardy contexts, the Sixth Amendment right to counsel includes offenses that, even if not formally charged, would be the "same offense" under *Blockburger*. When the defendant confessed to the murders, he was under indictment only for burglary. Because burglary and murder are not the same offense under applicable State law, e.g., murder requires a death, but burglary does not; once on the premises burglary requires a specific intent to commit a further crime, and murder does not, police were entitled to interrogate the defendant about the murders, and his confession to those crimes therefore was admissible.

Cobb reduces a defendant's Sixth Amendment protections. After a defendant is arraigned on one charge, the police may question him about other crimes, as long as those new charges do not constitute a lesser included or greater included offense of the crime with which he is currently charged. Police should consult with a prosecutor to ensure that courts do not regard the new charge as the "same offense" as the current charges. Combining *Cobb* with the *Henry/Kuhlman* cases suggests that a jail informant may actively initiate conversations with a cellmate about charges that differ from the charges that he has been arraigned on. That possibility could lead to pretext arrests for minor offenses, providing the prosecutor the opportunity to use an informer to ask the defendant about more serious crimes.

C. Comparing Fifth and Sixth Amendment Standards

There are two primary distinctions between a Fifth Amendment invocation of the right to counsel and a Sixth Amendment invocation of the right to counsel. First, a Sixth Amendment invocation may occur even before *Miranda* warnings. Second, *McNeil* suggests that the consequences of a Sixth Amendment invocation require that the

---

60 *Id.*, at 173.

61 *Id.*, quoting Blockburger v. United States, 284 U.S. 299, 304 (1932).

police may nevertheless continue questioning the suspect about uncharged offenses. As with the Fifth Amendment doctrine under *Miranda*, a defendant may invoke his right to counsel under the Sixth Amendment. The invocation must be unequivocal and the defendant must reinitiate communications with his police interrogators in order to waive his rights. Police should provide a *Williams* defendant in custody with *Miranda* warnings that function as "*Williams* warnings" under *Patterson v. Illinois*.

If a defendant who has been to court (and therefore entitled to counsel) invokes the right to counsel in response to such warnings, both *Miranda* and *Williams* rights to cut off police questioning will arise. The *Miranda* right will provide the defendant with the *Roberson* protection to "cut off" questioning about all crimes, while the *Williams* right will provide the redundant *Edwards* protection with a "cut off" of questioning about only the charged crime. However, if a defendant who has been to court fails to invoke the right to counsel in response to the warnings, then neither *Miranda* nor *Williams* "cut off" rights will arise. Only if the defendant is in custody and affirmatively has invoked the *Williams* right to counsel, does the *Williams* right provide him with the *Edwards* "cut off" right.

§ 13.5 Due Process Voluntariness Challenges

A. When Is a Confession Voluntary?

Before the decisions in *Miranda v. Arizona*, the admissibility of most confessions was tested by determining whether it was constitutionally "voluntary" under the Fourteenth Amendment Due Process Clause. If the statement was not voluntary, its admission into evidence was barred by Due Process. Currently, to be admissible in evidence, a defendant's statement must comply with the requirements of the Fifth and Sixth Amendments, as well as satisfy Due Process requirements. The concept of voluntariness bars any statement which was not the product of the defendant's free will as a result of police overreaching.

Voluntariness judgments are policy decisions about the type and amount of pressure that society finds tolerable in police interrogation. The focus is on the amount of pressure that the Constitution finds tolerable. If any pressure was prohibited, *all* confessions in response to police interrogation would be involuntary, because there is always some type of police pressure (even from the officer's badge on his uniform). If the pressure is irrelevant as long as the defendant is capable of making choice, most if not all confessions are voluntary because few defendants are deprived of the capacity for conscious choice. Choices made under the most trying of circumstances are still conscious choices. The case law rejects both the view that all confessions are involuntary and that all must be viewed as voluntary. Voluntariness is a legal term, subject to different interpretations.

If a confession is involuntary, the confession cannot even be used for impeachment or cross-examination, which might not be the case with a *Miranda* violation.[62] Consequently, prosecutors and defendants should seek both a determination as to admissibility under the Fifth and Sixth Amendments and a separate determination about the issue of voluntariness. "There is obviously no reason to require more in the way of a 'voluntariness' inquiry in the *Miranda* waiver context than in the Fourteenth Amendment confession context."[63] Unlike the Fifth Amendment or the Sixth Amendment, a Due Process challenge to a confession can be made anytime, regardless of when the defendant confessed.

Due Process's continued importance is that the Fifth Amendment and Sixth Amendment confession doctrines each have gaps in time that can be plugged only by reference to Due Process rules. For example, *Miranda* does not apply to undercover investigations, to impeachment evidence, or to defendants who have waived their *Miranda* rights.

B. Early Decisions

Beginning in the 1930s, the Court's confession cases addressed coercion, which included police brutality, and physical and psychological torture. *Brown v. Mississippi*[64] appears to be the first case where the Court ordered the suppression of a confession in a State criminal case. Because the police severely beat the suspects to obtain their confessions, the confessions' reliability under those circumstances was doubtful; there was a risk that those confessions were false. After reversing numerous convictions for the repulsive police misconduct, the Court remarked that

> Physical violence or threat of it by the custodian of a prisoner during detention serves no lawful purpose, invalidates confessions that otherwise would be convincing, and is universally condemned by the law. When present, there is no need to weight or measure its effects on the will of the individual victim.[65]

---

62 Mincey v. Arizona, 437 U.S. 385 (1978). See § 1.4(A), discussing Impeachment with Illegally Obtained Evidence.

63 See *Colorado v. Connelly*, 479 U.S. at 169–70.

64 Brown v. Mississippi, 297 U.S. 278 (1936).

65 Stein v. New York, 346 U.S. 156, 182 (1953).

Brown concluded that a Due Process violation had occurred because the convictions were based "solely" on those confessions; later cases clarified that simply using an illegally obtained confession at trial was unconstitutional.

Blackburn v. Alabama[66] stated that "a complex of values underlies the stricture against use by the state of confessions which, by way of convenient shorthand, this Court terms involuntary."[67] Courts reversed convictions based upon coerced confessions

> not because such confessions are unlikely to be true but because the methods used to extract them offend an underlying principle in the enforcement of our criminal law: that ours is an accusatorial and not an inquisitorial system.[68]

These cases used an exclusionary rule for illegally obtained confessions much like the Fourth Amendment exclusionary rule, to deter improper police conduct.

A defendant's "free and rational choice" became another basis for evaluating confessions. In *Townsend v. Sain*,[69] an ill defendant received a drug with the properties of a truth serum, and he soon confessed in response to questioning by police who were unaware of the drug's effect. Although the confession was reliable and there was no conscious police wrongdoing, its use in evidence was disallowed. "Any questioning by police officers which in fact produces a confession which is not the product of free intellect renders that confession inadmissible."[70]

C. *Mincey*, *Connelly*, and *Fulminante*

The Court followed a case-by-case approach to reach its finding of involuntariness in *Mincey v. Arizona*.[71] During a drug raid by undercover and plainclothes detectives on the defendant's apartment, an undercover agent was killed. The defendant and two others were wounded. A detective went to the hospital where the defendant was barely conscious and in the intensive care unit.

The defendant received *Miranda* warnings after which the detective questioned him for three hours, although the defendant asked three times for the questioning to stop until he could see an attorney. Homicide detectives also thoroughly searched the

---

66 361 U.S. 199 (1960).

67 Blackburn v. Alabama, 361 U.S. 199, 207 (1960).

68 Rogers v. Richmond, 365 U.S. 534, 540–41 (1961).

69 372 U.S. 293 (1963).

70 Townsend v. Sain, 372 U.S. 293, 309 (1963).

71 437 U.S. 385 (1978).

defendant's apartment for four days without a warrant. Prosecutors obtained indictments for murder, assault and drug offenses against the defendant. At trial, most of the prosecution's evidence was from the apartment search and the hospital interrogation. The State appellate court affirmed the drug convictions but reversed the other convictions.

The Court held that Due Process requires that the statements obtained from the defendant in the hospital not be used against him, because they were not "the product of his free and rational choice."[72] The detective took advantage of the defendant's physical trauma by interrogating him in his vulnerable state. The defendant's choice was to delay the questioning because he wanted an attorney present. His relative isolation from friends and family also supported the conclusion that the defendant's "will was simply overborne."[73] Building from earlier cases, the Court held that use of the involuntary statements, given the defendant's personal vulnerabilities, was a Due Process violation, whether introduced on the issue of guilt or for impeachment.

Then, *Colorado v. Connelly*[74] altered the judicial approach to these issues. The Court held that the purpose of the Due Process limitation on interrogation is not to ensure that all confessions are truly voluntary, but to deter police overreaching. Thus, factual information about the defendant that is unknown to the police is irrelevant to the Due Process analysis. The same policy that underlies the *Miranda* waiver issue, deterring the police from improper methods, applies to the Due Process approach to confessions.

In *Connelly*, the defendant walked up to a police officer and stated that he had murdered someone and wanted to talk about it. After the officer advised him of his *Miranda* rights, the defendant said he still wanted to discuss the murder even though he understood his rights. A detective arrived and advised the defendant of his rights again before taking the defendant to the police station. There, he described the location of the murder before being held overnight, after which he became disoriented during an interview when he confessed while talking to a public defender.

Police sent him to a state hospital for evaluation which indicated that the defendant believed he was following the "voice of God" by confessing. The police knew only that the defendant had been a

---

[72] Mincey v. Arizona, 437 U.S. 385, 401 (1978), quoting Greenwald v. Wisconsin, 390 U.S. 519, 521 (1968).

[73] *Mincey v. Arizona*, 437 U.S. at 401–02.

[74] 479 U.S. 157 (1986).

patient in several mental hospitals in the past but knew nothing of the auditory hallucinations that led him to confess; his symptoms of mental illness had manifested only the day after his confession during an interview with appointed counsel.

The trial court suppressed the defendant's statements as being involuntary, because (1) his conduct suggested that his statements were not the product of a free choice, even though the police had not violated his rights, and (2) his mental condition voided his attempted waiver of his Fifth and Sixth Amendment rights. The Court held that the lower court had committed reversible error when it excluded a confession volunteered to police by a defendant who suffered from a psychosis that interfered with his ability to make free and rational choices. The defendant's characteristics cannot alone "ever dispose of the inquiry into constitutional 'voluntariness.' "

> [W]hile [the defendant's] mental condition is surely relevant to an individual's susceptibility to police coercion, mere examination of the confessant's state of mind can never conclude the due process inquiry." Without "the crucial element of police overreaching, . . . there is simply no basis for concluding that any state actor has deprived a criminal defendant of due process of law.[75]

Connelly is grounded in the notion that, at a minimum, there must be "police conduct causally related to the confession," and that this conduct must be "coercive." A "statement rendered by one in the condition of [the defendant] might be proved to be quite unreliable, [but] this is a matter to be governed by the evidentiary laws of the forum . . . and not by the Due Process Clause."[76] The purpose of the Due Process requirement is "to prevent fundamental fairness in the use of evidence, whether true or false."[77]

The Court concluded that "coercive police activity is a necessary predicate to a finding of involuntariness."[78] Even if a defendant's free will is "overborne" by his mental illness, this does not make his confession involuntary in the absence of police coercion. While the defendant's free choice is relevant, its importance depends on the police having engaged in overreaching the suspect,[79] evaluated by the totality of circumstances. The defendant's personal characteristics are often relevant as they relate to police overreaching.

---

[75] Colorado v. Connelly, 479 U.S. 157, 163–64 (1986).

[76] *Id.*, at 167.

[77] *Id.*

[78] *Id.*

[79] *Id.*, at 170.

The method of taking the defendant's statements and their admission into evidence in *Connelly* did not violate Due Process. While a defendant's mental condition may be a significant factor in deciding the issue of voluntariness, it is not conclusive on the constitutional issue of voluntariness.[80] If the police are aware of the defendant's mental issues but nevertheless respectfully question the suspect, is there police overreaching? The next case suggests that there is, because the Court held that it is coercive for the police to exploit a situation that they did not create.

Five years after *Connelly*, the Court decided *Arizona v. Fulminante*,[81] where a group of inmates had threatened the defendant with violence because of rumors that he had killed a child. An informant-inmate played the role of sheriff, bargaining for the defendant's confession with a promise to provide him with protection from other inmates. The defendant admitted to the informant-inmate that he had killed the victim, supplying details of the crime. After the defendant was released from prison, he also confessed to the informant-inmate's future wife. Later, the defendant was indicted for murder; he filed a motion to suppress his confession to the informant-inmate based on a violation of Due Process; the trial judge denied the motion. The State appellate court reversed his conviction and the State appealed.

By applying its totality of circumstances Due Process test, the Court held that the defendant's fear of physical group violence provoked his confession, even with the promise of protection from the informant-inmate. The record showed that the threat of physical violence to the defendant was credible, i.e., the promise was a "credible threat of physical violence unless Fulminante confessed." His "will was overborne in such ways as to render his confession the product of coercion."[82] Using the totality of circumstances analysis, the Court found that the defendant's individual frailties as relevant to its finding that the confession was involuntary.

To summarize the current test for voluntariness, the prosecution has the burden of proof by a preponderance of the evidence. In determining whether a statement of the defendant is voluntary, the judge must examine the "totality of the circumstances" surrounding the giving of the statement.[83] The trial judge makes the voluntariness decision outside the presence of the jury. The "totality of the circumstances" can usually be divided into two categories: (1) the characteristics of the defendant such as: age, intelligence,

---

80 *Id.*

81 499 U.S. 279 (1991).

82 Arizona v. Fulminante, 499 U.S. 279, 287–88 (1991).

83 Haynes v. Washington, 373 U.S. 503 (1963).

education, criminal experience, and his mental and physical condition at the time of the interrogation, and (2) a careful assessment of the police conduct that preceded the confession, e.g., the methods of interrogation used by the police, including any physical or mental coercion, threats, promises or inducements, delay in bringing the defendant before a judge, and the extent to which the police used deceit or trickery in questioning the suspect.

The weighing of these factors to decide whether a statement is voluntary is imprecise. Except in certain obvious circumstances, such as where physical coercion is employed, it may not be possible to say that any one factor requires suppression of a statement. The defendant may always attempt to challenge the confession's veracity with the jury by showing its circumstances.

The "totality of the circumstances" rule for voluntariness is similar to the "totality of the circumstances" rule for a *Miranda* waiver. The following section discusses the various factors present in both traditional Due Process voluntariness cases and *Miranda* waiver cases. However, a "[d]etermination of whether a statement is involuntary 'requires more than a mere color-matching of cases.'" Instead, it "requires careful evaluation of all the circumstances of the interrogation."[84]

D. Defendant's Characteristics

The defendant's age is a factor in determining the voluntariness of a confession,[85] or a waiver of *Miranda*,[86] i.e., whether under the totality of the circumstances the juvenile's confession is freely and voluntarily given following a knowing and intelligent waiver of the right to counsel and the right to remain silent.[87] A minor should not be interrogated as long or as vigorously as an adult.[88]

Subnormal mentality is also a factor considered by the courts in the voluntariness determination,[89] although *Connelly* implies that the police could easily state the suspect did not appear to them to have any mental problems. Likewise, a suspect's relatively high

---

[84] *Mincey v. Arizona,* 437 U.S. at 401, quoting from Reck v. Pate, 367 U.S. 433, 442 (1961).

[85] See In re Gault, 387 U.S. 1 (1967).

[86] Fare v. Michael C., 442 U.S. 707 (1979).

[87] See Edwards v. Arizona, 451 U.S. 477 (1981).

[88] Gallegos v. Colorado, 370 U.S. 49 (1962) (14-year-old detained for five days; parent not allowed to see child); Haley v. State of Ohio, 332 U.S. 596 (1948) (15-year-old).

[89] Culombe v. Connecticut, 367 U.S. 568 (1961). The confession of a mentally ill defendant is involuntary and inadmissible See, e.g., Colorado v. Connelly, 479 U.S. 157 (1986); Blackburn v. Alabama, 361 U.S. 199 (1960); Fikes v. Alabama, 352 U.S. 191 (1957).

intelligence may be persuasive in a court's consideration of the circumstances surrounding the making of a statement.

The police interrogation of a suspect should be commensurate with his educational level. Where a suspect is illiterate, trial courts are more careful about whether the suspect understands the questions asked.[90] The police need not exhibit the same degree of care for a suspect who has attained a high level of education.[91]

There are two circumstances in which a defendant's level of intoxication may play a role in determining whether a confession was involuntary in terms of its reliability. First, intoxication may become relevant because an amount of police coercion is needed to overcome the will of an intoxicated defendant. Second, a confession may be suppressed when the defendant was intoxicated to the degree of mania or was hallucinating, functionally insane, or otherwise incapable of understanding the meaning of his statements. However, the recent emphasis on police coercion may have overshadowed the unreliability of an inebriated defendant's statement under Due Process analysis.

The police have wider latitude in questioning an experienced criminal than a suspect who has little or no criminal experience.[92]

E. Methods of Interrogation

The criteria used to determine whether a confession is the result of coercion are whether the police activity was objectively coercive, whether the coercion overbore the defendant's will, and whether the coercive activity was the crucial motivating factor behind the defendant's confession. Coercion may be psychological or physical. Any statement of the defendant which is the product of police violence,[93] the threat of physical violence,[94] or where the defendant is deprived of food[95] or sleep[96] will render the statement involuntary. Likewise, statements obtained from a defendant who has been

---

90 See Culombe v. Connecticut, 367 U.S. 568 (1961); Harris v. South Carolina, 338 U.S. 68 (1949); White v. Texas, 310 U.S. 530 (1940).

91 Crooker v. California, 357 U.S. 433 (1958), overruled in part by, Escobedo v. Illinois, 378 U.S. 478 (1964).

92 Haynes v. Washington, 373 U.S. 503 (1963) (confession involuntary; defendant had no prior experience with police).

93 Brown v. Mississippi, 297 U.S. 278 (1936) (brutally beating suspects).

94 Payne v. Arkansas, 356 U.S. 560, 566 (1958) (police told suspect "that there would be 30 or 40 people there in a few minutes that wanted to get him"); Malinski v. New York, 324 U.S. 401 (1945) (suspect kept naked for hours to indicate imminent beating); Chambers v. Florida, 309 U.S. 227 (1940) (threat of mob violence). See Arizona v. Fulminante, 499 U.S. 279 (1991) (confession motivated by fear of physical violence from other inmates; admission held harmless error).

95 Payne v. Arkansas, 356 U.S. 560, 566 (1958).

96 See Spano v. New York, 360 U.S. 315 (1959).

injured, is in pain, and may be confused are not voluntarily given. For example, in *Mincey*[97] the defendant's statement was involuntary because he was in great pain, confused, and periodically lapsed into unconsciousness.

The length of the interrogation is also a factor, i.e., the longer the period of interrogation before an incriminating statement was obtained, the less likely that it will be deemed voluntary.[98] Similarly, the use of more than one interrogator may weigh heavily against a finding of voluntariness.[99]

F. Improper Promises

Some confessions are induced by hope or fear resulting from promises by prosecutors, police, or others with authority over suspects. A promise to drop charges against the suspect in exchange for a confession may lead to suppression of that statement as involuntarily made. However, a suspect who solicited the non-prosecution promise is unlikely to find sympathy by arguing that he was the victim of compelling influences.

The truth or falsity of a promise should be irrelevant to a finding of involuntariness, if a court is looking at the pressure on the defendant that was generated by the police conduct. On the other hand, the gullibility of a defendant may suggest police overreaching if the defendant's reputation is that he'll believe anything. If a false promise bothers a trial judge, it may not be the pressure generated by the lie that troubles him as much as it is that the trial judge dislikes lying.

The totality of circumstances analysis may reveal that these circumstances were so compelling that they overcame the defendant's will. Certain promises are more influential than others in producing a confession. For example, *Rogers v. Richmond*[100] held that the police obtained the suspect's confession as a result of police coercion—a threat to take the defendant's spouse into custody. Similarly, *Lynumn v. Illinois*[101] decided that the police coerced the suspect's confession by informing her that she could lose custody of her children as well as her welfare payments unless she cooperated with the police.

---

97 437 U.S. 385 (1978).

98 See Reck v. Pate, 367 U.S. 433 (1961) (6–7 hours of questioning each day for four days); Fikes v. Alabama, 352 U.S. 191 (1957) (questioning for several hours at a time over five-day period); Turner v. Pennsylvania, 338 U.S. 62 (1949) (questioning from 4–6 hours per day for five days).

99 Ashcraft v. Tennessee, 322 U.S. 143 (1944) (36 hours of relay questioning).

100 365 U.S. 534 (1961).

101 372 U.S. 528 (1963).

Chapter 14

IDENTIFICATION PROCEDURES

Table of Sections

---

§ 14.1 Introduction

An eyewitness to a crime may testify that, prior to trial, he identified the defendant as the perpetrator of the crime. The event at which such an identification was made is frequently called a "pretrial confrontation." In addition, a police officer who was present at the pretrial confrontation may testify at trial about a pretrial identification made by the eyewitness. In addition, the eyewitness may be asked to identify the defendant in the presence of the jury. Such testimony is called an "in-court identification." This Chapter examines the admissibility of identifications under the Sixth Amendment right to counsel and the Due Process Clause.

§ 14.2 Challenges to Identifications

A. Psychological Research

Although most scientific study of eyewitness identification did not begin until after the 1967 Court decision in *United States v. Wade*,[1] the Court identified some of the dangers of eyewitness identification. Experimental psychologists trained to determine the causes of human behavior used staged crimes and other methods to determine what causes false identifications and how to reduce their occurrence.

The research reveals several problems that often create unreliable identifications. First, a person's confidence about an identification may grow from repeated exposure to a suspect, either through photos or personal observation. Second, one person's identification may influence another person's, as described in *Gilbert v. California*,[2] where crime victims and witnesses attended the same lineup and shouted their choice of which lineup participants had committed the crime, in each other's presence. Third, many people believe that, with respect to their own memory, "I am a camera," when their actual recall is often incorrect. For example, stress may reduce a person's ability to perceive accurately rather than "burn into memory forever" accurate observations.

Unfortunately, because courts are unlikely to adopt procedural rules that require (1) criminals to commit crimes in well-lit places, and (2) victims and witnesses not to forget what they observed, courts are left to apply concepts that (1) protect against suggestiveness, and (2) promote reliability of identifications. To minimize the risks of false identifications, empirical evidence supports four rules:[3]

- Police or prosecutors should inform eyewitnesses that the perpetrator of a crime might not be in a lineup that they observe.

---

1 388 U.S. 218, 228–32 (1967).

2 388 U.S. 263, 267 (1967).

3 Wells, G.L. & Seelau, E.P. (1995) "Eyewitness Identification: Psychological research and legal policy on lineups." *Psychology, Public Policy, and Law*, Volume 1, pages 765–791.

- The suspect should not be obvious as a distinctive member of a lineup.
- Persons who do not know which person is the suspect should administer the lineup.
- Prior to allowing other information to contaminate their judgment, witnesses should be asked how certain they are about their choices.

The research results have led to defendants calling expert witnesses to testify about the unreliability of identifications. Judges sometimes respond by excluding such expert testimony, either because the judge thinks that the expert will tell the jury what they already know, or the expert testimony will usurp the jury's role. In reality, many people do not know very much about the problems associated with eyewitness testimony, and expert testimony may provide information to assist the jurors in making a decision.

B. Legal Challenges to Out-of-Court Identifications

There are three possible, distinct legal challenges to an out-of-court identification. First, the identification may be challenged on the basis of the Sixth Amendment right to counsel rule requiring that defense counsel be present at the pretrial confrontation. Second, the pretrial identification may be challenged on the basis of the Fourteenth Amendment Due Process clause which excludes a pretrial confrontation between the defendant and the eyewitness that is so impermissibly suggestive as to give rise to a very substantial likelihood of misidentification.

If the defendant is successful in either of these two challenges, then proof of the pretrial identification is not admissible during the prosecution's case-in-chief. Similarly, a Fourteenth Amendment violation which meets the Due Process test will exclude an in-court identification, because the prosecution is not permitted to "rehabilitate" the unreliable pretrial identification.

A third possible challenge is that the identification is the fruit of an earlier illegality such as an illegal arrest, search or confession. Similar to a Sixth Amendment violation, the in-court identification will be permitted only if the prior "taint" of a pretrial identification has been removed by intervening events.[4] *Wade* was remanded by the Court to the trial court for a hearing to determine "whether the in-

---

4 See Chapter 1, discussing Fruit of the Poisonous Tree.

court identifications had an independent source"[5]—the third possible challenge.

§ 14.3 Categories of Identifications

A. Showup Identifications

A "showup" is a one-on-one presentation of the suspect to an eyewitness. Because it is considered inherently more suggestive than a lineup, a showup is not a generally approved method of securing an identification. Nevertheless, an identification based upon a showup is constitutionally acceptable if under the totality of circumstances it does not present a substantial likelihood of irreparable misidentification, e.g., tainting a later identification by allowing the witness to view photos or videos of the suspect committing the crime prior to the identifying the perpetrator in person.

An on-the-spot showup of a suspect detained near the scene of the crime shortly after its commission usually is upheld, because: (1) the investigating officers needed to make an immediate determination of probable cause to proceed further against the suspect; and (2) the witness's memory was so fresh as to minimize the danger of misidentification. Neither the nervousness or the handcuffing of the suspect nor a statement by the police that they thought they had captured the criminals compel suppression of the identification.

Similarly, as in *Stovall v. Denno*,[6] a hospital room showup of a suspect to a witness for identification is justified by the risk that the witness might not otherwise have an opportunity to make a proper identification, so long as the totality of circumstances do not suggest a substantial risk of misidentification.[7] Even a stationhouse showup may be upheld under the totality of the circumstances, regardless of whether the showup is police-initiated or the idea of the witness.

B. Photograph Identifications

Photographic identifications generally are used when the suspect is not yet in custody. Even when a suspect is in custody, a physical identification may not be conducted because corporal lineups are usually difficult to manage, i.e., it is sometimes difficult to find persons of the same race, age, height and weight who are willing to participate in a lineup. Facilities to conduct a corporal

---

5 *United States v. Wade*, 388 U.S. at 242.

6 388 U.S. 293 (1967).

7 Stovall v. Denno, 388 U.S. 293 (1967).

lineup are not always available. For these reasons it may be far easier for the police to conduct a photographic "lineup."

Lineups with photos are of several types. The first is the single photo of a suspect which is shown to a witness. This procedure is similar to a showup and is similarly received by the courts. The second type of photo lineup is like a physical lineup where the police have a suspect in mind and portray the suspect's photograph with several additional photos of similar looking people. The third use of photographs is the so-called "mug book" view. Here, the police have no firm suspect in mind and show a victim a book of many mug shots with hopes that the culprit is among the photos.

The most circumspect identification is where a single photo is presented. Where this occurs, courts assume suggestiveness and then inquire as to the totality of circumstances to see if the identification was otherwise reliable.[8] Where the defendant's photo is in a "lineup" of the photographs, the courts, in determining suggestiveness, look to whether elements in the photographs' other minor variations in the physical features of the individuals pictured misled witnesses in making their identifications. In addition, courts look to whether the police attempted to influence the witness or whether the same person's photo recurs. The disparity in appearance in persons depicted is often a major consideration although there is no requirement that the persons be identical. Differences in the photos themselves as well as apparent differences in the participants have been a source of litigation.

C. Physical Lineup

A physical lineup consists of presenting the defendant and several other similar looking persons to the witness for identification. This is to be distinguished from the showup where only the suspect is presented. A suspect or defendant has no constitutional right to appear in a lineup, and it is within the court's discretion or police discretion whether one is necessary or appropriate. Lineups are usually conducted behind one-way glass. The following is a suggested procedure for a lineup that would unlikely violate Due Process.

1. All persons in the lineup should be of the same race, sex, approximate age, height and weight.

2. The eyewitnesses should not view or know the suspect(s) before the lineup. The eyewitnesses should assemble in a closed room, so that they are unable to see the suspect being brought to the lineup in handcuffs or under other incriminating circumstances. Similarly, they

---

8 Manson v. Brathwaite, 432 U.S. 98, 110 (1977).

should not be permitted to see the other persons who are to be in the lineup prior to the lineup, since the eyewitnesses may realize that those persons are not suspects.

3. The accused should be allowed to choose his or her position, or number, in the lineup.

4. All persons in the lineup should wear the same type of clothing. For example, in *Foster v. California*,[9] the defendant was the only person in the lineup wearing a leather jacket similar to that worn by the robber. Where an eyewitness has informed the police that the perpetrator was wearing a particular item of clothing (e.g., a hat) either all or none of the persons in the lineup should be required to wear that item of clothing during the lineup.

5. Prior to being shown the lineup, each eyewitness should be told that: (a) several persons will appear in the lineup; (b) each person in the lineup will be wearing a large card with a number on the card, and the eyewitness should refer to the number in making an identification; (c) the fact that these persons appear in the lineup does not mean that the police believe that any of them is the perpetrator, and that the police are also interested in eliminating persons as suspects. After these initial instructions are given to the eyewitnesses, one officer should be assigned to stay with each eyewitness until the entire lineup procedure has been completed to confirm that there is no communication between the eyewitnesses until each has made his or her own independent decision.

6. The persons in the lineup can be required to speak the words spoken by the perpetrator.[10] The appearance of the suspect can also be altered, such as requiring him to wear certain clothing, shave a beard, put on glasses, or put on a false beard. To avoid suggestibility, all the persons in the lineup should be asked to speak the words spoken by the perpetrator or wear the items of clothing. Usually this means passing the item of clothing from person to person in the lineup.

7. The police should not allow more than one eyewitness to view the lineup at the same time. Each eyewitness should be brought, one at a time, to the area from which the lineup is to be viewed. After an eyewitness has viewed the lineup, the officer accompanying that eyewitness should take the

---

9 See Foster v. California, 394 U.S. 440 (1969).

10 *United States v. Wade*, 388 U.S. at 222–23.

eyewitness to a room to which no other eyewitness will be brought. Usually the police will have a form where the witness's identification is to be marked, along with comments as well as notations by the police as to the names of the other persons in the lineup. If the eyewitness can make an identification, he will probably complete the portion of the form by writing something like "number 5 is the person who held me up." If the eyewitness is unable to make an identification, he should so indicate in the same place on the form. The eyewitness should sign the form. After the eyewitness has inserted any comments and signed the form, the officer should complete the rest of the form including inserting the names of the persons in the lineup next to their respective numbers. The officer should also sign the form.

8. The lineup should be photographed to make a complete record of the out-of-court identification. When the persons in the lineup are required to put on an item of clothing, or glasses, then each person in the lineup should also be photographed wearing that item of clothing or glasses.

9. Where the lineup is to be conducted after a complaint has been filed against a suspect, the lineup should not be held unless defense counsel, or an assigned representative, is present.

10. Lineups cannot always be held in formal settings. Particularly where the defendant is not in custody, courts will allow reasonable alternatives consistent with the situation.

In determining the validity of a lineup, the question is one of suggestiveness. If the lineup is suggestive, then the *Neil v. Biggers*[11] five-factor test must be considered in determining whether an identification is reliable despite suggestiveness in the identification procedure. To determine the possible suggestiveness of a lineup, courts have looked to numerous factors such as the circumstances of the lineup, matters which occur prior to the lineup, and the number of lineups.[12] As to the other persons in the lineup, the defendant is not entitled to have identical-looking persons in the lineup.

---

11 409 U.S. 188 (1972).

12 See Foster v. California, 394 U.S. 440, 443 (1969).

D. Other Identification Procedures

When an inanimate identification occurs by the police display of physical objects for a witness to identify, the "lineup" may be deemed either suggestive as a matter of law or a matter for the jury.

A voice identification may be appropriate when a victim cannot make a visual identification because the attacker either covered the victim's eyes, or there was not enough light to see. It is not unusual for the attacker to talk to the victim for a considerable period of time, and therefore the police may wish to obtain a pretrial voice identification. Orders commanding voice examples do not violate either Fourth or Fifth Amendment protections.

All the principles which apply to visual identification also apply to voice identifications. The defendant does not have a right to counsel when his voice is taped for later listening by a witness. Where the witness is to listen to these tape recordings in an attempt to identify the voice of the perpetrator, there is no right to counsel at such a "voice spread" because it is the functional equivalent of a photographic lineup.

From a Due Process perspective, the same considerations as to suggestiveness govern voice identifications as visual ones.

However the role of counsel is defined at a lineup, *Wade* recognized that the right to counsel is inapplicable to scientific identification procedures, e.g., a blood sample taken from the defendant.

> Knowledge of the techniques of science and technology is sufficiently available, and the variables in techniques few enough, that the accused has the opportunity for a meaningful confrontation of the Government's case at trial through the ordinary processes of cross-examination of the Government's expert witnesses and the presentation of the evidence of his own experts. The denial of a right to have his counsel present at such analyses does not therefore violate the Sixth Amendment; they are not critical stages since there is minimal risk that his counsel's absence at such stages might derogate from his right to a fair trial.[13]

Similarly, *Gilbert v. California*[14] held that the taking of a handwriting sample is not a critical stage of a criminal proceeding, thereby entitling a defendant to the presence and assistance of counsel.

---

13 *United States v. Wade*, 388 U.S. at 227–28.

14 388 U.S. 263 (1967).

> The taking of the exemplars was not a 'critical' stage of the criminal proceedings entitling petitioner to the assistance of counsel. Putting aside the fact that the exemplars were taken before the indictment and appointment of counsel, there is minimal risk that the absence of counsel might derogate from his right to a fair trial. If, for some reason, an unrepresentative exemplar is taken, this can be brought out and corrected through the adversary process at trial since the accused can make an unlimited number of additional exemplars for analysis and comparison by government and defense handwriting experts. Thus, "the accused has the opportunity for a meaningful confrontation of the [State's] case at trial through the ordinary processes of cross-examination of the [State's] expert [handwriting] witnesses and the presentation of the evidence of his own [handwriting] experts."[15]

Assuming the evidence is otherwise lawfully obtained, scientific identification evidence requires only an adequate foundation for admissibility. The courts have considered the admissibility of various scientific identification techniques based on scientific acceptance rather than traditional identification questions. These techniques include fingerprint, footprint, voiceprint, bite mark, and blood analysis.[16]

§ 14.4 Sixth Amendment Right to Counsel

A. When a Defendant Has a Right to Counsel

At or after the initiation of adversary judicial criminal proceedings against the defendant, the defendant is entitled to have a lawyer present at any government-sponsored pretrial confrontation with an eyewitness. The reason for this rule is two-fold: (1) to enable the defense at trial to "meaningfully . . . attack the credibility of the witness' courtroom identification," and (2) to eliminate unfair pretrial confrontations which may result in persons being identified as the perpetrators of crime when, in fact, they are not.[17]

In *United States v. Wade*, a bank robbery occurred in September, 1964. A grand jury indicted Wade in March, 1965. He was arrested on the indictment ten days later, counsel was appointed in late April, and a lineup occurred two weeks later but without notice to defense counsel. The timeline suggests that the lineup was not held either to

---

15 Gilbert v. California, 388 U.S. 263, 267 (1967), quoting *United States v. Wade*, 388 U.S. at 227–28.

16 See, e.g., Daubert v. Merrell Dow Pharmaceuticals, 509 U.S. 579 (1993).

17 Kirby v. Illinois, 406 U.S. 682, 695 (1972).

(1) reduce the witnesses' memory loss, or (2) enable defense counsel to assist the defendant in recalling what occurred at the lineup. To help the witnesses, each person in the lineup wore two strips of tape on his face, as the actual robber wore eight months earlier. Both bank employees identified Wade at the lineup.[18]

After *Wade*, to suppress a pretrial identification, defense counsel had to show that: (1) the pretrial confrontation was one at which the presence of defense counsel was required because adversary judicial criminal proceedings had begun, and (2) the defense counsel was not present, then any proof that an identification was made of the defendant at that pretrial confrontation was not admissible.[19] The type of pretrial identification (at or after adversary proceedings have begun where the right to counsel applies) includes any lineup, showup, or other type of identification process where the defendant is required to submit to a corporal identification.

B. Photographic Displays

There is no right for a suspect or defendant to have counsel present when the police show photographs of the defendant and others to the victim. That holding applies any time, regardless of whether law enforcement has arrested the defendant, taken him to court, referred him to the prosecutor for indictment, or the defendant has already been indicted. In *United States v. Ash*,[20] the Court distinguished a photographic display from confrontations like showups and lineups, when "the function of the lawyer has remained essentially the same as . . . the function at trial," i.e., giving the suspect or defendant "aid in coping with legal problems or assistance in meeting his adversary."[21]

Photographic displays differ from showups and lineups for three reasons; without counsel at a photo display, (1) authorities cannot trick or take advantage of the accused, (2) there is no impairment to effective cross-examination because photographic identifications are relatively easy to reconstruct, and (3) there is no need for a trained observer to assist in performing trial-like functions, compared to a lineup or showup. On the other hand, photo display identifications often raise Due Process issues.[22]

---

18 *United States v. Wade*, 388 U.S. at 220.

19 United States v. Wade, 388 U.S. 218 (1967).

20 413 U.S. 300 (1973).

21 United States v. Ash, 413 U.S. 300 (1973).

22 See § 14.6, discussing Due Process Principles for identifications.

C. Rationale for Right to Counsel

As the *Wade* Court had recognized for any right to counsel situation, the presence of "counsel is necessary to preserve the defendant's basic right to a fair trial as affected by his right meaningfully to cross-examine the witnesses against him.[23] *Wade* also recognized the dangers inherent in pretrial identifications, especially without counsel.

> The vagaries of eyewitness identification are well-known; the annals of criminal law are rife with instances of mistaken identification. Mr. Justice Frankfurter once said: "What is the worth of identification testimony even when uncontradicted? The identification of strangers is proverbially untrustworthy. The hazards of such testimony are established by a formidable number of instances."
>
> . . . A major factor contributing to the high incidence of miscarriage of justice from mistaken identification has been the degree of suggestion inherent in the manner in which the prosecution presents the suspect to witnesses for pretrial identification. . . Suggestion can be created intentionally or unintentionally in many subtle ways. . . .
>
> Moreover, "[i]t is a matter of common experience that, once a witness has picked out the accused at the line-up, he is not likely to go back on his word later on, so that in practice the issue of identity may (in the absence of other relevant evidence) for all practical purposes be determined there and then, before the trial."[24]

While the defendant has the right to counsel at a pretrial lineup after commencement of adversary criminal proceedings, the role of counsel remains unclear. *Wade* implies that defense counsel as an observer might point out unfair aspects of the lineup to the police, and suggest corrective measures. Perhaps police are less likely to do prejudicial or suggestive things in defense counsel's presence. The most important advantage of counsel's observation is to decide the tactical wisdom of exposing the lineup identification in order to cast doubt. By observing, counsel will know better what questions to ask.

Lineups constitute a "critical stage" for the right to counsel's presence. As with *Miranda*, the *Wade* Court called on the legislative branch to enact appropriate reforms.

> Legislative or other regulations, such as those of local police departments, which eliminate the risks of abuse and

[23] *United States v. Wade*, 388 U.S. at 227.

[24] *Id.*, at 228–29.

> unintentional suggestion at lineup proceedings and the impediments to meaningful confrontation at trial may also remove the basis for regarding the stage as "critical." But neither Congress nor the federal authorities have seen fit to provide a solution. What we hold today "in no way creates a constitutional straitjacket which will handicap sound efforts at reform, nor is it intended to have this effect."[25]

In the late 1960s, Congress tried to statutorily "repeal" the *Wade* principle in federal criminal cases, by allowing the testimony of *any* witness who saw the defendant commit or participate in a crime.[26] The legislative attempt at repeal was hardly what the Court had in mind when it called for the adoption of identification reforms, and it did not have the desired "repeal" effect.

Several States have extended the *Wade* right to counsel beyond the viewing of the defendant by a witness to include the broader period when the witness communicates to the police the fact of identification. The wider period enables defense counsel to reconstruct at trial the whole process of pretrial identification, including cross-examining the witness who identified the defendant at a lineup. With a broader view, defense counsel can observe the witness to determine that person's initial certainty (or lack thereof), as well as any possibly suggestive words or conduct by the police to bolster the witness confidence.

Other courts take a more expansive view of defense counsel's role. In *United States v. Allen*,[27] the court indicated that:

> the presence of counsel at a lineup serves not only to allow an informed challenge to be made to identification evidence at trial, but also "to minimize the likelihood of an unduly suggestive confrontation." It would seem that appellant's counsel might best be able to serve his client's interest and the interest of justice if he is given in advance of the lineup the names of the witnesses who would attend; the time, place and nature of the crimes involved; and the descriptions of the suspect, if any, which the witnesses had given to the police. Counsel also might be allowed to have a role in setting up the lineup and proposing changes to avoid suggestive features. If such a procedure were followed, it might well be that, absent plain error or circumstances unknown to counsel at the time of the lineup, no challenges

---

25 *Id.*, at 239. See Miranda v. Arizona, 384 U.S. 436, 467 (1966).

26 18 U.S.C. § 3502.

27 408 F.2d 1287 (D.C.Cir. 1969).

to the physical staging of the lineup could successfully be raised beyond objections raised at the time of the lineup.[28]

As a result of *Wade*, police training in conducting lineups increased considerably, including better record-keeping of what occurred during the lineup itself. Adopting the findings of psychologists has contributed to better lineup practices, such as (1) informing eyewitnesses that the suspect might not be in the lineup, (2) to administer the lineup, selecting a person who does not know which person is the suspect, (3) asking witnesses to the lineup how certain they are about their initial choice, before allowing other information to affect their belief, and (4) conducting the lineups by having witnesses view each person one by one, instead of viewing all simultaneously. The last change requires the witness to compare each person to their memory, instead of comparing each person to each other. It is also likely that a videotape of a lineup is a better protection for a defendant than the presence of his attorney. The video may be used later to support directly some claims that a lineup was conducted unfairly.

Police departments use these improvements even though, as the next section suggests, *Kirby* eliminated for the most part the possibility that an attorney would be present at a lineup before the suspect went to court the first time.

D. When "Adversary Judicial Criminal Proceedings" Begin

In *Kirby v. Illinois*,[29] the issue was whether a suspect was entitled to counsel immediately upon being taken into custody. The Court answered in the negative, by holding that the right to counsel does not attach for identification purposes until the "initiation of adversary judicial criminal proceedings—whether by way of formal charge, preliminary hearing, indictment, information, or arraignment."[30] Unfortunately, the Court did not further specify when "adversary judicial criminal proceedings" begin. It was only clear from the opinion that a mere arrest will not trigger the Sixth Amendment right to counsel at a pretrial confrontation but that the indictment of the defendant will trigger that right.

Five years later, the Court decided *Moore v. Illinois*,[31] which held that "adversary judicial criminal proceedings" had begun by the time of a preliminary hearing. Therefore, an identification of an

28 United States v. Allen, 408 F.2d 1287, 1289 (D.C.Cir. 1969).

29 406 U.S. 682 (1972).

30 *Kirby v. Illinois*, 406 U.S. at 689.

31 434 U.S. 220 (1977).

unindicted defendant at a preliminary hearing at which he was not represented by counsel was held to violate the defendant's Sixth Amendment right to counsel. On the other hand, when an identification occurred before the preliminary hearing, the defendant had no right to the presence of counsel.

After three decades of uncertainty about the triggering event for the right to counsel, the Court decided *Rothgery v. Gillespie County*[32] to specify more clearly when the right to counsel attaches and why it attaches at that point. At the initial appearance, the "government's commitment to prosecute" is "sufficiently concrete" because the accusation "prompts arraignment and restrictions on the accused's liberty to facilitate the prosecution."[33] *Kirby* and *Rothgery* effectively undercut *Wade*, because the police may avoid the *Wade* counsel requirements simply by postponing the defendant's initial court appearance until after a lineup. In the five years between *Wade* and *Kirby*, all eight federal circuits that had faced the question had applied *Wade* to pre-adversary confrontations.

E. The "Rest of the Story" in *Wade*

While appearing in a lineup without an attorney, the police required all those in the lineup to speak the words of the person who robbed the bank, "Put the money in the bag." While holding that Wade's Sixth Amendment rights were violated, the Court denied his claim of a Fifth Amendment breach.

> We have no doubt that compelling the accused merely to exhibit his person for observation by a prosecution witness prior to trial involves no compulsion of the accused to give evidence having testimonial significance. . . . Similarly, compelling Wade to speak within hearing distance of the witnesses, even to utter words purportedly uttered by the robber, was not compulsion to utter statements of a 'testimonial' nature; he was required to use his voice as an identifying physical characteristic, not to speak his guilt.[34]

Hearing Wade's voice likely was important to the bank employees' identification, because Wade had worn distracting pieces of adhesive tape on his face during the robbery to distract eyewitnesses from focusing on his facial characteristics.

---

[32] 554 U.S. 191 (2008).

[33] Rothgery v. Gillespie County, Tex., 554 U.S. 191, 207 (2008).

[34] *United States v. Wade*, 388 U.S. at 222–23.

As discussed elsewhere,[35] a defendant's Fifth Amendment privilege is not violated by requiring a suspect or defendant to identify a physical characteristic like their voice or a handwriting sample. In *Wade*, there was an arguable difference between providing a voice sample and supplying that sample along with the same words as the robber. Perhaps the key distinction is that Wade was not the only person in the lineup who had to speak that phrase; all persons in the lineup had to utter that phrase, thereby helping those witnessing the lineup to focus on the sound of the voice rather than on the spoken words.

F. Remedy for Violation of Right to Counsel

Once a court determines that there was a Sixth Amendment violation in the pretrial confrontation, evidence about that out-of-court confrontation is excluded from evidence at trial. An in-court identification

> is the direct result of the illegal lineup "come at by exploitation of (the primary) illegality." The State is therefore not entitled to an opportunity to show that that testimony had an independent source. Only a *per se* exclusionary rule as to such testimony can be an effective sanction to assure that law enforcement authorities will respect the accused's constitutional right to the presence of his counsel at the critical lineup. . . . That conclusion is buttressed by the consideration that the witness' testimony of his lineup identification will enhance the impact of his in-court identification on the jury and seriously aggravate whatever derogation exists of the accused's right to a fair trial.[36]

The "fruit of the poisonous tree" doctrine[37] of *Wong Sun v. United States*[38] then becomes applicable to an in-court identification. The trial court will not permit the eyewitness to make even an in-court identification unless the prosecution can demonstrate, by "clear and convincing evidence" that the in-court identification will be based on the eyewitness's observations of the defendant at the scene of the crime and *not* at the pretrial confrontation.[39] Essentially, the

---

35 See § 16.4(E), discussing the Fifth Amendment's inapplicability to identifying physical characteristics.

36 Gilbert v. California, 388 U.S. 263, 272–74 (1967).

37 See § 1.7, discussing the Fruit of the Poisonous Tree Doctrine.

38 371 U.S. 471 (1963).

39 United States v. Wade, 388 U.S. 218 (1967).

prosecution must prove the witness's trial identification has an origin independent of the pretrial confrontation.[40]

Wade identified "various factors" that a trial court must consider in deciding whether to permit the eyewitnesses to make an in-court identification, despite the Sixth Amendment violation. The Court offered examples such as

> the prior opportunity to observe the alleged criminal act, the existence of any discrepancy between any pre-lineup description and the defendant's actual description, any identification prior to lineup of another person, the identification by picture of the defendant prior to the lineup, failure to identify the defendant on a prior occasion, and the lapse of time between the alleged act and the lineup identification. It is also relevant to consider those facts which, despite the absence of counsel, are disclosed concerning the conduct of the lineup.[41]

If the trial court is satisfied that there is an independent basis for an in-court identification, the prosecution may introduce testimony from an identifying witness.

Even with an in-court identification, the defendant may be able to rebut the independent basis for the in-court identification as well as impeach the witness by questioning the fairness of the earlier identification procedure.[42] To rebut the independent basis, defense counsel will attempt to show that the witness's original description of the witness was so inaccurate or limited that he could not have made the in-court identification without the benefit of the illegal lineup, i.e., his certainty was the result of his lineup memory rather than his memory of the crime. In addition, counsel may point out that the witness in court was not immediately certain. For example, before identifying him, the witness requested that the defendant speak or turn around.

For impeachment, counsel will attempt to prove that the witness was more interested in making an in-court identification than in being certain about it. Counsel may raise multiple issues relating to police influence prior to or during the lineup. For example, did they tell the witness that they had reason to believe that the perpetrator of the crime would be in the lineup? Especially with video evidence of the lineup, counsel may try to show the length of time it took for the witness to identify the suspect after first observing him. How closely

---

[40] See Chapter 1, discussing the Fruit of the Poisonous Tree Doctrine.

[41] *United States v. Wade*, 388 U.S. at 241. Some of these factors are similar to those for determining whether a pretrial identification violates Due Process.

[42] See Watkins v. Sowders, 449 U.S. 341 (1981).

did the witness's original account of the suspect match the suspect's actual description? Were other lineup participants similar in appearance to the suspect? If not, were there compelling reasons for not waiting until others with similar appearance could be found? Were other witnesses present at the lineup, and if so was this witness aware that others had also identified the suspect?

§ 14.5 Waiver of Right to Counsel

> [F]or Wade the post-indictment lineup was a critical stage of the prosecution at which he was 'as much entitled to such aid [of counsel] . . . as at the trial itself. . . .Thus both Wade "and his counsel should have been notified of the impending lineup, and counsel's presence should have been a requisite to conduct of the lineup, absent an intelligent waiver."[43]

Without counsel's presence, *Wade* was unclear about how the defendant waived his right to counsel for an impending lineup, unless he was aware of his right to counsel and knew enough to understand whether he should nonetheless waive that right. Tactically, the waiver standard for lineup counsel is parallel to the interrogation cases. Any waiver must be knowing, intelligent, and voluntary (adding that the waiver will be more effective if it is written).[44] Because the right involved is the Sixth Amendment right to counsel, the standard of proof for a waiver of counsel is identical to the Fifth Amendment analysis.[45]

§ 14.6 Due Process Principle

Even if there is no infringement of the Sixth Amendment right to counsel, there still may be potential that an identification procedure was conducted unfairly, i.e., it was unnecessarily suggestive *or* the identification itself was unreliable. A second, broader line of attack upon an out-of-court identification is based on the Due Process Clause of the Fourteenth Amendment (or the Fifth Amendment for federal cases) which is separate and distinct from the Sixth Amendment approach. A Due Process violation may exist even where the pretrial confrontation took place *before* adversary judicial criminal proceedings began, and it may also exist even though defense counsel was present at the pretrial confrontation. Due Process also may be used to challenge a pretrial photo identification, regardless of when it occurred.

---

43 *United States v. Wade*, 388 U.S. at 237.

44 Johnson v. Zerbst, 304 U.S. 458, 464 (1938).

45 Brewer v. Williams, 430 U.S. 387, 404 (1977). See § 13.5, discussing Due Process Voluntariness Challenges for confessions.

A. *Stovall* and *Foster*

The Due Process challenge to the admissibility of an out-of-court identification arises from the Court's decision in *Stovall v. Denno.*[46] The defendant was arrested the day after a homicide. Police took him to a hospital where the victim's wife, who was wounded during her husband's homicide, was a patient. After she observed the suspect and heard him speak, she identified him as her husband's murderer. At trial, she also made an in-court identification.

The Court held that a pretrial confrontation violates Due Process if it is "unnecessarily suggestive and conducive to irreparable mistaken identification."[47] "[T]he record in the present case reveals that the showing of Stovall to Mrs. Behrendt [the murder victim's spouse who also had been seriously wounded in the knife attack] in an immediate hospital confrontation was imperative."

> Here was the only person in the world who could possibly exonerate Stovall. Her words, and only her words, "He is not the man" could have resulted in freedom for Stovall. The hospital was not far distant from the courthouse and jail. No one knew how long Mrs. Behrendt might live. Faced with the responsibility of identifying the attacker, with the need for immediate action and with the knowledge that Mrs. Behrendt could not visit the jail, the police followed the only feasible procedure and took Stovall to the hospital room. Under these circumstances, the usual police station line-up, which Stovall now argues he should have had, was out of the question.[48]

In order to decide whether there was a Due Process violation, the "totality of the circumstances" must be considered.

Perry v. New Hampshire,[49] explained *Stovall*: there was no Due Process violation even though the defendant was the only person presented to the victim for identification in a showup in the victim's hospital room and even though the defendant was presented wearing handcuffs. The suggestive showup used was necessary, because the victim was the only eyewitness, and it was uncertain that she would survive long enough for the identification to be conducted under less suggestive conditions.

In *Perry*, the identification process did not include the police. The police had seen the defendant standing in a parking lot of an

---

46 388 U.S. 293 (1967).

47 Stovall v. Denno, 388 U.S. 293, 302 (1967).

48 *Id.*

49 Perry v. New Hampshire, 565 U.S. 228 (2012).

apartment building holding two amplifiers that he had just stolen from nearby vehicles. One officer stayed with the defendant while another went to interview an eyewitness who lived in the building. When the officer asked the eyewitness for a specific description of the thief, she looked out her window and identified the person still in the parking lot standing next to the officer there. The trial court denied the motion to suppress the spontaneous identification, because the officer did not tell her that the thief was standing in the parking lot and did not tell her to go to her window to look. "The fallibility of eyewitness evidence does not, without the taint of improper state conduct, warrant a due process rule requiring a trial court to screen such evidence for reliability before allowing the jury to assess its creditworthiness."[50] The Court held

> that the Due Process Clause does not require a preliminary judicial inquiry int the reliability of an eyewitness identification when the identification was not procured under unnecessarily suggestive circumstances arranged by law enforcement.[51]

In *Foster v. California*,[52] the defendant was convicted of robbing a Western Union office. His height differed from the others in a lineup, and he was the only participant wearing a leather jacket like the one worn by the robber. Yet, there was no positive identification. The police immediately permitted a one-on-one showup between the suspect and the witness, but even then the witness's identification was tentative. The police waited a few days before conducting another lineup, in which the suspect was the only person who also had appeared in the first lineup. In that suggestive lineup, the witness finally identified the suspect. The Court had no difficulty holding that the suspect's Due Process rights were violated.

> The suggestive elements in this identification procedure made it all but inevitable that [the witness] would identify [the suspect] whether or not he was in fact "the man." In effect, the police repeatedly said to the witness, "This is the man." This procedure so undermined the reliability of the eyewitness identification as to violate Due Process.[53]

B. The Due Process Exclusionary Rule

If the confrontation was so unfair that there was a Due Process violation, any reference to an out-of-court identification must be excluded, i.e., no proof of an out-of-court identification may be

---

50 *Id.*, at 245.

51 *Id.*, at 248.

52 394 U.S. 440 (1969).

53 Foster v. California, 394 U.S. 440, 443 (1969).

presented to the jury.[54] Specifically, neither the eyewitness who made the identification nor persons who were present when the eyewitness made the identification, may testify before the jury that such an out-of-court identification was made. A ruling that there was a Due Process violation also means that the eyewitness will not be permitted to rehabilitate the identification by making an in-court identification.

C. Unnecessarily Suggestive Identifications

In *Stovall's* companion case of *United States v. Wade*, the Court stated that a suggestive physical lineup occurs when:

> all in the lineup but the suspect were known to the identifying witness, [when] the other participants in a lineup were grossly dissimilar in appearance to the suspect, [when] only the suspect was required to wear distinctive clothing which the culprit allegedly wore, [when] the witness is told by the police that they have caught the culprit after which the defendant is brought before the witness alone or is viewed in jail, [when] the suspect is pointed out before or during a lineup, and [when] the participants in the lineup are asked to try on an article of clothing which fits only the suspect.[55]

Similarly, in a photo display, the relevant factors for its suggestiveness include the size of the array, the officer's manner of presenting it, and the details of the photos themselves. The Court has recognized that photo displays may be necessarily suggestive.

> [I]t is not suggested that it was unnecessary for the FBI to resort to photographic identification in this instance. A serious felony had been committed. The perpetrators were still at large. The inconclusive clues which law enforcement officials possessed led to [two suspects]. It was essential for the FBI agents swiftly to determine whether they were on the right track, so that they could properly deploy their forces in Chicago and, if necessary, alert officials in other cities.[56]

Merely because a more reliable identification procedure could have been used does not make the procedure that *was* used unnecessarily suggestive or unreliable. In *Neil v. Biggers*, a showup was deemed *unnecessarily* suggestive even though the police could

---

54 Gilbert v. California, 388 U.S. 263 (1967).

55 *United States v. Wade*, 388 U.S. at 233.

56 Simmons v. United States, 390 U.S. 377, 384–85 (1968).

not assemble a lineup because they could not locate anyone who fit a physical description comparable to the prime suspect.

> In this case it appears to the Court that a line-up, which both sides admit is generally more reliable than a show-up, could have been arranged. The fact that this was not done tended needlessly to decrease the fairness of the identification process to which petitioner was subjected.[57]

The Due Process approach to an unnecessarily suggestive out-of-court identification has several component parts. First, was there any suggestion inherent in the identification, e.g., the robber was wearing an earring, and only one person in the lineup wore an earring? Second, if there was suggestion, was it unnecessarily suggestive? Typical types of suggestion to avoid are differences in race or gender among lineup participants, statements by the police that the perpetrator is present in the lineup, and witnesses making identifications in each other's presence. If any suggestion was unnecessary, there is no Due Process violation. If there was unnecessary suggestion, the analysis moves to the next step, which analyzes the reliability of the unnecessarily suggestive identification, based upon the factors discussed in the next section.

D. Reliable Identifications

In *Neil v. Biggers*,[58] the Court changed the test for determining whether a pretrial confrontation violated Due Process. Even though a showup may have been unnecessarily suggestive, in-court and out-of-court identifications are still admissible if the identification nonetheless was reliable, i.e., there was "no substantial likelihood of misidentification."[59] An out-of-court identification does not violate Due Process if under the " 'totality of the circumstances' the identification was reliable."[60] Whereas the emphasis in *Stovall* was on the suggestiveness of the confrontation, it shifted in *Neil* to the reliability of the identification itself.

Because the trial in *Neil* preceded the date of the decision of the Court in *Stovall*, the exclusionary rule of *Stovall* was not applicable to the case. *Neil* stated that the *per se* exclusionary rule of *Stovall* "would have no place in the present case, since both the confrontation and the trial preceded *Stovall v. Denno*, . . . when we first gave notice that the suggestiveness of confrontation procedures was anything

57 Neil v. Biggers, 409 U.S. 188, 199 n.6 (1972).

58 409 U.S. 188 (1972).

59 Neil v. Biggers, 409 U.S. 188, 201 (1972).

60 *Id.*, at 199.

other than a matter to be argued to the jury."[61] The new test was set forth in *Neil*:

> We turn, then, to the central question, whether under the "totality of the circumstances" the identification was reliable even though the confrontation procedure was suggestive. As indicated by our cases, the factors to be considered in evaluating the likelihood of misidentification include the opportunity of the witness to view the criminal at the time of the crime, the witness' degree of attention, the accuracy of the witness' prior description of the criminal, the level of certainty demonstrated by the witness at the confrontation, and the length of time between the crime and confrontation. Against these factors is to be weighed the corrupting effects of the suggestive evidence itself.[62]

E. Manson v. Brathwaite

Any uncertainty about the applicable Due Process test ended five years later, when the Court held in *Manson v. Brathwaite*[63] that the test previously announced in *Neil* was to be used in determining whether a pretrial confrontation violated Due Process even when the identification took place after *Stovall.*

An undercover police officer purchased drugs from Brathwaite, after observing him for several minutes preceding the transaction. After the purchase, the officer soon described the seller to another officer who suspected that he knew the seller's identity. Two days after the drug sale, the undercover officer identified the seller from a lone photograph. At the seller's trial, the officer also made an in-court identification of the seller, now the defendant. After his conviction, the defendant appealed, alleging that the identifications had violated his Due Process rights. The Court rejected his claim.

The Court identified three interests in deciding to prefer a totality of circumstances analysis over *Stovall*'s *per se* approach to Due Process cases. First, a jury should hear identification testimony only if it has aspects of reliability.[64] Because the *Stovall* test emphasizes suggestiveness only, it prevents a jury from hearing evidence that is reliable and relevant. Even in *Stovall*, the Court had stated that despite the suggestiveness of the showup, the fact that the only witness to the murder was dying had provided reliability

61 *Id.*, at 199.

62 *Id.*, at 199–200.

63 432 U.S. 98 (1977).

64 Manson v. Brathwaite, 432 U.S. 98, 112 (1977).

and saved the identification from violating Due Process, because the suggestiveness of the hospital identification was necessary.

Deterrence on police behavior was the second of the three factors identified by the Court to support the addition of reliability to the analysis.

> Although the *per se* approach has the more significant deterrent effect, the totality approach also has an influence on police behavior. The police will guard against unnecessarily suggestive procedures under the totality rule, as well as the *per se* one, for fear that their actions will lead to the exclusion of identifications as unreliable.[65]

The totality method influences police behavior, and provides a safeguard against "unnecessarily suggestive procedures" by enabling them to be offset by the reliability of the identification.

The final interest discussed by the Court was a concern for the administration of justice, though the Court seemed to use this interest as another way of focusing on the issue of reliable evidence.

> Here the *per se* approach suffers serious drawbacks. Since it denies the trier reliable evidence, it may result, on occasion, in the guilty going free. Also, because of its rigidity, the *per se* approach may make error by the trial judge more likely than the totality approach. And in those cases in which the admission of identification evidence is error under the *per se* approach but not under the totality approach cases in which the identification is reliable despite an unnecessarily suggestive identification procedure reversal is a Draconian sanction. Certainly, inflexible rules of exclusion that may frustrate rather than promote justice have not been viewed recently by this Court with unlimited enthusiasm.[66]

When the Court concluded that reliability is the linchpin in determining the admissibility of identification testimony, it was choosing the totality approach over the narrower *per se* analysis. The totality of the circumstances view permits the admission of the confrontation evidence if, despite the unnecessarily suggestive aspect, the out-of-court identification possesses certain features of reliability. To prove suggestiveness or reliability, *Perry* recognized the admissibility of eyewitness identification testimony by experts to address problems like cross-racial identification, identification after long delays or under stress, and psychological phenomena. There are

---

65 *Id.*

66 *Id.*, at 112–13.

alternative devices to test reliability, regardless of whether law enforcement has engaged in improper activity: "counsel at post-indictment lineups, vigorous cross-examination, protective rules of evidence [e.g., Fed.R.Evid. 403], and jury instructions on both the fallibility of eyewitness identification and the requirement that guilt be proved beyond a reasonable doubt."[67]

From *Stovall* to *Brathwaite*, the Court discussed its concern for in-court identification reliability by referring to an "irreparable mistaken identification"[68] or an "irreparable misidentification."[69] However, the Court did not offer a clarification about the relevance of that phrase to the Due Process test. Perhaps the use of "irreparable" cautions a trial court about deciding that, despite an unreliable *out*-of-court identification, a prosecutor's offer of an *in*-court identification could be reliable.

F. Applying the *Brathwaite* Factors

To determine whether a pretrial confrontation violates Due Process, a trial court will conduct a hearing on a motion *in limine* by the defense to prohibit any testimony about the identification. The first part of the *Brathwaite* test is to ask whether the pretrial identification procedure was suggestive? By itself, the suggestiveness of an identification procedure does not require suppression of the eyewitness evidence, even if that increases the risk of mistaken identification. If it was not suggestive, then proof of the fact of the out-of-court identification is admissible.

If it was suggestive, was it *unnecessarily* suggestive? If the identification is unnecessarily suggestive, there must be a preliminary judicial inquiry into the reliability of the identification, i.e., was the identification unnecessarily suggestive and *arranged by* law enforcement?[70]

Suppression of the identification is required only if the unnecessary suggestiveness creates a very substantial risk of misidentification. Trial courts will hear proof of the five-factor *Neil* test to determine reliability, which are similar to the *Wade* independent source factors.

The first reliability factor is the opportunity of the witness to view the criminal at the time of the crime. The courts look to the

---

[67] *Perry v. New Hampshire*, 565 U.S. at 233, 247.

[68] *Stovall v. Denno*, 388 U.S. at 302.

[69] Manson v. Brathwaite, 432 U.S. 98, 116 (1977), quoting Simmons v. United States, 390 U.S. 377, 384 (1968).

[70] *Perry v. New Hampshire*, 565 U.S. at 248.

lighting conditions, the amount of time for the view, the quality of the person's eyesight, and the degree of view by the victim.

The second factor is the witness's degree of attention. Was the person trained to observe or was the person a casual passing observer? In many cases, the person making the identification is in neither category, but is the victim who is likely to be especially alert.[71]

The third reliability factor is the accuracy and extent of the witness's prior description of the criminal, ranging from poor to not detailed, but reasonably accurate to be complete and accurate. A somewhat related factor is the discrepancy between the defendant's appearance at the time of the crime and at the time of identification.

The fourth factor is the level of certainty of the witness at the confrontation. This factor seems in large part to be a function of the extent of the description. The level of certainty can run from nonexistent to virtual certainty. Highly relevant to the level of certainty is where the witness has previously observed other physical or photographic displays and has or has not picked out someone else.

The final reliability factor is the time between the crime and the confrontation. While this is also a variable, the other factors appear to be given more weight. Scientific evidence suggests that most memory loss occurs in the first forty-eight hours after a crime is committed.

After weighing these five factors, if the trial court concludes that an unnecessarily suggestive procedure created a "very substantial risk of misidentification," there is a Due Process violation and neither the out-of-court identification nor an in-court identification is admissible. On the other hand, if the trial court decides that the reliability of the identification outweighs the unnecessary suggestiveness, the identification is admissible through testimony about either the out-of-court identification or an in-court identification.

G. Lack of State Action

One of the purposes of the Due Process approach to identifications is to deter improper police behavior so that the police might "fear that their actions will lead to the exclusion of identifications as unreliable."[72] Private confrontations therefore do not give rise to the same considerations as police-initiated identifications.[73] Therefore, the suggestibility of confrontations is not

---

71 *Manson v. Brathwaite*, 432 U.S. at 112.

72 *Id.*

73 See § 1.3(A), discussing Private Actors.

a legitimate issue where there is no State action involved. A somewhat related principle is relevant where the witness has a "chance encounter" with the defendant who is in police custody. Unless these confrontations are rigged or planned, they do not rise to the level of a Due Process violation.

Chapter 15

RIGHT TO COUNSEL

Table of Sections

---

§ 15.1 Introduction

The Sixth Amendment provides that "in all criminal prosecutions, the accused shall enjoy the right . . . to have the assistance of counsel for his defense." Courts have assumed that a defendant in a criminal case always had a right to retained counsel, but it was not until well into the 20th century that courts began to recognize the importance of counsel for all defendants, i.e., an obligation to provide an attorney at public expense for an indigent defendant.

For a citizen who is arrested, accused, questioned, and put on trial, we say to this person, "Defend yourself!" But a layperson does not know the rules of law, how to construe a statute, apply court decisions and perhaps distinguish them from each other, take advantage of available defenses, and know how a particular judge reacts to situations. With those odds, a layperson will not have a fair trial, except by accident. Even for the greatest of trial lawyers, the first thing they realize when accused of a crime is the need for their own attorney.

This Chapter discusses several aspects of the right to counsel, including the defendant's right to effective assistance of counsel, the right to waive that right, and conflicts of interest.

§ 15.2 Right to Counsel

A. Case Law Before *Gideon*

In *Powell v. Alabama*,[1] nine Black minors were charged with raping two white girls near Scottsboro, Alabama. Eight were convicted and sentenced to death. On appeal, they raised two claims: they had a right to counsel at trial, and a right to appointed counsel if they lacked the funds to retain counsel. Although the trial court had appointed "all members of the bar"[2] at their arraignment to represent the defendants, it was an empty gesture because

> they would have not. . .been given that clear appreciation of responsibility or impressed with that individual sense of duty which should and naturally would accompany the appointment of a selected member of the bar. . . .[3]

The Court upheld both claims on Due Process grounds. Due Process provided the defendants a right to representation by retained counsel, giving them a reasonable opportunity to employ an attorney. The Court reviewed the history of counsel through the practices of the States since adoption of the Bill of Rights. The right to counsel fit within Due Process, meaning that the importance of counsel related to a defendant's right to a fair hearing in court.

---

1 287 U.S. 45 (1932).

2 Powell v. Alabama, 287 U.S. 45, 49 (1932).

3 *Id.*, at 56.

While the Congress had passed a statute for appointed counsel in death penalty cases, more than half of the States had not provided to appointed counsel in most felony cases. The Court reiterated its reliance on Due Process to support a right to appointed counsel. To secure a fair hearing, an indigent defendant had the same rights to a fair hearing as the affluent defendant, and that included a right to counsel.

> The right to be heard would be, in many cases, of little avail if it did not comprehend the right to be heard by counsel. Even the intelligent and educated layman has small and sometimes no skill in the science of law. If charged with crime, he is incapable, generally, of determining for himself whether the indictment is good or bad. He is unfamiliar with the rules of evidence. Left without the aid of counsel he may be put on trial without a proper charge, and convicted upon incompetent evidence, or evidence irrelevant to the issue or otherwise inadmissible. He lacks both the skill and knowledge adequately to prepare his defense, even though he have a perfect one. He requires the guiding hand of counsel at every step in the proceedings against him. Without it, though he be not guilty, he faces the danger of conviction because he does not know how to establish his innocence.[4]

The Court's holding in *Powell* was narrowly drawn, confined to the facts of the case.

> All that it is necessary now to decide, as we do decide, is that in a capital case, where the defendant is unable to employ counsel, and is incapable adequately of making his own defense because of ignorance, feeble-mindedness, illiteracy, or the like, it is the duty of the court, whether requested or not, to assign counsel for him as a necessary requisite of due process of law; and that duty is not discharged by an assignment at such a time or under such circumstances as to preclude the giving of effective aid in the preparation and trial of the case.[5]

In *Johnson v. Zerbst*,[6] federal prosecutors charged two defendants with counterfeiting. Although the trial court declined to appoint counsel for the defendants because they were not charged with a capital crime, the Court held that the right to appointed counsel as well as to retained counsel are both part of the Sixth

---

4 *Id.*, at 68–69.

5 *Id.*, at 65.

6 304 U.S. 458 (1938).

Amendment. Trial without counsel violated the Sixth Amendment, which explicitly applies to "all criminal prosecutions," and which

> embodies a realistic recognition of the obvious truth that the average defendant does not have the professional legal skill to protect himself. [It therefore] withholds from the federal courts, in all criminal proceedings, the power and authority to deprive an accused of his life or liberty unless he has or waives the assistance of counsel.[7]

The Court focused on the value of the right to be heard in the absence of counsel, whose importance corresponded with other Sixth Amendment basics like a jury trial, notice, confrontation, and compulsory process. A court's responsibility to guarantee access to counsel extended to defendants unable to afford counsel's financial cost. The only exception to the right to counsel for an indigent defendant was a knowing and intelligent waiver of his Sixth Amendment right to appointed counsel.

An extension of *Johnson*'s holding to State cases took another quarter century. Because *Powell* indicated that State cases were to be decided by Due Process principles, *Betts v. Brady*[8] held that Due Process required appointed counsel only when the circumstances of a case suggested that an indigent defendant needed counsel to receive a fair trial, e.g., due to "ignorance, feeblemindedness, illiteracy, or the like."[9]

> Asserted denial (of due process) is to be tested by an appraisal of the totality of facts in a given case. That which may, in one setting, constitute a denial of fundamental fairness, shocking to the universal sense of justice, may, in other circumstances, and in the light of other considerations, fall short of such denial.[10]

Despite its reference to "other circumstances," the Court in *Betts* found that they were absent in a robbery trial where the trial comprised a "simple issue [of] the veracity"[11] about testimony that Betts could ably address on his own.

---

7 Johnson v. Zerbst, 304 U.S. 458, 462, 463 (1938).

8 316 U.S. 455 (1942).

9 Betts v. Brady, 316 U.S. 455, 463 (1942).

10 *Id.*, at 462.

11 *Id.*, at 472.

B. Gideon v. Wainwright

Gideon v. Wainwright[12] held that a defendant in a criminal case has an absolute right to counsel for charged felonies.[13] The Court applied the Sixth Amendment right to defense counsel at trial to the States through the Fourteenth Amendment. *Gideon* also provided appointed counsel for indigent defendants, and the failure to appoint counsel for indigents became reversible error.

Prosecutors in Florida charged the defendant with the felony of breaking and entering a poolroom with the intent to commit a misdemeanor. At his initial appearance, the trial court denied the defendant's request for counsel, telling him that Florida law entitled him to appointed counsel only if he was charged with a capital offense. At his trial, the defendant "conducted his defense about as well as could be expected from a layman."[14] The jury convicted him, and he was sentenced to serve five years in a State prison.

Ironically, the Court appointed counsel for the Gideon on his appeal where the question posed to counsel was "Should this Court's holding in *Betts v. Brady* be reconsidered?" In the twenty plus years between *Betts* and *Gideon*, the appellate brief from the Americans for Civil Liberties Union found that of the 139 State appellate cases litigated about the existence of special circumstances under *Betts*, only eleven decisions had found reversible error because the circumstances of the case required counsel for an indigent defendant. Plus, not one case was halted in midstream in order to appoint counsel. At the time the Court decided *Betts*, fewer than half the States required counsel for indigents, whether by statute, court rule, or court decision. Twenty years later, when *Gideon* was decided, 45 States required appointed counsel. The coming change in *Gideon* was approved by the States themselves, i.e., the Court merely followed what the States had done.

States were hoping that the Court in *Gideon* would reaffirm *Betts*'s use of special circumstances, limit *Gideon*'s application to indigents charged with felonies only, limit its application to the trial portion of a felony prosecution, and not make the decision in *Gideon* retroactive, regardless of what the Court decided. The Court chose *none* of the alternative courses.

---

12 372 U.S. 335 (1963).

13 See Texas v. Cobb, 532 U.S. 162 (2001) (the Sixth Amendment right to counsel attaches only to charged offenses, and there is no exception for uncharged crimes that are "factually related" to a charged offense).

14 Gideon v. Wainwright, 372 U.S. 335, 337 (1963).

The Court emphasized its *Betts* mistake in discussing fundamental fairness. Counsel was always "essential to a fair trial."[15] The right to counsel is a necessity due to the State's belief that attorneys are essential to the public's prosecutorial interest. Defendants who can afford attorneys hire them, but a fair and impartial system can be a reality only if indigents face their accusers with the assistance of an attorney.

> [R]eason and reflection require us to recognize that in our adversary system of criminal justice, any person hauled into court, who is too poor to hire a lawyer cannot be assured a fair trial unless counsel is provided for him. . . . Lawyers to prosecute are everywhere deemed essential . . . [and] there are few defendants . . . who fail to hire the best lawyers they can get to prepare and present their defenses.[16]

Powell had highlighted that the decision to retain counsel was critical to the defendant. Even a genius layperson might need counsel in order to get a fair hearing. However, for appointed counsel, *Powell* did not regard the assistance of counsel as vital to a fair hearing in all cases. *Powell*'s casual approach to appointed counsel may explain why it referred to Due Process with its case-by-case examination of circumstances rather than using the Sixth Amendment's bright line method.

By contrast, *Gideon* identified the right to appointed counsel for all under the Sixth Amendment as part of the array of rights like notice, jury, and confrontation, each of which is essential to a fair hearing in an adversary system of justice. A defendant who is an "intelligent and education layperson," whether indigent or not, needs counsel to provide a fair trial. If the Sixth Amendment has a counsel requirement to ensure a fair trial, no distinction should exist between a well-to-do defendant and an indigent defendant. If the Court labels a proceeding as a critical stage in a criminal prosecution, all defendants have a right to counsel regardless of the financial ability to pay counsel. Conversely, if a proceeding is not critical, no one has a right to counsel.

The right to counsel should depend on the nature of the proceeding, rather than on the defendant's financial situation. The later cases finding that the Sixth Amendment right to retained or appointed counsel did not apply looked at whether the proceeding

---

[15] *Id.*, at 342.

[16] *Id.*, at 344.

was not part of a "criminal prosecution" or did not present a "critical stage" of the criminal prosecution.[17]

C. Right to Retain Counsel of Choice

Retained counsel must be admitted to practice law in the place of the criminal proceedings, unless the trial court exercises discretion to grant counsel special admission to the Bar of that jurisdiction for the limited purpose of representing defendant in a specific criminal proceeding ("*pro hac vice* admission"). The trial court's authority is discretionary, because "the Constitution does not require that because a lawyer has been admitted to the bar of one State, he or she must be allowed to practice in another."[18]

When a defendant has a right to counsel, the right includes the "right to retained counsel of his choosing" as part of the "right to spend his own money to obtain the advice and assistance . . . of counsel."[19] For example, *Luis v. United States*[20] held that the defendant's right to spend his money to retain counsel of choice was unconstitutionally impaired where a pretrial asset freeze order included assets that were unrelated to the alleged crimes.

The purpose of the right to counsel "is to guarantee an effective advocate for each criminal defendant, rather than to ensure that a defendant will inexorably be represented by the lawyer whom he prefers."[21] A Sixth Amendment violation of the right to representation by counsel of choice requires automatic reversal of a subsequent conviction, because it is a "structural defect" and not subject to harmless error.[22]

Appropriate governmental interests may restrict the defendant's right to counsel of choice. *United States v. Gonzalez-Lopez*[23] held that there is a distinction between the effective assistance of counsel and the right to representation by counsel of choice.

> The right to select counsel of one's choice . . . has never been derived from the Sixth Amendment's purpose of ensuring a fair trial. It has been regarded as the root meaning of the constitutional guarantee. . . .Where the right to be assisted

---

[17] See § 15.2(D), discussing Critical Stage of a Criminal Prosecution.

[18] Leis v. Flynt, 439 U.S. 438 (1979).

[19] Caplin & Drysdale, Chartered v. United States, 491 U.S. 617, 626 (1989).

[20] 578 U.S. 5 (2016). See United States v. Lillard, 57 F.4th 729 (9th Cir. 2023) (no Sixth Amendment violation when the government seized defendant's funds from his inmate accounts; the government had a property interest in the funds).

[21] Wheat v. United States, 486 U.S. 153, 159 (1988).

[22] *Id.*, at 152.

[23] 548 U.S. 140 (2006).

> by counsel of one's choice is wrongly denied, therefore, it is unnecessary to conduct an ineffectiveness or prejudice inquiry to establish a Sixth Amendment violation. Deprivation of the right is "complete" when the defendant is erroneously prevented from being represented by the lawyer he wants regardless of the quality of the representation he received. To argue otherwise is to confuse the right to counsel of choice—which is the right to a particular lawyer regardless of comparative effectiveness—with the right to effective counsel—which imposes a baseline requirement of competence on whatever lawyer is chosen or appointed.[24]

The governmental interest restricting the choice of retained counsel usually relates to a fundamental feature of the adversary system. Common examples of a court overriding a defendant's right to retain counsel of choice relate to whether the chosen person is a member of the bar,[25] or is not a member of the bar in the particular State.[26] A court may reject representation by a person who is not a current member of the bar, "regardless of his persuasive powers."[27] A trial court may also use its discretion to evaluate the interests of counsel or the parties, as in *Wheat v. United States*,[28] when the Court upheld the trial court's exercise of discretion to prohibit representation by an attorney who also represented other defendants and the defendant wanted to waive having conflict-free counsel.

D. Critical Stage of a Criminal Prosecution

The Sixth Amendment right to appointed counsel applies only to "critical stages" of a criminal prosecution. The definition of a "critical stage" necessarily involves a retrospective inquiry as to how counsel would have benefited the defendant. In *United States v. Wade*,[29] the Court described a critical stage as when "potential substantial prejudice to the defendant's rights inheres in the particular confrontation," and "the ability of counsel [can] help avoid that prejudice."[30] The Court has found the right to counsel to apply to a critical stage such as when a criminal defendant appears at his preliminary hearing, at a guilty-plea hearing, and at a sentencing proceeding.

---

24 United States v. Gonzales-Lopez, 548 U.S. 140, 147–48 (2006).

25 Wheat v. United States, 486 U.S. 153 (1988).

26 Leis v. Flynt, 439 U.S. 438 (1979).

27 *Wheat v. United States*, 486 U.S. at 159.

28 486 U.S. 153 (1988).

29 388 U.S. 218 (1967).

30 United States v. Wade, 388 U.S. 218, 227 (1967).

Most cases applying this test concerned pretrial proceedings. For pretrial proceedings, "critical stage" analysis looks at the significance of the proceeding in relation to the trial and whether the defendant personally participates in that "trial-like confrontation."[31] For example, a person indicted by a grand jury has no right to have his counsel participate in that grand jury's proceedings even though the proceeding follows his status as an "accused," usually after adversary judicial proceedings have begun through his arrest or the filing of a complaint. The Court has held that an "accused" has the right to the assistance of counsel at a preliminary hearing,[32] at some pretrial identification procedures (but not others),[33] and when subjected to police or prosecutor efforts to elicit confessions.[34]

In determining whether a judicial proceeding meets the "critical stage" standard, a court asks whether the proceeding has an adverse or beneficial effect for the disposition of the charge, if counsel had represented the defendant, and whether that effect could have been avoided or regained by counsel later provided. For example, in *Hamilton v. Alabama*,[35] the Court held that an indigent defendant was entitled to appointed counsel at an arraignment because, under State law, defenses not raised then were considered waived. In *White v. Maryland*,[36] the Sixth Amendment right to counsel applied where the defendant was asked to enter a non-binding guilty plea at the initial appearance, but his plea of guilty, though later withdrawn, could still be used against him at trial.

> The Sixth Amendment requires effective assistance of counsel at critical stages of a criminal proceeding. Its protections are not designed simply to protect the trial, even though "counsel's absence [at critical stages] may derogate from the accused's right to a fair trial. . . ." The constitutional guarantee applies to pretrial critical stages that are part of the whole course of a criminal proceeding, a proceeding in which defendants cannot be presumed to make critical decisions without counsel's advice. This is consistent, too, with the rule that defendants have a right to effective assistance of counsel on appeal, even though that cannot in any way be characterized as part of the trial . . . . The precedents also establish that there exists a right to counsel during sentencing in both noncapital . . . and

---

31 Rothgery v. Gillespie County, 554 U.S. 191, 212 n.16 (2008).

32 Coleman v. Alabama, 399 U.S. 1 (1970).

33 See Chapter 14, discussing Identification Procedures.

34 See § 13.2, discussing Sixth Amendment Confession Challenges.

35 368 U.S. 52, 53 (1961).

36 373 U.S. 59, 60 (1963).

capital cases. . . . Even though sentencing does not concern the defendant's guilt or innocence, ineffective assistance of counsel during a sentencing hearing can result in *Strickland* prejudice because "any amount of [additional] jail times has Sixth Amendment significance."[37]

Defining the point at which a defendant becomes an "accused" in a criminal prosecution for Sixth Amendment purposes, *United States v. Gouveia*[38] held that a person is not an accused if he is merely detained by the Government which intends to file criminal charges against him. That person becomes an accused at the time of his initial court appearance. More explicitly, in *Rothgery v. Gillespie County*,[39] the Court held that the defendant's initial appearance was a "critical stage," because its "sufficiently concrete" commitment to prosecute constitutes an "adversary judicial proceeding." *Rothgery* added that a defendant's right to appointed counsel must occur within a reasonable time "to allow for adequate representation at any critical stage before trial, as well as at trial itself."[40]

Coleman v. Alabama[41] discussed why a preliminary hearing is a "critical stage" under the Sixth Amendment. The purpose of this hearing had two primary purposes; (1) the preliminary hearing determines whether the evidence justified charging the defendant with an offense, and (2) the suspect has the right to confront and cross-examine prosecution witnesses at the preliminary hearing. A defense on the merits could be compromised if the defendant had no legal assistance for exploring or preserving the witnesses' testimony. In addition, the Court noted that counsel "can also be influential . . . in making effective arguments for the accused on such matters as . . . bail."[42]

The Sixth Amendment's "criminal prosecution" continues until the end of the trial and includes a right to counsel at sentencing. A criminal prosecution ends when the defendant pursues his first appeal as a matter of right (sometimes known as a first-tier review) from the conviction.[43] The right to appointed counsel also extends to

---

[37] Lafler v. Cooper, 566 U.S. 156, 165 (2012), quoting United States v. Wade, 388 U.S. 218, 226 (1967) and Glover v. United States, 531 U.S. 198, 203 (2001).

[38] 476 U.S. 180 (1984).

[39] 554 U.S. 191 (2008).

[40] Rothgery v. Gillespie County, 554 U.S. 191, 212 (2008).

[41] 399 U.S. 1 (1970).

[42] Coleman v. Alabama, 399 U.S. 1, 9 (1970).

[43] See, e.g., Evitts v. Lucey, 469 U.S. 387 (1985) (Equal Protection requires counsel); Ross v. Moffitt, 417 U.S. 600 (1974) (no counsel for a discretionary second appeal); Douglas v. California, 372 U.S. 353 (1963) (Equal Protection requires counsel). There is no right to appointed counsel for filing a collateral attack. Murray v. Giarratano, 492 U.S. 1 (1989); Pennsylvania v. Finley, 481 U.S. 551 (1987).

the first appeal should defendant later seek to overturn his guilty plea, even if allowing that appeal is discretionary under state law.[44]

When a trial judge places a defendant on probation without fixing the imprisonment that would be imposed if probation were later revoked, the later sentencing decision requires the presence of counsel. In *Mempa v. Rhay*,[45] the Court held that a probation revocation proceeding months after conviction is a part of the "criminal prosecution," thus requiring counsel, because it relates to fixing the defendant's prison term for the crime much like a sentencing immediately after trial.

By contrast, when a judge imposes a prison sentence but suspends the sentence in favor of probation, *Gagnon v. Scarpelli*[46] held that a probation revocation hearing is not part of the criminal prosecution and thus does not require counsel. The only issue presented in such a hearing is whether to revoke probation, and that determination is based on the defendant's conduct after trial rather than the commission of the original offense.

E. Appointed Counsel and Actual Imprisonment

Argersinger v. Hamlin[47] placed limits on *Gideon*. While the trial court in *Argersinger* applied a line between "petty" and "serious" crimes that the Court had adopted in the right-to-jury-trial cases, the Court rejected that distinction in the right-to-counsel setting: (1) "We are by no means convinced that legal and constitutional questions involved in a case that actually leads to imprisonment even for a brief period are any less complex than when a person can be sent off for six months or more,"[48] and (2) "the volume of misdemeanor cases, far greater in number than felony cases, may create an obsession for speedy dispositions, regardless of the fairness of the result."[49]

After *Argersinger*, whether an indigent defendant is entitled to appointed counsel is dependent upon whether he is sentenced to serve at least a "day in jail" in his misdemeanor case. If he does, he has a right counsel; if he does not, there is no such right. The Court suggests that if there is any chance that the judge is going to sentence the defendant to at least a day in jail before hearing the facts, counsel should be appointed, i.e., judges should resolve any doubts about

---

[44] See Halbert v. Michigan, 545 U.S. 605 (2005) (defendant pled nolo contendere to a felony, and later appealed his conviction, but the appellate court refused to appoint counsel for his first appeal; Court held that he was denied due process).

[45] 389 U.S. 128 (1967).

[46] 411 U.S. 778 (1973) (Due Process).

[47] 407 U.S. 25 (1972).

[48] Argersinger v. Hamlin, 407 U.S. 25, 33 (1972).

[49] *Id.*, at 34.

imprisonment in favor of the indigent defendant and appoint counsel. If the judge makes the wrong choice and denies an indigent's request for counsel, imprisonment is not a possibility after *Argersinger* if the facts turn out to be more serious than the judge previously believed. Specifically, *Argersinger* held that "absent a knowing and voluntary waiver, no person may be imprisoned for any offense, whether classified as petty, misdemeanor, or felony, unless he was represented by counsel at trial."[50] If an indigent defendant were to be imprisoned, the judge must ensure that the defendant was offered appointed counsel but waived that right.

By focusing on the result of a trial to activate the right to counsel before trial, *Argersinger* obviously created a problem of implementation. How should a judge decide eligibility for counsel, if it is to be based on a predetermination of a trial's result? Judges should not attempt to decide which defendants would be sent to jail if found guilty. For example, before trial the judge should not know about the defendant's prior record until guilt has been found. The resolution should be comparable to the right-to-jury trial cases: appoint counsel for all indigents if imprisonment is an authorized or permissible sentence, even if rarely imposed. Counsel is essential to a fair trial; most defendants are incapable of preparing a legal defense and the judge cannot also be an advocate for the defendant.

In *Scott v. Illinois*,[51] the defendant was convicted of shoplifting with a maximum penalty of one year of imprisonment and a $500 fine, but he actually was not sentenced to prison and was fined only $50. The Court concluded that the "federal constitution does not require a State trial court to appoint counsel for a criminal defendant such as [Scott]."[52] Because *Argersinger* had relied on the "conclusion that incarceration was so severe a sanction that it should not be imposed . . . unless an indigent has been offered appointed counsel," it had "delimit[ed] the constitutional right to appointed counsel in State criminal proceedings."[53]

"The central premise of *Argersinger*—that actual imprisonment is a penalty different in kind from or the mere threat of imprisonment"—was not altered by the fact that the misdemeanor in *Scott* had a *potential* penalty in excess of the petty offense category of a six-month maximum incarceration. The key for the right to counsel on any misdemeanor charge is whether the trial court imposes a sentence of even one day's imprisonment after conviction.

---

50 *Id.*, at 37.

51 440 U.S. 367 (1979).

52 Scott v. Illinois, 440 U.S. 367, 369 (1979).

53 *Id.*, at 373.

In *Nichols v. United States*,[54] the Court held that an uncounseled misdemeanor conviction that was valid under *Scott* (because no term of incarceration was imposed) nevertheless could be used to enhance an actual imprisonment sentence for a later offense. Because the uncounseled misdemeanor conviction itself was valid, a sentencing court can consider that conviction later, just like other facets of a defendant's criminal record that are used to assess the appropriate sentence.

Alabama v. Shelton held that the Sixth Amendment does not allow later activation of a suspended sentence that was imposed along with probation in a proceeding where the defendant had no counsel. The Court characterized the suspended sentence as an incarceration "actually imposed," i.e., the incarceration that would result after a probation revocation hearing would be from the underlying offense rather than from the later probation violation. In other words,

> a suspended sentence that may "end up in the actual deprivation of a person's liberty" may not be imposed unless the defendant was accorded "the guiding hand of counsel" in the prosecution for the crime charged.[55]

Courts probably can create probation-only sentences for defendants and thus shift incarceration decisions (and the accompanying right to counsel) to later probation revocation hearings after which a court decides whether incarceration is appropriate.

§ 15.3 Indigency for Appointed Counsel and Other Matters

A. Indigent Defendants

If a defendant requests court-appointed counsel, the court may question the defendant directly or examine an affidavit of poverty which is compiled by a pretrial release officer based on answers from the defendant. Or, the judge may simply ask the defendant whether the information in the affidavit is accurate, reminding the defendant about the penalties for perjury as a result of making false statements in the affidavit. If the defendant qualifies as financially unable to hire counsel, the court appoints counsel.

The exact point on the economic scale at which a defendant becomes indigent and therefore entitled to appointed counsel is not subject to precise measurement. Indigency is determined for each individual in the light of all pertinent circumstances, according to

---

54 511 U.S. 738 (1994).

55 535 U.S. 654, 658 (2002).

State statutes,[56] court rules, and administrative regulations. These provisions define indigency as the "financial inability to obtain counsel," sometimes with an added phrase such as "without substantial hardship for the defendant or the defendant's family."

The form used in an affidavit of indigency asks about issues such as current and anticipated sources of income, assets (especially those that can be quickly sold), fixed expenses, employment, dependents, debt, credit score, prior charges, and the current charges. The trial court's knowledge about the customary fees charged for different crimes is useful to an informed decision, as is the defendant informing the court about whether he has looked for an attorney but could not afford the quoted fee. Examining the form provides the trial court with guidance about how to exercise its discretion for deciding whether to appoint counsel. Because the indigency decision occurs early in the case, the court usually is unable to explore other relevant factors, such as the complexity of the case.

Most States try to avoid forcing the defendant to choose between affording pretrial release and retaining an attorney. The indigency decision may occur after deducting the likely cost of posting cash for pretrial release from the defendant's disposable assets, and making the appointed-counsel decision based on that net remainder. In many States, the trial court defers to the decision of the Public Defender's office on the indigency issue.

Indigent defendants do not have the right to choose which defense attorney will be appointed to represent the defendant,[57] because a defendant has no right to a "meaningful attorney-client relationship" with appointed counsel. *Morris v. Slappy*[58] recognized a trial court's broad discretion to compel a substitution of counsel when the delay for appointed counsel to become available would disrupt the trial court's schedule. There, the Public Defender assigned to the case initially was hospitalized for emergency surgery. The Court held that the Sixth Amendment does not guarantee a meaningful attorney-client relationship. The Court also stressed the "broad discretion that must be granted trial courts on matters of continuance."[59]

A judge may use discretion to appoint a particular attorney desired by an indigent defendant, *if* (1) that attorney is available, (2) he is willing to accept the appointment, and (3) he is agreeable to accepting the (typically low) compensation made available for

---

56 See, e.g., 18 U.S.C. § 3006(A); Ky.Rev.Stat. § 31.120.

57 Wheat v. United States, 486 U.S. 153 (1988).

58 Morris v. Slappy, 461 U.S. 1 (1983).

59 *Id.*, at 11.

providing such appointed services. When a defendant facing a death sentence requests that his appointed counsel be replaced, the correct standard is for the trial court to use its discretion and determine whether the "interests of justice" justify the request.[60]

B. Transcripts for Indigents

In *Griffin v. Illinois*[61] the defendant's right to an appeal of his conviction was dependent on his ability to submit a trial record that was difficult to assemble in the absence of a stenographic transcript. The indigent defendant unsuccessfully requested the State to furnish a free transcript so that he could prepare his appeal. The Court held that the State's refusal denied him Due Process and Equal Protection. While noting that the defendant had no constitutional right to a transcript, the State could not condition his exercise of his right of appeal on a basis that discriminated against him based upon his indigency.

> In criminal trials a State can no more discriminate on account of poverty than on account of religion, race, or color [since] the ability to pay costs in advance bears no rational relationship to defendant's guilt or innocence and could not be used as an excuse to deprive a defendant of a fair trial. . . . There can be no equal justice where the kind of trial a man gets depends on the amount of money he has.[62]

This "*Griffin* principle" also applies to requests for a trial transcript to be used (1) in a collateral attack upon a conviction,[63] (2) in a habeas proceeding to be used on appeal from a denial of habeas relief,[64] (3) in a habeas proceeding to be used in filing a second habeas petition,[65] and (4) in preparing for trial.[66]

Griffin noted that a transcript need not be provided if the State can find other ways to provide "adequate and effective appellate review to indigent defendants."[67] Transcripts for use on appeal are generally required where they are the preferable means of presenting a claim of the type urged by the indigent defendant.[68] Courts will look more closely at alternatives, however, where a transcript is no longer available through no fault of the Government. For example, in

---

60 Martel v. Clair, 565 U.S. 648 (2012).

61 351 U.S. 12 (1956).

62 Griffin v. Illinois, 351 U.S. 12, 17–18, 19 (1956).

63 United States v. MacCollom, 426 U.S. 317 (1976).

64 Long v. District Court, 385 U.S. 192 (1966).

65 Gardner v. California, 393 U.S. 367 (1969).

66 Roberts v. LaVallee, 389 U.S. 40 (1967).

67 Griffin v. Illinois, 351 U.S. 12, 20 (1956).

68 See, e.g., Long v. District Court, 385 U.S. 192 (1966).

Norvall v. Illinois,[69] where no trial transcript was available, the State may deny relief to defendants who had counsel at the time of trial and who presumably had counsel's continuing services for purposes of an appeal, but failed to pursue an appeal.

Courts have not discounted alternatives when the transcript was desired for use in preparing for trial. In *Britt v. North Carolina*,[70] the Court upheld a State court's refusal to grant a defendant a transcript of his first trial that had ended in a mistrial, noting that there was available "an informal alternative which appears to be substantially equivalent."[71]

Griffin also applies to the denial of remedies to indigent defendants who cannot afford filing fees for appeals or post-conviction proceedings. In *Burns v. Ohio*,[72] the refusal to permit an indigent defendant to file a motion for permission to appeal to a State appellate court due to his inability to pay docket and filing fees violated Due Process and Equal Protection. And in *Smith v. Bennett*,[73] a State that made the writ of habeas corpus available only to prisoners who could pay the necessary filing fees violated Equal Protection by denying the writ to indigent prisoners.

C. Expert Witnesses for Indigents

When an indigent defendant makes a preliminary showing of a need for the assistance of an expert, Due Process requires that the Government provide access to the expert's assistance. In *Ake v. Oklahoma*,[74] the Court held that an indigent must have the "basic tools" necessary to present a defense that would be "seriously in question" at trial. The Court applied its three-part Due Process test from *Mathews v. Eldridge*[75] to examine the (1) defendant's interest in presenting a workable defense, (2) the State's fiscal interest as affected by the need for a fair and accurate process, and (3) the role of the witness in presenting the defense.[76]

The State's failure in *Ake* to heed a "preliminary showing" that the defendant needed access to a psychiatrist's assistance about his sanity at the time of the offense to prove a significant issue at trial constituted reversible error.

---

69 373 U.S. 420 (1963).

70 404 U.S. 226 (1971).

71 Britt v. North Carolina, 404 U.S. 226, 230 (1971).

72 360 U.S. 252 (1959).

73 365 U.S. 708 (1961).

74 470 U.S. 68 (1985).

75 424 U.S. 319 (1976).

76 Ake v. Oklahoma, 470 U.S. 68, 78–79 (1985).

> [W]ithout the assistance of a psychiatrist to conduct a professional examination on issues relevant to the defense, to help determine whether the insanity defense is viable, to present testimony, and to assist in preparing the cross-examination of a State's psychiatric witnesses, the risk of an inaccurate resolution of sanity issues is extremely high. With such assistance, the defendant is fairly able to present at least enough information to the jury, in a meaningful manner, as to permit it to make a sensible determination.[77]

However, the Court minimized what it required of the State to satisfy Due Process. The State's obligation was to provide the assistance of a competent psychiatrist of its *own* choosing; the defendant's Due Process rights did not include the ability "to choose a psychiatrist of his personal liking or to receive funds to hire his own."[78]

McWilliams v. Dunn,[79] held that *Ake* "requires more than just an examination; it requires that the State provide the defense with 'access to a competent psychiatrist who will conduct an appropriate *examination* and assist in *evaluation*, *preparation*, and *presentation* of the defense.' "[80] Even though the defendant was able to procure State-paid neuropsychological testing before sentencing, *Ake* was violated because the trial court rejected a request for a second expert to interpret the test, assist with preparing a defense strategy, and testify at trial.

D. Indigent Criminal Appeals

When a defendant appeals his conviction, his appointed counsel may encounter the ethical obligation not to assert nonfrivolous claims. In *Anders v. California*,[81] the Court attempted to resolve the tension between defense counsel's ethical obligation to assert only nonfrivolous claims and the indigent defendant's constitutional right to appointed counsel on the first appeal of right.[82] The State's procedure permitted appointed counsel to withdraw from representation, after reviewing the record and "conscientiously concluding . . . that there are no meritorious grounds for appeal," and then consulting with the defendant.

---

77 *Id.*, at 82.

78 *Id.*, at 83.

79 582 U.S. 183 (2017).

80 McWilliams v. Dunn, 582 U.S. 183 (2017) (emphasis in original).

81 386 U.S. 738 (1967).

82 Pennsylvania v. Finley, 481 U.S. 551 (1987) disallowed the *Anders* standard in State post-conviction proceedings, because there was no constitutional right to appointed counsel in those proceedings.

In *Anders*, appointed counsel sent a conclusory "no merit" letter to the State appellate court, which reviewed the record, and considered any contrary statement filed by the defendant. When the State court agreed with defense counsel's conclusion, the defendant's appeal went forward without other counsel. The Court agreed that defendant's right to appointed counsel did not preclude withdrawal, but it concluded that the California procedure undermined the defendant's constitutional right to counsel.

The *Anders* Court set up a "framework" for allowing appointed counsel to withdraw from representing an indigent appellant: (1) after a "conscientious examination" of the appeal, counsel must determine that the appeal is "wholly frivolous" and "so advise the court and request permission to withdraw"; (2) "that request must be accompanied by a brief referring to anything in the record that might arguably support the appeal"; (3) "a copy of counsel's brief should be furnished the indigent [defendant] and time allowed him to raise any points that he chooses"; and (4) the appellate court, "after a full examination of all the proceedings," must find that "the case is wholly frivolous."[83]

McCoy v. Court of Appeals of Wisconsin[84] held that a variation of the *Anders* procedure is acceptable when appointed appellate counsel presents a statement of the strongest arguments for the client's contentions, plus an explanation of the contrary authority that persuaded counsel to conclude that defendant's contentions were frivolous. Requiring counsel to cite contrary authority provides a safeguard against attorneys concluding that an appeal is frivolous without diligent research, i.e., "no constitutional deprivation occurs when the attorney explains the basis for that conclusion."[85]

In *Smith v. Robbins*,[86] the Court upheld a California withdrawal procedure that dispensed entirely with substantive briefing by appointed appellate counsel. After concluding that the appeal was frivolous, counsel filed a brief that "summarizes the procedural and factual history of the case with citations of the record," "attests that he has reviewed the record, explained his evaluation of the case to his client, provided the client with a copy of the brief, and informed the client of his right to file a *pro se* supplemental brief."[87] Counsel asked the appellate court to examine the record for arguable issues. The appellate court next examined the entire record, and affirmed if

---

83 Anders v. California, 386 U.S. 738, 744 (1967).

84 486 U.S. 429 (1988).

85 McCoy v. Court of Appeals of Wisconsin, 486 U.S. 429, 443 (1988).

86 528 U.S. 259 (2000).

87 Smith v. Robbins, 528 U.S. 259, 265 (2000).

the appeal was frivolous, but directed further briefing for any nonfrivolous issue.

Commenting that *Anders* set up a "prophylactic framework" for withdrawal, not as a constitutional mandate but as an example of "one method of satisfying the requirements of the Constitution for indigent criminal appeals,"[88] the Court upheld this procedure that "reasonably ensures that an indigent's appeal will be resolved in a way that is related to the merit of the appeal."[89] After reviewing this California procedure, the Court concluded that it did not contain the problems identified in *Anders* that deprived the indigent appellant of the fair opportunity to appeal.

When *Anders* applies, but an appellate court allows withdrawal without complying with *Anders*'s prerequisites, the mandatory remedy is to require a new appeal. *Penson v. Ohio*[90] held that applying harmless error analysis instead of a new appeal as a "remedy" would "render meaningless" the *Anders* protections. Suppose that counsel used an acceptable State procedure for asserting the frivolous nature of an appeal, but the defendant claimed in a later collateral attack that counsel was incompetent in failing to recognize a non-frivolous issue. *Smith v. Robbins* held that the defendant must meet the two-pronged standard of a traditional *Strickland* ineffective assistance claim,[91] including a showing of deficient performance and prejudice to the defendant.

§ 15.4 Effective Assistance of Counsel

The right to effective assistance of counsel applies to both a criminal trial and to guilty pleas, sentencing, and a first appeal of right, i.e., all proceedings for which there is a right to counsel.[92] The standard of review applied to all types of ineffectiveness claims does not vary with the status of counsel as retained or appointed.[93] Whether a defendant has a right to effective assistance of counsel during State post-conviction proceedings is still an open question.[94] To gain relief, the defendant must prove that counsel's defective performance was likely to have caused significant prejudice to the

---

88 *Id.*, at 276.

89 *Id.*, at 278.

90 488 U.S. 75 (1988).

91 See § 15.4, discussing Effective Assistance of Counsel.

92 United States v. Cronic, 466 U.S. 648, 654 (1984).

93 Cuyler v. Sullivan, 446 U.S. 335 (1980).

94 Martinez v. Ryan, 566 U.S. 1 (2012).

defendant's case.[95] The remedy for ineffective assistance is automatic reversal of the defendant's conviction.

A. *Per Se* Ineffective Counsel

Until 1984, the Court had not articulated an ineffective assistance of counsel standard that applied beyond the facts of the case before it. In *Powell v. Alabama*,[96] the Court stated that the Sixth Amendment right to counsel included the right to the effective assistance of counsel. A defendant whose counsel was unable to provide effective representation in no better off than a defendant who had no counsel at all. Then, more than fifty years later, the Court decided two major ineffective assistance of counsel cases on the same day, *United States v. Cronic*[97] and *Strickland v. Washington*.[98]

In *Cronic*, after counsel's appointment, the defendant's trial-inexperienced, young, real estate attorney had only twenty-five days to prepare a complicated case that the prosecution had investigated for four and one-half years and which involved thousands of documents. *Cronic* raised the issue of *per se* ineffectiveness, when a defendant claims that his defense counsel was guilty of "extrinsic ineffectiveness," i.e., some factor or factors *extrinsic* to counsel's actual performance created a permissible inference of Sixth Amendment ineffectiveness. *Cronic* created criteria for evaluating when claims of extrinsic ineffectiveness establish ineffective assistance of counsel, e.g., counsel's age, inexperience overall or in criminal cases, disability, personal or emotional problems, alcoholism or substance abuse problems, problems with the law, insufficient preparation time, or disciplinary issues with the Bar.

The Court refused either to make an inference of ineffective assistance *or* to accept a hypothetical basis for finding ineffectiveness, concluding that ordinarily a defendant can "make out a claim of ineffective assistance only by pointing to specific errors made by trial counsel."[99] The Court's past cases provided three examples of when a presumption of ineffectiveness is appropriate:

> (1) "counsel was either totally absent or prevented from assisting the accused during a critical stage of the proceeding," e.g., the trial court had unconstitutionally refused to appoint counsel or had restricted counsel's

---

95 See *United States v. Cronic*, 466 U.S. at 662. There may be surrounding circumstances so likely to prejudice the accused that ineffectiveness of counsel may be presumed.

96 287 U.S. 45 (1932).

97 466 U.S. 648 (1984).

98 466 U.S. 668 (1984).

99 United States v. Cronic, 466 U.S. 648, 666 (1984).

> assistance; (2) "if counsel entirely fails to subject the prosecution's case to meaningful adversarial testing;" and (3) "occasions when, although counsel is available to assist the accused during trial, the likelihood that any lawyer, even a fully competent one, could provide effective assistance is so small that a presumption of prejudice is appropriate without inquiry into the actual conduct of the trial."[100]

The Court commented that every attorney has a "first jury trial," twenty-five days is adequate preparation time, and real estate experience in a white-collar crime trial may be "useful."[101] These criteria made it almost impossible for a criminal defendant to make a successful claim.

> The right to effective assistance is the right of the accused to require the prosecution's case to survive the crucible of meaningful adversary testing. When a true adversarial criminal trial has been conducted—even if defense counsel may have made demonstrable errors—the kind of testing envisioned by the Sixth Amendment has occurred. The critical question therefore is whether counsel's performance was so deficient that the process "lost its character as a confrontation between adversaries," producing an "actual breakdown of the adversary process."[102]

However, *Cronic* recognized exceptions to the general rule that ineffectiveness cannot ordinarily be established extrinsically. Besides a complete denial of counsel at a critical stage of the trial, "if counsel entirely fails to subject the prosecution's case to a meaningful adversarial testing, then there has been a denial of Sixth Amendment rights that makes the adversary process itself presumptively unreliable."[103] Despite the exceptions, appellate courts rarely reverse a conviction for extrinsic ineffectiveness. For example, extrinsic ineffectiveness did not exist when defense counsel conceded his client's guilt of the murder with which he was charged. A "concession of . . . guilt does not rank as a 'fail[ure] to function in any meaningful sense as the Government's adversary.' "[104]

Allegations of a defense counsel's failures at specific points (e.g., failure to introduce mitigating evidence, waiver of closing argument) may raise issues of *actual* ineffectiveness under *Strickland*

---

100 *Id.*, at 659, 660 n.25.

101 *Id.*, at 665.

102 *Id.*, at 654–58.

103 *Id.*, at 659.

104 Florida v. Nixon, 543 U.S. 175, 190 (2004).

(discussed in the next section), but not under *Cronic*. Similarly, a trial court's order denying a defendant the opportunity to consult with his attorney during a fifteen-minute recess taken while the defendant was continuing to testify was not extrinsic ineffective assistance because the order did not amount to "[a]ctual or constructive denial of the assistance of counsel altogether."[105]

B. Strickland v. Washington

In *Strickland v. Washington*,[106] the Court established criteria for ineffective assistance of counsel when claims of *actual* episodes of ineffectiveness are alleged. Counsel's action or inaction as to a particular matter must be judged both in the context of his total representation (at the time of representation) and the strength of the Government's evidence. In other words, the effectiveness of the representation is based on what defense counsel encountered at the time, rather than evaluating in retrospect what counsel should have done.

Defendant ignored his counsel's advice, and pleaded guilty to all offenses for which he was indicted, including three counts of first-degree murder. During his guilty-plea colloquy, in which he "accepted responsibility for the crimes," the trial judge told defendant that he respected people like the defendant who admitted their criminal responsibility "but that he was making no statement at all about his likely sentencing decision." The trial judge later sentenced the defendant to death at his capital sentencing hearing.

Defense counsel admitted to having done little preparation for the capital sentencing hearing: his client discussed his background, and he spoke by phone with defendant's wife and mother. He did not otherwise seek out character witnesses or request a psychiatric examination, because the conversations with his client gave no indication that the defendant had psychological problems. He also decided to rely on the plea colloquy for evidence about the defendant's background and his claim of emotional stress, in order to prevent the prosecutor from cross-examining defendant at a sentencing hearing.

"Counsel also excluded from the sentencing hearing other evidence he thought was potentially damaging,"[107] e.g., he did not request preparation of a presentence report which would have included his client's criminal history. On the basis of the record, the Court concluded that the defendant had *not* proved ineffective assistance of counsel. Despite the holding, the court did refer to a

---

105 Perry v. Leake, 488 U.S. 272, 280 (1989), quoting *Strickland v. Washington*, 466 U.S. at 692.

106 *Id.*

107 Strickland v. Washington, 466 U.S. 668, 673 (1984).

defense counsel's "duties to consult with the defendant on important decisions and to keep the defendant informed in the course of the prosecution."[108]

> When a convicted defendant complains of the ineffectiveness of counsel's assistance, the defendant must show that counsel's representation fell below an objective standard of reasonableness.
>
> More specific guidelines are not appropriate. The Sixth Amendment refers simply to "counsel," not specifying particular requirements of effective assistance. It relies instead on the legal profession's maintenance of standards sufficient to justify the law's presumption that counsel will fulfill the role in the adversary process that the Amendment envisions. The proper measure of attorney performance remains simply reasonableness under prevailing professional norms.[109]

The goal of the Sixth Amendment right to counsel is to provide the "basic elements of a fair trial." A key component of that fair trial is an adversarial system of litigation. The assistance of counsel guarantee "envisions counsel playing a role that is critical to the ability of the adversarial system to produce just results."[110] The " 'very premise of our adversary system . . . is that partisan advocacy on both sides of a case will best promote the ultimate objective that the guilty be convicted and the innocent go free.' " That " 'very premise' . . . underlies and gives meaning to the Sixth Amendment."[111] "The benchmark for judging any claim of ineffectiveness must be whether counsel's conduct so undermined the proper functioning of the adversarial process that the trial cannot be relied on as having produced a just result."[112]

Justice Marshall was the lone dissenter, objecting to the prejudice standard as unworkable. To him, a showing of deficient performance should suffice for a Sixth Amendment violation.

> [I]t is often very difficult to tell whether a defendant convicted after a trial in which he was ineffectively represented would have fared better if his lawyer had been competent. . . . The difficulties of estimating prejudice after the fact are exacerbated by the possibility that evidence of

---

108 *Id.*, at 688.

109 *Id.*, at 687–88.

110 *Id.*, at 685.

111 *United States v. Cronic*, 466 U.S. at 655–56.

112 *Strickland v. Washington*, 466 U.S. at 685–86.

> injury to the defendant may be missing from the record precisely because of the incompetence of defense counsel.[113]

The Court's standard involves a fact-sensitive analysis that measures the quality and effect of counsel's representation under the circumstances of the case. The constitutional standard for finding ineffective assistance of counsel requires a finding of an error in counsel's performance, and prejudice resulting from that error which had an adverse effect on the outcome. The definition of prejudice is: but for counsel's unprofessional errors, a reasonable probability exists that the result of the proceeding would have been different or that the defendant would have chosen a different course of action. The two parts of the test are independent of one another, but a defendant must show *both* that his defense counsel performed deficiently *and* that the deficient performance actually prejudiced his defense.

C. Effective Assistance of Appointed Counsel

Consistent with *Gideon*, appointed counsel has the same duty of effectiveness as retained counsel.[114]

> A proper respect for the Sixth Amendment disarms petitioner's contention that defendants who retain their own lawyers are entitled to less protection than defendants for whom the State appoints counsel. We may assume with confidence that most counsel, whether retained or appointed, will protect the rights of an accused. But experience teaches that, in some cases, retained counsel will not provide adequate representation. The vital guarantee of the Sixth Amendment would stand for little if the often uninformed decision to retain a particular lawyer could reduce or forfeit the defendant's entitlement to constitutional protection. Since the State's conduct of a criminal trial itself implicates the State in the defendant's conviction, we see no basis for drawing a distinction between retained and appointed counsel that would deny equal justice to defendants who must choose their own lawyers.[115]

A defense lawyer representing an indigent on appeal from a criminal conviction does not have a constitutional duty to raise every nonfrivolous issue requested by the defendant.[116] In *Pennsylvania v.*

---

113 *Id.*, at 711.

114 Cuyler v. Sullivan, 446 U.S. 335 (1980).

115 *Id.*, at 344–45.

116 Jones v. Barnes, 463 U.S. 745 (1983).

Finley,[117] the Court held that, because a prisoner has no Equal Protection or Due Process right to appointed counsel in a post-conviction proceeding, he had no constitutional right to insist on an *Anders* procedure for withdrawal of appointed counsel when that attorney found the case to be frivolous on direct appeal.

McCoy v. Court of Appeals of Wisconsin, Dist. 1,[118] contains an extensive discussion of procedures to be followed in the event that appointed counsel determines to withdraw in an appellate court. In *Penson v. Ohio*,[119] the Court found reversible error when an appellate court denied an appointed counsel's motion to withdraw. The court had no basis for determining whether counsel had searched carefully for arguable error, it should have made its own examination of the record before acting on the motion, and it failed to appoint new counsel after deciding that "several arguable claims" that were in the record.

D. Strategic Decisions

Decisions within the client's control are simply described as involving "fundamental rights," while those within the lawyer's control are said to involve matters requiring the "superior ability of trained counsel" in assessing "strategy." In *Harrington v. Richter*,[120] the failure to present certain forensic evidence did not constitute ineffective assistance of counsel because the Court instead viewed it as a strategic decision. A competent attorney may choose a strategy that did not require using expert witnesses because "counsel is entitled to balance limited resources in accord with effective trial tactics and strategies." Although the strategy did not work out as hoped, it was not an unreasonable or unprofessional strategy, viewed objectively. A reviewing court, in determining whether counsel was ineffective, is highly deferential in scrutinizing counsel's performance.

> It is all too tempting for a defendant to second-guess counsel's assistance after conviction or adverse sentence, and it is all too easy for a court, examining counsel's defense after it has proved unsuccessful, to conclude that a particular act or omission of counsel was unreasonable. A fair assessment of attorney performance requires that every effort be made to eliminate the distorting effects of hindsight, to reconstruct the circumstances of counsel's challenged conduct, and to evaluate the conduct from

---

117 481 U.S. 551 (1987).

118 486 U.S. 429 (1988).

119 488 U.S. 75, 76 (1988).

120 562 U.S. 86 (2011).

> counsel's perspective at the time. Because of the difficulties inherent in making the evaluation, a court must indulge a strong presumption that counsel's conduct falls within the wide range of reasonable professional assistance; that is, the defendant must overcome the presumption that, under the circumstances, the challenged action "might be considered sound trial strategy." There are countless ways to provide effective assistance in any given case. Even the best criminal defense attorneys would not defend a particular client in the same way.[121]

However, the Court cautioned about giving too much importance to counsel's inability to describe the precise process that drove his strategic decisions. Trial courts should not require that

> counsel confirm every aspect of the strategic basis for his or her actions. There is a "strong presumption" that counsel's attention to certain issues to the exclusion of others reflects trial tactics rather than "sheer neglect." After an adverse verdict at trial even the most experienced counsel may find it difficult to resist asking whether a different strategy might have been better, and, in the course of that reflection, to magnify their own responsibility for an unfavorable outcome. *Strickland,* however, calls for an inquiry into the objective reasonableness of counsel's performance, not counsel's subjective state of mind.[122]

The Court has held or stated in dicta that counsel (not the defendant) has the ultimate decision regarding whether or not to advocate the following: barring prosecution use of unconstitutionally obtained evidence,[123] obtaining dismissal of an indictment on the ground of racial discrimination in the selection of the grand jury,[124] challenging an improper jury instruction,[125] including a particular nonfrivolous claim among the issues briefed and argued on appeal,[126] foregoing cross-examination, calling a possible witness (other than defendant) to testify, providing discovery to the prosecution (even where the failure to do so risks possible sanctions of exclusion),[127] and being tried within the 180-day time period specified in the Interstate Agreement on Detainers.[128] In evaluating whether defense counsel

---

121 *Strickland v. Washington*, 466 U.S. at 689–90.

122 Harrington v. Richter, 562 U.S. 86, 109–10 (2011).

123 Wainwright v. Sykes, 433 U.S. 72 (1977).

124 Tollett v. Henderson, 411 U.S. 258 (1973).

125 Engle v. Isaac, 456 U.S. 107 (1982).

126 Jones v. Barnes, 463 U.S. 745 (1983).

127 Taylor v. Illinois, 484 U.S. 400 (1988).

128 New York v. Hill, 528 U.S. 110 (2000).

has discharged this duty, the trial court must determine whether the decision was tactical or strategic. If the decision was tactical or strategic, counsel's decision is presumed correct, and the inquiry ends.

In addition to decisions about pleading guilty,[129] the "accused has the ultimate authority to make certain fundamental decisions regarding the case, as to whether to waive a jury, testify in his own behalf, or take an appeal."[130] For example, in *Garza v. Idaho*,[131] when defense counsel refused his client's request to appeal his conviction after he had waived his appeal rights as part of a guilty plea agreement, counsel rendered deficient performance by not filing a notice of appeal in light of the client's clear requests.

In *Florida v. Nixon*,[132] the Court held that a capital client's counsel's performance was not presumptively deficient by failing to obtain the client's express approval of a strategy to concede guilt and focus instead on urging mercy during the penalty phase.

> [I]n a capital case, counsel must consider in conjunction both the guilt and penalty phases in determining how best to proceed. When counsel informs the defendant of the strategy counsel believes to be in the defendant's best interest and the defendant is unresponsive, counsel's strategic choice is not impeded by any blanket rule demanding the defendant's explicit consent. Instead, if counsel's strategy, given the evidence bearing on the defendant's guilt, satisfies the *Strickland* standard, that is the end of the matter. . .[133]

McCoy v. Louisiana[134] stated in a capital case that "[t]he Sixth Amendment guarantees a defendant the right to choose the objective of his defense and to insist that his counsel refrain from admitting guilt, even when counsel's experienced-based view is that confessing guilt offers the defendant the best chance to avoid the death penalty." Thus, "when a client makes it plain that the objective of 'his defense' is to maintain innocence of the charged criminal acts and pursue an acquittal, his lawyer must abide by that objective and may not override it by conceding guilt."[135]

---

129 Brookhart v. Janis, 384 U.S. 1 (1966) (counsel cannot enter guilty plea inconsistent with client's express desire).

130 Jones v. Barnes, 463 U.S. 745, 751 (1983).

131 586 U.S. 232 (2019).

132 543 U.S. 175 (2004).

133 Florida v. Nixon, 543 U.S. 175, 192 (2004).

134 584 U.S. 414 (2018).

135 McCoy v. Louisiana, 584 U.S. 414 (2018).

E. Deficient Counsel Performance

Strickland rejected the use of a checklist to measure the competency of counsel.

> [T]he performance inquiry must be whether counsel's assistance was reasonable considering all the circumstances... No particular set of detailed rules for counsel's conduct can satisfactorily take account of the variety of circumstances faced by defense counsel or the range of legitimate decisions regarding how best to represent a criminal defendant. Any such set of rules would interfere with the constitutionally protected independence of counsel and restrict the wide latitude counsel must have in making tactical decisions... [T]he purpose of the effective assistance guarantee of the Sixth Amendment is not to improve the quality of legal representation, although that is a goal of considerable importance to the legal system. The purpose is simply to ensure that criminal defendants receive a fair trial.[136]

A critical performance factor focuses on defense counsel's challenged conduct on the facts of the particular case, viewed as of the time of counsel's conduct. Courts find incompetency far more readily where there has been an abdication rather than an exercise of professional judgment, i.e., a lack of diligence is more likely to establish deficient performance. In *Maryland v. Kulbicki*,[137] for example, because there was no reason for counsel to have questioned the credibility of ballistics evidence at the time of trial, defense counsel was not ineffective for having failed to question that evidence even though later it was viewed as questionable. The crucial factor is how far a court is willing to go in assuming that counsel's actions are strategic, in accord with a general presumption of competence. The record should substantiate that counsel's handling of the case was reasonably calculated to be in the defendant's best interest.

In *Hinton v. Alabama*,[138] defense counsel's mistaken belief that State law allowed him to request and receive limited funding for expert witnesses was "a quintessential example of unreasonable performance." His ignorance on the point of law was both fundamental to the case and could have been resolved with a cursory investigation into the relevant statutes. The Court remanded the case for a determination of whether the errors had prejudiced the

136 *Strickland v. Washington*, 466 U.S. at 688–89.

137 577 U.S. 1 (2015).

138 571 U.S. 263 (2014).

outcome of the trial. In *Evitts v. Lucey*,[139] counsel failed to follow a simple court rule about filing a statement of appeal with the appellate brief. The drastic consequences from that failure required a finding of ineffective assistance of counsel.

Another example of deficient performance was *Wiggins v. Smith*,[140] when defense counsel in a capital case decided not to expand the penalty phase investigation beyond presentence investigation and social services reports. The Court held that his performance was below standard practices and prevailing professional norms in the State at the time of the trial. Standard practice at that time in Maryland included preparation of a social history report. Although funds existed to retain a forensic social worker, a report was not commissioned. Because counsel knew from the social services report about the defendant's alcoholic mother and his problems in foster care, the decision to cease investigating was unreasonable.[141]

Wiggins found that a reasonably competent attorney would have known that those leads would assist in making an informed choice among possible defenses. In addition, counsel had discovered nothing to suggest that mitigation evidence would have been counterproductive or that further investigation would have been fruitless. This distinguished the case from precedents in which this Court had found limited investigations into mitigating evidence to be reasonable. The record showed that counsel's failure to investigate thoroughly resulted from inattention, not a strategic judgment.

Similarly, in *Rompilla v. Beard*,[142] trial counsel failed to present mitigating evidence during the penalty phase about the defendant's childhood, mental capacity and health, and alcoholism. The Court, noting that the case called for "specific application of the standard of reasonable competence required on the part of defense counsel by the Sixth Amendment," held that

> even when a capital defendant's family members and the defendant himself have suggested that no mitigating evidence is available, his lawyer is bound to make reasonable efforts to obtain and review material that

---

[139] 469 U.S. 387 (1985).

[140] 539 U.S. 510 (2009).

[141] Cullen v. Pinholster, 563 U.S. 170 (2003) was another case where the Court used state practices and norms as reference points instead of a national consensus. The Court discussed the "family sympathy: mitigation defense as it was "known to the defense bar in California at the time and had been used by other attorneys."

[142] 545 U.S. 374 (2005).

counsel knows the prosecution will probably rely on as evidence of aggravation at the sentencing phase of trial.[143]

An additional example of deficient performance is *Padilla v. Kentucky*.[144] Defendant was a lawful permanent resident in the United States for more than 40 years when he pled guilty to drug trafficking charges and faced deportation. He later claimed that his lawyer told him not to worry about deportation because he had lived in the United States for so long, and he did not advise him about the possibility of deportation. The State Supreme Court had denied the defendant post-conviction relief because, unlike all other States, it believed that deportation was merely a "collateral" consequence of a conviction.

The Court reversed, holding that prevailing professional norms supported the view that counsel must advise his client regarding the deportation risk. The consequences of the defendant's plea could easily be determined from reading the relevant removal statute, his deportation was presumptively mandatory, and his counsel's advice was incorrect. Because the deportation consequence was truly clear, the duty to give correct advice was clear. Accepting the defendant's allegations as true, the Court found that he had sufficiently alleged constitutional deficiency for a Sixth Amendment violation.

Courts often view errors of judgment as part of practicing law, rather than constitutional in nature. For example, in *Burger v. Kemp*,[145] counsel's decision not to mount an extensive investigation into his client's background in search of mitigating circumstances, was supported by counsel's reasonable professional judgment which courts afford a heavy measure of deference. In *Knowles v. Mirzayance*,[146] defense counsel recommended after the guilt phase that his client withdraw his insanity defense. The Court held that was not deficient performance, but instead was based on counsel's reasonable belief that the defense was doomed (because medical testimony about the defense had already been rejected and the defendant's parents were unavailable to testify). Other cases like *Nix v. Whiteside*[147] found nothing deficient about defense counsel's refusal to cooperate with his client in presenting perjured testimony.

F. Prejudice to Client

The second component of the *Strickland* test is prejudice, focusing on whether counsel's deficient performance renders the

143 Rompilla v. Beard, 545 U.S. 374, 377 (2005).

144 559 U.S. 356 (2010).

145 483 U.S. 776 (1987).

146 556 U.S. 111 (2009).

147 475 U.S. 157 (1986).

result of the trial unreliable or the proceeding fundamentally unfair, i.e., whether the defendant was deprived of a substantive or procedural right. In an allegation of ineffectiveness due to a failure to raise an issue, a reviewing court will refuse to find prejudice to a defendant who cannot show that counsel's errors deprived the defendant of a fair and reliable trial.[148] "It is not enough for the defendant to show that the errors had some conceivable effect on the outcome of the proceeding."[149]

> The defendant must show that there is a reasonable probability that, but for counsel's unprofessional errors, the result of the proceeding would have been different. A reasonable probability is a probability sufficient to undermine confidence in the outcome.[150]

In *Weaver v. Massachusetts*,[151] during the trial of the accused, "the courtroom was occupied by potential jurors and closed to the public for two days of the jury selection process." Defense counsel made no objection during the trial nor on direct review. When the defendant raised the issue in a post-conviction proceeding for an ineffective assistance claim, *Weaver* held that the defendant must show either a reasonable probability of a different outcome or that the violation was so serious as to render the trial fundamentally unfair.

Prejudice is often difficult to prove, but at times the injustice from counsel's ineffectiveness is simple to demonstrate. For example, in *Glover v. United States*,[152] counsel's deficient performance consisted of failing to object to a legal error that affected the calculation of the defendant's prison sentence. A mistake that resulted in additional imprisonment, regardless of its length, obviously harmed the defendant. From the *Argersinger* line of cases, discussed earlier in this Chapter, any (added) incarceration is significant under the Sixth Amendment.

In *Strickland*, the Court condoned counsel's need to make quick decisions that excluded certain leads in the case based on speculation, as well as protecting those decisions from judicial evaluation by saying the magic words "strategy" and "tactics." If the fear of possible rebuttal by a prosecutor justifies not even investigating what evidence there might be, even the most inept lawyer will have a solid position to a charge of ineffective assistance.

---

148 Strickland v. Washington, 466 U.S. 668 (1984).

149 *Id.*, at 693.

150 *Id.*, at 694.

151 582 U.S. 206 (2017).

152 531 U.S. 198 (2001).

Although in *Rompilla*, the defense counsel received advance notice of the prosecutor's intent to use defendant's prior rape-assault conviction and its similar *modus operandi* to prove the aggravator of "history of violence," they never looked at that file until shortly just before the sentencing hearing. Perhaps worse, they did not read the rest of the file that showed the defendant's history of severe mental illness, child abuse, and alcoholism. Until defense counsel investigates the entire case to learn as much as possible about the relevant circumstances, e.g., the relative strength of the grounds for defenses to pursue and to concede, "counsel [are] not in a position to make a reasonable strategic choice."[153]

Prejudice also may be presumed when State statutes or trial court rulings prohibit counsel from making full use of traditional trial procedures.[154] *Cronic* identified three situations in which prejudice may be presumed: (1) a complete denial of counsel at a critical stage; (2) "counsel *entirely* fails to subject the prosecution's case to meaningful adversarial testing"[155] and (3) the circumstances make it highly unlikely that competent counsel could render assistance. Otherwise, the prejudice standards announced in *Strickland v. Washington* apply.

State interference with the right to counsel is judged by whether the interference denies counsel the opportunity to participate fully and fairly in the adversary factfinding process. In *Geders v. United States*,[156] the trial court ordered the defendant not to consult with counsel during an overnight recess between defendant's direct and cross-examination. That order constituted reversible error that deprived the defendant of his right to assistance of counsel. In *Perry v. Leake*,[157] by contrast, the Court upheld the trial court's discretion to deny the defendant an opportunity to confer with defense counsel during a brief recess between the conclusion of the defendant's direct examination and the start of cross-examination.

Other examples of State interference affect defense counsel's ability to assist the client. In *Herring v. New York*,[158] because a state statute gave the trial court in a bench trial the discretion of denying a closing argument before returning a verdict, the Court held that the statute deprived the defendant of his right to assistance of

---

153 Wiggins v. Smith, 539 U.S. 510, 536 (2003).

154 United States. v. Cronic, 466 U.S. 648 (1984).

155 Before the decision in Bell v. Cone, 535 U.S. 685 (2002), lower courts had applied the presumption to a variety of situations. *Bell* cautioned, however, that a presumption of prejudice is permissible only when the "failure is complete," rather than when counsel fails to take certain steps to contest the government's case.

156 Geders v. U.S., 425 U.S. 80 (1976).

157 488 U.S. 272 (1989).

158 See, e.g., Herring v. New York, 422 U.S. 853 (1975).

counsel. Similarly, in *Brooks v. Tennessee*[159] a State statute required that a defendant in a criminal proceeding "desiring to testify shall do so before any other testimony for the defense is heard by the court trying the case." The Court held that the statute violated the defendant's Fifth Amendment privilege against self-incrimination by penalizing him for remaining silent by excluding his testimony later in the trial. In addition, the statute deprived him of the Sixth Amendment's "guiding hand of counsel" in deciding whether to testify and, if so, at what point during the defense's case-in-chief.

Issues of ineffective counsel also arise on appeal. To prove ineffective assistance of appellate counsel, "[d]efendant must first show that his counsel was objectively unreasonable . . . in failing to find arguable issues to appeal—that is, that counsel unreasonably failed to discover nonfrivolous issues and to file a merits brief raising them."[160]

> [A]ppellate counsel who files a merits brief need not (and should not) raise every nonfrivolous claim, but rather may select from among them in order to maximize the likelihood of success on appeal. . . . [I]t is still possible to bring a *Strickland* claim based on counsel's failure to raise a particular claim, but it is difficult to demonstrate that counsel was incompetent.[161]

"If [defendant] succeeds in such a showing, he then has the burden of demonstrating prejudice. That is, he must show a reasonable probability that, but for his counsel's unreasonable failure to file a merits brief, he would have prevailed on his appeal."[162]

When deficient performance costs a defendant an appeal that the defendant would have otherwise pursued, prejudice to the defendant is presumed "with no further showing from the defendant of the merits of his underlying claims."[163] In *Garza v. Idaho*,[164] defense counsel refused his client's request to appeal his conviction after he had waived his appeal rights as part of a guilty plea agreement. The Court applied a presumption of prejudice, and held that the Sixth Amendment ineffective assistance of counsel applied

---

159 406 U.S. 605 (1972).

160 Smith v. Robbins, 528 U.S. 259, 285 (2000).

161 *Id.*, at 288.

162 *Id.*, at 285.

163 Roe v. Flores-Ortega, 528 U.S. 470 (2000).

164 586 U.S. 232 (2019). See also Pope v. Taylor, 100 F.4th 918 (7th Cir. 2024) (28-year delay in resolving appeal, including appointed counsel's abandonment of defendant, resulting in loss of transcripts of trial deprived petitioner of his due process right to meaningful direct appeal).

regardless of whether defendant had signed and waived his appeal rights.

G. Plea Bargaining

While there is no constitutional right to plea bargain, the practical reality of the criminal justice system requires oversight of defense counsel in plea negotiations. Defense counsel is ineffective if he fails to properly inform the defendant of a beneficial plea agreement offered by the prosecution.[165] "[A]s a general rule, defense counsel has the duty to communicate formal offers from the prosecution to accept a plea on terms and conditions that may be favorable to the accused."[166] To prove ineffectiveness, the defendant must show that (1) but for the ineffective advice of counsel there is a reasonable probability that the plea offer would have been accepted and presented to the court; (2) the court would have accepted its terms; and (3) the conviction or sentence would have been less than under those imposed after trial.[167]

> Disparities in a defendant's comparative sentence exposure between the actual sentence faced and a more favorable sentence he could have received if his counsel had been effective are an important factor in the reasonable-probability inquiry where a defendant claims he would have accepted a plea but for his counsel's error. In combination with a defendant's statement that he would have accepted a plea agreement but for his counsel's error, significant disparities in sentence exposure can be sufficient to establish a reasonable probability the defendant would have made an agreement.
>
> This treatment of sentence-exposure disparities makes good sense. It offers an objective piece of evidence in an inherently speculative inquiry that requires us to imagine a counterfactual scenario in which a defendant possessed information relevant to his plea calculus that he did not actually have due to an error by counsel.[168]

In *Baker v. United States*,[169] the defendant did not understand the "full scope" of the disparity between his sentence under an offered plea (15–17 years total) and on all counts at trial (57 years). Defense counsel had told defendant that his exposure at a trial was 21 years instead of the 57-year mandatory minimum sentence. The Third

---

165 Missouri v. Frye, 566 U.S. 134 (2012).

166 *Id.*, at 145.

167 *Id.*, at 147.

168 Baker v. United States, 109 F.4th 187, 197 (3d Cir. 2024).

169 109 F.4th 187 (3d Cir. 2024).

Circuit held that the defendant had "demonstrated a reasonable likelihood he would have taken the plea offer but for his counsel's error in calculating his sentence exposure," and remanded the case in order for the Government to reoffer the original plea agreement.[170]

Counsel also is ineffective if he incorrectly advises the defendant on the state of the law, leading the defendant to reject a beneficial plea agreement.[171] The proper remedy is not specific performance of the original plea. Instead, the prosecution should re-offer the plea deal and if the defendant accepts it, the trial court can decide how to amend the original sentence. If the trial court finds that accepting the plea deal would have resulted in conviction of a lesser offense, it may require the prosecution to re-offer the plea, vacate the trial conviction, and accept the plea.[172]

A formal plea bargain offer means that its terms and its processing can be documented so that what took place in the negotiation process becomes clearer if some later inquiry turns on the conduct of earlier pretrial negotiations.

> The prosecution and the trial courts may adopt some measures to help ensure against late, frivolous, or fabricated claims after a later, less advantageous plea offer has been accepted or after a trial leading to conviction with resulting harsh consequences. First, the fact of a formal offer means that its terms and its processing can be documented so that what took place in the negotiation process becomes more clear if some later inquiry turns on the conduct of earlier pretrial negotiations. Second, States may elect to follow rules that all offers must be in writing, again to ensure against later misunderstandings or fabricated charges. Third, formal offers can be made part of the record at any subsequent plea proceeding or before a trial on the merits, all to ensure that a defendant has been fully advised before those further proceedings commence.[173]

To prove prejudice in the guilty plea context, the inquiry is whether there is a reasonable probability that, but for counsel's errors, the defendant would not have pleaded guilty and would have insisted on going to trial. A reasonable probability exists if the defendant convinces "the court that a decision to reject the plea bargain [and instead proceed to trial] would have been rational under

---

170 *Id.*, at 204.

171 Lafler v. Cooper, 566 U.S. 156 (2012).

172 *Id.*, at 171.

173 *Missouri v. Frye*, 566 U.S. at 146.

the circumstances."[174] In *Padilla v. Kentucky*, the Court held that effective counsel must advise the client about the deportation consequences of a conviction, and also establish that he was prejudiced by counsel's misadvice.[175] In *Hill v. Lockhart*,[176] like the later cases, the Court held that prejudice during plea bargaining relates to the "reasonable probability that, but for counsel's errors, [defendant] would not have pleaded guilty and would have insisted on going to trial."[177]

H. Conflicts of Interest

The constitutional right to effective assistance of counsel entitles the defendant to the "undivided loyalty" of counsel. The defendant does not receive the full benefit of the adversary process when defense counsel's decisions are influenced by obligations owed to persons (including defense counsel) other than the defendant. While a division of loyalty can result from various defense arrangements, the situation producing the most frequent conflict claims is the representation of more than one codefendant by the same attorney.

Although codefendants may start out with identical concerns, a divergence of interests may develop at almost every point in the progress of the litigation. One defendant may receive an attractive plea bargain, while the other may receive a less attractive offer or none at all. Codefendants may raise conflicting defenses, or have different levels of culpability, which may affect defense counsel's closing arguments or counsel's approach to sentencing. One defendant's decision to testify may highlight the lack of testimony from the other.

A lawyer also may be placed in a conflict situation when there is a professional relationship with both the defendant and a third party who has some interest in the case. Or, a conflict arises when someone with an interest in the case pays the legal fees of defense counsel. For example, in *Wood v. Georgia*,[178] when an employer of an alleged criminal enterprise provides legal assistance to employees, defense counsel is acting as an agent of the employer and the risk of conflict of interest is evident. Conflicts of interest may arise between the defendant and defense counsel, as when a compensation agreement includes counsel's interest in royalties received from a book or movie portraying the trial or related events.

---

174 Padilla v. Kentucky, 559 U.S. 356, 372 (2010).

175 *Id.*, at 374.

176 474 U.S. 52 (1985).

177 Hill v. Lockhart, 474 U.S. 52, 59 (1985).

178 450 U.S. 261 (1981).

Joint representation is not *per se* violative of the constitutional guarantee of effective assistance. However, each defendant is entitled to representation free of an actual conflict of interest. A trial court's failure to take adequate steps to resolve a potential conflict of interest, despite statements by counsel that a conflict exists, deprives defendants of effective assistance of counsel. Reversal of the ensuing conviction is necessary even in the absence of a showing of prejudice. In the absence of a supported finding by the trial court that the asserted conflict does not exist or was no more than a remote possibility, there is a presumption of prejudice to the defendants.

Unconstitutional multiple representation is never harmless error. In *Holloway v. Arkansas*,[179] when a trial court improperly required joint representation of multiple defendants over their timely objection, prejudice was presumed and reversal was automatic. The Court viewed the infraction of the right to assistance of counsel as so basic to a fair trial that it could never be viewed as harmless error. On the other hand, when defense counsel fails to request separate counsel, the trial judge is not required to inquire into the propriety of multiple representation.

> *Holloway* requires state trial courts to investigate timely objections to multiple representation. But nothing in our precedents suggests that the Sixth Amendment requires state courts themselves to initiate inquiries into the propriety of multiple representation in every case. . . Absent special circumstances, therefore, trial courts may assume either that multiple representation entails no conflict or that the lawyer and his clients knowingly accept such risk of conflict as may exist. Indeed, as the Court noted in trial courts necessarily rely in large measure upon the good faith and good judgment of defense counsel.[180]

In the absence of an objection by defense counsel or the defendant, an inquiry is not constitutionally mandated unless the trial judge knows or reasonably should know that a particular conflict exists.[181]

Mickens v. Taylor[182] held that when the trial judge does not inquire into a potential conflict of interest about which the judge knew or reasonably should have known, the defendant must prove that the conflict of interest adversely affected counsel's performance. Instead of automatically reversing the defendant's conviction, the appellate court instead should remand for a hearing about whether

---

179 Holloway v. Arkansas, 435 U.S. 475 (1978).

180 Cuyler v. Sullivan, 446 U.S. 335, 346–47 (1980).

181 *Id.*, at 347.

182 Mickens v. Taylor, 535 U.S. 162 (2002).

an actual conflict affected the defense counsel's performance. *Mickens* did confirm an automatic reversal for a failure to inquire where defense counsel raised an objection to continuing his representation due to a conflict.

The prevailing standard of review for post-conviction conflict claims is whether an actual conflict of interest adversely affected defense counsel's performance.[183] In *Burger v. Kemp*,[184] the defendant failed to prove an actual conflict of interest when law partners represented separately tried defendants, when one lawyer prepared appellate briefs for both defendants, and when the defendant's lawyer did not argue his client's lesser culpability in the briefs.

A defendant may waive a conflict of interest with regard to his attorney, and a trial judge must recognize a presumption in favor of a defendant's counsel of choice, but that presumption may be overcome by either a demonstration of an actual conflict or a showing of a serious potential for conflict, without actually violating a defendant's Sixth Amendment right to his counsel of choice.[185]

I. Raising the Issue of Ineffective Assistance

Ineffective assistance of counsel is one of the most common claims asserted on direct appeal or as a collateral attack on a conviction. In *Massaro v. United States*,[186] the Court concluded that "an ineffective assistance of counsel claim may be brought in a collateral attack proceeding under § 2255, regardless of whether the petitioner could have raised the claim on direct appeal."[187] In a federal collateral attack proceeding, counsel's ineffectiveness may excuse the procedural default that related to counsel's performance at trial or during the post-conviction proceeding itself.[188]

If the defendant claims that counsel was ineffective by failing to comply with the jurisdiction's contemporaneous objection rule, e.g., failing to object to the admissibility of evidence or to a jury instruction, the defendant must show "cause" for that failure. To constitute cause, the defendant usually must prove that counsel's error amounted to a Sixth Amendment violation. An ineffective assistance of counsel claim that is asserted as cause for the

---

183 Cuyler v. Sullivan, 446 U.S. 335 (1980).

184 483 U.S. 776 (1987).

185 Wheat v. United States, 486 U.S. 153, 163 (1988).

186 538 U.S. 500 (2003).

187 Massaro v. United States, 538 U.S. 500, 504 (2003).

188 Martinez v. Ryan, 566 U.S. 1 (2012).

procedural default of another claim may *itself* be barred by a procedural default.[189]

Inadequate assistance of counsel in State post-conviction proceedings also may excuse a procedural default.[190] By contrast, when a State prisoner fails in State post-conviction proceedings to challenge the effectiveness of his *direct appeal* lawyer, he may not raise that claim in a federal habeas petition—even if the failure was caused by ineffective assistance of his post-conviction counsel. *Davila v. Davis*[191] limited the claim to circumstances in which the underlying ineffectiveness claim involved the prisoner's *trial* lawyer.

§ 15.5 Waiver of Counsel

A. Faretta v. California

Before *Gideon*, it was common for defendants to represent themselves because courts were telling them that they had no right to counsel. Perhaps, then, it would not have occurred to anyone to argue that a given defendant did not have the right to proceed *pro se* because that was a common procedure. After *Gideon*, the issue of whether a person *should* be allowed to represent himself stood out. In *Faretta v. California*,[192] the defendant requested the trial court to permit him to represent himself, and after a hearing, the trial court denied the request and appointed counsel for the defendant. After his conviction and appeal, the Court held that a defendant has a Sixth Amendment right to represent himself, i.e., proceed *pro se*.

Although the Sixth Amendment does not refer to self-representation explicitly, the right is implicit in the structure of the Amendment that refers to rights of "the accused." Those rights are available to the defendant who may apply them himself to present his own case. The Sixth Amendment language also refers to an accused having the "assistance" of counsel. The right to counsel is the defendant's to implement on his own, or with the "assistance" of counsel.

Despite the expertise of a lawyer, "it is not inconceivable that in some rare instances, the defendant may in fact present his case more effectively by conducting his own defense."[193] Because "the defendant, and not his lawyer or the State, will bear the personal consequences of the conviction,"[194] he should be free to decide

[189] Edwards v. Carpenter, 529 U.S. 446 (2000).

[190] Trevino v. Thaler, 569 U.S. 413 (2013); Martinez v. Ryan, 566 U.S. 1 (2012).

[191] 582 U.S. 521 (2017).

[192] 422 U.S. 806 (1975).

[193] *Id.*, at 834.

[194] *Id.*

whether his is such a case. Although his decision may not be wise, his "choice must be honored out of 'that respect for the individual which is the lifeblood of the law.' "[195] The Court identified the limitation of self-representation by stating:

> Neither is . . . [the right of self-representation] a license not to comply with relevant rules of procedural and substantive law. Thus, whatever else may or may not be open to him on appeal, a defendant who elects to represent himself cannot thereafter complain that the quality of his own defense amounted to a denial of "effective assistance of counsel."[196]

The trial court in *Faretta* had erred in forcing the defendant to accept appointed counsel.[197]

In *Martinez v. Court of Appeal of California*,[198] the Court refused to extend *Faretta* to *pro se* representation on appeal. Because on appeal, a defendant's position shifts from an accused to a convicted appellant, "the autonomy interests" of the defendant are only "those that survive a felony conviction," and therefore are "less compelling than those motivating the decision in *Faretta*."[199]

B. Standard for Waiver

In response to a defendant's request, the trial court must hold a hearing to determine whether the defendant is competent to make the decision to waive the right to counsel completely or partially, and whether to appoint standby counsel. A defendant who proceeds *pro se* must act "knowingly and intelligently" in giving up the "traditional benefits associated with the right to counsel."[200] "Although a defendant need not himself have the skill and experience of a lawyer in order to competently and intelligently choose self-representation, he should be made aware of the dangers and disadvantages of self-representation, so that the record will establish that 'he knows what he is doing and his choice is made with eyes open.' "[201] A trial court's determination in this regard is reviewed for an abuse of discretion.

---

195 *Id.*, quoting Illinois v. Allen, 397 U.S. 337, 350–51 (1970).

196 *Id.*, at 834 n.46.

197 McKaskle v. Wiggins, 465 U.S. 168 (1984) later included a footnote that self-representation analysis is never subject to harmless error analysis.

> Since the right of self-representation is a right that when exercised usually increases the likelihood of a trial outcome unfavorable to the defendant, its denial is not amenable to "harmless error" analysis. The right is either respected or denied; its deprivation cannot be harmless.

Id., at 177 n.8.

198 528 U.S. 152 (2000).

199 Martinez v. Court of Appeal of California, 528 U.S. 152, 163 (2000).

200 *Faretta v. California*, 422 U.S. at 835.

201 *Id.*

The *Faretta* defendant showed that he was "literate, competent, and understanding, and that he was voluntarily exercising his informed free will."[202] That he may not have mastered the intricacies of the hearsay rule, or that he lacked other "technical legal knowledge," was "not relevant to an assessment of his knowing exercise of the right to defend himself."[203]

If the defendant makes a clear request to waive counsel, *Faretta* suggests possible grounds for denying such a request: (1) the request is untimely; (2) the defendant is inclined to engage in serious and obstructionist conduct; (3) defendant is unable to gain the understanding, or exercise the reasoning, needed for an acceptable waiver under *Faretta*; and (4) the defendant due to disabilities will be unable to take the actions needed to conduct his own defense.

Faretta stated that a request in that case was made "well before the date of trial."[204] At some point, a late request may disrupt the schedule of proceedings and thus justify rejection. It also noted that "the trial judge may terminate self-representation by a defendant who engages in serious and obstructionist misconduct."[205] The Court also recognized that a trial court can refuse the request when, despite its efforts to explain the consequences of a waiver, the defendant does not appreciate what is needed for a knowing and intelligent waiver.[206] *Faretta* makes clear, however, that a defendant does not need legal expertise nor unusual intelligence to meet its standard of awareness of the dangers and disadvantages of self-representation.

In *Indiana v. Edwards*,[207] the Court recognized a trial court's authority to deny *pro se* representation in cases where the defendant's mental illness interferes with self-representation, even when the defendant is mentally competent to stand trial and understands the disadvantages of self-representation described in *Faretta*.

Much of the language in *Godinez v. Moran*[208] indicated that the traditional standard for determining whether a defendant is competent to stand trial is also applicable to the competency to waive counsel and proceed to trial *pro se*, as well as when the defendant seeks a waiver of counsel and plead guilty. But while the standard for competency to stand trial requires that the defendant have a "sufficient present ability to consult with his lawyer with a

[202] *Id.*, at 835.
[203] *Id.*, at 836.
[204] *Id.*, at 807.
[205] *Id.*, at 834 n.46.
[206] *Id.*, at 835–36.
[207] 554 U.S. 164 (2008).
[208] 509 U.S. 389 (1993).

reasonable degree of rational understanding" and "a rational as well as factual understanding of the proceedings against him," it does not show that the defendant understands and can exercise the judgment needed for the waiver of counsel. There remains the trial courts' "serious and weighty responsibility" to determine whether, in fact, the waiver was "intelligent and voluntary." "In this sense," the Court noted, "there is a heightened standard for pleading guilty and for waiving the right to counsel, but it is not a heightened standard for competence."[209]

C. *Pro Se* Representation to Plead Guilty

While *Faretta* approved the concept of and focused on self-representation at trial, *Iowa v. Tovar*[210] held that a defendant who wants to plead guilty on his own does not need awareness of the disadvantages of being without counsel that *Faretta* required for proceeding to trial *pro se*. A trial court does not need to warn the defendant about the risks that proceeding *pro se* may overlook viable defenses or lose out on the value of advice about pleading guilty.

The Court described its approach to counsel waivers as "pragmatic," asking in each situation "what purposes a lawyer can serve at the particular stage of the proceedings in question the proceedings in question, and what assistance [counsel] could provide to an accused at that stage."[211] For a guilty plea, what an attorney does for the client requires "less rigorous warnings"[212] to ensure that the defendant understands how the waived right "would apply in general in the circumstances."[213] Courts "indulge in every reasonable presumption against waiver."[214]

> [N]either warning is mandated by the Sixth Amendment. The constitutional requirement is satisfied when the trial court informs the accused of the nature of the charges against him, of his right to be counseled regarding his plea, and of the range of allowable punishments attendant upon the entry of a guilty plea.[215]

The Court's past decisions had noted that

> [t]he information a defendant must possess in order to make an intelligent election . . . will depend on a range of

[209] Godinez v. Moran, 509 U.S. 389, 396, 401 (1993).

[210] 541 U.S. 77 (2004).

[211] *Id.*, at 90.

[212] *Id.*, at 90.

[213] *Id.*, at 92, quoting United States v. Ruiz, 536 U.S. 622, 629 (2002).

[214] Brookhart v. Janis, 384 U.S. 1, 4 (1966).

[215] Iowa v. Tovar, 541 U.S. 77, 81 (2004).

> case-specific factors, including the defendant's education or sophistication, the complex or easily grasped nature of the charge, and the stage of the proceeding.[216]

The Court concluded that it was sufficient that the defendant is aware of the availability of counsel's assistance, without exploring the various aspects of that assistance. The Court referred to a standard from *United States v. Ruiz*[217] that

> the law ordinarily considers a waiver knowing, intelligent, and sufficiently aware if the defendant fully understands the nature of the right and how it would likely apply in general in the circumstances—even though the defendant may not know the specific detailed consequences of invoking it.[218]

The Court cited *Patterson v. Illinois*,[219] as another waiver of counsel case where the Court stated that a defendant does not need "a full and complete appreciation of all the consequences flowing from his waiver" to satisfy "the constitutional minimum."[220]

D. Stand-By Counsel

Faretta stated that

> a state may—even over objection by the accused—appoint a "standby counsel" to aid the accused if and when the accused requests help, and to be available to represent the accused in the event that termination of the defendant's self-representation is necessary.[221]

Thus, if counsel is expected to assist in the defense in any way, the court may appoint standby counsel, even over defendant's objection. *McKaskle v. Wiggins*,[222] permitted appointment of standby counsel over the defendant's objection. The Court noted that "the *pro se* defendant is entitled to preserve actual control over the case he chooses to present to the jury" and that "standby counsel's participation without the defendant's consent should not be allowed to destroy the jury's perception that the defendant is representing himself."[223]

---

[216] *Id.*, at 88.

[217] 536 U.S. 622 (2002).

[218] *United States v. Ruiz,* 536 U.S. at 629.

[219] 487 U.S. 285 (1988).

[220] Patterson v. Illinois, 487 U.S. 285, 292 (1988).

[221] *Faretta v. California*, 422 U.S. at 834 n.46.

[222] 465 U.S. 168 (1984).

[223] McKaskle v. Wiggins, 465 U.S. 168 (1984).

In determining whether standby counsel's participation would undermine the defendant's *Faretta* rights, the Court prescribed a two-pronged test. First, did

> standby counsel's participation over defendant's objection effectively allow counsel to make or substantially interfere with any significant tactical decisions, or to control the questioning of witnesses, or to speak instead of the defendant on any matter of importance?[224]

Such action necessarily undermines the defendant's right of self-representation because it deprives him of the "actual control over the case he chooses to present to the jury."[225] Second, even if the defendant was able to present his case in his own way, did the additional unsolicited participation of counsel "destroy the jury's perception that the defendant is representing himself"?[226]

The Court stated that the trial court has the authority, despite defendant's objection, to both appoint standby counsel and to direct that counsel to "steer defendant through the basic procedures of the trial."[227] The judge could "relieve [himself] of the need to explain and enforce the basic rules of court room protocol or to assist the defendant in overcoming routine [procedural] obstacles that stand in the way of defendant's achievement of his own clearly indicated goals."[228]

The purpose of standby counsel is to have someone other than the judge explain basic rules of courtroom protocol to assist defendant in overcoming routine procedural or evidentiary problems. A defendant who exercises hybrid representation is entitled to assert a claim of ineffective assistance of counsel, but only for those parts of the representation that were explicitly undertaken by trial counsel. To avoid future claims of ineffective assistance of counsel, the court should make a record of the nature of the limited representation which defendant is to receive. The record should include a ruling on the role of counsel at each stage of trial, including: (1) the role of counsel in the preservation of error for appellate review; and (2) the nature of any advice given.

---

224 *Id.*, at 178.

225 *Id.*

226 *Id.*

227 *Id.*, at 184.

228 *Id.*

Chapter 16

INVESTIGATIVE GRAND JURY

Table of Sections

---

§ 16.1 Introduction

The requirement that serious criminal prosecutions be based upon an indictment by a grand jury is specifically embodied in the federal constitution.[1] However, the federal requirement of a grand jury indictment is not applicable to the States. In *Hurtado v. California*,[2] the Court held that the words "Due Process of law" in the Fourteenth Amendment do not require an indictment by a grand jury in a State murder prosecution.[3] All States and the federal system use grand juries, but only two States use the grand jury for investigative purposes only. If a state uses a grand jury, the proceedings must be conducted in a manner which will guarantee Due Process and Equal Protection to persons who are affected by its proceedings.

In the criminal justice system when grand juries are used for most felony cases, a grand jury usually convenes after an initial appearance and a preliminary hearing (aka preliminary examination), to consider whether probable cause supports the issuance of an indictment against the target of the investigation. When a prosecutor seeks to proceed in secret, there may be no arrest and the issuance of an indictment may be the first occurrence in a criminal case.[4] Historically, a formal charge returned by a grand jury on its own is generally known as a Presentment. When a prosecutor assists the grand jury, usually by dominating the presentation of evidence, the charging document is known as an Indictment. Without a grand jury's participation (and instead of an indictment), a prosecutor may complete a form called an Information and claim that probable cause supports the charges. Slightly more than half the States permit the use of an Information.

§ 16.2 What Grand Juries Do

A. Nature of Grand Jury

The grand jury is a prosecutorial organ which acts both (1) as a "sword" to initiate formal charges based upon probable cause, and (2) as a "shield" to protect and insulate citizens from official harassment

[1] U.S. Const. Amend. V; Ex parte Bain, 121 U.S. 1 (1887), overruled on other grounds by, United States v. Cotton, 535 U.S. 625 (2002).

[2] 110 U.S. 516 (1884).

[3] Hurtado v. California, 110 U.S. 516, 538 (1884).

[4] If an accused was arrested, but the grand jury indicts a defendant before a preliminary hearing occurs, the indictment supersedes the need for a preliminary hearing because probable cause supports the formal charge. But see Hawkins v. Superior Court, 586 P.2d 916 (Cal. 1978) (defendants is denied Equal Protection when an indictment is returned before a preliminary hearing).

By statute, a Michigan prosecutor with probable cause may request that a judge conduct an inquiry into a matter by subpoenaing witnesses and issuing arrest warrants. In effect, the judge becomes a one-person-grand-jury. However, after an arrest warrant issues using that process, a different judge must conduct a preliminary hearing as though no *judicial* investigation had preceded the arrest, People v. Peeler, 984 N.W.2d 80 (Mich. 2022) held that charges issued under the statutory procedure did not prevent the need for a preliminary hearing.

based upon groundless charges. As the Court stated in *Wood v. Georgia*,[5] the grand jury serves the invaluable function of standing between the accuser and the accused.[6]

In the vast majority of cases, the grand jury is a formal arm of the prosecution. "A grand jury is clothed with great independence in many areas, but it remains an appendage of the court, powerless to perform its investigative function without the court's aid, because [the grand jury is] powerless itself to compel the testimony of witnesses."[7] However, the Court noted in *United States v. Williams*[8] that "[a]lthough the grand jury normally operates. . . under judicial auspices, its institutional relationship with the Judicial Branch has traditionally been, so to speak, at arm's length."[9]

The prosecutor is in a unique position to bring matters to the attention of the grand jury and to influence its deliberations. However, the grand jury may subpoena witnesses on its own; it may elect to hear defense testimony; its deliberations are secret. Prosecutors exert substantial influence over the grand jury; the prosecutor selects the witnesses the grand jury will subpoena, the evidence it will hear, and the documents it will examine. The prosecutor also explains the law to the grand jurors, instructs them as to the amount of proof necessary to justify an indictment, and usually prepares indictments for the grand jury foreperson to sign. While the grand jury as a practical matter often follows the lead of the prosecutor, it potentially has sufficient independence to prevent it from becoming a "rubber stamp."

However, the grand jury may act to protect citizens from groundless prosecutions in some instances. The grand jury will generally insulate the citizen against oppressive prosecution in cases in which there is no evidence whatsoever to support an indictment. More importantly, it has broad, independent investigative powers[10] which enables it to expose official misconduct and neglect as well as criminal activities committed or concealed by public officials.[11]

---

5 370 U.S. 375 (1962).

6 Wood v. Georgia, 370 U.S. 375, 390 (1962).

7 Brown v. United States, 359 U.S. 41, 49 (1959), overruled on other grounds, Harris v. United States, 382 U.S. 162 (1965).

8 504 U.S. 36 (1992).

9 United States v. Williams, 504 U.S. 36, 47 (1992).

10 "A grand jury may consider an extraordinarily broad range of evidence, and the scope of its inquiries is not to be limited narrowly." In re Grand Jury Investigation, 966 F.3d 991, 994 (9th Cir. 2020).

11 "A grand jury has the authority and duty to inquire into all information that might possibly bear on its investigation until it has identified an offense or has satisfied itself that none has occurred." Trump v. Vance, 977 F.3d 198, 206 (2d Cir. 2020).

B. Grand Jury Duties

The primary duty of the grand jury is to investigate charges of criminal misconduct which are within its knowledge or brought to its attention. To be effective and impartial, the grand jury has a duty to maintain secrecy regarding its investigations. It has a duty to return an indictment against anyone for whom it decides there is sufficient evidence to justify a charge. The grand jury also has a duty to report on its actions regarding all matters pending before it.

In *Bank of Nova Scotia v. United States*,[12] the Court refused to use its supervisory authority to dismiss an indictment for the Government's misconduct, without considering the possible prejudicial effect on the grand jury's decision to indict. The Court reasoned that the grand jury's supervisory authority must be consistent with statutory and rule standards, including the harmless error standard to disregard errors "not affect[ing] substantial rights."

A federal court cannot dismiss an indictment (as the lower court had done), simply "to declare with unmistakable intention that [prosecutorial misconduct] will not be tolerated."[13] Any dismissal must be based on a finding of a sufficient likelihood of prejudice so as not to constitute harmless error. Prejudice requires a showing that a "violation substantially influenced the grand jury's decision to indict," or that there existed a " 'grave doubt' that the decision to indict was free from the substantial influence of [the] violations."[14] The only guidance about the meaning of "grave doubt" is that it requires more than raising a "substantial question" about the likely effect in the mind of the reviewing court.[15]

C. Constitutional Selection of Grand Jury

A grand jury is selected from a source that is representative of the local population, e.g., private property taxpayers or persons with a driver's license, in order for the grand jury to reflect a cross-section of the community. However, the grand jury that actually hears a particular case need not actually "mirror" the community.[16] The constitutional rules regarding the selection process are essentially the same for both a petit jury and a grand jury and apply to the members of both bodies.[17] To establish a *prima facie* violation of the Sixth Amendment right to an impartial jury, a defendant must show

---

12 487 U.S. 250 (1988).

13 Bank of Nova Scotia v. United States, 487 U.S. 250, 263 (1988).

14 *Id.*, at 256.

15 *Id.*, at 263.

16 Taylor v. Louisiana, 419 U.S. 522 (1975).

17 See Vasquez v. Hillery, 474 U.S. 254 (1986).

that: (1) the community contains a distinct group;[18] (2) the distinct group was not represented fairly in the venire from which the jury was chosen; and (3) the underrepresentation was due to systematic exclusion of the group in the jury selection process.[19] The defendant need not be a member of the underrepresented group to have standing to raise this claim. The prosecution can rebut a *prima facie* violation by showing that the systematic exclusion manifestly and primarily advances a significant state interest that is incompatible with the fair cross-section requirement.[20]

When grand jurors are selected in an intentionally discriminatory fashion, Equal Protection provides an additional basis for challenging the composition of the grand jury. As with a Due Process challenge, a criminal defendant has standing to object to Equal Protection discrimination against persons of a different race or gender in the selection of grand jurors.[21] In order to prove an Equal Protection violation, the defendant must: (1) establish that the group is a recognizable class; (2) prove the degree of underrepresentation; and (3) show that the selection process is susceptible to abuse. The prosecution can rebut the prima facie case by showing an absence of discriminatory intent.[22]

Challenges based on the grand jury's composition allege Equal Protection violations, because "the structural protections of the grand jury have been so compromised" as to require a "presumption of prejudice;" "any inquiry into harmless error" in such cases would require "ungrounded speculation."[23] If the manner of selection of grand jurors or the foreperson is shown to be the result of unconstitutional selection methods, an indictment returned by that grand jury is void.[24]

§ 16.3 Investigative Advantages of a Grand Jury

A. Grand Jury's Authority

A grand jury's investigative authority rests on "the longstanding principle that 'the public has a right to every man's evidence.' "[25] Courts have the right to compel the testimony of anyone, subject only to "constitutional, common law or statutory privilege."[26] The Court

---

18 Duren v. Missouri, 439 U.S. 357 (1979).

19 Taylor v. Louisiana, 419 U.S. 522 (1975).

20 Duren v. Missouri, 439 U.S. 357 (1979).

21 Campbell v. Louisiana, 523 U.S. 392 (1998).

22 Castaneda v. Partida, 430 U.S. 482 (1977).

23 *Id.*, at 257.

24 Vasquez v. Hillery, 474 U.S. 254 (1986).

25 Branzburg v. Hayes, 408 U.S. 665, 688 (1972).

26 *Id.*

has described a grand jury's authority to compel testimony as "[a]mong the necessary and most important of the powers. . . [that] assure the effective functioning of government in an ordered society."[27] Effective law enforcement requires the cooperation of the public, because the grand jury must be free to conduct wide-ranging investigations.

The grand jury may investigate "merely on suspicion that the law is being violated, or even just because it wants assurance that it is not."[28] The grand jurors must be able to act on "tips, rumors, evidence proffered by the prosecutor, or [their own] personal knowledge."[29] They must have the capacity to "run down every available clue" and to examine "all witnesses. . . in every proper way."[30]

A grand jury cannot be burdened "with minitrials and preliminary showings [that] would assuredly impede its investigation and frustrate the public's interest in the fair and expeditious administration of the criminal laws."[31] It must be left "free to pursue its investigations unhindered by external influence or supervision so long as it does not trench upon the legitimate rights of a witness called before it."[32] Grand jury appearances may be difficult at times and require answers that are embarrassing. They are "part of the necessary contribution of the individual to the welfare of the public."[33]

As an agent of the court which it serves, a grand jury has no greater power nor jurisdiction than the court possesses. It is dependent upon the court for the enforcement of all its powers. However, the grand jury is intended to have a certain independence from the court, and it is improper for a court to attempt to control or interfere with lawful investigations.

The grand jury has broad powers to compel the cooperation of witnesses and potential defendants in its investigations. When alleged abuses may occur, the grand jury acts as an alternative to an unsupervised police investigation. It is difficult for the potential for abuse to be removed without destroying the function of the grand jury as a citizen's committee for the investigation of official misconduct or neglect.

---

27 Kastigar v. United States, 406 U.S. 441, 445 (1972).

28 United States v. Morton Salt, 338 U.S. 632, 643 (1950).

29 *Branzburg v. Hayes*, 408 U.S. at 701.

30 United States v. Dionisio, 410 U.S. 1, 13 (1973).

31 *Id.*, at 17.

32 *Id.*

33 Blair v. United States, 250 U.S. 273, 281 (1919).

Compared to police investigations, grand jury investigations are expensive, time consuming, and cumbersome. Police investigations generally work well and are far less costly. Grand jury investigations of certain cases justify the extra costs: e.g., a factually complex organizational structure, victims and other witnesses refusing to cooperate, information located in extensive business records, investigating in secret, or counteracting suspicion about political manipulation of the case.

B. Power to Investigate

The grand jury has broad power to investigate the possibility of criminal misconduct. It is not limited to the investigation of matters which are brought to its attention by prosecutorial agents, or to matters which give it probable cause to believe a crime has been committed. Grand juries may properly investigate any matter which it believes or suspects may lead to the institution of criminal charges. In *Blair v. United States*,[34] the Court stated that the grand jury is a body with powers of investigation and inquisition; the scope of its inquiries cannot be limited by forecasting how it will decide matters presented to or initiated by it.[35] Years after *Blair*, *Branzburg v. Hayes*[36] noted that the investigative power of the grand jury is necessarily broad, and an investigation is not complete until every available clue is investigated and all witnesses are examined to determine if a crime has been committed.[37]

United States v. R. Enterprises, Inc.[38] was a challenge to the scope of a grand jury investigation on relevancy grounds. Fed.R.Crim.P. 17(c) permitted a subpoena to be quashed "if compliance would be unreasonable or oppressive." The defendant relied heavily on *United States v. Nixon*,[39] which had dealt with a subpoena *duces tecum* requiring items subpoenaed for use at trial.[40] The *R. Enterprises* Court, though, held that the *Nixon* standard for a subpoena did not apply to a motion to quash a *grand jury* subpoena. A grand jury

> may compel the production of evidence or the testimony of witnesses as it considers appropriate, and its operation

---

34 250 U.S. 273 (1919).

35 *Blair v. United States*, 250 U.S. at 282.

36 408 U.S. 665 (1972).

37 *Branzburg v. Hayes*, 408 U.S. at 701.

38 498 U.S. 292 (1991).

39 418 U.S. 683 (1974).

40 *Nixon* had held that a party seeking to enforce a subpoena must show that the documents sought are relevant, admissible in evidence, and adequately specified.

> generally is unrestrained by the technical procedural and evidentiary rules governing the conduct of criminal trials.[41]

Permitting a recipient of a subpoena to challenge a grand jury investigation would be unwise, inviting "procedural delays and detours while courts evaluate the relevancy and admissibility of documents sought by a particular subpoena." "Requiring the Government to explain in too much detail the particular reasons underlying a subpoena" would "compromise 'the indispensable secrecy of grand jury proceedings,' " and it would "afford the targets of the investigation far more information about the grand jury's internal workings. . . than the Federal Rules of Criminal Procedure appear to contemplate."[42]

The Court decided that what was needed was a standard of reasonableness that

> gives due weight to the difficult position of subpoena recipients but does not impair the strong governmental interests in affording grand juries wide latitude, avoiding minitrials on peripheral matters, and preserving a necessary level of secrecy.[43]

"[A] grand jury subpoena issued through normal channels is presumed to be reasonable, and the burden of showing unreasonableness must be on the recipient who seeks to avoid compliance."[44] R. Enterprises "did not challenge the subpoena as being too indefinite, nor did [it] claim that compliance would be overly burdensome."[45] The challenge was strictly on relevancy grounds and for such a challenge, the Court applied the following standard:

> "[T]he motion to quash must be denied unless the district court determines that there is no reasonable possibility that the category of materials the Government seeks will produce information relevant to the general subject of the grand jury's investigation."[46]

Recognizing that the above standard imposed an "unenviable task" upon the party making the challenge, the Court suggested that the district court could ease that task through appropriate procedures.

---

41 United States v. R. Enterprises, Inc., 498 U.S. 292, 298 (1991).

42 *Id.*, at 299.

43 *Id.*, at 300.

44 *Id.*, at 301.

45 *Id.*

46 *Id.*

> [A] court may be justified in a case where unreasonableness is alleged in requiring the Government to reveal the general subject of the grand jury's investigation before requiring the challenging party to carry its burden of persuasion . . . In cases where the recipient of the subpoena does not know the nature of the investigation, we are confident that district courts will be able to craft appropriate procedures that balance the interests of the subpoena recipient against the strong governmental interests in maintaining secrecy, preserving investigatory flexibility, and avoiding procedural delays. For example, to ensure that subpoenas are not routinely challenged as a form of discovery, a district court may require that the Government reveal the subject of the investigation to the trial court *in camera*, so that the court may determine whether the motion to quash has a reasonable prospect for success before it discloses the subject matter to the challenging party.[47]

C. Subpoena Authority

The basic investigative advantage of the grand jury stems from its ability to use the subpoena authority of the court that impaneled it. Upon the request of the grand jury foreperson or the prosecutor, the federal district court issues subpoenas, but the grand jury is dependent upon the court for enforcement. The grand jury may use a subpoena *duces tecum* to obtain tangible evidence and a subpoena *ad testificandum* to obtain testimony. Because it is an abuse of the grand jury process to use grand jury subpoenas for the purpose of preparing an already pending indictment for trial, grand juries may delay the issuance of indictments even if probable cause to indict already exists. Until the grand jury returns an indictment, it may continue to hear from more witnesses, examine more documents, and build the Government's case.

The grand jury is especially useful in obtaining statements from persons who refuse voluntarily to furnish information to law enforcement. While an individual has the right to refuse to cooperate with law enforcement, refusal to comply with a subpoena *ad testificandum* may subject an individual to a possible jail sentence for contempt. Faced with that threat, a reluctant witness often decides to give the grand jury information that he has refused to give to law enforcement. If the information sought through the subpoena could be incriminating, the witness may still refuse to cooperate by relying on his constitutional privilege against self-incrimination. The grand jury subpoena *ad testificandum* also has the advantage of requiring

---

[47] *Id.*, at 302.

witnesses to give information under oath. A witness who fails to tell the truth may be prosecuted for perjury.

The grand jury subpoena *duces tecum* offers several advantages over a search warrant, which is the primary device available to the police for obtaining records and physical evidence. Unlike the search warrant, the subpoena *duces tecum* can issue without a showing of probable cause. Even where probable cause could be established, a subpoena may have other advantages. With a subpoena, for example, the party served may gather records covered by the subpoena from other persons and locations. Other grand juries advantages include lay participation, most participants are sworn to secrecy, use of immunity from prosecution and the threat of contempt to compel cooperation, and they may counteract suspicions of political manipulation associated with police investigations.

Grand jury witnesses in several contexts have argued that even where the testimony or documents demanded of them clearly would be relevant, the grand jury should be required to show a "compelling need" for that information where the impact of its inquiry would be to chill the exercise of a constitutionally protected right. Witness claims about the oppressiveness of a subpoena also involve the alleged chilling impact of the grand jury subpoenas on their exercise of First Amendment rights.

Branzburg v. Hayes was a First Amendment challenge to subpoenas issued to newspaper reporters by federal and State grand juries. Articles by the subpoenaed reporters suggested that they knew of specific criminal activities, based upon their personal observation or interviews with the alleged parties. One subpoena *duces tecum* directed a reporter to produce his notes and tape recordings of an interview intended for publication. Without a showing of a compelling need for the information, the reporters claimed that their promises of confidentiality to their sources of information protected them from testifying. The Court rejected their First Amendment objection, because standard grand jury practice is that a subpoena is not conditioned on a "preliminary showing" by the Government that "a crime had been committed."

While noting that requiring the reporters to testify could deter future sources, the public interest in the grand jury's investigation of crime outweighed any negative impact on news gathering. The Court tried to assure the press that "news gathering" deserved "First Amendment protections."[48] Judicial control of the grand jury process always is available to provide an appropriate remedy if the grand jury process misuses its powers to harass the press. A concurring

48 *Branzburg v. Hayes*, 408 U.S. at 707.

opinion by the majority's fifth vote attempted to offer hope to the press.

> [T]he Court states that no harassment of newsmen will be tolerated. If a newsman believes that the grand jury investigation is not being conducted in good faith he is not without remedy. Indeed, if the newsman is called upon to give information bearing only a remote and tenuous relationship to the subject of the investigation, or if he has some other reason to believe that his testimony implicates confidential source relationships without a legitimate need of law enforcement, he will have access to the court on a motion to quash and an appropriate protective order may be entered.
>
> The asserted claim to privilege should be judged on its facts by the striking of a proper balance between freedom of the press and the obligation of all citizens to give relevant testimony with respect to criminal conduct. The balance of these vital constitutional and societal interests on a case-by-case basis accords with the traditional way of adjudicating such questions.
>
> In short, the courts will be available to newsmen under circumstances where legitimate First Amendment interests require protection.[49]

Branzburg established that the government interest in investigating crime is *per se* a compelling interest.

Claims challenging grand jury subpoenas also may be based on other sources of constitutional protection, as indicated by *Trump v. Vance*,[50] in which the Court rejected the claim that a "heightened need standard" was needed to protect a President's exercise of executive authority when a state grand jury subpoenas "a President's private papers."

On behalf of a state grand jury, the New York County District Attorney's Office issued a subpoena duces tecum on Trump's accounting firm, seeking financial records, including tax returns. A motion to quash the subpoena was filed. When the case reached the Court, it conceded that a President "is not 'relegated' only to the challenges available to private citizens" and can challenge the subpoena as an attempt to influence the performance of his official duties or requiring "compliance . . . [that] would impede his constitutional duties.

---

49 *Id.*, at 709–10 (Powell, J., concurring).

50 591 U.S. 786 (2020).

The Court cited *R. Enterprises* to affirm its protections against arbitrary fishing expeditions that "apply with special force to a President, in light of the office's unique position as the head of the Executive Branch." Those protections also are enforceable in federal courts despite the usual policy against federal interference in state criminal proceedings. Thus, "grand juries ae prohibited from engaging in 'arbitrary fishing expeditions' and initiating investigations 'out of malice or an intent to harass.' "[51] Federal officials can be protected from harassment even from state grand juries acting to harass or engage in bad faith.

D. Questioning Based on Illegally Obtained Evidence

In *United States v. Calandra*,[52] prosecutors asked a grand jury witness about records that were seized from his office. Without answering the questions, the witness was able to postpone his appearance and file motions to suppress the records and retrieve them. The trial court granted his motion and also ordered that he not have to answer any grand jury "questions based on the suppressed evidence."[53] The Court reversed, and held that a grand jury witness cannot raise the exclusionary rule to prevent questioning based on evidence that was unconstitutionally seized. The Court applied a balancing test to weigh the effect of applying the exclusionary rule in grand jury proceedings against the deterrence of illegal searches.

> Permitting witnesses to invoke the exclusionary rule before a grand jury would precipitate adjudication of issues hitherto reserved for the trial on the merits and would delay and disrupt grand jury proceedings. Suppression hearings would halt the orderly progress of an investigation and might necessitate extended litigation of issues only tangentially related to the grand jury's primary objective. . . In some cases the delay might be fatal to the enforcement of the criminal law.[54]

The incremental deterrent effect from applying the exclusionary rule was "uncertain at best." The Court refused to "embrace a view that would achieve a speculative and undoubtedly minimal advance in the deterrence of police misconduct at the expense of substantially impeding the role of the grand jury."[55] Using the same balancing test, lower courts have expanded the application of *Calandra* to include

---

51 *Trump v. Vance*, 591 U.S. at 805.

52 414 U.S. 338 (1974).

53 United States v. Calandra, 414 U.S. 338, 341–42 (1974).

54 *Id.*, at 349.

55 *Id.*, at 352.

questioning based on other constitutional violations. Even if *Calandra* prevents a grand jury witness from raising the issue, that witness could refuse to answer based on the Fifth Amendment privilege, discussed in the next two sections.

In *Gelbard v. United States*,[56] grand jury witnesses refused to answer questions, because the questions resulted from illegal electronic surveillance. Unlike *Calandra*, however, the Court held that the surveillance violated 18 U.S.C. § 2515, which refers specifically to grand jury proceedings in which "no evidence derived [from an illegal interception] may be received."[57] Under the federal civil contempt statute, the statutory violation was "just cause" for refusing to testify.

E. Warnings to Grand Jury Witnesses

United States v. Mandujano[58] held that, even if *Miranda*-type warnings to grand jury witnesses about the privilege were required, the failure to give the warnings is not a defense to a perjury charge based on the witness's false grand jury testimony. The Court's plurality opinion also rejected the trial court's reasoning that as a putative defendant the witness should have been given full *Miranda*-type warnings; *Miranda* applied only to "custodial interrogation," which clearly did not include questioning before the grand jury. Because prosecutors gave Mandujano a type of self-incrimination warning, there was no need to rule on warnings as a constitutional requirement. In addition, the Court in *United States v. Wong*[59] held that failure to "Mirandize" a grand jury witness is not a constitutional prerequisite to the use of the testimony against the witness in a subsequent perjury trial.

In the federal system, United States Attorneys have followed the practice of notifying all witnesses of Fifth Amendment privilege rights to all witnesses as a matter of internal policy. Justice Department guidelines require that all witnesses be advised of their right to exercise their self-incrimination privilege.[60] That notification is also contained in an "advice of rights" form that commonly is attached to all federal subpoenas. and contains the following information:

> (A) The grand jury is conducting an investigation of possible violations of federal criminal laws involving: (State here the general subject matter of inquiry, e.g., the

---

56 408 U.S. 41 (1972).

57 Gelbard v. United States, 408 U.S. 41, 43 n.2 (1972).

58 425 U.S. 564 (1976).

59 431 U.S. 174, 178 (1977).

60 United States Attorneys Manual, § 9–11.150.

conducting of an illegal gambling business in violation of 18 U.S.C. § 1955; (B) You may refuse to answer any question if a truthful answer to the question would tend to incriminate your; (C) Anything that you do say may be used against you by the grand jury or in a subsequent legal proceeding; (D) If you have retained counsel, the grand jury will permit you a reasonable opportunity to step outside the grand jury room to consult with counsel if you do so desire.[61]

In *United States v. Washington*,[62] the Court refused to recognize that a target witness had the right to be warned about his target status. The witness received full *Miranda*-type warnings before appearing in the grand jury room, but he was not warned about a possible indictment in connection with possessing a stolen motorcycle. Department of Justice guidelines provide advice to "known targets" that "their conduct is being investigated for possible violation of federal criminal law."[63] The failure to give a potential defendant a target warning did not put the witness at a "constitutional disadvantage," because his status as a target "neither enlarg[ed] nor diminish[ed]" the scope of his constitutional protection. He "knew better than anyone else"[64] whether his answers would be incriminating, and he also knew that anything he did say, after failing to exercise the privilege, could be used against him.

In *Mandujano*, the grand jury witness was told that he could have a lawyer outside the room with whom he could consult,[65] but he was not offered an appointed attorney. The Court stated that the advice about the availability of counsel was consistent with constitutional decisions. Because "no criminal proceedings had been instituted," the "Sixth Amendment right to counsel had not come into play."[66] The lack of any "initiation of adversary judicial proceedings" made the Sixth Amendment inapplicable. Under "settled principles[,] the witness may not insist upon the presence of his attorney in the grand jury room."[67]

F. Assertion of Fifth Amendment Privilege

The privilege against self-incrimination is available in grand jury proceedings. *Counselman v. Hitchcock*,[68] held that a grand jury

---

61 See *id.*

62 431 U.S. 181 (1977).

63 United States Attorneys Manual, § 9–11.151.

64 United States v. Washington, 431 U.S. 181, 189 (1977).

65 United States v. Mandujano, 425 U.S. 564, 568 (1976).

66 *Id.*, at 581.

67 *Id.*

68 142 U.S. 547 (1892).

witness may assert his privilege against self-incrimination. When the Fifth Amendment states that a person cannot be compelled to be a witness against himself "in a criminal case," that phrase refers to the proceeding in which the compelled testimony is eventually used, not the proceeding in which the testimony is compelled. The privilege thus applies to a witness "in any proceeding" who is being compelled to give grand jury testimony that might incriminate him later in a criminal case.

Because subpoenaing targets of a grand jury investigation is inherent in the grand jury's investigative role, targets of the investigation may assert their Fifth Amendment privilege. "The obligation to appear" before the grand jury "is no different for a person who may himself be the subject of the grand jury inquiry."[69] When the target appears before the grand jury and exercises the privilege against self-incrimination, the Government cannot use his silence to impeach the defendant at a later trial.[70]

The witness may not assert the privilege of anyone but himself,[71] and courts give the benefit of the doubt when a witness claims protection of the privilege for himself. In *Hoffman v. United States*,[72] the Court ruled that questions about a witness's current job and his contacts with a fugitive witness were covered by the privilege in a racketeering investigation. The Court described the applicable standard.

> This provision of the [Fifth] Amendment must be accorded liberal construction in favor of the right it was intended to secure.
>
> The privilege afforded not only extends to answers that would in themselves support a conviction. . . but likewise embraces those which would furnish a link in the chain of evidence needed to prosecute the claimant for a federal crime. . . [T]his protection must be confined to instances where the witness has reasonable cause to apprehend danger from a direct answer. . . However, if the witness, upon interposing his claim, were required to prove the hazard in the sense in which a claim is usually required to be established in court, he would be compelled to surrender the very protection which the privilege is designed to guarantee. To sustain the privilege, it need only be evident from the implications of the question, in the setting in

---

69 *United States v. Dionisio*, 410 U.S. at 10 n.8.

70 Grunewald v. United States, 353 U.S. 391, 423 (1957).

71 Bellis v. United States, 417 U.S. 85, 88 (1974).

72 341 U.S. 479 (1951).

> which it is asked, that a responsive answer to the question or an explanation of why it cannot be answered might be dangerous because injurious disclosure could result.[73]

Questions about the witness's current job could prompt answers about gambling law violations, and contacts with a fugitive could result in information about hiding that person from law enforcement. Because a witness may assert the privilege in response to questions where answers either "would in themselves support a conviction [or] would furnish a link in the chain of evidence," a trial court seldom rejects a claim of privilege by a grand jury witness who refuses to testify.

Malloy v. Hogan[74] reversed a lower court's rejection of a privilege claim by a witness who had pled guilty to gambling. The privilege claim related to the circumstances of his arrest and plea, and the questions were devised to determine the identity of the witness's employer. As the Court observed, if the employer "were still engaged in unlawful activity, disclosure of his name might furnish a link in a chain of evidence sufficient to connect the [witness] with a more recent crime for which he still might be prosecuted."[75]

Even a person who swears to his innocence may claim the privilege. In *Ohio v. Reiner*,[76] although the suspect claimed unawareness about the victims' injuries, she conceded that she had spent extended periods of time with the child abuse victims. The privilege protects "innocent men . . . who otherwise might be ensnared by ambiguous circumstances," and "truthful responses of an innocent witness . . . may provide the Government with incriminating evidence from the speaker's own mouth."[77]

When a witness answers a question, a "testimonial waiver" of the privilege is automatically assumed. By answering and providing certain incriminating information, a witness may relinquish the right to raise the privilege for additional questions that seek incriminating information about the same topic. In *Rogers v. United States*,[78] the witness testified before a grand jury that, as treasurer of the Communist Party of Denver, she had been in possession of party records, but she had subsequently delivered those records to another person. She refused to identify the recipient of the records, asserting that the information would be incriminating. The Court

---

73 Hoffman v. United States, 341 U.S. 479, 486–87 (1951).

74 378 U.S. 1 (1964).

75 Malloy v. Hogan, 378 U.S. 1, 13 (1964).

76 532 U.S. 17 (2001).

77 Ohio v. Reiner, 532 U.S. 17, 21 (2001).

78 340 U.S. 367 (1951).

affirmed her contempt conviction, holding that the privilege was inapplicable. By answering one question about the records, she had waived her right to claim the privilege about answering other records-related questions, i.e., she had already incriminated herself by admitting her party membership and past possession of the records. In effect, *Rogers* refused to permit a witness to disclose a basic incriminating fact and then claim the privilege as to "details" about that fact.

A witness may claim the Fifth Amendment privilege and refuse to testify for other reasons. The court appears to have the inherent power to limit other inquiries which might otherwise invade the privacy of the witness or subject him to harassment for no legitimate purposes. For example, in *Branzburg v. Hayes*, the Court stated that grand juries must operate within constitutional limits, and official harassment for any purpose other than law enforcement is not justified.[79]

G. Immunity from Prosecution

1. Generally

An immunity grant is a court order granting a witness sufficient immunity from future prosecution to supersede the self-incrimination privilege. Once a witness is granted immunity, he no longer can rely upon the privilege. The immunity grant may be used to gain information from various types of recalcitrant witnesses, e.g., from less important crime participants, or from witnesses who do not want to give testimony that could harm others. Because immunity grants follow invocation of the privilege, persons who simply refuse to give a statement to the police are unlikely to receive immunity. The most likely method for receiving immunity is in connection with a subpoena *ad testificandum* directing an uncooperative witness to testify before the grand jury. The scope of immunity is co-extensive with Fifth Amendment privilege at trial.[80]

When a witness invokes the privilege against self-incrimination, the prosecutor may seek an immunity order from the judge overseeing the grand jury to grant immunity to the witness and thus force an answer. In the federal system and many States, the role of the trial court in issuing an immunity order is limited.

Under the federal immunity statute,[81] the trial court must issue the immunity order after the prosecutor for the Government complies with two requirements. First, the request for immunity is approved

---

79 See *Branzburg v. Hayes*, 408 U.S. at 707–08.

80 See Kastigar v. United States, 406 U.S. 441, 448 (1972).

81 18 U.S.C. § 6003.

by one of the top officials in the United States Department of Justice. Second, approval of the request for an immunity order reflects a judgment of the local United States Attorney that "testimony or other information. . . [from the witness] may be necessary to the public interest," [and the witness] "has refused or is likely to refuse to testify or provide other information on the basis of his privilege against self-incrimination." Without an immunity order, the witness is unlikely to respond to the prosecutor's questions other than to assert his Fifth Amendment privilege.

After complying with the foregoing requirements, the trial court cannot refuse to grant the order of immunity on the ground that it disagrees with the Government's conclusion that the immunity may be necessary to the public interest. At a hearing on the Government's request for immunity, the only challenge from the witness relates to the procedural regularity of the application, e.g., the scheduling of the hearing did not enable the witness the opportunity to consult counsel. To protect the witness's rights, counsel for the witness should request any past statements to the Government, even outside the grand jury context, in order to avoid inadvertently committing perjury when he is questioned after the immunity grant.

The common types of immunity used by the State and federal judicial systems are transactional immunity and use/derivative use immunity. Transactional immunity protects a grand jury witness from prosecution based upon any transaction about which he is questioned and testifies. Use/derivative use immunity has been used in federal courts since the late 1960s. Its scope is narrower than transactional immunity, because a grand jury witness with use/derivative use immunity may still be prosecuted. However, with use/derivative use immunity, the witness's grand jury testimony and any information derived from that testimony cannot be used against the witness in a later criminal prosecution. However, other information may be admissible if it has a source independent of the grand jury testimony. The constitutionality of the federal use/derivative use immunity was upheld in *Kastigar v. United States*.[82]

In *Murphy v. Waterfront Commission*,[83] the Court held that a witness who was granted use/derivative use immunity from State prosecution cannot be compelled to give incriminating testimony under federal law *or* State law. The Fifth Amendment's "policies and purposes" required that the scope of the privilege protect "a State witness against incrimination under federal as well as State law and a federal witness against incrimination under State as well as federal law," i.e., immunity granted to replace the privilege must extend to

---

82 406 U.S. 441 (1972).

83 378 U.S. 52 (1964).

both potential State and federal prosecutions. Regardless of the type of immunity order issued by the court, i.e., transactional or use/ derivative use immunity, a witness may be prosecuted for perjury based upon his grand jury testimony.

The contempt sanction makes the grand jury subpoena particularly useful in obtaining statements from persons who would not voluntarily furnish information to the police. If an immunized witness refuses to testify before the grand jury, the court may issue an order to the witness requiring him to show cause why he should not be held in contempt of the court's immunity order. The witness risks being jailed for civil contempt, which he can end simply by testifying, or for criminal contempt that carries a sentence for a time certain, e.g., six months. A witness held in civil contempt cannot be jailed past the end of the current grand jury's term, but may be subject to being held in contempt again by refusing to testify to another grand jury.

2. *Presidential Immunity*

After President Donald Trump was indicted for trying to overturn the 2020 election results, specifically for conspiracy to defraud the United States, conspiracy to obstruct an official proceeding, obstruction of an official proceeding, and conspiracy to violate constitutional rights, he moved to dismiss the indictment on grounds of Presidential immunity. Although lower courts denied his motion, the Supreme Court in *Trump v. United States* held that Presidents enjoy absolute immunity from criminal prosecution for conduct that falls within their "conclusive and preclusive constitutional authority."[84] Such absolute immunity encompasses Presidents' authority to confer with Justice Department officials on potential investigations and their power to remove or reassign subordinates.

In addition, Presidents also enjoy rebuttable "presumptive immunity" for conduct that falls within the "outer perimeter"[85] of their official duties, e.g., conferring with the Vice-President on questions relating to the scope of their official powers. The Government may rebut the presumption on a showing that "applying a criminal prohibition to that act would pose no dangers of intrusion on the authority and functions of the Executive Branch."

Presidential immunity is an objective inquiry that cannot explore subjective motives. Neither type of immunity permits

---

84 603 U.S. 593, 609 (2024).

85 *Trump v. United States*, 603 U.S. at 614, 618.

evidentiary use of official acts to indicate corrupt motive. Conversely, there is no immunity for presidential "private" acts.

H. Secrecy

Most jurisdictions' grand jury secrecy provisions describe who can be present in the grand jury room and to which of those persons the secrecy rules apply. In addition to the grand jurors, usually only the prosecutor, stenographer, an interpreter needed for a witness, and the witness who is testifying (plus the parent, guardian, or custodian of a minor witness or other person under disability) may be present when the grand jury is in session. Subject to written exceptions, grand jurors, stenographers, and interpreters are prohibited from disclosing the proceedings and any testimony before the grand jury. Significantly, testifying witnesses are not bound by secrecy prohibitions. Other provisions provide whether prosecutors may reveal to other government personnel what occurred during the grand jury proceedings.[86]

In *United States v. Procter & Gamble Company*,[87] the Court listed five objectives of the secrecy requirements that contribute to the success of the grand jury's investigative and screening purposes:

> (1) to prevent the escape of those whose indictment may be contemplated; (2) to insure the utmost freedom to the grand jury in its deliberations, and to prevent persons subject to indictment or their friends from importuning the grand jurors; (3) to prevent subornation of perjury or tampering with the witnesses who may testify before grand jury and later appear at the trial of those indicted by it; (4) to encourage free and untrammeled disclosures by persons who have information with respect to the commission of crimes; (5) to protect the innocent accused who is exonerated from disclosure of the fact that he has been under investigation, and from the expense of standing trial where there was no probability of guilt.[88]

Butterworth v. Smith[89] supported a First Amendment challenge to a State statute imposing secrecy on a grand jury witness after the grand jury had completed its investigation. A newspaper reporter testified before the grand jury about public officials' improprieties. After the grand jury was discharged, he sued for a violation of his civil rights, because he intended to write a book about the

---

[86] See, e.g., Fed.R.Crim.P. 6(e)(3)(B). Defendants are entitled only to their own grand jury testimony. Fed.R.Crim.P. 16(a)(1)(A).

[87] 356 U.S. 677 (1958).

[88] United States v. Proctor & Gamble Company, 356 U.S. 677, 681 n.6 (1958).

[89] 494 U.S. 624 (1990).

investigation that included his grand jury appearance. The Court ruled for the plaintiff, distinguishing an earlier precedent because in the case at bar, the plaintiff had the requested information in his possession *before* he testified. The Court rationalized that traditional functions of grand jury secrecy were not served after the grand jury's investigation; those functions were especially insufficient "to overcome [the witness's] First Amendment right to make a truthful statement of information he acquired on his own."[90]

In some situations, such as commission of perjury by a grand jury witness, the policy of secrecy may yield to more pressing interests. For example, in *Dennis v. United States*,[91] the Court ruled that a trial court did not err when it permitted State prosecutors to testify about the contents of a witness's grand jury testimony after the witness refused to repeat such statements at trial. A prosecutor could refer to the transcript of the witness's testimony in the course of questioning at trial. In short, the policy of secrecy is not absolute, and the veil of secrecy may disappear in the interest of justice.

Requests for court-ordered disclosure of grand jury transcripts to third parties has produced frequent litigation about secrecy issues. *Douglas Oil Co. of California v. Petrol Stops Northwest*[92] describes the legal standard of "particularized need" to order disclosure of grand jury transcripts to third parties.

> Parties seeking grand jury transcripts under Rule 6(e) must show that the material they seek is needed to avoid a possible injustice in another judicial proceeding, that the need for disclosure is greater than the need for continued secrecy, and that their request is structured to cover only material so needed. Such a showing must be made even when the grand jury whose transcripts are sought has concluded its operations as it had in *Dennis [v. United States]*. . . [T]he interests in grand jury secrecy, although reduced, are not eliminated because the grand jury has ended its activities. . . It is equally clear that as the considerations justifying secrecy become less relevant, a party asserting a need for grand jury transcripts will have a lesser burden in showing justification. . . In sum, as so often is the situation in our jurisprudence, the court's duty in a case of this kind is to weigh carefully the competing

---

90 Butterworth v. Smith, 494 U.S. 624, 636 (1990).

91 384 U.S. 855 (1966).

92 441 U.S. 211 (1979).

> interests in light of the relevant circumstances and the standards announced by this Court.[93]

Courts commonly describe the disclosure standard as setting forth three prerequisites: "(1) the material sought to be disclosed is needed to avoid a possible injustice, (2) the need for disclosure is greater than the need for continued secrecy, and (3) the request to disclose covers only materials so needed."[94]

§ 16.4 Production of Evidence

A. Fifth Amendment Inapplicable to Organizations

Court decisions during the past fifty years have reduced the Fifth Amendment's protection. The Court has noted that the privilege against self-incrimination is designed to protect interests unique to individual persons, and the Government must be free to regulate organizational entities effectively. Because the privilege applies only to natural persons, its protections are not available to incorporated organizations. *Hale v. Henkel*[95] held that the Fifth Amendment privilege is personal to a witness, who cannot claim the privilege of another person or of a corporation even as a corporate officer or employee.

A person who is subpoenaed to produce entity records may be incriminated by the contents of such records. In *Braswell v. United States*,[96] the person subpoenaed to produce corporate records was a corporate president and its only shareholder. The Court held that the custodian of entity records has no personal Fifth Amendment privilege to resist a grand jury subpoena for *entity* records, and cannot claim the Fifth Amendment privilege on behalf of the entity. The person holding the records acts in a representative rather than in an individual capacity, even if the subpoena is directed to the custodian by name. By voluntarily possessing the records, he assumes the entity's responsibility for making the records available to a government agency (or even a grand jury) entitled to see them.

Because the custodian's act of production is an act of the entity, the government "may make no evidentiary use of the 'individual act' against the individual."[97] For example,

---

[93] Douglas Oil Co. of California v. Petrol Stops Northwest, 441 U.S. 211, 221–24 (1979).

[94] In re Criminal Investigation No. 437, 557 A.2d 235 (Md. 1989).

[95] 201 U.S. 43 (1906), overruled in part by Murphy v. Waterfront Com'n, 378 U.S. 52 (1964).

[96] 487 U.S. 99 (1988).

[97] Braswell v. United States, 487 U.S. 99, 118 (1988).

> in a criminal prosecution against the custodian, the Government may not introduce into evidence before the jury the fact that the subpoena was served upon and the corporation's documents were delivered by one particular individual, the custodian.[98]

Braswell probably does not apply to *former* employees who possess entity documents and are subpoenaed, because a former employee is no longer an agent of the entity and not a custodian of the entity records.[99] However, even though a trial jury cannot be told that he produced the records, it is free to infer that the custodian possessed the documents. By contrast, an entity employee may claim Fifth Amendment protection to avoid giving *oral* testimony.[100]

The Fifth Amendment privilege also is not available for use by unincorporated organizations. *United States v. White*[101] held that the privilege is essentially personal and cannot be used by or on behalf of any organization. An individual cannot rely on the privilege against self-incrimination to avoid producing records of a collective entity, when the records are in the individual's possession in a representative capacity, even if those records might incriminate the individual personally.[102]

Baltimore City Department of Social Services v. Bouknight[103] shows the possible scope of the act of production doctrine. A mother suspected of child abuse objected on Fifth Amendment grounds to a subpoena to produce her infant son. She could not base her objection on what a physical examination might reveal, because that would be a claim based upon the contents of what was produced, i.e., the child. She could, however, claim the privilege because "the act of production would amount to testimony regarding her control over and possession of" him, thereby assisting the State in prosecuting the mother for child abuse. The Court had no need to decide whether "this limited testimonial assertion is sufficiently incriminating and sufficiently testimonial for purposes of the privilege."[104] Through custody from the juvenile court, the mother had "assumed custodial duties related to production" (analogous to an entity agent) and had done so as part of a noncriminal regulatory scheme which included a production

---

98 *Id.*

99 See, e.g., In re Three Grand Jury Subpoenas, 191 F.3d 173 (2d Cir. 1999).

100 Curcio v. United States, 354 U.S. 118 (1957).

101 322 U.S. 694 (1944).

102 Bellis v. United States, 417 U.S. 85 (1974) (partnership).

103 493 U.S. 549 (1990).

104 Baltimore City Department of Social Services v. Bouknight, 493 U.S. 549, 555 (1990).

component (analogous to regulations under the required records doctrine).

B. Required Records

A person cannot claim the Fifth Amendment privilege in order to avoid disclosing required records of certain business activities and to make those required records available for government inspection. In *Shapiro v. United States*,[105] a subpoena recipient objected to a subpoena for business records that were required to be maintained under the federal Emergency Price Control Act. While the Court recognized that "there are limits which the Government cannot constitutionally exceed in requiring the keeping of records which may be inspected by an administrative agency and may be used in prosecuting statutory violations committed by the record-keeper himself,"[106] it chose not to define those limits; whatever limits existed, this subpoena did not surpass them.

The subpoena in *Shapiro* was not excessive as long as there was "a sufficient relation between the activity sought to be regulated and the public concern so that the Government can constitutionally regulate or forbid the basic activity concerned."[107] That broad language became the foundation of the required records doctrine. Although dissenting Justice Frankfurter stated that "all records which Congress may require . . . fall outside the protection of the Fifth Amendment,"[108] later cases clarified that the doctrine was not so broad. The Court has described the three elements of the required records doctrine.

> [F]irst, the purpose of the United States' inquiry must be essentially regulatory; second, information is to be obtained by requiring the preservation of records of a kind which the regulated party has customarily kept; and third, the records themselves must have assumed "public aspects" which render them at least analogous to public documents.[109]

Marchetti v. United States[110] and *Grosso v. United States*[111] clarified that subpoenas are proper in prosecutions for failing to comply with statutory schemes that include a reporting requirement, e.g., requiring gamblers to register with the Government and to pay an occupational tax. As in *Shapiro*, the Court refused to describe the

---

105 335 U.S. 1 (1948).

106 Shapiro v. United States, 335 U.S. 1, 32 (1948).

107 *Id.*

108 *Id.*, at 37 (Frankfurter, J., dissenting).

109 Grosso v. United States, 390 U.S. 62, 67 (1968).

110 390 U.S. 39 (1968).

111 390 U.S. 62 (1968).

limits of the required records doctrine, but the Court did find that *Shapiro*'s three elements were missing in *Marchetti* and at least two were missing in *Grosso*.

Applying the first *Shapiro* element, the wagering tax standards did not constitute "an essentially non-criminal and regulatory area," and their disclosure mandates related to a "selective group inherently suspect of criminal activities."[112] For the second element, at least in *Marchetti*, the disclosure standards did not involve records that the person otherwise would have kept. In *Shapiro*, the recorded transaction was "one in which [the subpoena recipient] could lawfully engage solely by virtue of the license granted to him under the statute."[113] In these later cases, however, no such "public aspect" (the third requirement of the required records doctrine) existed for the gambling records.

California v. Byers[114] upheld a "hit and run" statute requiring a driver in an accident to stop at the scene and leave his name and address. In assessing regulatory schemes with disclosure requirements possibly leading to criminal prosecutions, the Court had to "balanc[e] the public need on the one hand, and the individual claim to constitutional protections on the other."[115] A balancing approach thus is part of the required records doctrine.

C. Records Possessed by Third Persons

The Fifth Amendment privilege does not apply to a subpoena for the records of a client held by a third person who is served with a subpoena requiring production of those records. *Couch v. United States*[116] held that, because the Fifth Amendment privilege is personal and belongs to the person and not to the information that may incriminate the person, there is no violation of the Fifth Amendment privilege in obtaining production of a taxpayer's business and tax records in his accountant's possession. Then, in *Fisher v. United States*,[117] the Court held that, because a summons issued to a taxpayer's lawyer to produce documents belonging to the taxpayer does not compel the taxpayer to do anything, the summons does not violate the taxpayer's privilege against self-incrimination.

Both taxpayers conceded that the summons required their agents rather than the taxpayers to produce the documents, but argued that was irrelevant because they had a legitimate expectation

---

112 Marchetti v. United States, 390 U.S. 39, 57 (1968).

113 *Shapiro v. United States*, 335 U.S. at 35.

114 402 U.S. 424 (1971).

115 California v. Byers, 402 U.S. 424, 427 (1971).

116 409 U.S. 322 (1973).

117 425 U.S. 391 (1976).

of privacy in the documents even after delivering them to their agents. The Court rejected the taxpayers' argument, because the Fifth Amendment applies only to personal compulsion and there was none. These taxpayers were not themselves required "to do anything" in response to the summons. The Fifth Amendment "protects against 'compelling testimony, not the disclosure of private information.' "[118]

D. Act of Producing Documents

The grand jury has the power to compel a witness to produce evidence to assist in its investigation. *Warden v. Hayden*[119] stated that compulsory production of a person's personal papers for use against that person is equivalent to that person being compelled to be a witness against himself and is within the Fifth Amendment's prohibition. However, for documents and things, the Fifth Amendment relates to the act of production, not to their incriminating content.

Instead of the documents' content, what matters to the judicial analysis about the act of production is whether the person producing the documents was compelled to produce those documents. A judge will find compulsion if the prosecutor cannot show that, at the time the subpoena issued, it did not know that the (1) subpoenaed papers existed, (2) papers sought were authentic, and (3) papers were possessed by the recipient of the subpoena.

Because the documents in *Fisher* had been transferred from the taxpayer to his attorney, the Court had to consider whether the taxpayer had a valid Fifth Amendment privilege claim if he personally had received the IRS summons. Under the attorney-client privilege, the attorney could refuse to turn over documents that "would have been privileged in the hands of the client by reason of the Fifth Amendment."[120] Thus, whether the attorney could claim attorney-client privilege depended on whether his client-taxpayer could validly claim the Fifth Amendment privilege.

When *Fisher* refers to knowledge, what type of information qualifies as knowledge? The government must prove knowledge, not just inferences, about the documents' existence, possession, and authenticity. The government may use circumstantial evidence (e.g., for a bank account, it may be assumed that a party received the bank's customary account documents) to establish knowledge, but its knowledge cannot be based on general assumptions about matters such as recordkeeping practices, e.g., documentation of one

118 Fisher v. United States, 425 U.S. 391, 401 (1976).

119 387 U.S. 294 (1967).

120 Fisher v. United States, 425 U.S. 391, 402 (1976).

transaction verifies the presence of comparable documents for other transactions.[121]

The act of production "has communicative aspects of its own, wholly aside from the contents of the papers produced."[122] Compliance with a subpoena "tacitly concedes the existence of the papers demanded and their possession or control by the [subpoenaed party]." It also would indicate that party's "belief that the papers are those described in the subpoena," and in some instances this would constitute authentication of the papers.[123] Relying upon what became known as the "foregone conclusion" standard, *Fisher* reasoned:

> It is doubtful that implicitly admitting the existence and possession of the papers rises to the level of testimony within the protection of the Fifth Amendment. The papers belong to the accountant, were prepared by him, and are the kind usually prepared by an accountant working on the tax returns of his client. Surely the Government is in no way relying on the "truthtelling" of the taxpayer to prove the existence of or his access to the documents. The existence and location of the papers are a foregone conclusion and the taxpayer adds little or nothing to the sum total of the Government's information by conceding that he in fact has the papers. Under these circumstances by enforcement of the summons "no constitutional rights are touched. The question is not of testimony but of surrender."[124]

The Court concluded that the taxpayer did not have a valid self-incrimination claim.

> In light of the records now before us, however incriminating the contents of the accountant's workpapers might be, the act of producing them the only thing which the taxpayer is compelled to do would not itself involve testimonial self-incrimination.[125]

"To be 'testimonial,' a communication or act must itself, explicitly or implicitly, relate a factual assertion or disclose information."[126] In *Doe v. United States*,[127] the Court held that a court

---

121 What is the source of testimony about these matters? The government may rely on testimony from third persons familiar with the type of document, comparing the documents with a prior version of the document, or making a comparison to other related documents.

122 *Fisher v. United States,* 425 U.S. at 410.

123 *Id.*

124 *Id.*, at 411.

125 *Id.*, at 410–11.

126 Doe v. United States, 487 U.S. 201, 210 (1988).

127 487 U.S. 201 (1988).

order to sign a form consenting to disclosure of foreign bank records was not a testimonial communication that violated Doe's Fifth Amendment privilege. "By signing the form, Doe made no statement, explicit or implicit, regarding the existence of a foreign bank account or his control over any such account."[128]

United States v. Doe[129] involved a subpoena ordering a sole proprietor to produce his business records for grand jury use. Because the business records, like the accountant's workpapers in *Fisher*, were prepared voluntarily, only their production and not their creation was compelled. Even if a prosecutor is unable to prove the three elements of existence, possession and authenticity, the production of the documents still can be compelled by granting use/derivative-use immunity to the subpoena recipient. *Doe* held that the act of producing records was privileged (because the prosecutor could not prove all three "act of production" elements) and therefore he could not be compelled to produce the records without a statutory grant of use/derivative use immunity.[130]

Doe also declined to treat all "private papers" as *per se* protected by the Fifth Amendment. Justice O'Connor's concurrence specifically addressed the issue of compelled production of private papers.

> [T]he Fifth Amendment provides absolutely no protection for the contents of private papers of any kind. The notion that the Fifth Amendment protects the privacy of papers originated in *Boyd v. United States*, but our decision in *Fisher v. United States* wounded the death knell for *Boyd*. "Several of *Boyd*'s express or implicit declarations [had] not stood the test of time[,] and its privacy of papers concept "had long been a rule searching for a rationale. . . ."[131]

In *United States v. Hubbell*,[132] the defendant had produced documents after being granted use/derivative use immunity. The Court affirmed the dismissal of criminal charges after the Government was unable to show that immunized subpoenaed documents produced by the defendant did not assist the Government in locating other evidence supporting additional criminal charges. The Court stated that it was "apparent from the text of the subpoena itself that the prosecutor needed Hubbell's assistance both to identify potential sources of information and to produce those sources."

---

128 *Id.*, at 215–16.

129 465 U.S. 605 (1984).

130 United States v. Doe, 465 U.S. 605, 617 n.17 (1984).

131 *Id.*, at 618. (O'Connor, J., concurring).

132 530 U.S. 27 (2000).

It was "unquestionably necessary for Hubbell to make extensive use of 'the contents of his own mind' in identifying the hundreds of documents responsive to the subpoena." Therefore,

> [g]iven the breadth of description of the eleven categories of documents called for by the subpoena, the collection and production of the materials demanded was tantamount to answering a series of interrogatories asking a witness to disclose the existence and location of particular documents fitting certain broad descriptions.[133]

The Court then described the critical connection between Hubbell's act of production and the Government's evidence supporting the added charges.

> It is abundantly clear that the testimonial aspect of [Hubbell's] act of producing subpoenaed documents was the first step in a chain of evidence that led to this prosecution. The documents did not magically appear in the prosecutor's office like "manna from heaven." They arrived there only after respondent asserted his constitutional privilege, received a grant of immunity, and-under the compulsion of the District Court's order—took the mental and physical steps necessary to provide the prosecutor with an accurate inventory of the many sources of potentially incriminating evidence sought by the subpoena. It was only through [Hubbell's] truthful reply to the subpoena that the Government received the incriminating documents of which it made "substantial use . . . in the investigation that led to the indictment."[134]
>
> . . .
>
> [H]ere the Government has not shown that it had any prior knowledge of either the existence or the whereabouts of the 13,120 pages of documents ultimately produced by [Hubbell]. The Government cannot cure this deficiency through the overbroad argument that a businessman such as [Hubbell] will always possess general business and tax records that fall within the broad categories described in this subpoena.[135]

The Court may have been incredulous about the Government's misunderstanding about either the nature of use-derivative use immunity, or the need for its evidence to have a source independent

---

[133] United States v. Hubbell, 530 U.S. 27, 41 (2000).

[134] *Id.*, at 42–43.

[135] *Id.*, at 44–45.

of the thousands of pages turned over by Hubbell in his "truthful reply" to the Government's subpoena.

E. Physical Characteristics v. Mental Process

A grand jury may require a witness to produce voice samples, handwriting samples, hair samples, and other samples indicating a person's physical characteristics that are "constantly exposed to public view." In *United States v. Dionisio*,[136] the grand jury subpoenaed about twenty persons to give voice exemplars for comparative scientific testing with recorded conversations that had been received in evidence. In *United States v. Mara*,[137] a witness was told to produce handwriting exemplars to determine whether he authored certain writings. Both subpoena recipients claimed that the subpoenas were unreasonable under the Fourth Amendment, because they had not been supported by any showing of reasonableness.

The Court had little patience for the Fourth Amendment challenge directed at a grand jury subpoena. "It is clear that a subpoena to appear before a grand jury is not a 'seizure' in the Fourth Amendment sense." The Court explained the difference between the "compulsion exerted" by a subpoena as opposed to an "arrest or even an investigative stop."

> The latter is abrupt, is effected with force or the threat of it and often in demeaning circumstances, and, in the case of arrest, results in a record involving social stigma. A subpoena is served in the same manner as other legal process; it involves no stigma whatever; if the time for appearance is inconvenient, this can generally be altered; and it remains at all times under the control and supervision of a court.[138]

As physical characteristics "constantly exposed to the public," subpoena directives for a voice sample and a handwriting sample are distinguishable, for example, from the taking of a blood sample.

> Like a man's facial characteristics, or handwriting, his voice is repeatedly produced for others to hear. No person can have a reasonable expectation that others will not know the sound of his voice, any more than he can reasonably expect that his face will be a mystery to the world.[139]

---

136 410 U.S. 1 (1973).

137 410 U.S. 19 (1973).

138 *United States v. Dionisio*, 410 U.S. at 10.

139 *Id.*, at 14.

Unlike physical characteristics, in *Pennsylvania v. Muniz*,[140] the police violated a defendant's Fifth Amendment rights by asking him to use his mental recollection (rather than showing a physical characteristic) to disclose the date of his sixth birthday. The suspect's failure to recall a personal fact[141] supported the prosecution's DUI case against the suspect.

§ 16.5 Enforcement Powers

The attendance of a witness before the grand jury in obedience to a subpoena or other lawful court order may be enforced in the same manner as in other judicial proceedings. Once a witness is voluntarily before the court, testimony may be coerced the same as if the witness had been subpoenaed to appear. If a witness refuses to testify or cooperate with a grand jury, the court may order the witness to do so under penalty of contempt. There are two types of contempt, civil and criminal.

Civil contempt is used to coerce the recalcitrant witness into cooperating with the grand jury. The witness usually is sentenced to jail time, and he may purge himself of the contempt simply by complying with the court's order to cooperate, i.e., he has the jailhouse keys "in his pocket," pending his compliance. The civil contemnor who refuses to purge himself remains under sentence until the term of the grand jury expires. In *Shillitani v. United States*,[142] grand jury witnesses refused to answer questions even after the trial court granted immunity and the court imposed conditional sentences giving witnesses the right to be released when they obeyed the order to testify. The Court held that the actions of the trial court constituted a civil contempt proceeding, for which neither an indictment nor a jury trial is constitutionally required.

An alternative to civil contempt is criminal contempt, when the trial court with the oversight for that grand jury imposes punishment for violation of its order to cooperate with the grand jury. The contemnor is sentenced to a specific fine or period of imprisonment and has no opportunity to purge himself. However, the contemnor can appeal the contempt citation. For example, in *Maness v. Meyers*,[143] a contemnor sought review of a State court judge's finding of criminal contempt where he as defense counsel had advised his client during a civil case to refuse on Fifth Amendment grounds to produce material that the counsel believed in good faith would tend to incriminate the client. The Court held that the lawyer was not

---

140 496 U.S. 582 (1990).

141 Pennsylvania v. Muniz, 496 U.S. 582, 593–94 (1990).

142 384 U.S. 364 (1966).

143 419 U.S. 449 (1975).

subject to the penalty of contempt for advocating on behalf of his client without disrupting the proceedings.

§ 16.6 Judicial Review of Grand Jury's Work

A. Costello v. United States

Courts may have the opportunity to evaluate how well the indicting process works when indicted persons challenge the evidence considered by the grand jury to support the formal charge. After his indictment for tax evasion, Costello filed two motions: (1) to examine the grand jury minutes and (2) to dismiss the indictment, alleging that the grand jury did not consider sufficient competent evidence to return the indictment. After the trial court denied the motions, the case went to trial, when the prosecution called 144 witnesses. Cross-examination of all the witnesses revealed that only three people—all Government agents—testified before the grand jury. Defendant renewed his motion to dismiss, claiming that this new information clearly showed that the grand jury lacked sufficient competent evidence to indict. The trial court again denied the motions, and the defendant was subsequently convicted.

The Court in *Costello v. United States*[144] emphasized the "history" and "traditions" of the grand jury. English grand jurors were not "hampered by rigid procedural or evidentiary rules," and could act on "such information as they deemed satisfactory," including "their own knowledge." They acted independently and were "free from control by the Crown or the judges." Early decisions in this country likewise recognized that a court could not "revis[e] the judgment of the grand jury upon the evidence, . . . whether or not [the grand jury's] finding was founded upon sufficient proof." The Court denied the defendant's Fifth Amendment claim because it conflicted with "the whole history of the grand jury institution."[145]

The Court also noted that the defendant's challenge, if successful, would inflict administrative costs. "If indictments were to be held open to challenge on the ground that there was inadequate or incompetent evidence before the grand jury, the resulting delay would be great indeed,"[146] enabling defendants to "insist on a kind of preliminary trial to determine the competency and adequacy of the evidence before the grand jury." Defendants could wait until trial for "a strict observance of all the rules designed to bring about a fair verdict." There was no need to adopt "a rule which would result in

---

144 350 U.S. 359 (1956).

145 Costello v. United States, 350 U.S. 359, 363 (1956).

146 *Id.*, at 363.

interminable delay, but add nothing to the assurance of a fair trial."[147]

The reasoning of the *Costello* opinion was broader than the defendant's evidentiary challenge. The defendant complained that the basis for the indictment was hearsay. While the lower court had stressed that hearsay often is quite reliable, and that the inability to cross examine the witness was irrelevant to the *ex parte* nature of the grand jury, the Court instead relied generally on the grand jury's freedom to act on incompetent evidence. The Court isolated one principle to control this and future challenges: "An indictment returned by a legally constituted and unbiased grand jury, like an information drawn by the prosecutor, if valid on its face, is enough to call for a trial of the charge on the merits."[148]

In a brief concurring opinion, Justice Burton expressed concern about the Court's holding.

> [I]t seems to me that if it is shown that the grand jury had before it no substantial or rationally persuasive evidence upon which to base its indictment, that indictment should be quashed. To hold a person to answer to such an empty indictment for a capital or otherwise infamous federal crime robs the Fifth Amendment of much of its protective value to the private citizen.[149]

How much evidence or what type of evidence is required to indict? Most indictments are supported by a combination of first-hand evidence and hearsay. *Costello* upheld the return of an indictment based wholly on hearsay. *Calandra*'s holding suggested that an indictment is valid although it is based entirely on answers to questions based on illegally obtained evidence. An indictment even supported in part by perjured testimony probably would withstand scrutiny if probable cause existed even after the perjured proof was removed from consideration.

B. No Duty to Present Exculpatory Evidence

United States v. Williams[150] held that a federal district court cannot dismiss an indictment based on the prosecutors' failure to comply with a court-created standard that requires that they present known exculpatory evidence to the grand jury. *Williams* tested the scope of the *Bank of Nova Scotia*[151] ruling about the courts'

---

147 *Id.*, at 364.

148 *Id.*, at 363.

149 *Id.*, at 364. (Burton, J., concurring).

150 504 U.S. 36 (1992).

151 See § 16.2(B), discussing duties of a grand jury.

supervisory power to outlaw prosecutorial acts not specifically prohibited by "Rule, statute, or Constitution."

> We did not hold in *Bank of Nova Scotia* that the courts' supervisory power could be used, not merely as a means of enforcing or vindicating legally compelled standards of prosecutorial conduct before the grand jury, but as a means of prescribing those standards of prosecutorial conduct in the first instance—just as it may be used as a means of establishing standards of prosecutorial conduct before the courts themselves. It is this latter exercise that respondent demands. Because the grand jury is an institution separate from the courts, over whose functioning the courts do not preside, we think it clear that, as a general matter at least, no such "supervisory" judicial authority exists.[152]

Judicial supervision over the grand jury is limited to the use of the subpoena power, and does not extend to "prescribing modes of grand jury procedure."[153] Federal courts' authority to devise procedural rules "not specifically required by regulation the Constitution or Congress" is limited.

"[A]s a general matter at least," no supervisory authority existed to independently create standards for judging prosecutorial conduct in the grand jury. For example, mandatory disclosure of exculpatory evidence was inconsistent with the "grand jury's historical role" as an "accusatory body," and would necessitate "judicial reshaping of the grand jury institution, substantially altering the traditional relationships between the prosecutor, the constituting court, and the grand jury itself."[154]

An obligation to present exculpatory evidence to the grand jury would be unjustified even if federal courts could prescribe grand jury procedures as part of a "common law of the Fifth Amendment." Requiring disclosure of even substantial exculpatory evidence "would neither preserve nor enhance the traditional functioning" of the federal grand jury, but instead "alter the grand jury's historical role, transforming it from an accusatory body to an adjudicatory body."[155] "The grand jury sits not to determine guilt or innocence, but to assess whether there is adequate basis for bringing a criminal charge." For that purpose, the grand jury "hear[s] only the prosecutor's side."[156]

---

152 United States v. Williams, 504 U.S. 36, 46–47 (1992).

153 *Id.*, at 50.

154 *Id.*

155 *Id.*

156 *Id.*, at 51.

Contrary to the purpose and history of the grand jury, requiring that the grand jury hear exculpatory evidence would provide a target defendant with a role in the proceedings. It would surely

> invite the target to circumnavigate the system by delivering his exculpatory evidence to the prosecutor, whereupon it would have to be passed on to the grand jury—unless the prosecutor is willing to take the chance that a court will not deem the evidence important enough to qualify for mandatory disclosure.[157]

---

[157] *Id.*, at 52.

Table of Cases

Index

References are to Pages